1008

NOTE

Oxford Historical Monographs will consist of books which would formerly have been published in the Oxford Historical Series. As with the previous series, they will be carefully selected studies which have been submitted, or are based upon theses submitted, for higher degrees in this University. The works listed below are those still in print in the Oxford Historical Series.

The Medieval Administration of the Channel Islands, 1199–1399.
By J. H. LE PATOUREL. 1937.

The Corporation of Leicester, 1689–1836. By R. W. GREAVES. 1939.

Durham Jurisdictional Peculiars. By FRANK BARLOW. 1950.

English Monasteries and their Patrons in the Thirteenth Century.
By SUSAN WOOD. 1955.

The Estates of the Percy Family, 1416–1537. By J. M. W. BEAN. 1958.

The Radical Duke. Career and Correspondence of Charles Lennox, third Duke of Richmond. By ALISON GILBERT OLSON. 1961.

The Norman Monasteries and their English Possessions.
By DONALD MATTHEW. 1962.

Edward III and the Scots. The Formative Years of a Military Career, 1327–1335. By RANALD NICHOLSON. 1965.

A Medieval Oxfordshire Village: Cuxham: 1240 to 1400.
By P. D. A. HARVEY. 1965.

Cardinal Bainbridge in the Court of Rome 1509–14.
By D. S. CHAMBERS. 1965.

The Later Lollards 1414–1520. By JOHN A. F. THOMSON. 1965.

The Impeachment of Warren Hastings. By P. J. MARSHALL. 1965.

The Passing of the Irish Act of Union. By G. C. BOLTON. 1966.

The Miners and British Politics 1906–1914. By ROY GREGORY. 1968.

VICTORIAN QUAKERS

BY

ELIZABETH ISICHEI

OXFORD UNIVERSITY PRESS

1970

Oxford University Press, Ely House, London W.1

GLASGOW NEW YORK TORONTO MELBOURNE WELLINGTON
CAPE TOWN SALISBURY IBADAN NAIROBI DAR ES SALAAM LUSAKA ADDIS ABABA
BOMBAY CALCUTTA MADRAS KARACHI LAHORE DACCA
KUALA LUMPUR SINGAPORE HONG KONG TOKYO

MADE AND PRINTED IN GREAT BRITAIN
BY WILLIAM CLOWES AND SONS, LIMITED
LONDON AND BECCLES

FOR

UCHE PETER ISICHEI

PREFACE

A LTHOUGH the historian's most serious biases are perhaps not those that one can recognize and summarize oneself, I should perhaps say a word about my own attitude to the subject matter of this book. I am a Christian, though not a Friend, but find myself in sympathy with many of Friends' views.

This study is based on a thesis submitted for the Oxford Doctorate of Philosophy. I rejoice to have the opportunity of thanking the individuals and institutions which made it possible for me to write it.

The award of a Commonwealth Scholarship, and the grant of admission by Somerville College, made it possible for me to study at Oxford. Subsequently, the Warden and Fellows of Nuffield College, by electing me first to a Studentship and later to a Research Fellowship, have provided me with the best imaginable conditions for study and writing. This book is the first substantial product of this research; I hope that another volume, on a different theme, will appear shortly. I am most grateful to them for their confidence in me, and especially for the complete freedom they have given me.

So many of my friends and colleagues at Nuffield have helped me, at different times and in different ways, that it is difficult for me to particularize. Nevertheless I should like to thank my College supervisor, Dr. A. F. Madden, an unfailing source of help and encouragement; Dr. R. M. Hartwell, who guided my first steps in nineteenth century history; and Dr. Brian Harrison (now a Fellow of Corpus Christi College), who helped me especially in my work on philanthropy.

I am particularly grateful to my university supervisor, Dr. B. R. Wilson of All Souls College, who read and criticized draft after draft of voluminous typescript. He was unfailingly generous with his time and I am deeply in his debt for his patience, helpfulness and illuminating suggestions. I am also grateful to Dr. J. D. Walsh, of Jesus College, whose advice has guided so many post-graduate students and who shaped my understanding of evangelicalism. Dr J. Kent was kind enough to read and criticize an early version of chapter I.

I could not have written this book without the co-operation of Friends and the help of many archivists and librarians. To all who have helped me, my grateful thanks are due.

I have yet another debt to acknowledge, of quite another nature and degree. It is to my beloved husband, Dr. Uche Peter Isichei, whose unfailing unselfishness, generosity and love, over the years, have made it possible for me to remain a historian, while becoming a wife and mother.

Nuffield College, Oxford   ELIZABETH ISICHEI
February 1969

CONTENTS

PART TWO: THE QUAKERS AND SOCIETY

LIST OF FIGURES

NOTE ON ABBREVIATIONS AND TERMINOLOGY

THROUGHOUT this book, the practice has been followed of using those terms to refer to religious bodies with which they prefer to describe themselves. Thus, the terms 'Friend' and 'Quaker' are used interchangeably, and the Society of Friends is often referred to simply as 'the Society'. All references to Quakerism, unless otherwise specified, refer to England only. In referring to passages in Quaker letters and diaries, the standard form of dating has been used, instead of reproducing such Quakerisms as '2mo'. Manuscript journals and diaries, which frequently have no titles, are always referred to as 'Journal'. Unofficial manuscript accounts of Yearly Meeting Proceedings, which likewise usually lack a title, are referred to as 'Account of . . . Yearly Meeting'.

In addition to those which are generally accepted, the following abbreviations are used in footnotes:

Correspondence—letters containing the reminiscences of aged Quakers, in the possession of the writer.

F.F.D.S.A.	The Friends First Day School Association
FHL	Friends House Library, Euston Road, London N.W.1.
FQE	*The Friends Quarterly Examiner*
JFHS	*The Journal of the Friends Historical Society*
MM, QM, YM	Monthly Meeting, Quarterly Meeting, Yearly Meeting
YM Proceedings	*Extracts from the Minutes and Proceedings of the Yearly Meeting of Friends held in London* (printed annually, from 1857). The official manuscript minutes of Yearly Meeting are referred to as *YM Minutes*.

INTRODUCTION

'VICTORIAN England was religious.'[1] All accounts of Victorianism echo a judgement of this kind, yet our knowledge of the religious history of the period is curiously uneven. Much of the existing literature is biographical—the writing of massive biographies was a very characteristic Victorian industry, and many modern scholars have chosen the biographical approach. This, indeed, has much to commend it, for religion is essentially an individual and inward phenomenon. But the concentration on personalities, rather than on the wider issues of social history, means that we know, for example, every facet of the psychology of Newman, but singularly little about the corporate history of the half million odd Congregationalists who went to church on the morning of Census Sunday, 1851.[2] Most histories of the individual denominations have been written by their members, in a spirit of filial piety.[3] Characteristically, they choose a wide time span. Such studies are often not without their excellences, but the spirit which inspires them is not conducive to critical scholarship, nor to a concern with the broader issues of nineteenth century history. A recent book which appeared after this study was finished, Robert Currie's *Methodism Divided*, marks a new departure in Victorian religious history, though it deals with a large and complex topic—the history of the various branches of Methodism over a hundred and thirty years—in necessarily brief compass, and the animus it displays towards its sub-

[1] The opening sentence of Owen Chadwick, *The Victorian Church* (London, 1966).
[2] Here and subsequently, in this *Introduction* statistics come from *Census of Great Britain, 1851, Religious Worship* (Parl. Papers, 1852–3, lxxxix). These returns are of attendances, in the morning, afternoon and evening, not of members. They are difficult to interpret, as some individuals attended twice or more, while a count of those who attended in, for example, the morning, excludes those who attended later in the day. But the general picture they give of the relative strength of the denominations is a valuable one.
[3] For two examples of the genre, cf. R. Tudur Jones, *Congregationalism in England, 1662–1962* (London, 1962); G. A. Beck (ed.) *The English Catholics, 1850–1950* (London, 1950).

ject is perhaps as misleading as the more common tendency
to hagiography. But in general, the scholar seeking a modern
analysis of the Victorian history of the Catholics, the Congregationalists, the Baptists, or the Unitarians, not to mention smaller groups like the Mormons or the Sweden-
borgians, will look in vain.[1] Impressionistic accounts of the
religious sensibilities of the Victorians are no substitute for
this kind of detailed and systematic research.

Yet if it is true that many Victorians were deeply preoccupied with religion, and that a religious frame of reference
pervaded public life in a way which would seem astonishing
today, it is equally true that religion was very much a
minority concern. The great stronghold of religion was the
middle classes. The attitude of the aristocracy ranged from
the intense evangelical piety which G. W. E. Russell
remembered from his Anglican childhood[2] to the distaste for
Enthusiasm in all its manifestations which had characterized
an earlier day. But it was the 'labouring classes'—at least
seventy per cent of the population—who were, in the main,
cut off from the corporate life of the churches, partly by
social barriers, partly by the exhausting demands of their
grim struggle to survive. Horace Mann wrote that 'the
masses of our working population . . . are *unconscious Secu-
larists*',[3] a verdict which Charles Booth echoed, at a later
date, after his monumental survey of life in London.[4] All
thoughtful denominational leaders were aware of his exclusion of the poor from their ranks, and to a greater or lesser
extent troubled by it. Two of the few modern studies of the
social history of Victorian religion concentrate on this
theme.[5] Mayhew's interviews with the London street population bring it vividly to life—as in the words of the boy who

---

[1] The same is true, to some extent of Anglicanism, despite Chadwick's substantial study. The subject is so complex and various that a number of detailed
monographs are necessary.

[2] G. W. E. Russell, *A Short History of the Evangelical Movement* (London, 1915).

[3] Horace Mann, *Sketches of the Religious Denominations of the Present Day* (London,
1854), p. 93.

[4] Charles Booth, *Life and Labour of the People in London*, 3rd Series, *Religious
Influences*, vol. vii, pp. 399–400 and 424–8.

[5] Kenneth S. Inglis, *The Churches and the Working Classes in Victorian England*
(London, 1963). E. R. Wickham, *Church and People in an Industrial City* (London,
1957).

told him 'yes he had heer'd of God who made the world. Couldn't exactly recollec' when he's heer'd on him, but he had, most sarten-ly . . .Knew there was a book called the Bible; didn't know what it was about; didn't mind to know.'[1]

If religion was a minority concern, the Quakers formed only a minuscule part of this minority. 14,016 Quakers went to Meeting on the morning of Census Sunday—a smaller attendance than that recorded by the Unitarians, or the Countess of Huntingdon's Connection. The Church of England recorded a morning attendance of two and a third million, the various branches of Methodism, 694,000, the Congregationalists, 515,000, the various branches of the Baptists, 353,000.

Yet although religion preoccupied only a minority, this minority formed the so-called 'political nation'. The importance of the Quakers in Victorian England, and the impact they made on contemporaries, was quite disproportionate to their numbers. The names of many leading Quaker industrialists became household words; John Bright and Joseph Sturge were only the most eminent of those engaged in politics, both in and out of Parliament. But their most characteristic contribution to society lay in philanthropy. In an age when taxation was low, and social legislation minimal, it was through philanthropy that wealth was redistributed in society, and the sufferings of the poor alleviated. Victorian England had many competing philanthropic agencies, often disposing of large incomes and forming powerful political pressure groups. Yet with one or two exceptions, we know little of their history, their organization, their finances, the geography and class-structure of their support, and their impact on the problems they sought to solve. An understanding of Victorian Quakerism is central to an understanding of Victorian philanthropy. The Quakers founded some charitable organizations, and formed the core of support for many others. The annual general meetings of many of these societies—the famous May Meetings—were held in May to coincide with the Quakers' Yearly Meeting.

[1] Henry Mayhew, *London Labour and the London Poor*, vol. i. *The London Street Folk* (London, 1851), p. 474.

It is the aim of this book, first to analyse the Victorian history of the Quakers, and secondly to describe, in a necessarily selective way, their impact on the society in which they lived. The first two chapters deal with their intellectual history, with the theological changes which faced them, and on occasion divided them. The pattern of schisms and divisions is always significant in the history of a religious movement, for the pathological extreme tells us much, obliquely, about the nature of orthodoxy. Under the general heading of *Organization*, in chapter three, there follows a discussion of the qualifications for membership, the way in which the Quakers reached decisions, how power was distributed in their church, the characteristics of the Quaker ministry and of their religious services, the ways in which money was raised and spent, and finally, of the formal and actual position of women. The subsequent chapter deals with *Exits and Entrances*, a dimension of religious history hitherto little studied by historians, but one which sheds much light both on the church's image in the rest of society and on its attitude towards its individual members. The concluding chapter of Part One deals with Quaker social life, with their gradual abandonment of isolationism and their rapprochement with 'the World'.

The second section of the book deals with their impact on society in business and economic life, and through politics and philanthropy, giving especially detailed attention to a branch of philanthropy they made peculiarly their own—the education of adults—which had important consequences for their own future as a church.

The differences between politics and philanthropy, in the Quaker context, were more apparent than real. The same qualities of mind and conscience led Joseph Sturge to be active in both. Many Quakers regarded politics primarily as a way of doing good, while ambition could influence the actions of the vice-president of a great charitable society as effectively as those of an aspiring M.P. The changing pattern of Friends' attitudes towards philanthropy and towards politics was essentially the same. In the eighteenth century, most Friends were quietists. Although they often acted as a highly effective pressure group, in defence of their corporate interests, they abhorred preoccupation with secular politics as spiritually dangerous. Even philanthropy was suspect, both for the close contact with other denominations it involved, and because it was feared that concern with outward activities could distract the individual from the inward life of the soul. By the beginning of the nineteenth century, the distrust of philanthropy was breaking down, largely under the impact of evangelicalism. This led Friends into closer sympathy with evangelicals of other denominations, and gave them a vivid awareness of the importance of proselytising work of all kinds, and of the need to do those good works which are the outward signs of a man's sanctification. The part which evangelical Friends played in the establishment of the British and Foreign Bible Society in 1804, and in its subsequent support, is symptomatic of the change. The distrust of politics was eroded more slowly, and it was not until the 1830s that some evangelically minded Friends began to take an active part in political life.

Scholars have hitherto paid little attention to Victorian Quakerism. The only account of the subject is to be found in the relevant portions of Rufus M. Jones, *The Later Periods of Quakerism*, which covers American as well as English Quakerism and was published in 1921. Jones was an American Quaker theologian and religious leader, and his work, understandably enough, was biographical in approach and didactic in intent. Several aspects of the subject have been studied since—notably the Friends' network of boarding-schools, in which they educated their own children, and their work in foreign missions, from the mid 1860s onwards. These are omitted from the present study, for this reason. But in the main, little attention has been devoted to the subject, despite its importance.

Since Friends were a highly articulate and relatively leisured middle-class group, their history is exceptionally well documented, and their periodicals, their numerous memoirs and biographies, the minutes of their meetings, which were carefully made and preserved both at the local and the national level, provide a mass of information about their history. The voluminous manuscript journals of some Friends, such as Elizabeth Fry, J. J. Gurney and J. B.

Braithwaite, survive, and a number of large manuscript collections, such as the Gurney Papers in Friends' House Library, and the Bright, Cobden and Sturge Papers in the British Museum, shed further light on their past. In the writing of particular chapters, these sources were supplemented by much material from outside the denominational context. Thus the chapter on the Quakers' economic composition draws on material in the original census returns of 1851, in the Public Record Office, and in trade directories. The chapter on philanthropy is based on the periodicals and annual reports of the movements studied.

This book is an essay in social history, not in sociology. It seeks to describe a particular institution at a particular period in time, rather than to contribute to sociological theory about the development of religious bodies. Nevertheless, it owes much to sociology, both in the questions asked and in the methods used. The approach throughout is analytic, rather than biographical and anecdotal. In the pursuit of exactitude, quantitative methods have been used wherever possible and appropriate. An attempt has been made to recreate the corporate life of the church, rather than the lives and achievements of notable individuals who happened to be Quakers. But any such study involves methodological problems of great complexity.

It is impossible to think and write about the past without using a large number of abstract concepts, such as Victorianism, Dissent, or Quakerism. The validity of the kind of association underlying any given concept may be criticized, but we cannot discuss the past without them. Yet Victorian Quakerism was not, of course, a holistic entity. It consisted of some thousands of individual Quakers, for each of whom religion was only one of many elements in life. Each saw himself in many different roles, in different situations. John Bright for instance, saw himself, in different contexts, as a Quaker, a Rochdale man, a manufacturer, a Radical, a member of Parliament, a Free Trader, an Englishman, or a husband and father—and the list is not exhaustive. As long as a study is confined to the corporate characteristics of a church—its organization and economic structure—no great difficulties arise. But when one attempts to analyse the

role of 'Quakers' in philanthropy or politics, one has to consider whether religious affiliation was indeed the dominant
consideration in an individual's life. Can one meaningfully
isolate the Quakers from the other supporters of the temperance movement and discuss their work in denominational
terms? It is because of methodological difficulties of this
kind that the greater part of the book deals with the Quakers'
internal history. Chapter IV, analysing *Exits and Entrances*,
provides a glimpse of the great variety of individuals and
attitudes which for most of the study are necessarily sub-
sumed under the generalization 'Quaker'. These difficulties,
of course, are less serious in the case of the Quakers than
they would be in the case of a larger church with a more
amorphous membership, with less sense of corporate identity and less control over its members' lives.

All churches change with the passage of time, but few
have changed as visibly and dramatically as the Society of
Friends. Both its spirit and its external manifestations, in the
early Victorian period, were almost unrecognizably different
both from what they had been in the seventeenth century and
what they were destined to become in the twentieth.

Its founder, George Fox (1624–1691), was essentially a
prophet and mystic. Our best source of knowledge about him
is his own *Journal*, one of the classics of Puritan autobiography.
As a young man, he went through a period of prolonged
religious search, occasioned by his dissatisfaction with the
state of the Puritan churches and their ministers. He passed
through a succession of mystical experiences, which impressed him with the central insight that knowledge of God
and holiness come from direct communion with His Spirit,
with the Seed of God in every man: 'But as I had forsaken
all the priests, so I left the separate preachers also ... for I
saw there was none among them all that could speak to my
condition. . . . Oh then, I heard a voice which said, "There
is one, even Christ Jesus, that can speak to thy condition",
and when I heard it my heart did leap for joy.'[1] This central
insight was full of implications for the church he founded.
He saw existing churches and their ministers as corrupt and

---

[1] *The Journal of George Fox* (ed. John L. Nickalls), Cambridge, 1952, p. 11.

plunged in error: 'the black earthy spirit of the priests wounded my life' and the church at Nottingham seemed 'a great idol and idolatrous temple'.[1] Baptism and the communion service were rejected as empty external rites, and even the scriptures were less important than spiritual contact with the Spirit Who inspired their contents. 'Yet I had no slight esteem of the Holy Scriptures.'[2] Since the Seed of God dwelt in all men's hearts, he rejected artificial hierarchies and social distinctions, refusing to doff his hat, and addressing all men as 'Thou'. Such practices were to crystallize into inherited shibboleths for his spiritual descendants. His view of the churches led naturally to an opposition to tithes and church rates. He rejected the swearing of oaths on scriptural grounds, and refused a post in the army which was offered him, for 'I lived in the virtue of that life and power that took away the occasion of all wars . . .'[3]

Fox's message appealed to a number of communities of the like-minded, some of the many little independent congregations which flourished under the Commonwealth. Quakerism, as it came to be called, evolved in the late 1640s and in the 1650s. Quakers themselves often chose 1652 as their date of origin—the year of Fox's vision on Pendle Hill. It seems that their first members were not drawn from the very poor, but rather from yeomen, small craftsmen, and so on.[4]

Fox and his fellow missionaries went through England, often in circumstances of great hardship, preaching their message. They thought that their mission was to convert the world: 'I was to bring people off from all the world's religions, which are vain.'[5] This belief of the early Friends in their own monopoly of truth, and the corruption of 'all the world's religions' had completely disappeared, as we shall see, by Victorian times. Fox's zeal sometimes led him into extravagance and eccentricity—as when he walked in stockinged feet through Lichfield crying 'Woe to the bloody city of Lichfield.' The early Friends sometimes went naked 'as a sign', and their religious meetings had on occasion

---

[1] *The Journal of George Fox*, Cambridge, 1952, p. 39. [2] ibid., p. 34. [3] ibid., p. 65.
[4] Alan Cole, 'The Social Origins of the Early Friends', *JFHS*, 1957, pp. 99ff.
[5] *Journal*, p. 35.

strange pentecostal-type manifestations of 'the power'. Not surprisingly, they were viewed as a sect of dangerous vision-ary fanatics, and were often persecuted or imprisoned. Yet their movement flourished. By 1680, according to one care-ful estimate, they had 60,000 members.[1]

When Victoria came to the throne, the Society of Friends had changed beyond recognition. Their total numbers had shrunk alarmingly. An unofficial census in 1840 showed that they had 16,227 members. The decline was partly due to extensive emigration, partly to their loss of a missionary spirit, partly to their readiness to expel delinquents, especi-ally those who married non-members. The prophetic and revolutionary vision had become quietism in the eighteenth century. This had produced its own saints and mystics, and a number of remarkable travelling ministers.[2] But by the 1830s it was in decline, giving way to evangelicalism. Despite Fox's distrust of church organization, the Quakers had developed a remarkably complex organization of their own. They had become prosperous and respected, and reached a *modus vivendi* with the powers that be on most of the issues where their 'testimonies' brought them into con-flict with the state. Their distinctive dress and speech, their tendency to shun 'the world' rather than convert it, their increasing readiness to co-operate with Christians of other denominations—all these are changes which have often been observed in the history of religious bodies.[3]

The changes which Quakerism underwent in the nine-teenth century are fully discussed in the pages which follow. But if Victorian Quakerism had moved far from the spirit of Fox, it was equally different from the Quakerism of our own time. All the barriers which marked Friends off as a 'Peculiar People'—the distinctive dress and speech, the embargo on marrying outsiders—have gone. The long Meetings for worship, held mainly in silence, and broken

---

[1] cf. p. 112, below.

[2] The Quaker 'Minister' was very different from that of other churches; Cf. pp. 94ff, below.

[3] This 'sect to denomination' pattern has been much studied. I discuss the rele-vance of Quaker history to it in my article, 'From Sect to Denomination in English Quakerism', *British Journal of Sociology*, 1964, pp. 207–22. This was reprinted in a revised form in *Patterns of Sectarianism* (ed. B. R. Wilson), (London, 1967).

by highly stylized ministry, claiming direct inspiration, have given way to wider participation and a more conversational tone. The patterns of world history have made pacifism, which was of peripheral importance in the nineteenth century, one of Quakerism's most central beliefs, and, for some, its most essential element. The theological battles of the nineteenth century have given way to a general liberalism, to an emphasis on the concept of the Light Within, and to a renewed interest in the writings of the early Friends. The spirit which inspired so much philanthropy survives, very often, in a noteworthy corporate and individual concern for peace and social justice.

Victorian Quakers differed both from their predecessors and from their descendants. They had much in common with the members of other churches, yet in some respects were *sui generis*. The analysis of their history, which follows, is a contribution to our understanding of Victorian religion, and, to a lesser extent, of Victorian politics and philanthropy. Yet to the writer, the changing problems and preoccupations of this little church have a fascination quite distinct from their objective importance in the Victorian world. And 'Time which antiquates antiquities, and hath an art to make dust of all things, hath yet spared us these minor monuments.'[1]

---

[1] Thomas Browne, *Urn Burial*, ch. 4.

PART ONE

The Quakers

I

THEOLOGY: SOME PATTERNS OF
BELIEF AND ACTION

INTRODUCTION

THE study of the formal beliefs of a religious movement is a conventional starting-point for an analysis
of its history. But it is one that demands more than a
conventional justification, for the relevance of theology to
the social history of religion is clearly variable. It is possible
to be a devoted member of a church and know very little of
its formal beliefs. Such ignorance, however, was probably
rare among Victorian Quakers. They could not but be aware
of their so-called 'distinguished views', which affected them
constantly in daily life. These rules and prohibitions, of
which pacifism would prove the most enduring, are analysed
in a later chapter. Theology, in its narrower sense, was
forced upon their attention by the co-existence of several
rival schools of thought among them. Joseph John Gurney
once observed that the advantage of the multiplicity of
Christian churches was that men were forced to consider
their respective merits.[1] The same was true within the small
world of English Quakerism, though none of the advocates
of contending schools of thought would have considered this
multiplicity an advantage: 'each is haunted by an unduly

---

[1] Joseph John Gurney, *Observations on the Distinguishing Views & Practices of
the Society of Friends*; 7th ed., London, 1834, p. 68.

coloured picture of its opposite.'[1] The quietist John
Wilbur was moved to tears by the evangelical complexion
of London Yearly Meeting, in 1832. Yet the diversity
of traditions within the sect, and the relatively advanced
education of its members, meant that every Quaker was
placed in a position of real intellectual choice. An understanding of the different kinds of theology current among
Victorian Friends is necessary for an understanding of their
history.

These theological patterns, in their turn, were largely a
reflection of currents of thought in the wider society.
Victorian Quakerism produced no theologian of sufficient
originality and power to make any mark outside the
movement itself. There were obvious reasons for this—
lack of access to the universities, until 1871, and the absence of a professional ministry. Among Victorian Quaker
theologians of note, J. J. Gurney was a banker; J. B.
Braithwaite a lawyer; Ash a rentier, who trained as a
doctor but never practised; Worsdell a school teacher; and
J. W. Rowntree a director of the cocoa works. Their
writings were the products of their leisure, admittedly often
abundant.

The most important reason why Victorian Quakers
failed to produce original theological thought lay in the
sect's ancient distrust of formal doctrinal statement.
Quietists were especially suspicious of the application of the
intellect to religion, but evangelicals often laid equal stress
on the fact that religion was a matter of experience rather
than of intellectual subtlety. As the leading Quaker evangelical put it, 'It is the frequent device of Satan to transplant
the religion of the believer from the *heart* to the *head*.'[2] The
theological liberalism which became popular among Friends
in the 1890s often appeared much like a rejection of
theology, and distrust of formal theology was to be very
characteristic of twentieth-century Quakerism. Elizabeth
Cadbury later complained: 'Friends are so inclined to pride
themselves on the nebulousness of their faith. There is a
danger of our becoming something like the balloons that

---

[1] Joseph John Gurney, *Journal*, 22 June 1834 (MS. transcript in FHL).
[2] *Idem, Hints on the Portable Evidence of Christianity* (London, 1832), p. 179.

are at present swaying backwards and forwards round every big city.'[1]

The dissensions of Victorian Quakers must be understood against the background of the schisms which rent American Quakerism at this period. The complex and troubled story of American Quakerism lies beyond the scope of this book. Suffice it to say that the first of many schisms took place in Philadelphia in 1827, when the supporters of the aged minister, Elias Hicks, withdrew from the Orthodox or evangelical party. Hicks appears much like antichrist in evangelical writings of the day, but it seems that he was a man of great piety whose thought was influenced both by mystical traditions and by the rationalism of the Enlightenment. He was apparently a Unitarian, and rejected the literal inspiration of the Bible, and the doctrines of Original Sin and the Atonement.[2] His views alarmed English evangelicals and quietists alike—they led evangelicals to a desire for more precise theological commitment. Quietists began to pick an uneasy path between the Scylla of Hicksism and the Charybdis of evangelicalism. The bitterness and even violence which characterized the American schisms had a profound effect on English Friends, a constant reminder of alarming possibilities for themselves.

THE EVANGELICALS

By the 1830s, evangelicalism was in the ascendant among Friends, and quietism was the preserve of a small band of ageing prophets, such as Sarah Lynes Grubb, George and Ann Jones, and Thomas Shillitoe. Inevitably, they defined their own position largely through their criticisms of evangelicalism. It therefore seems profitable to invert chronological order and begin with the later movement.

Any account of the beliefs of Quaker evangelicals must be drawn largely from the writings of Joseph John Gurney (1788–1847). He was so pre-eminent in the movement that

[1] Elizabeth Cadbury to Carl Heath, 13 Sept. 1940 (MS in Bournville Cocoa Works Archives).
[2] The most recent study of Hicks (very sympathetic to him) is: Bliss Forbush, *Elias Hicks Quaker Liberal* (New York, 1956).

its opponents often called Quaker evangelicalism 'Gurney-ism'. His erudition, eloquence, and fluent pen, his wealth and social standing, made him an obvious leader. His constellation of talents even moved a Quaker poetaster to verse:

> Gamaliel's self his book might con
> At the blest feet of Joseph John.[1]

The sources of Quaker evangelicalism were various. Transatlantic influences worked in two directions, but the most important factor was the eloquence and prestige of contemporary Anglican evangelicalism. The Gurneys of Earlham felt more at home in the company of Anglicans than they did with the poorer members of their own meeting. They were attracted, not only by the piety of the great evangelicals, but by their comparable wealth and social position. Quaker critics were fully aware of the social factors which attracted their wealthier members to evangelicalism. One of them explained the progression of a prosperous hat manufacturer to evangelicalism in these terms: 'his altered views are no doubt ascribable with those of many others, to too much association with the worldly, the rich and great.'[2]

Gurney was the friend of Edward Edwards, of Simeon and of Wilberforce. Simeon read his *Essays on Christianity* 'with great delight and edification',[3] and Wilberforce exhorted his family to be duly grateful for the privilege of intimacy with the family at Earlham.[4] Anglican evangelicalism was probably the decisive influence on Gurney. But he read widely in nonconformist sources, and recognized the similarity between some Quaker doctrines and the teachings of Wesley—his dcotrine, for instance, of the prevenient grace in all men, making them free to accept or reject salvation,

---

[1] Poem by Jeremiah Wiffen, c. 1820, in *JFHS* (1916), 175–6. For a less enthusiastic verse account, see the relevant stanza of *Quakerieties for 1838 by an Embryo 'Harvest Man'* (London, 1838).

[2] John Southall on Joseph Cooper, at 1836 YM, *JFHS* (1920), 84.

[3] David E. Swift, *Joseph John Gurney Banker, Reformer, and Quaker* (Middletown, Connecticut, 1962) p. 129.

[4] Robert Isaac Wilberforce and Samuel Wilberforce, *The Life of William Wilberforce*; 2nd ed., London, 1839, vol. iv, p. 298.

and his belief that holiness, and even perfection, are possible for the regenerate man.[1]

Evangelical theology was rooted in the concept of Original Sin. Through the Fall, the image of God in man is totally effaced so that it is impossible for man to please God or obey His Law by his own efforts. 'We are by nature the children of wrath. Prone to iniquity, and transgressors from the womb, we are alienated from God who is the source of all happiness; and in the world to come, eternal separation from him, and, therefore eternal misery, is the appointed consequence of our evil doings.'[2] From this terrible impasse, man is rescued by the Atonement. The evangelicals expounded the forensic view of the Atonement: as all men suffered through Adam's fall, so the world's sins were laid on Christ, whose perfect righteousness satisfied God's Law. Through faith, the believer appropriates to himself the merits of Christ. This faith is to be distinguished from the nominal Christian's 'notional' knowledge of God, 'a saving faith in Jesus is not merely intellectual—it springs from the heart, works by love'.[3] Here evangelicals, Quaker and non-Quaker alike,[4] lay great emphasis on the work of the Spirit, who works to effect the true conversion of sinners: '"The Comforter, who is the Holy Ghost," *dwells* not in an unrenewed heart. He pleads with the sinner, convincing him of sin, and leading him to repentance.'[5]

Although good works do not make a good man, it is the crucial paradox of evangelicalism that a converted man does good works. They are the essential proof of the possession of justifying faith, for without it, it is impossible to do good. 'Alas! that any should be so deluded into self-sufficiency, as to fancy that without a living faith in the Lord Jesus Christ, they can do justly, love mercy, and walk humbly with

[1] He quotes the Wesleyan, Adam Clarke, in his *Observations on the Society of Friends*, pp. 62–3. The account of Wesleyan and moderate Calvinist theology, in the pages that follow, is based on J. D. Walsh, *The Yorkshire Evangelicals in the Eighteenth Century: with special reference to Methodism* (Cambridge Univ. Ph.D. thesis, 1956).

[2] Joseph John Gurney, *Essays on the Evidences, Doctrines, and Practical Operation, of Christianity* (London, 1825), p. 510.

[3] *Ibid.*, 509

[4] Cf. Walsh, *op. cit.*, p. 15.

[5] YM Epistle, 1878.

God.'[1] Gurney's account of the process of justification and sanctification has more in common with Wesleyanism than with the moderate calvinism of the Anglican evangelicals. Where the calvinist taught that Justification effected a relative change in the relationship between God and man, Wesley claimed that at the moment of Justification a real change took place in the soul, which is freed from the power of sin and made holy. Although Gurney frequently speaks of 'imputed righteousness',[2] he describes the converted as 'the *regenerate* children of God. They are introduced to a new world, and are animated by new principles of action. A "new heart" is given to them, and a "new spirit" is put within them. They are born a second time.'[3]

The Bible was of central importance for the evangelical, the only source of knowledge of God, and a miraculously flawless document. 'Friends now assert that if the Bible says anything, *it* is certainly right',[4] commented a critic of evangelicalism in the sixties. To accept the Bible as the only vehicle of knowledge of God, was to abandon the traditional Quaker doctrine of the Light Within, enlightening every man. Thus, when Yearly Meeting, in 1829, in reaction against Hicksism, issued an epistle maintaining the paramount authority of scripture, it was rightly seen as an important mark of evangelical supremacy. John Wilkinson, a former Yearly Meeting Clerk who later resigned his membership, records that 'I was weak enough to imagine it was a first step'[5]—in, of course, an evangelical direction.

The evangelical, believing that salvation came through the possession of (evangelical) faith, was confronted by a troubling moral problem—what was the fate of the heathen, who had no opportunity of obtaining this faith? One common answer was that of simple agnosticism: 'the wisest and safest course . . . is to leave the question of his manner of

---

[1] Isaac Crewdson, *A Beacon to the Society of Friends* (London and Manchester. 1835), p. 152.
[2] e.g. *Essays on Christianity*, p.437.
[3] ibid., p. 465.
[4] Joseph B. Forster, *On Liberty* (London, 1867), p. 21.
[5] *Quakerism Examined: In a Reply to the Letter of Samuel Tuke* (London, 1836), p. 314.

dealing with those who never hear the gospel message, as one among his "secret things".[1] Gurney took a positively optimistic view of the fate of the heathen, in a doctrine which, though probably drawn from traditional Quaker sources, bears a striking resemblance to the theology of Wesley. Gurney begins with the concept of the universality of the Atonement (which is, of course, to be distinguished from a theory of universal salvation). Since Christ died for all men, 'so, on the other hand, *all* men have received a *measure* of that divine influence, through which alone they can permanently enjoy the mercy of God'.[2] Elsewhere he formulates this concept in a way which corresponds precisely to Barclay's Light Within: 'in the midst of his ruin by the fall, he is visited with a ray of heavenly light independently of any outward revelation."[3]

Yet there was a clear tendency among evangelicals to neglect the theory of the Light Within—the core of earlier Quakerism. Those who left the Society, Crewdson and Wilkinson, stigmatized the doctrine frankly as 'this delusive notion',[4] and Gurney himself clearly had mental reservations on the subject. Ash traced his first doubts on the soundness of Barclay to Gurney's criticisms of the doctrine of Universal Light made in casual conversation.[5] An evangelical at 1861 Yearly Meeting went so far as to recommend the discontinuance of the term Inward Light, 'as it had been grievously misinterpreted out of the Society, and was not found in Scripture'.[6]

Quaker evangelicals, like many non-Quakers, were troubled by the mysterious doctrines of Election and Predestination. Gurney refused to discuss Predestination, con-

[1] Edward Ash, *Seven Letters to a Member of the Society of Friends* (London, 1855), p. 7.

[2] Joseph John Gurney, *Observations on the Society of Friends*, p. 35; cf. p. 62 for an approving reference to the views of Wilberforce and of the Wesleyan Methodists.

[3] Joseph John Gurney, *Portable Evidence of Christianity*, p. 134. For Barclay's thought, cf. p. 17ff. below. Gurney's sister, Elizabeth Fry, who hated the doctrine of predestination, marked with a 'u' the passages in her Bible which supported the doctrine of universal grace. Her granddaughter Elizabeth Fry's *Journal*, 1844, *JFHS*, 1953, p. 22.

[4] *Beacon*, p. 77; *Quakerism Examimed*, Ch. II, *passim*.

[5] Edward Ash, *A Retrospect of My Life* (Bristol, 1874), p. 23.

[6] *The Friend* (1861), 139.

sidering it to be among the hidden things of God,[1] but in his private journal he noted that the doctrine seemed untenable,[2] and in *Chalmeriana* he quoted Wilberforce with warm approval, to the effect that a real offer of salvation is made to every man.[3] Edward Ash, his friend and in many respects his disciple, was deeply concerned with Election and Predestination. He felt that their scriptural authority was too clear to be doubted, and even viewed Predestination as 'a precious source of comfort and strength'.[4] He rejected the doctrine of Reprobation; salvation is wholly of God, but men's damnation is wholly of themselves[5]—a common moderate calvinist position. Even so, he went further than most evangelical Friends. When *The Friend* reviewed his essay on Election, it called it the first Quaker defence of the doctrine, and added, 'thus to represent [Election] is to confute it'.[6]

The heyday of Quaker evangelicalism extended from perhaps 1830 to perhaps 1885. It is possible to find many landmarks of evangelical supremacy during these years, such as the declarations of Yearly Meeting on the supremacy of scripture, in 1829 and 1835, or the trial of strength between quietists and evangelicals, in 1837—which the latter won—as to whether to authorize Gurney's projected journey to America.[7] It is not necessary to discuss the involved debates and disputes of those years in any detail here—suffice it to say that the 1830s were the period of transition. Although evangelicals were in a majority, quietists were still vocal and influential; and evangelicals themselves were not always united, as the Beacon controversy showed.

In 1835, a Manchester manufacturer, Isaac Crewdson, a dedicated evangelical, published *A Beacon to the Society of*

---

[1] *Essays on Christianity*, p. 195.

[2] *Journal*, 24 July 1820.

[3] *Chalmeriana: or, Colloquies with Dr. Chalmers* (London, 1853, written 1830–3), p. 4.

[4] *Seven Letters*, p. 10.

[5] *Four Essays on Theological Subjects* (London, 1864), pp. 58–61.

[6] *The Friend* (1864), 291.

[7] When a Quaker minister wished to pay an official visit to other countries, he had to gain the approval of the Yearly Meeting of Ministers and Elders. In Gurney's case, quietists opposed the project strongly, but without success.

Friends. This was intended as an answer to Elias Hicks, but it went to an extreme which even Quaker evangelicals could not countenance, attacking the doctrine of the Light Within, and Quaker traditions of mysticism and silent worship.[1] The book caused a furore, a pamphlet war ensued, and the Yearly Meeting of 1835, itself strongly evangelical, set up a committee of inquiry which was dominated by evangelicals. The members of this committee found themselves in fundamental agreement with Crewdson—their criticisms of him were peripheral and unconvincing, and their final decision equivocal.[2] Crewdson decided to resign, founding a schismatic sect, the fortunes of which are studied in the next chapter. Later, evangelicals mourned over the episode, realizing the fundamental agreement between Crewdson, and those who sat in judgment on him.[3]

The great quietist leaders, such as Sarah Grubb and Thomas Shillitoe, were already old in the 1830s. When they died, no younger Friends of any note took their place. All the eminent and 'weighty' Friends of the mid-Victorian era were evangelicals. Quietists remained vocal, and waged sporadic attacks on evangelicalism at Yearly Meeting, but they were few in number, and their voices had the accents of despair: 'William Graham & Jos. Armfield occupied considerable time in discourses of the most lugubrious tone. No ray of light or comfort could they discern in any direction.'[4] Evangelicals regarded them as at the best misguided, at the worst, eccentrics. Their references to quietist speeches at this time often carry unmistakable overtones of affectionate contempt.

Quaker evangelicalism was destined to fall, not before the attacks of quietists, but before the gradual inroads of liberal theology. In 1887, a conference was held at Richmond, Indiana, which was intended to mark the triumph of Quaker evangelicalism, but which, in the event, proved a landmark of its decline in England. With remarkable unanimity, the

---

[1] *A Beacon*, 65, 77, 96 and 153.

[2] *The Whole Correspondence between the Committee of the Meeting of Friends, and Isaac Crewdson* (London, 1836), pp. 22ff. cf. p. 46 below.

[3] Edward Ash, 'The Beacon Controversy, and the Yearly Meeting's Committee of 1835–7', *The Friend* (1870), 207–11.

[4] J. S. Rowntree, *Account of 1871 YM*, p. 35 (MS in FHL).

American Quakers who attended, adopted the Richmond Declaration, an evangelical statement of faith drafted by J. B. Braithwaite, the leader of the English deputation. On returning home to England, the deputation naturally expected that the Declaration would be officially endorsed by their own Yearly Meeting. A passage in Braithwaite's diary describes their disappointment: 'I find on coming home a *strong* feeling against the Declaratn. which is decried as a creed. This . . . is evidently a feeling that is widely spread. It has occasioned me—shall I confess—no little anxiety.'[1] Some of its opponents approved of the Declaration's contents, but disliked the adoption of what was, in effect, a creed; but much of the opposition came from advocates of liberal theology, such as J. W. Rowntree and Edward Worsdell, who were appalled by a doctrinal statement which 'assert(s) explicitly all the characteristic and most objectionable dogmas of traditional Theology'.[2] In the event, Yearly Meeting did not endorse the Declaration, simply printing it in its minutes, without comment. The decision was of great significance, for it marked the beginnings of evangelicalism's decline. As the twentieth century progressed, Quaker evangelicals would become a small and rather eccentric minority presenting an image very like that of the quietists during the 1860s.

The rise of evangelicalism had a profound effect on mid-Victorian Quakerism. It is, of course, difficult to be sure of the real impact of doctrine upon other attitudes and upon behaviour, to understand the connection between developments in theology and social changes, but some of the consequences of the widespread adoption of evangelical views by Friends seem fairly clear. One of the most important was that it helped destroy the concept of the Society of Friends as a Peculiar People, especially called to follow a distinctive way of life in partial isolation from a corrupt environment. Evangelicals were to campaign successfully in the 1850s for the abolition of many of the barriers which separated Quakers from their fellow Christians—such as their unusual

---

[1] J. B. Braithwaite, *Journal*, 31 Dec. 1887 (MSS in FHL).
[2] Edward Worsdell, *The Gospel of Divine Help*; 2nd ed., London 1888, p. 24, 'Note to Chapter I', dated Dec. 1887.

costume and patterns of speech, and the rule forbidding
them to marry non-Quakers—a campaign which is analysed
in Chapter V. A Quaker evangelical felt himself closer to a
non-Quaker evangelical than to a quietist from his own
church. The great Congregationalist, R. W. Dale, claimed
that 'The Evangelical movement encouraged what is called
an undenominational temper. It emphasized the vital importance of the Evangelical creed, but it regarded almost with
indifference all forms of Church polity that were not in
apparent and irreconcilable antagonism to that creed.'[1] The
friendship which men such as Gurney felt for Anglican
clergymen was in the strongest possible contrast with the
attitudes of the quietists of an earlier generation, with the
outlook summed up in the dying words of Thomas Shillitoe:
'The clergy of this country, to a man, every one of them, are
antichrist so long as they wear the gowns and receive the
pay.'[2]

Many Quaker evangelicals left Friends, and many more
considered such a step, repelled by the opposition of quietists
to evangelical faith, worried by doubts on baptism, and
attracted, very often, by the eloquence and piety of some
evangelical clergyman. It is significant that the three leading
Quaker exponents of evangelicalism, Gurney, Edward Ash,
and Joseph Bevan Braithwaite, all came close to leaving
Friends. Gurney opted for the Quakerism of his birth only
after a protracted period of doubt.[3] His friend, Ash, actually
resigned his Quaker membership in 1852, and became a
communicating Congregationalist, though a lifetime's associations were to draw him back to Friends.[4] J. B. Braithwaite, Gurney's biographer, and a 'Quaker Bishop' in his
later years,[5] was on the point of resigning in 1840. He
decided to attend one more Yearly Meeting, and tributes
paid there to the lives of ministers who had recently died

---

[1] R. W. Dale, *The Old Evangelicalism and the New* (London, 1889), p. 17.
[2] Quoted in William Hodgson, *The Society of Friends in the Nineteenth Century: A Historical View of the successive Convulsions and Schisms therein during that period.* (Philadelphia, 1875), vol. i, p. 314.
[3] *Journal*, 22 Sept. 1826; 2 Aug. 1838.
[4] Ash, *A Retrospect*, pp. 48ff.
[5] A. T. Alexander, 'Yearly Meeting Attenders—Familiar Personalities', *JFHS* (1930), 15–16.

moved him so much that he decided to stay a Quaker. The elements which bound such men to Friends are discussed more fully later; suffice it here to say that the Society of Friends was not only a church, but also a closely interwoven group of kinsmen, sharply differentiated in many of their habits and customs from the wider society. To a birthright Friend such as Gurney, Quakerism was almost a hereditary distinction, an intrinsic element in his personality. Rather than cut himself off from it, he would try to remodel it in an evangelical image.

This *rapprochement* with other evangelical Christians had other implications. For a time, from the 1870s onwards, evangelicals tended to remodel their traditional silent worship and inspirational ministry on the lines of a nonconformist chapel, at least in their Sunday evening meetings. The development of so-called mission meetings, with hymn singing and a prepared address, was little short of revolutionary. The Home Missioners appointed in country districts in the 1880s acted very much like nonconformist clergymen, and it became quite common for ardent Quaker evangelicals to hold what were, in effect, revival meetings.[1] Such developments went much further among Quaker evangelicals in America, who adopted a paid pastorate, and most of the externals of other protestant churches—a pulpit, bells, stained glass, and so on.

The adoption of evangelicalism had a definite impact on Quaker philanthropy. It was not the only source of philanthropy—the Anti-Slavery agitation antedates the triumph of evangelicalism among Friends by many years—but it made Quakers more ready to co-operate with other Christians in interdenominational enterprises. Until perhaps the 1850s, many, however, even among evangelicals, clung to the ideal of a Peculiar People, and feared 'the increased intercourse with others wch takes place through benevolent institns'.[2] Evangelicalism, in itself, often seemed to be a fulcrum of philanthropic action. All the notable Victorian Quaker

[1] These changes are discussed more fully, with references, in pp. 93ff. and 99ff. below.

[2] Benjamin Seebohm. Josiah Forster, *Notes on Yearly Meeting from 1828 to 1870 with some exceptions* (MSS. in FHL), *Account of 1841 YM*, f.9.

philanthropists were evangelicals, inasmuch as they had theological opinions at all. It is difficult to see quite why evangelicals were so often active in good works, though it is easy to see why quietists, with their fear of 'creaturely activity', were not. Evangelicalism often seemed to produce great earnestness and strenuousness, an awareness of life as a battlefield, with unthinkably great rewards to be won or lost, a desire to do those good works which were seen as the necessary fruit of saving grace.

There is a more obvious link between evangelicalism and Quaker entry into foreign mission work. Quietists had been opposed to mission work, because of their distrust of human organization, and their belief in the universality of the Light Within. Quakers entered this field remarkably late, in comparison with other denominations—it was not until 1866 that the first Quaker missionary left for India.[1] Foreign mission work, when it was finally taken up, was the direct result of the evangelical's belief in the need for the possession of the right kind of faith. Ignorance, in *A Pilgrim's Progress*, is refused admission to the Celestial City. In 1896, a Quaker missionary expounded that polarized vision of the world which underlay so much evangelical support for home and foreign missions, Bible and tract societies: 'I think it is a wonderfully significant thing that in all these pictures of the missionary field and of the state of the world, we see heathenism painted black. That is the colour that it should be painted.'[2] A leading advocate of liberal theology immediately stated what was both an older and a more recent Quaker doctrine—which was ultimately to lead to the abandonment of foreign missions—the duty of the missionary is to read 'the palimpsest of the human soul' and the characters which God has traced on it.[3] The growth of liberal theology was to go hand in hand with the rise of a sympathetic interest in eastern religions, and of distrust for conventional mis-

---

[1] Rachel Metcalfe. She was the first permanent resident missionary, with regular financial support; there had always been Quaker itinerant ministers, who travelled from place to place under 'concern' for a limited time.

[2] *Proceedings Darlington Conference on Foreign Missions, 1896* (London, 1897), p. 17.

[3] ibid., p. 23.

sionary endeavour. In the sphere of foreign missions, one can discern the impact of theological ideas on action with exceptional clarity.

One of the problems which confronted evangelicals was the difficulty of reconciling their beliefs with the writing of the early Friends, especially the quietism of Barclay's *Apology*, which had always been regarded as authoritative. It is usual for members of a church to idealize its origins, and regard the teachings of its founders as inspired by God. Their inability to do this left Quaker evangelicals with a difficulty, which they never satisfactorily solved.

Sometimes they ignored the whole question—Isaac Braithwaite told his son, who was searching the works of early Quakers for evangelical doctrines: 'thou hast nothing to do with our early Friends further than as they endeavoured to follow Christ.'[1] Sometimes they boldly claimed that the early Friends had been guilty of theological error,[2]—they opposed the republication of Barclay's *Apology*, an opposition which led to many bitter disputes with quietists. The rise of liberal theology was to coincide with a revived interest in the early history of Quakerism—the aged evangelical J. B. Braithwaite learnt of the establishment of the Friends Historical Society, in 1903, with real anxiety and dismay.[3]

Evangelicalism had implications for the psychology of the individual, as well as for the corporate life of the church. It often produced a measure of fear and anxiety—it was impossible to be certain of the reality of one's conversion, the sufficiency of one's faith, and yet the highest imaginable stakes depended on it. The conversion experience, which typically occurred in late adolescence,[4] was often accom-

---

[1] Quoted in *J. Bevan Braithwaite: A Friend of the Nineteenth Century, By his Children* (London, 1909), p. 83.

[2] Edward Ash, *The Christian Profession of the Society of Friends, commended to its Members* (London, 1837), pp. 29–30.

[3] J. B. Braithwaite, *Journal*, 10 Sept. 1903.

[4] Not all evangelicals claimed to pass through a conversion experience. Some Quaker evangelicals thought it essential, others believed conversion could be gradual. For a clash on the subject, see Anne Vernon, *A Quaker Business Man: The Life of Joseph Rowntree 1836–1925* (London, 1958), p. 22; cf. *Friends of a Half Century; Fifty Memorials with Portraits of Members of the Society of Friends, 1840–1890*, ed. William Robinson (London, 1891), p. 273.

panied by extreme fear—*primus in orbe deos fecit timor*. One such experience was described many years later by a Quaker M.P., a wealthy industrialist: 'I seemed to see things in a different perspective. I got frightened and things that never cost me a thought before seemed red sins. What would profit me in exchange for my soul? . . . I was near mad with confusion and fright and tried to get away alone.'[1] Edward Worsdell, in his evangelical days, used to wake up at night overcome with horror at the thought of the fate of the unconverted.[2] It is difficult to say how typical such experiences were—they belong, perhaps, to the pathology of evangelical history—but the strongly marked fear of death which characterized many Quaker evangelicals, including J. J. Gurney and Elizabeth Fry, was probably rooted in such eschatological terrors.

Another source of anxiety lay in the consciousness of post-conversion sin. Edmund Gosse, in his account of his childhood among the Plymouth Brethren, recalls his father's anxiety at the contradiction between his son's 'unquestionable sanctification by faith and . . . equally unquestionable naughtiness'.[3] Evangelicals drew on the comforting concept of 'continued recourse to the fountain', but since righteousness was the necessary fruit of conversion, lapses were a natural source of disquiet. As a young child, the Quaker philanthropist, Peter Bedford, was so disturbed by an act of profanity he committed that he intentionally burnt his hands with live coals, to bring home the realization of the consequence of sin.[4]

The nature of his faith meant that an evangelical faced with intellectual doubts was in a position of terrible psychological strain. If salvation depends on the possession of the right kind of faith, doubts about the details of faith appear as perilous temptations. If the evangelical's faith were true, and he abandoned it, he would be embracing his own damnation. As a Quaker society put it, in 1900, 'ignorance & fear largely keep Evangelicals from seeing further than

[1] Quoted in Charlotte Fell Smith, *James Nicholson Richardson of Bessbrook* (London, 1925), p. 147.
[2] *The Gospel of Divine Help*, pp. 74–5.
[3] Edmund Gosse, *Father and Son* (London, 1958, first published 1907), p. 146.
[4] *Friends of a Half Century*, p. 73

their creed.'[1] Worsdell described his own progression from evangelicalism to theological liberalism in these terms: 'he resolved to run all risks, and to follow only such teachings as his conscience could accept, wherever they came from'.[2] It is the use of the word 'risks' which is so remarkable and significant here. It is this attitude which inspired the real alarm with which J. B. Braithwaite viewed liberal theology. Heightened to the hallucinatory intensity of childhood, it appears in Logan Pearsall Smith's early recollections of the Hicksites: 'I remember climbing the wall that surrounded one of the Hicksite meeting-houses, and gazing in on those precincts with all the horror of one who gazes into Hell.'[3] But the late Victorian evangelical, if he was an educated man, could not but be aware of the difficulties of his position, of the findings of biblical criticism, for instance, or the wide-spread acceptance of criticisms of the substitutionary theory of the atonement. A Quaker evangelical, at least, could not ignore them—he heard them constantly expounded at Quaker meetings,[4] and read them in Quaker periodicals. The inevitable result, for many, was a feeling of insecurity and strain—as Jonathan Grubb, a veteran evangelical minister, put it, when confronted with Quaker expositions of liberal theology, 'he could not but feel that an attempt was being made to sweep away the ground of his hope.'[5]

THE QUIETISTS

Perhaps the most striking single characteristic of the small group of Victorian Quaker quietists was their unquestioning and uncritical reverence for the writings of the early Friends. In particular, Barclay's *Apology*, first published in 1676, a massive scholastic exposition of quietism, was their *Summa*, to be read and quoted the way evangelicals read and quoted the Bible. 'Fox and Barclay became in a small way

---

[1] *Socialist Quaker Society Minutes* (MSS in FHL), 26 July 1900.
[2] *The Gospel of Divine Help*, p. 75.
[3] Logan Pearsall Smith, *Unforgotten Years* (London, 1938), p. 26.
[4] There is an interesting account of this process, in Yorkshire, in Edward Grubb, 'Some Personal Experiences', *FQE* (1938), 302–3. Many YM debates also reflect it.
[5] *The Friend* (1885), 144 (speech during the 1885 YM debate on *A Reasonable Faith*). Jonathan Grubb was Edward's father.

Saint Fox and Saint Barclay—they became objects of worship—the brazen serpents of Quakerism.' [1] Difficulties, such as the difference between the thought of Barclay and Fox, never troubled them. They were not intellectuals, and produced no theological treatises. Their thought must be garnered from the writings of Barclay himself, from their correspondence, and from unofficial transcripts of their sermons.

The formative influence on Victorian quietism must undoubtedly be found in the writings of the early Friends. Many quietists read non-Quaker mystical writings, but they were regarded as private devotional aids to deepen and strengthen a position already held. The writings of Madame de Guyon were popular—Sarah Lynes Grubb studied French to be able to read them in the original. In 1838, *The Irish Friend* claimed that Friends had always valued, *inter alia*, the writings of Guyon, Fenelon, Molinos, and William Law.[2] Samuel Botham's daughter claimed that her father used to 'value highly and read industriously' the life and works of Guyon, Fenelon, Francis de Sales, Thomas a Kempis, Boehme, and Molinos—as well as the Bible.[3] The list is interesting because Botham was an obscure Friend, not a religious leader, but such energetic eclecticism can hardly have been typical.

All Victorian quietists regarded Barclay as 'the sheet anchor of our principles',[4] and an understanding of their thought is best obtained from an analysis of the *Apology*. For Barclay, the primary source of knowledge of God is immediate revelation, the Light Within the heart of every man. This Light is distinguished from reason and from conscience [5] (a distinction many later thinkers were to find meaningless).[6] Despite his own excellent education, and his

---

[1] Forster, *On Liberty*, p. 23.

[2] *The Irish Friend* (1838), 101.

[3] Samuel Botham, 1758–1823. Mary Howitt *An Autobiography*, ed. Margaret Howitt (London, 1889), vol. i, p. 49; Amice Lee, *Laurels and Rosemary, The Life of William and Mary Howitt* (London, 1955), p. 26.

[4] *The Friend* (1846) 209.

[5] Robert Barclay, *An Apology for the true Christian Divinity, as the same is held forth and preached by the people, in scorn, called Quakers;* 14th ed., Glasgow, 1886, pp. 12, 102.

[6] cf. p. 36 below.

zeal in writing controversial works, he foreshadows the anti-intellectualism of later quietists in his depreciation of reason, 'the soaring airy head-knowledge'.[1] He valued the Bible, but thought it had only a subordinate and relative impor-tance as a source of religious knowledge,[2] pointing out the problems involved in its interpretation, and the variety of Christian creeds which have been erected on the same Biblical foundation. The paramount source of knowledge of God is the Light Within.

Barclay's theology rests on the postulate of Original Sin. He sees the fall of man as a radical corruption of human nature: 'All Adam's posterity, or mankind . . . is fallen, degenerated, and dead . . . subject unto the power, nature, and seed of the serpent, which he soweth in men's hearts, while they abide in this natural and corrupted estate.'[3] Despite this ruined condition, the death of Christ obtained for all the possibility of salvation. Salvation is available to all, whether they have heard the Christian message or not,[4] but it is not necessarily obtained by all. Salvation depends on obedience to the Light or Seed of grace within the heart. This is universally present, and all men are free to obey or to reject its intimations: '*God, in and by this Light and Seed, invites, calls, exhorts, and strives with every man, in order to save him:* which, as it is received and not resisted, works the salvation of *all*, even of those who are ignorant of the death and sufferings of Christ.'[5] This Light is wholly super-natural; the natural man grows closer to God by the suppres-sion of his own will and reason, so that he can be entirely dominated by this Light. Barclay's theology 'wholly excludes the natural man from having any place or portion in his own salvation',[6] and salvation is 'a passiveness rather than an act'.[7]

Despite his quietism, Barclay emphasized the need for real righteousness, in order to obtain salvation. He made elaborate attempts to avoid what he called Arminianism, and to reconcile his belief in the need for individual sanctifica-tion with his quietist views of grace and human nature, speaking of 'the *formation of Christ in us, Christ born and*

---

[1] *Apology*, p. 12.   [2] ibid., pp. 46ff.   [3] ibid., p. 66.
[4] ibid., pp. 76ff.   [5] ibid., p. 93.   [6] ibid., p. 94.   [7] ibid., p. 104.

brought forth in us, from which good works as naturally proceed as fruit from a fruitful tree'.[1] He taught the doctrine
of Perfection. As he put it in his eighth Proposition:

In whom this pure and holy *birth* is fully brought forth, the body of
death and sin comes to be crucified and removed, and their hearts
united and subjected to the *truth*; so as not to obey any suggestions or
temptations of the evil one, but to be free from actual sinning and
transgressing of the *law of God*, and in that respect *perfect*: yet doth
this perfection still admit of a growth; and there remaineth always in
some part a possibility of sinning.[2]

The writings of nineteenth-century quietist Friends mirror the thought of Barclay. Paradoxically, they treasured his
scholastic exposition, but condemned religious learning as
tending to 'promote the creature' and deflect the individual
from the search for true inward experience of God. Biblical
or theological learning was 'a carnal wisdom, a head knowledge, an outward learning'.[3]

This anti-intellectualism was a persisting trait of quietism
and one of its main lines of demarcation from evangelicalism. In 1872 a critical account of a sermon by an American quietist at Manchester noted that 'The purport of his
petition was, that pride of intellect might humble itself, and
by the time-honoured methods of ceasing to think, forbear-
ing to inquire, and abstaining from examination, effect a
return to the peace and joy of faith.'[4] In its extreme form,
quietism opposed the application of conscious intelligence,
not only to doctrine and preaching, but to the most mundane
aspects of the church's corporate life—thus, in 1854, the
proposal to call a conference to discuss the declining numbers of English Quakers was attacked by a quietist in these
terms: 'The very idea of changes and plans made in the
wisdom that is of the earth, earthy, strikes at the root of true
spirituality.'[5]

Most typically, the theology of the quietist minister[6] was

---

[1] *Apology*, p. 144.   [2] ibid., p. 171.
[3] Ann Jones, at Men's Yearly Meeting 1836, quoted in Hodgson, *The Society of
Friends in the Nineteenth Century*, vol. i, p. 298.
[4] *The Manchester Friend* (1872), 184.
[5] *The British Friend* (1854), 161.
[6] For an account of the Quaker ministry, which differed in most respects from
that of other churches, see pp. 94–99 below.

revealed through his use of traditional sermon images—
'centring down', 'digging deep', avoiding 'the willings and
the runnings'—an inherited and stereotyped language intended to represent mystical experience. Nineteenth-century
quietists were led to greater precision of theological language
by their fear of being identified with the Hicksites. Matters
to which earlier quietists had devoted little articulate speculation and probably little conscious thought—the nature of
Christ, the atonement, the role of scripture[1]—were now defined. Formerly, vague, unitarian-type beliefs had probably
been fairly common;[2] now, quietists defended the doctrine
of the deity of Christ. Some quietist ministers, including
Shillitoe and John Barclay, expounded the doctrine of the
Atonement in terms that would have satisfied any evangelical: 'We also own all that the Scriptures speak of, respecting
His most satisfactory sacrifice, and that he tasted death for
every man, purchased eternal redemption for us.'[3] Not all
quietists, however, were prepared to accept the doctrine of a
vicarious Atonement—the conservative Daniel Pickard
noted, after hearing an evangelical address, 'I was pained to
hear him say that our Saviour was *punished in our stead*—for
excess of truth pays tribute unto error.'[4]

Like Barclay, nineteenth-century quietists believed that
human nature was ruined by original sin.[5] Man's way from
this impasse was to obey the Light Within, the supernatural
Seed of grace in his heart.[6] The core of the quietist message
was emptying and passivity, so that the Seed of grace could
grow unhampered by natural 'willings and runnings'.

now the work that is wanted, as far as I have in this and some other
favoured seasons had capacity to see, is a sinking down and bowing

[1] William Sturge, *Some Recollections of a Long Life* (privately printed, 1893)
pp. 39–40.
[2] Mary Howitt, *An Autobiography*, pp. 46–7; *Friends of a Half Century*, p. 218.
[3] John Barclay, a nineteenth-century quietist, belonged to the same family as
the Apologist, Robert, from whom, of course, he should be distinguished. *A
Selection from the Letters and Papers of the late John Barclay* (1st American ed.,
from 2nd London ed., Philadelphia, 1847), p. 193; cf. *Journal of the Life, Labours
and Travels of Thomas Shillitoe* (2nd ed., London, 1839), vol. ii, pp. 424–5.
[4] Daniel Pickard, *Journal*, 26 Jan. 1870 (MSS in FHL).
[5] Sarah Grubb, quoted in Hodgson, *The Society of Friends in the Nineteenth
Century*, vol. i, p. 295.
[6] *Barclay Letters and Papers*, p. 35.

down yet lower and deeper than many of us have hitherto humbled ourselves,—even under the government and dominion of the holy seed, Christ Jesus; that so we may, through subjection to Him, be led to 'cease from our own works', and to let him do and work all things in us according to his own divine will.[1]

To the quietist, the intellectual understanding of Christian doctrines is insufficient, for they can only be truly understood if Christ is experienced in the heart. This was the ground of the dying Shillitoe's indictment of J. J. Gurney: 'I apprehend J. J. Gurney is no Quaker in principle. . . . I love the man, for the work's sake, so far as it goes; but he has never been emptied from vessel to vessel, and from sieve to sieve, nor known the baptism of the Holy Ghost and of fire, to cleanse the floor of his heart from his Episcopalian notions.'[2]

John Barclay considered that the evangelicals were 'crucifying unto themselves the Son of God afresh',[3] even when their theology was formally correct, because their beliefs were rooted 'in the notion and dead apprehension'[4] rather than in mystical experience. It was common for quietists to stigmatize evangelicalism as 'an easy worldly religion'[5] because of its neglect of mysticism.

Nineteenth century quietists stressed that real personal righteousness is not only possible, but essential for salvation, and that perfection is attainable in this life. They believed that evangelicals neglected the doctrine of holiness,[6] apparently misinterpreting evangelicalism, for they often spoke as if the evangelical doctrine of imputed righteousness made personal sanctification unnecessary. Thus, Daniel Pickard records a conversation with an evangelical and notes as a postscript: 'all *true experience* is plain—there is no man justified but he who is also sanctified at least in measure.'[7]

---

[1] *Barclay Letters and Papers*, p. 139.
[2] Hodgson, vol. i, p. 313.
[3] *Barclay Letters and Papers*, p. 135.
[4] ibid., He goes on to point out that evil spirits can testify of Christ!
[5] Hodgson, vol. ii, p. 358.
[6] For a quietist statement of the doctrine of Perfection, see *Journal of Thomas Shillitoe*, vol. i, p. 37. For an (American) allegation of its neglect by Friends, Hodgson, vol. i, p. 230.
[7] *Journal*, 5 Feb. 1870.

Sarah Grubb had made this criticism of evangelicalism in a letter of 1834: 'Faith in the atoning sacrifice is abundantly enforced, while there is little said inviting us to yield up the *will*, with the *affections and lusts, to be crucified.*'[1]

The quietists' emphasis on the Light Within had several implications. They believed firmly in the universal offer of salvation, in contra-distinction to some evangelicals—Sarah Grubb told the extreme American evangelical, Elisha Bates, that she could not recognize his ministry because 'I have never once heard thee preach universal grace.'[2] They believed that the guidance of the indwelling Spirit, and not the Bible, was the primary source of religious knowledge and condemned the evangelical attitude to scripture: 'The exalting of the Holy Scripture to a place in our estimation which they do not assign to themselves, has been a device fruitful of vast injury to our religious Society.'[3] Shillitoe explained this doctrine for the edification of a tribe of American Indians: 'I consider such, as tell you that they [the scriptures] are the only rule or means of salvation, to be under the influence of a wrong spirit; for if we are to believe such sentiments as these, what must have become of millions of our fellow-creatures before the Scriptures were in existence?'[4] The fear of identification with Hicksism led conservatives to stress the value and excellence of the Bible, but they firmly refused to accept it as the primary source of knowledge of God.

The similarities between quietist and evangelical doctrine were greater than either side was willing to recognize. Both parties accepted the doctrines of Original Sin and of man's rescue from this state by the Atonement. Many evangelicals, including the whole body of Wesleyan Methodists, accepted the doctrines of the inner Light and of the universal offer of salvation. All evangelicals stressed the need for sanctifica-

---

[1] *A Selection from the Letters of the late Sarah Grubb (formerly Sarah Lynes)* (Sudbury, 1848), p. 299.

[2] ibid., 308. Some seventy-three years later, a quietist expressed similar views through the improbable channels of the *Harrogate Herald*, FHL Cuttings, CC 126.

[3] Daniel Pickard, *An Expostulation on Behalf of the Truth against Departures in Doctrine, Practice, and Discipline* (London, 1864), pp. 32–3.

[4] *Journal of Thomas Shillitoe*, vol. ii, p. 213 (a letter to the Seneca tribe, dated 9 Mar. 1827).

tion, and Wesley taught the doctrine of Perfection. The
essential points of difference, within the Quaker fold, were
the status accorded 'our ancient primitive worthies'; the
relative roles of the inner light and of the Bible, as sources of
revelation; and the attitude taken to mysticism.

The quietists' indictment of evangelicalism was as much
sociological as theological. They realized that evangelicalism spread in the Society largely through increased co-
operation with other denominations in good works, that the
leaders of Quaker evangelicalism were men of wealth and
status, attracted to Anglican evangelicals partly by social
factors. Men such as Shillitoe and John Barclay deplored
the spread of wealth in the Society, and its gradual assimilation to 'the World'. Shillitoe was, by choice, a shoemaker,
with a business consience of neurotic scrupulousness, and
Barclay had rejected the prospect of a successful business
career. From such a vantage point they denounced the
wealth and learning of the evangelicals, in the accents of the
epistle of James. According to the quietist interpretation,
evangelicals were men who had succumbed to the temptation
of accepting the values and pleasures of 'the World'. The
natural corollary of this was that they had absorbed the
theological views then current in English society. As John
Barclay put it: 'It is the distinguishing feature of this heresy,
that it runs among the rich, and the great, and learned, and
the eloquent, and the gifted, and experienced.'[1] The doctrine of inspiration meant, in practice, that conservatives were
confident of the validity of their own inspiration, and took it
for granted that they could pronounce upon the validity
of the inspiration of others. Thus they were essentially indifferent to their declining numbers, and to the numerical
and intellectual strength of their opponents, appropriating
to themselves the New Testament promises to 'little ones'.

Quietist theology had many implications for the social
life of Quakerism. Some of these have already been noted—
the anti-intellectual bias; the fear of organization, even for
missionary or philanthropic purposes; the clinging to the
concept of a 'Peculiar People', who should live in isolation
from the wider society. Quietist theology tended to be

---

[1] *Barclay Letters and Papers*, p. 271.

associated with a particular type of ministry. The quietist minister believed that the words he spoke were literally inspired, that he was a passive instrument of divine communication (this attitude was also held by some evangelical ministers). They were often concerned by the problem of distinguishing inspired messages from natural fluency in public speaking. One of the solutions to this problem was involved unconsciously—the adoption of a highly stereotyped style of ministry, marked by traditional phraseology and a curious chanting intonation. This kind of delivery was equated with inspiration, and its adoption had the merit of reassuring speaker and audience as to the validity of the message. The great quietist ministers of the eighteenth and early nineteenth centuries tended to conform to a psychological type—emotional and scrupulous, passing through successive phases of exaltation and of 'plungings' and 'baptisms'. Despite their fear of human arrangements, quietist ministers travelled great distances to preach to Quaker and non-Quaker audiences. They often claimed telepathic gifts, the power to read minds and see events at a distance. Inspiration was held to determine the daily details of life—Sarah Lynes Grubb insisted on moving, with her husband and children, from Clonmel, Ireland, to England, leaving behind family ties and economic interests, because she felt that 'the Lord . . . was drawing my mind to a residence in England'.[1] Later the Lord directed two more changes of residence.

The doctrine of inspiration meant that all religious communications, even within the family circle, needed to be immediately inspired. Thus, in many quietist homes, family prayer, Bible reading, and religious instruction were avoided, though they became the regular practice of evangelicals. Mary Howitt (1799–1888), in her recollections of her childhood, gives a picture which has many parallels: 'neither she [her mother] nor our father ever gave or permitted us to receive religious tuition. . . . So fearful were they of interfering with His workings, that they did not even teach us the Lord's Prayer.'[2]

[1] *Letters of Sarah Grubb*, p. 11.
[2] Mary Howitt, *An Autobiography*, p. 46.

Some of the teachings of the quietists were resuscitated in the anti-evangelical reaction which was to be embodied in works such as Worsdell's *Gospel of Divine Help*. The leaders of this reaction—which became an orthodoxy—saw the doctrine of the Light Within as the core of Quakerism. They believed in the universality of the offer of salvation, and refused to regard the Bible as the primary source of doctrine. The differences were many and significant—they rejected quietism, welcomed the intellectual study of religion and organized social action, and on the whole discarded the doctrines of Original Sin and of the Atonement. Yet the element of continuity was a strong one, and it would be interesting to find evidence that quietists recognized this. The diaries and papers of conservative Quakers, at the time of the Manchester Conference, for instance, suggest that the relationship escaped them. But it is interesting to note the relatively benign attitude which some conservatives displayed towards the rationalist movement among Manchester Friends in the 1870s,[1] which was rooted in the apprehension that for both schools of thought, evangelicalism was the common enemy.

THE UNITARIAN ELEMENT

Throughout the late eighteenth and nineteenth centuries, there was always an element of Unitarianism in English Quakerism. It did not form a cohesive and continuous movement; its manifestations were sporadic, and whenever it became articulate it was always condemned. But there can be no doubt of its existence.

The first phase of Unitarianism among British Friends came at the end of the eighteenth century, and was the product of the Enlightenment. It was strongest in Ireland, where 'a number in different parts of the nation, were in a disposition to lay waste in great measure the Holy Scriptures, disputed the divinity of Christ, and were not united with the present ministry or discipline of our religious Society, but yet professed to exalt the divine light and im-

---

[1] cf. Joseph Armfield at 1869 YM, in *The Friend* (1869), 125-6.

mediate revelation very highly.'[1] The movement in Ireland led to many resignations and disownments. It had an indirect consequence for English Quakerism, for William Rathbone of Liverpool was disowned for writing a sympathetic account of it—and the Unitarianism of the famous family of philanthropists and merchant princes dates from this time.[2]

It is clear that Rathbone had long been a Unitarian at heart[3]—before his disownment he had educated his son at a school 'for well-to-do Arians'[4]—and there is evidence that the winds of the Enlightenment touched many who never gave public expression to their views, and so never incurred the penalty of expulsion. Catherine Gurney, for instance, recalled that in 1797–8 'the volumes of Godwin, Paine, &c, had fallen into our hands, so that we were truly in the wilderness of error.'[5] The Gurneys' sojourn in the wilderness was a brief one, but it is certain that such views were fairly widely diffused.

On three occasions in less than a hundred years, London Yearly Meeting was called on to give a formal verdict on Unitarianism. On each occasion the verdict was adverse, but the successive trials—for so in effect they were—are of great interest. The first test case was that of Hannah Barnard, a visiting American minister who in 1798 was attacked for heterodoxy. She held that parts of the Old Testament were neither authentic nor edifying, and doubted the miraculous elements in the life of Christ. She was silenced as a minister by London Yearly Meeting, and American Friends subsequently confirmed the sentence by expelling her. She joined the Unitarians.

In 1812 there was a second test case when an English

---

[1] *A Journal of the Life, Travels, and Religious Labours, of William Savery*, ed. Jonathan Evans (London, 1844), p. 293. cf. William Rathbone, *A Narrative of Events that have lately taken place in Ireland, among the Society called Quakers* (London, 1804), Appendix, p. 32.

[2] William Rathbone, *A Memoir of the Proceedings of the Society called Quakers, belonging to the Monthly Meeting of Hardshaw, in Lancashire, in the case of the Author of a Publication entitled A Narrative of Events, etc.* (Liverpool, 1805), passim.

[3] Eleanor F. Rathbone, *William Rathbone A Memoir* (London, 1905), pp. 25–7.

[4] Emily A. Rathbone, *Records of the Rathbone Family* (privately printed, 1913), p. 166.

[5] Augustus J. C. Hare, *The Gurneys of Earlham* (London, 1895), vol. i, p. 82.

Quaker, Thomas Foster, appealed to Yearly Meeting against a sentence of disownment for subscription to the Unitarian Book Society, and for 'low views of the person of Christ'. His disownment was confirmed, and J. J. Gurney, recalling the incident many years later, claimed that the verdict was unanimous, and that this proved 'that in the year 1812, Friends were not Unitarians'.[1] It is significant that he thought the statement in need of proof.

In 1873, there was a third test case, similar to Foster's, when Edward Bennett appealed to Yearly Meeting against a sentence of disownment. He was a Unitarian by conviction; the immediate occasion of offence was that he had given active support to Charles Voysey, who was expelled from the Church of England for Unitarianism, and founded the Theistic Church. Bennett held his views openly, if not aggressively—he circularized his evangelical judges[2] with a questionnaire beginning, 'If Christ be not God, is it not the sin of idolatry to worship him as God?'[3] He was condemned with great unanimity, but some speakers stressed that his offence lay less in his views than in the openness with which he expounded them. One observed, 'Many there knew what it was to be sorely harassed with doubts in the Divinity of our Lord.'[4]

The evidence suggests that these widely separated test cases spring from a long-continued, albeit subterranean, element in Quakerism. In 1852 an editorial in *The Friend* condemned the interest of Friends in 'Unitarian or Deistical' literature.[5] In that year, a visiting American minister gave an impassioned address to Yearly Meeting on the same subject: 'She seemed deeply exercised for some present, who were speculating on religion—who were disposed not to believe anything but what they could prove—who only admitted that Jesus Christ was 'a great prophet' & that he

---

[1] *Chalmeriana*, p. 56.

[2] If a Quaker was disowned by his Monthly Meeting, he could appeal to his Quarterly Meeting, and then, if necessary, to Yearly Meeting. Yearly Meeting was thus the highest court of appeal; all present took part. But the right of appeal was seldom exercised.

[3] *Daylight in Dusty Corners*, given in full in *The Manchester Friend* (1873), 106–7.

[4] *The Friend* (1873), 126.

[5] ibid. (1852), 30.

was commissioned to perform the wonderful miracles which we read of.'[1]

In the late 1860s, Manchester Meeting became a stronghold of such views. Manchester was a long-established centre of Unitarianism, and since Quakers and Unitarians belonged to the same social class it is likely that they were thrown into considerable contact. There is little positive evidence on the matter, but it is perhaps significant that when the Quaker dissidents decided to form a schismatic movement, they met on Unitarian premises,[2] and the only one of their number whose subsequent religious history can be traced joined the Unitarians, returning to Friends in his old age.[3]

The history of the Manchester schismatics, and the personalities involved, are discussed in the next chapter—here we are concerned solely with their theological opinions. They did not form an ideologically united movement; an anonymous member of the Yearly Meeting committee which was set up to investigate them described their views in these terms:

It was apparent that the Friends whose views and objections have been referred to were far from being of one mind on important points. . . . Bearing in mind that this is merely a record of *impressions* it may be stated that there were some whose belief seemed to include little that is distinctively Christian: others whose views appeared to be Socinian, or rather perhaps Hicksite. Others again unwillingly involved in mental perplexity, desirous to grasp the great doctrine of salvation by Christ, while struggling with doubts about 'the miraculous conception', and possibly of other miracles. There were also those who, with honest intent, would describe themselves Friends of the original school. . . . The bond of union among these various classes was a claim to exercise freedom of thought . . .[4]

It is clear that not all the members of the group were Unitarians, though this was the aspect which alarmed Quaker evangelicals most strongly. Perhaps for this reason,

[1] Sybil Jones, address given in Samuel Alexander, *Account of 1852 YM* (MSS. in FHL), pp. 37d–38 (every fourth page numbered). There is much other evidence on this matter.

[2] The Memorial Hall, opened in 1862 to mark the bicentenary of the 1662 ejections.

[3] cf. p. 64 below.

[4] MSS. in FHL, Box 9.4 (3), f. 8.

some of the dissidents avoided giving unequivocal expression to their views on the nature of Christ—this was true of David Duncan, the movement's leader until his death in 1871. A Friend who attended his public lectures stated that 'the language used by DD in public discussion has for a long time been altogether inconsistent with a belief in the divine attributes of our Lord Jesus Christ.'[1] and J. B. Braithwaite, after interviewing Duncan, recorded in his diary that 'it was evidt. that his views were not those held by Friends on the authority of S.S. on the person of the Ld Jesus Xt. and on the efficacy of His atoning sacrifice'.[2]

Apart from their Unitarianism, the Manchester dissidents anticipated, in the details of their thought, the views which would become common currency among Friends some twenty years later. As in the case of an earlier Manchester schism, the Beaconite, the heretics of one generation anticipated the orthodoxy of the next. They unhesitatingly rejected two keystones of evangelicalism—the literal inspiration and infallibility of the Bible, and the substitutionary view of the Atonement:

One of these avowed his inability to accept the whole of the Old Testament, or to believe that a God of love commanded or approved the exterminating wars against the Canaanites. Another asked if the influence of the Holy Spirit would necessarily lead to the acceptance of the doctrine of the atonement. Another could not see why it was needful that there should be a mediator between God & us.[3]

They were stout defenders of what they knew of the conclusions of Higher Criticism—the fullest statement of their position is to be found in Duncan's *Can an Outward Revelation be Perfect?* This is not, of course, a contribution to scriptural exegesis, but rather an attempt to point out the significance of biblical criticism for a Quaker audience: 'How rash and unthinking and irreverent is the dogmatism, which rests all possibility of faith in God upon writings

---

[1] Letter to J. S. Fry (20 April, 1871, MSS in FHL, Box 9.3 (121)).

[2] *Journal*, 1865–76 vol., p. 172; cf. *The Manchester Friend* (1873), 162; Frederick Cooper, *The Crisis in Manchester Meeting. With a Review of the Pamphlets of David Duncan and Joseph B. Forster* (Privately printed, 1869), pp. 5–6.

[3] MSS in FHL, Box 9.4 (3), f.7.

notoriously incomplete; the portion which we do possess, shrouded in doubt and uncertainty.'[1]

They were unanimous in rejecting the substitutionary interpretation of the Atonement. They were deeply influenced by the anti-evangelical reaction which had rejected the idea of vicarious suffering as morally unacceptable. It had found definitive expression in Jowett's essay on 'The Atonement' (1855) and John McLeod Campbell's *The Nature of Atonement* (1856), and the Manchester dissidents accepted it fully: 'it is immoral to desire immunity through the pains or obedience of another, from the eternal consequences of error.'[2] The traditional concept of Christ as a mediator was unacceptable: 'I feel no need of approaching God through Christ, God may be worshipped in Himself.'[3] They were also unanimous in rejecting the doctrines of the everlasting punishment of the wicked[4]—an attitude which had cost F. D. Maurice his chair at King's College, London, in 1853.

Their attitude to the early Friends was at once more enthusiastic and more iconoclastic than that of the evangelical. They spoke of their 'insane or highly blameable extravagances' and 'frivolous, short-sighted, and foolish fears and scruples'.[5] Yet they realized how close the early Friends were to certain views of their own in, for instance, the relative rather than absolute value they accorded scripture. In particular, they recognized the harmony between the concept of the Light Within and their own insistence on intellectual freedom. Joseph B. Forster, the leader of the movement after Duncan's death, declared '. . . every law which fixes a limit to free thought, exists in violation of the very first of all doctrines held by the Early Quakers,—the doctrine of the 'Inner Light'.[6] They believed that formal

---

[1] David Duncan, *Can an Outward Revelation be Perfect? Reflections upon the Claim of Biblical Infallibility* (London, 1871), p. 11.

[2] *The Manchester Friend* (1873), 30.

[3] An interview noted in J. B. Braithwaite, *Journal*, no date (1865–76 vol., p. 173).

[4] *The Manchester Friend* printed a series of articles on the subject, entitled 'An Appeal to the Orthodox'.

[5] *The Manchester Friend* (1872), 68—in an article entitled 'The Value of Reading the Works of Early Friends, Contested'.

[6] *On Liberty*, p. 26.

agreement upon dogma was not necessary in a church, and urged an ideal of complete intellectual freedom among church members united only by good will and amity. The short life of the schism they founded provides a commentary on the utopian nature of their reaction against the vehemence of contemporary theological disagreements. Their attitude has parallels in the loose and subjective church polity described by Harnack some thirty years later.[1]

Like other theological movements among Friends, the thought of the Manchester dissidents was a reflection of currents of thought in the wider society. Their ideas were those current among English liberal theologians of the day, channelled to them in the first instance by the lectures of David Duncan, a former Presbyterian minister, and therefore one of the very few Quakers with a formal theological training. The movement probably began in 1861, with Duncan's lecture on *Essays and Reviews*.[2] In the years that followed, Duncan's supporters studied *Essays and Reviews*, the writings of Colenso, 'and other books of the same description'. As Samuel Davidson wrote, reflecting on the intellectual genesis of the movement: 'No book properly embodies it. It is dispersed in the general mind of thinkers which it has leavened.'[3]

The movement in Manchester was rapidly forgotten by Quakers—it is not mentioned in the quasi-official volumes of Jones, *The Later Periods of Quakerism*.[4] Its significance however was twofold. In the 1870s, it was the visible part of an iceberg. A letter to a Quaker periodical in 1871 complained:

As we grow up, come into contact with those who are not Friends, and read the literature of the day, we gradually find that there are many earnest thoughtful men who entirely disbelieve the theology which we

[1] J. Rendel Harris (a convert to Quakerism, and a leading Quaker thinker) noted this parallel in 1899, when he suggested that McGiffert's *History of Christianity in the Apostolic Age* would make a good Quaker tract! (in *Present Day Papers* (11 May 1899), p. 46). McGiffert was Harnack's pupil.

[2] Published as *Essays and Reviews: A Lecture* (Manchester, 1861).

[3] *The Manchester Friend* (1872), 200.

[4] The only account by a Quaker historian is to be found in Richenda C. Scott's short article, 'Authority or Experience. John Wilhelm Rowntree and the Dilemma of 19th Century British Quakerism', *JFHS* (1960), 75ff.

have been taught that it is right to believe. This fact leads us to think and inquire for ourselves, and the subject is so enormous that when once entered upon, it is very long before we again feel that our convictions are at all settled. . . . And yet if we speak out, we are, I presume, much in the same position as the Friends who have lately been obliged to resign at Manchester.[1]

Except for their Unitarianism, the Manchester rebels were essentially pioneers, prophets of the liberal theology which would become widely accepted among Friends in the 1890s. John Wilhelm Rowntree, the leader of the later movement, headed a section of his notes, for the history he did not live to write, 'The Rise of Modern Thought—the Lancashire trouble'. The forgotten Friends of Manchester, who welcomed liberal views in the 1860s, instead of the 1890s, deserve to be rescued from oblivion—they followed what they believed to be the truth in the face of what amounted to persecution,[2] with remarkable courage, tenacity, and openness of mind.

THE SPREAD OF LIBERAL THEOLOGY

Since in many respects the Manchester rebels were the precursors of the Quaker liberal thinkers of the eighties and nineties, an analysis of the thought of the latter involves a certain measure of repetition. But there was one major difference—none of the thinkers discussed in the pages that follow was a Unitarian. The authors of *A Reasonable Faith* called the divinity of Christ the 'chief cornerstone' of a Christian's faith.[3]

The first important Quaker statements of liberal theology[4] are to be found in *A Reasonable Faith*, published anonymously in 1884, and Edward Worsdell's *The Gospel of Divine Faith*, which appeared two years later. *The British Friend* became a vehicle for liberal opinions in 1891, when the three authors of *A Reasonable Faith*, Francis Frith,

---

[1] *The British Friend* (1871), 277.

[2] cf., pp. 62ff. below.

[3] *A Reasonable Faith, Short Essays for the Times, By Three 'Friends'*. (London, 1884), p. 30; cf. Edward Grubb on Unitarianism, in *FQE* (1938), 301.

[4] I.e. by those who remained Quakers, and exercised real influence over Quaker thought.

William Pollard, and William Edward Turner, became associated with its publication. A younger Friend, Edward Grubb, advocated liberal theology in many reviews and articles in Quaker periodicals, but it is John Wilhelm Rowntree who first rose into prominence in 1893, who has always been regarded by Quakers as the prophet of the movement. It is difficult to tell why, from his published writings, since Worsdell expounded the same ideas, earlier and more strikingly. The explanation probably lies in his ebullient and lovable personality, in the energy which organized Summer Schools and *Present Day Papers*, and especially, one suspects, in his premature death.

All these thinkers came to liberal theology through a severe personal crisis. Turner adopted it in his forties, when he was already an established evangelical minister, and suffered much obloquy in consequence.[1] Rowntree and Grubb were scions of well-known evangelical families. Both went through a phase of doubt and near-agnosticism, and painful isolation in the company of the devout.[2] Grubb has recorded his sufferings at the Yearly Meeting of 1880, 'in tears because I felt myself utterly alone. I seemed to be living in a different world from all that company.'[3] They found a release from their difficulties by rejecting formal theology in favour of a religion grounded on personal experience.

The ideas of the leading Quaker liberal theologians seem to have been largely shaped by two factors—the Darwinian theory of evolution, and the popularization of the findings of biblical criticism, which produced a consciousness of the difficulties and ambiguities inherent in the evangelical attitude to scripture. Edward Worsdell stated the assumptions which they held: 'the essay pre-supposes that an evolutionary interpretation of outward nature may be true, and that in the records contained in the Old Testament there may be an admixture of the legendary, and of survivals from a previous heathendom.'[4]

[1] *The Annual Monitor* (1913), 172.
[2] *John Wilhelm Rowntree Essays and Addresses* (ed. Joshua Rowntree) (London, 1905), Introduction, pp. xii–xiii; Edward Grubb, 'Some Personal Experiences', *FQE* (1938), 300–1.
[3] ibid., p. 301.
[4] *The Gospel of Divine Help*, pp. 13–14.

Quaker liberals usually regarded the Bible as inspired to a certain extent, but did not accept all parts of it as equally authoritative. The authors of *A Reasonable Faith* believed that it differed from the writings of other men of religious insight in degree of inspiration, but not in essential character: 'the Bible is unique only in degree.'[1] Quaker liberals usually adopted the theory of progressivism[2] to explain the fact that supposedly inspired writings contained parts which their own consciences found unacceptable, such as the command to exterminate the Canaanites, which had troubled Hannah Barnard at the end of the eighteenth century. The theory of progressive revelation was one of the key concepts of nineteenth-century theology. Traceable to Lessing and Herder, it played a key role in the thinking of liberal Anglicans such as Thomas Arnold, Stanley, Hare, and Milman.[3] According to this view, God's truths are timeless and unchanging, but God's revelation of them to humanity is gradual. At any given time, God's revelation of Himself to men is adapted to the current condition of human thought and behaviour. As Lessing put it, 'What education is to the individual man, revelation is to the whole human race.'[4] Quaker liberals seized upon this concept as the clue to the problems of the Old Testament. They welcomed it all the more readily because the Darwinian theory of physical evolution had hardened into a fashionable orthodoxy. Darwin's theories were referred to repeatedly by speakers at the Manchester Conference,[5] and sometimes had the status of an intellectual panacea—one speaker suggested that Elias Hicks would have been spared his theological errors had he lived in the post-Darwinian era: 'A little knowledge of evolution would have saved him all that false doctrine.'[6]

Liberal expositions of the doctrine of progressivism often

---

[1] *A Reasonable Faith*, p. 98.

[2] The earliest Quaker statement of this theory is probably an anonymous, privately printed pamphlet, *Work of the Future for the Society of Friends* (1874). It is reviewed in *The Friend* (1875), 55.

[3] cf. Duncan Forbes, *The Liberal Anglican Idea of History*, (Cambridge, 1952), *passim*.

[4] Quoted in Henry Chadwick, *Lessing's Theological Writings* (London, 1956), p. 82.

[5] For which, see pp. 40–1 below.

[6] *Proceedings of Manchester Conference, 1895* (Manchester, 1896), p. 220.

carry the unwitting implication that it was to the detriment of the biblical writers that they were not born nineteenth-century Englishmen. Yet whatever the overtones of the theory, it offered an escape from the bewildering problems offered by scriptural exegesis. Worsdell added an ingenious hypothesis of his own—God made His revelation intentionally obscure and contradictory, in order to preserve a dimension of human freedom, some scope for choice and decision.[1]

Regarding the Bible as fallible, liberal Quakers had no certain source of theological knowledge. They were profoundly aware of this: 'To stake Christianity on that which further knowledge may show to be doubtful, is to prepare the way for unbelief. Common honesty, as well as common prudence, forbids us to assert, as indisputably true, anything that we are conscious that we do not know.'[2] Their reaction was in part to condemn metaphysical and dogmatic religion,[3] and in part to seek a basis for knowledge of God in personal intuition and experience. In his paper, 'May we believe in God?', J. W. Rowntree rejects attempts to establish the existence of God by philosophical means, and claims that the road to knowledge of God lies through individual experience. Silvanus Thompson made the same point at the Manchester Conference:

in that middle region of thought, where neither the scientific nor the critical method is available to discover truth, all is not darkness or confusion. . . . To every man there comes a consciousness, not to be analysed in the test-tube of the chemist, nor probed with the scalpel of the physiologist, not to be touched by the syllogism of the critic, nor disposed of the reading of a codex, a consciousness of something quite other than those things which are to be apprehended by the physical senses. Not to the intellect but to the soul of man does the voice of God speak.[4]

This emphasis on religious experience as the foundation of faith was easily integrated with the early Friends' doctrine of the Light Within. Where the evangelical viewed the writings of the early Friends with doubt and hesitation, the

[3] *The Gospel of Divine Help*, pp. 48–9.
[1] ibid., p. 17.
[2] cf.; for example, John William Graham's paper at the Manchester Conference, *passim* (*Manchester Conference*, pp. 240ff.).
[4] *Manchester Conference*, p. 232.

late Victorian liberal came to them in a spirit of enthusiastic re-discovery. Whether this sense of identification rested on real similarities of thought is a question which lies beyond the scope of this book, though it is clear that there was a gulf between the prophetic and revolutionary outlook of Fox, and that of Victorian liberalism. But the sense of identification was strong, and destined to produce much re-editing of texts and research into early Quaker history.

The doctrine of the Light Within now became the core of Quaker theology. The Liberals claimed that any attempt to distinguish this Light from natural reason and conscience rendered the doctrine meaningless,[1] and condemned Barclay, who made precisely this distinction, for dualism. All consciences are enlightened, though in different degrees, and conscience is always a spiritual faculty of man.[2]

The revival of the concept of the Light Within was closely linked with an optimistic view of man. The Quaker liberals taught the possibility of—and need for—real righteousness, and liked to contrast their teaching with the evangelical doctrine of imputed righteousness: 'Scripture bids us "put on Christ" and be "clothed with humility"—in fact, not in fiction'.[3] They tended to reject the doctrine of Original Sin: 'The Quaker doctrine of the seed of God in the heart is a flat contradiction of the doctrine of original sin.'[4] In fact, all systems of Christian theology have stressed that the believer must seek real righteousness. For the evangelical, good works were the indispensable fruit of grace; Wesley taught the doctrine of Perfection, and it is clear that the Quaker liberals' summary of evangelical belief in this respect was a travesty of evangelicalism—a not uncommon failing in converts. Nevertheless, an emphasis on the moral and ethical aspects of religion, a confidence in the spiritual capacities of man, were especially characteristic of this school.

---

[1] *The Gospel of Divine Help*, p. 36. Edward Grubb, *Authority and the Light Within* (2nd ed., London, 1909), pp. 8off.; *The Friend* (1923), 538. Evangelicals had tended to distinguish the Inner Light from reason and conscience (this distinction is made in, for instance, the 1879 YM epistle). Hicks condemned the distinction (*Journal of Thomas Shillitoe*, vol. ii, p. 156, footnote).

[2] *The Gospel of Divine Help*, pp. 36–42.

[3] ibid., p. 161.

[4] E. Vipont Brown, *The Friend* (1923), 685.

The late Victorian Quaker liberals, like the Manchester dissidents, rejected the substitutionary view of the Atonement as morally unintelligible. As the authors of *A Reasonable Faith* put it, 'They have been told that God is angry, and must be propitiated that He is just and cannot forgive their debt, unless indeed (strange contradiction!) some one pay it for them. They are then assured that Jesus Christ has intervened and borne the Father's wrath.'[1] For these thinkers, the substitutionary theory of the Atonement was contrary to charity and justice, and posited an inadequate, if not actually blasphemous, idea of God. They believed that it assumed an unreal antagonism between the intentions of the Father and the Son, and placed the Father in a light which fell short of human standards of goodness—and they loved to quote the words of Whittier, that 'nothing can be good in Him/Which evil is in me.' In 1893, at Yearly Meeting, Sylvanus Thompson attacked the doctrine in words which showed little concern for evangelical susceptibilities: "That notion of a bloody sacrifice was a piece of heathenism, a piece of Judaism."[2]

Their rejection of the evangelical theory of the Atonement left them with an intellectual difficulty—how else could they explain the Incarnation, and, more especially, the sufferings and death of Christ? Their usual explanation was that God wished to reveal Himself to men. Christ was a mediator in the sense of being a means of communication. The purpose of his earthly life was to show men how to live, and make holiness attractive to them by power of example.[3] His death was not a propitiatory sacrifice, but a lesson in self sacrifice: 'Christ's sufferings touch the heart of mankind at a point which is nearest to that of contrition and love.'[4]

Many evangelicals had agonized over the fate of the unbeliever, but the late Victorian Quaker liberals believed in the universality of salvation. Worsdell stated that the doctrine of Hell posits immorality in God, and in '"the saved" [who] will be happily unconcerned about the sin-

---

[1] *A Reasonable Faith*, pp. 49–50.
[2] *The British Friend* (1893), 150A.
[3] *The Gospel of Divine Help*, pp. 30ff.; *A Reasonable Faith*, pp. 26ff.; *John Wilhelm Rowntree, Essays and Addresses*, ed. Joshua Rowntree (London, 1905), pp. 269ff.
[4] *A Reasonable Faith*, p. 79.

fulness of the "lost"'.[1] Furthermore, it is irrational: 'It fails to show any purpose whatsoever in the perpetual prolongation of a sinful existence. . . . It neglects the fact that . . . no such line can be drawn as to justify conditions so opposed as entire happiness and entire misery.'[2] He criticised the doctrine of eternal punishment, too, on practical grounds, for encouraging dead-bed repentance, just as he attacks the doctrine of imputed righteousness for producing delusive complacency in those of mediocre life.[3]

What are the sources of the thought of the Quaker liberals? In their rejection of dogma, and their emphasis on religious consciousness, they had much in common with Ritschl and his followers, but although some of Ritschl's works were translated into English as early as 1872, his ideas do not appear to have become current in England until the 1890s—too late to be a formative influence on Quaker liberals. Undoubtedly, it was English liberal theologians who were important—Grubb and Rowntree both stated that Caird had influenced them decisively; Rowntree paid tribute to the biblical exegesis of Robertson Smith, and Grubb to the writings of Erskine.[4] Quaker periodicals in the 1870s contain several sympathetic accounts of Erskine[5] (1788–1870). He was a Scottish layman who rebelled against the harshness of Presbyterian Calvinism, and emphasized the Fatherhood of God, and the divine illumination of the soul. John McLeod Campbell's writings on the Atonement exercised much influence[6] and a number of influential Friends were familiar with the thought of F. W. Robertson.[7] Another strong influence was the poetry of the American Quaker, Whittier, who stated many of the teachings of liberal theology in a form easily remembered and understood.[8]

---

[1] *The Gospel of Divine Help*, p. 79.

[2] ibid., pp. 79–80.

[3] ibid., p. 81 (death-bed repentance), and p. 124 (imputed righteousness).

[4] Introduction, *John Wilhelm Rowntree, Essays and Addresses*, p. xvi; FQE (1938), 302.

[5] FQE (1878), 296–313; *The Friend* (1879), 131–2 (a defence provoked by an attack on pp. 94–5).

[6] FQE (1879), 600–609; *The Friend* (1873), 113ff.; (1877), 328–30.

[7] See the review, ibid. (1866), 27–9, and the controversy that followed.

[8] FQE (1938), 302; Whittier figures prominently in the bibliography of *The Gospel of Divine Help*.

Both within the Quaker fold and outside it, emphasis on religious experience as the basis of faith naturally quickened interest in mysticism. This was a living tradition in Quakerism—the 'siftings' and 'diggings deep' of quietist ministers. An interest in mysticism among non-Quakers produced such works as Inge's *Christian Mysticism* (1899), Von Huegel's *The Mystical Element in Religion* (1908) and Evelyn Underhill's *Mysticism* (1911), as well as a new, nine-volume edition of the works of William Law. Among Quakers, Summer School lectures included accounts of mystics such as Tauler, Boehme and Madame Guyon[1]—recalling the favourite reading matter of the early Victorian quietists.[2] *Present Day Papers* contained an article by Inge, and an enthusiastic review of Inge's book.[3] J. W. Graham recognized how Quaker tradition and the current preoccupations of non-Quaker theologians coalesced: 'the religious world has come round to the Indwelling Voice as its central conception, and so essential Quakerism holds the future in the hollow of its hand.'[4] Similarly, liberal Quakers rejoiced at the appearance of William James' *Varieties of Religious Experience*, because its pragmatism confirmed what they already believed—it was 'a treasure-house for "Friends"'.[5]

One of the most striking aspects of the intellectual history of Victorian Quakerism was the rapidity and completeness with which liberal theology spread. It is difficult to chart its progress with any precision—one can only note significant landmarks on the way. In 1870 a Quaker conference seriously debated whether only the converted should be allowed to be Sunday School teachers.[6] In 1893 an evangelical brought down a storm of outraged protest on his head when he asked Quaker school children whether they had been saved.[7] It is obvious that an intellectual revolution had taken place among Friends in the twenty-three years that lie between.

---

[1] Birmingham Summer School report in *The British Friend* (1899), 282.
[2] cf., p. 17 above.
[3] *Present Day Papers*, iii (1900), pp. 149ff. and pp. 155ff.
[4] *Manchester Conference*, p. 241.
[5] *Present day Papers*, v (1902), p. 292.
[6] *Proceedings Dublin Conference, F.F.D.S.A., 1870* (London, 1871), pp. 6off.
[7] Howard Nicholson; *The British Friend* (1893), 223–6.

In the mid-1880s, when *A Reasonable Faith* and *The Gospel of Divine Help* were published, their authors saw themselves as daring pioneers, bound to suffer for their opinions: 'The writers knew what they would have to suffer, the opprobrium that would be cast upon them.'[1] And indeed, they did suffer—*A Reasonable Faith* led to energetic attacks at Yearly Meeting and in the correspondence columns of Quaker periodicals, while Worsdell's book cost him the headship of a Quaker school.[2] But the tide was turning; indeed, before either book was published, it had already begun to turn.

At Yearly Meeting, in 1880, an evangelical complained that 'taking away the terrors of the world to come' was having a deadening effect on Quaker spirituality.[3] At Yearly Meeting the following year, the same Friend stated that theological doubt was becoming fashionable among Friends: 'Young men who have doubts are made so much of, invited about and patted on the back as intellectually superior.'[4] Five years later, Francis Frith declared, doubtless prematurely, that his status among Friends had changed from that of a dangerous radical to that of a conservative.[5] When his co-author, Pollard, died in 1893, a Quaker tribute reflected on his changing reputation: 'It is clear . . . that the standpoint of "A Reasonable Faith" increasingly appeals to the thoughtful and devout among ourselves.'[6]

But the most important landmarks, which showed that liberal theology had turned into an orthodoxy, were the Manchester Conference of 1895, and the series of Summer Schools which began in 1897. In 1895, a conference was held, appropriately enough at Manchester, to discuss the relationship of the Society of Friends to modern thought. It attracted an attendance ranging from 1,000 to 1,300; this included some non-Quaker observers, but it was a remarkable total for a church which had, at the time, less than 16,500 members, including children. Both the papers read,

1 William Pollard at 1885 YM, *The Friend* (1885), 144.
2 Information from Miss A. Worsdell.
3 Henry Hipsley; *The Friend* (1880), 142.
4 ibid. (1881), 144.
5 ibid. (1886), 148.
6 J.W.G., in *The British Friend* (1893), 299.

and the discussions which followed them, showed the shift of opinion which had taken place among Friends. Four out of five addresses on theology, for instance, were given by well-known liberals. In this case, the organizers of the conference curtailed the usual discussion, but such papers, delivered at an official Quaker conference, were a portent. Two years later, Scarborough Summer School was held, to bring Friends into contact with 'modern thought', and, in particular, to provide a crash course in the conclusions of modern Biblical criticism. Extremists called it 'Satan's Sinful Snare', but 528 participant tickets were sold,[1] and for some of the attenders it proved a revelation.[2] Liberals noted with surprise and pleasure that the Summer School was not attacked at Yearly Meeting, and that it was benignly reported by the (evangelical) *Friend*.

The liberal theology which silently and invisibly became an orthodoxy among Friends was destined to remain so. The reaction which is associated with the names of Barth and Niebuhr, which began to affect English church members in the 1930s, had no influence on Friends. In 1940, Charles Roden Buxton told his brother that he had been reading Barth, but was uninfluenced—otherwise 'I should have had to leave the Society of Friends'.[3] Twenty years later, a Quaker noted that Barth's 'very name seems to be anathema to Friends'.[4] It is not difficult to see why Friends, with their doctrine of the Light Within, could not accept Barth's view of the complete transcendence of God—but these questions, of course, lie far beyond the time span of this book.

Some of the implications of liberal theology for the social history of Quakerism have already been considered. It has been noted that many liberals were critical of foreign missions, and of proselytizing work in general—and indeed the

[1] *The British Friend* (1897), 197.

[2] 'Recollections of Lawrence Richardson', *JFHS* (1953), 42, gives an account of a transformation in outlook resulting from the second summer school.

[3] Victoria de Bunsen, *Charles Roden Buxton, A Memoir* (London, 1948), p. 104. His reaction to Kierkegaard was identical.

[4] Richard K. Ullman, 'Peacemakers, Churchmen and Friends' in *Then and Now. Quaker Essays Historical and Contemporary by friends of Henry Joel Cadbury on his Completion of Twenty-Two years as Chairman of the Friends Service Committee*, ed. Anna Brinton (Philadelphia, 1960), p. 276.

subjectivity of a theology which makes experience of God
the proof of His existence makes it unstable ground for
proselytizing. But although they were relatively uninterested
in missions, they were deeply interested in social questions.
Many of those, such as Edward Grubb, who took a leading
part in introducing liberal theology to Friends, were equally
prominent in discussing 'The Social Problem'. It does not
seem likely that an interest in social questions was inherent
in liberal theology, but rather that the kind of intellectual
who eagerly studied new developments in the theological
sphere was equally receptive to contemporary currents of
thought on social questions—on the inadequacy of philanthropy, the magnitude of the problem of poverty, and so on.
And there was a tendency to turn from the insoluble intellectual difficulties latent in a religion based on subjective
experience, and tackle humanitarian work, which could be
faced with an undivided mind. As John Wilhelm Rowntree wrote, quoting Robertson, 'There are many problems
insoluble except, in active life.'[1]

It is a seeming paradox that men who rejected much
traditional theology and emphasized the primary importance of religious experience and intuition should have laid
such stress on the intellectual study of religion. Evangelicals had criticized quietists for their anti-intellectualism.
Liberals made much the same charges against evangelicals,
accusing them of intellectual timidity, of blindness to the
theological issues of the day: 'He who neglects his intellectual powers or refuses to be guided by them in the discovery
of truth, is not only an intellectual coward, he is defying the
purposes of the Almighty.'[2] Not only did John Wilhelm
Rowntree establish the Summer Schools, but he suggested
the foundation of a permanent Quaker college for religious
studies—an idea which became reality in 1903, as the result
of a gift from George Cadbury. Rowntree had hoped that
such a college would produce a well-informed ministry
among Friends. Whether the college, Woodbrooke, fulfilled
the hopes it aroused has sometimes been questioned, but its
establishment was of considerable significance at the time.

---

[1] *John Wilhelm Rowntree Essays and Addresses*, Introduction, p. xvii.
[2] *Manchester Conference*, p. 235.

This account of the theological views of Friends forms a lengthy prolegomenon to a social history. To what extent do theological opinions affect social behaviour? Are the more obvious correlations—such as have been indicated here—cause and effect, or simply coincidental? Or are the effects of religious beliefs on behaviour more far-reaching, subtle and profound that those which strike the historian as immediately significant? There is no easy answer to such questions, but perhaps the best way to study the impact of ideas on behaviour, in this context, is to study the records of schisms which are ideological in origin. Then it is possible to see how a modification in the beliefs of a church produces or fails to produce changes in church practice and social orientation.

II

BELIEF DIVIDED: THREE SCHISMS

INTRODUCTION

THE schisms which took place in the little world of Victorian Quakerism have long since been almost forgotten, even by Friends. Schisms in a church which had less than 14,000 members, at the time of its first census, were necessarily minuscule. The first, that of the Beaconites, was the largest—300 friends resigned, in different parts of England, but probably fewer than a hundred of these actually joined a schismatic Quaker meeting.[1] The second, the Fritchley schism, is still in existence, but it has never numbered more than perhaps eighty adherents, and for most of its existence they have been much fewer.[2] The third schism, that of the Manchester free-thinkers who met at Memorial Hall, was the smallest and the most ephemeral, and is now the least known—in its heyday, its meetings attracted perhaps thirty attenders.[3] But the real loss of members was greater than these figures suggest, if one includes the descendants of the original seceders. For twenty years, after the Beaconite schism, the records of the relevant Monthly Meeting list a steady trickle of resignations from young Crewdsons, Boultons, Ransomes, and so on—the children of those who resigned in 1836.

Each schism was the expression of a distinctive theological viewpoint. The Beaconite schism, established in the mid-1830s was the child of evangelicalism; the Fritchley

---

[1] For the total of 300 resignations (a rough estimate), see *J. Bevan Braithwaite, A Friend of the Nineteenth Century*, pp. 50–1. 52 Friends resigned in Manchester (*Hardshaw East MM Minutes*, vol. ii, pp. 378, 433, 440) but to these should be added their dependants.

[2] 80 members and attenders were present when Fritchley Meeting House was opened, in 1897 (*The Friend* (1897, 692). This was the period of the movement's greatest strength.

[3] *The Manchester Friend* (1872), 100. Only 13 Friends resigned their membership (*Hardshaw East MM Minutes*, vol. vii, pp. 69, 73, 87–8).

schism, which evolved gradually in the late 1860s, was the expression of quietist conservatism. The Manchester seceders of the early 1870s accepted the findings of liberal theology and contemporary biblical criticism, and tended to unitarianism.

There are a number of points of similarity between the movements. Each was localized in a single place—the first and third in Manchester, the second in an obscure Derbyshire village. Each was largely the work of a single leading figure. The Fritchley schism seems to have caused hardly a ripple in contemporary Quakerism, but the Beaconite secession, and that of the Manchester dissidents some thirty-five years later, caused deep alarm and concern among Friends. The diaries and correspondence of Friends in the 1830s are full of comments and speculation about the seceders, and they were almost equally troubled by the dissensions in Manchester in the early 1870s. But perhaps the most interesting thing about the schisms is not the crisis they created among contemporary Friends, but the way in which they evolved forms of church organization and of worship to correspond with their respective theological starting-points.

AN EVANGELICAL SCHISM: THE BEACONITES

The Beaconite schism was the most important of the three, both in the numbers and status of the seceders, and in the significance which was attached to it by contemporary Friends. It was occasioned by the publication of *A Beacon to the Society of Friends* in 1835. Isaac Crewdson, the author of the *Beacon*, would have been surprised if anyone had foretold that it would produce a schism.[1] When his book appeared, he was in his middle fifties, a wealthy silk and cotton manufacturer who was born in Kendal but had spent all his adult life in Manchester. He was respected and loved, both by Quakers and in Manchester generally, for his piety and philanthropy.[2] As a young man he had been a quietist, but like so many of his contemporaries he had found release

---

[1] Memoir of Isaac Crewdson, prefixed to his *Glad Tracts for Sinners* (privately printed, 1845), p. 12.
[2] cf. Leo H. Grindon, *Manchester Banks and Bankers* (Manchester, 1877), p. 125.

from his religious anxieties in the doctrines of the Atonement and of substitutionary righteousness. His evangelicalism, strengthened by a dangerous illness, and clarified by his labours of love in abridging and publishing Puritan classics, was held with a convert's fervour. J. J. Gurney once told him that they had started from opposite points, but had met and crossed on the road.[1]

The appearance of the *Beacon* gave an objective focus to the tension between evangelicals and conservatives which already existed in Manchester meeting. A letter from a visitor to Manchester in February 1835 reveals how this tension had produced a state of disorder truly remarkable in a Quaker meeting: 'I never beheld a Meeting in such a state. Very many were in tears on both sides the meeting and it was really a most distressing season.'[2] Three months later, Yearly Meeting spontaneously intervened and set up a committee of inquiry. This committee saw the *Beacon* as the real point of issue. After repeated visits to Manchester, they finally made recommendations which revealed the ambiguity of their position, as evangelicals passing judgment on an evangelical. They advised the Monthly Meeting not to proceed against Crewdson for doctrinal unsoundness, but recommended Crewdson, who was a minister, to be silent in Meetings for Worship. In 1836, Crewdson, his brother-in-law, William Boulton, and fifty sympathizers resigned from Manchester Meeting in protest.

Their action sparked off a chain of resignations throughout England. Many of those who resigned, both at Manchester and elsewhere, were linked to Crewdson by kinship, marriage, or friendship—there are only 22 different surnames among the 52 members who resigned at Manchester.[3] J. B. Braithwaite recalled:

The influence of the controversy was wide-spread owing largely to family connections among Friends at Kendal and Manchester and a few at Birmingham. The meeting at Manchester was deprived of some who might have been its most valuable members, and Kendal

[1] Joseph Bevan Braithwaite, *Memoirs of Joseph John Gurney* (London, 1854), vol. ii, p. 151.
[2] James Clark to Eleanor Stephens (15 Feb. 1835), *JFHS* (1919), 130.
[3] *Hardshaw East MM Minutes*, vol. ii, pp. 378, 433, 440.

was greatly reduced. Some also who might have been ornaments to the Society at Tottenham and in the neighbourhood of London withdrew from it.[1]

The bitterness which had disfigured meetings at Manchester was duplicated elsewhere in England. At Bristol, a minister began a sermon with the words, 'Friends, what is the state of this Meeting? There is spiritual wickedness in high places'—referring to two eminent evangelicals on the ministerial benches beside her.[2] When the committee which had dealt with Crewdson reported to Yearly Meeting, an impassioned debate followed which showed the strength of Crewdson's supporters, though in the end the Committee's work was confirmed.[3] The resignations meant a crisis of conscience for many Quaker evangelicals, doubtful as to where their loyalties should lie. They created a storm in the normally tranquil world of English Quakerism—Gurney wrote sadly in his diary of 'these days of commotion of Beacons and Anti-Beacons'.[4]

The seceders troubled those who remained, not only by their numbers, but by their wealth and eminence. They included a former Yearly Meeting Clerk, John Wilkinson, who immediately wrote a lengthy polemic against the church he had left, and the famous philanthropist and scientist, Luke Howard.

Most of the seceders joined other churches, but those in Manchester decided to form a separate organization of their own. Several factors probably account for their decision— Crewdson's leadership, their relatively great numbers, and their desire to have the links of kinship and friendship which bound them mirrored in a religious organization, as they had been in Quakerism.

In November, 1836, the Evangelical Friends, as they were called, held their first meeting, in an empty infant school room.[5] But they did not lack energy, or financial

1 *J. Bevan Braithwaite, A Friend of the Nineteenth Century*, p. 65.

2 William Sturge, *Some Recollections of a Long Life* (privately printed), 1893), p. 41.

3 John to William Dymond, 8 June 1837 (transcript in FHL, Port. 34/3).

4 *Journal*, 3 Mar. 1835.

5 *The Inquirer* (1839), 73. This account (pp. 73–7) supplies the details given in this and the following paragraph.

resources. They began to publish a periodical, *The Inquirer*, and to build a church with seating capacity for 600. Within a year, the church, in Grosvenor Street, Chorlton on Medlock, was completed; they chose to call it a 'Chapel' rather than a 'meeting house', symbolizing their move away from Quakerism, their rapprochement with other denominations.

On the third of December 1837, the Evangelical Friends met to consider what form of church polity they should adopt—the fact that they found it necessary to discuss the matter, instead of automatically adopting Quaker forms, shows how far they had moved from the church of their birth. They decided 'carefully to examine the New Testament, in order to ascertain what was the practice of the churches in the days of the apostles, deeming it a duty to follow their example as closely as practicable.'[1] The *tabula rasa* mentality they displayed—as though no form of church government had existed since apostolic days—was extraordinary. After searching their New Testaments for three weeks, they decided that there were two offices in the early church—the positions of deacon and elder—and appointed deacons and elders accordingly.[2] They looked in vain for precise instructions on the method of appointment: 'there is a total absence of any direction on the subject.'[3]

They made several more significant departures from Quaker practices. They rejected the ministry of women, as unscriptural,[4] and birthright membership as non-evangelical, for their insistence on the saving act of faith made inherited church membership a contradiction in terms. Later in the century, Quaker evangelicals were to wage a spirited campaign on birthright membership, for the same reason, regarding the practice of granting membership automatically to Quaker children as a fruitful source of nominal members. Meanwhile, the Beaconites drafted an evangelical statement of faith, which prospective members had to accept.[5]

---

[1] *The Inquirer* (1839), 75.
[2] ibid., 77. Crewdson and Boulton were made 'Elders, Bishops or Pastors' and four deacons were appointed.
[3] ibid.
[4] ibid. (1838), 84–9 and 105–8; (1840), pp. 437–9.
[5] ibid. (1839), 73–4.

The Beaconites abandoned the Quaker Meeting for Worship, and replaced it by a form of service practically indistinguishable from that of a dissenting chapel. An early eye-witness account gives both an invaluable picture of their church services and an explanation of their rapid decline.

When the Meeting House in Grosvenor-street was opened for public worship, though not a dissident Friend, I attended at one of the earliest services. The room was by no means well filled. It was plain and unassuming with a low platform and rostrum, but no pulpit. There were seats on the platform and in the room, and from the rostrum one of the leaders conducted the service, which was rather tame and frigid. There was hymn singing, Bible reading, prayer, and an address; altogether, in form, just such a service as the Rev. James Griffin would be conducting in Rusholme Road hard by, without the prestige of a recognised status, or a historical name from Cromwellian times. It is no wonder that the cause languished and eventually 'scattered'.[1]

This change in form of service was closely connected with the Beaconites' theological beliefs. The traditional Quaker meeting, with its silence and unpremeditated and spontaneous ministry, rested on the doctrine of the Light Within, the belief that God spoke directly to the heart of the believer. When the Beaconites rejected this doctrine, they naturally moved away from the form of service which it had led to.

The Beaconites' most radical break with Quakerism was their adoption of the rites of baptism and the Lord's Supper. It has always been one of the most fundamental teachings of Quakerism that these are empty external rites, and that the true baptism and the true communion are purely spiritual realities, taking place in the heart. But many Quaker evangelicals were troubled by their neglect of practices which scripture clearly enjoins, and the Beaconites adopted both rites. In 1837 an aged Quaker wrote to his niece that a 'Minister who I also much esteemed has commenced the typical cerimony [sic] of water babtism [sic] and that some of the Members of our Society have been to Manchester to have this cerimony performed upon them'.[2] *The Inquirer* regularly printed accounts of public baptisms; they were,

---

1 *Manchester City News*, 18 Mar. 1905 (*FHL Press cuttings*, CC 86).
2 Richard Cockin to Mary Fox, 19 May 1837, *JFHS* (1925), 71.

however, restricted to adults.[1] Similarly, Crewdson cele-
brated the rite of the Lord's Supper, first in his home, and
then when the chapel was opened, publicly.

In 1837 and 1838 a number of Quakers were baptized,
either by Crewdson or by a clergyman. Some of these
resigned their membership, or were expelled, but others
were intensely reluctant to leave 'the religious Society to
which they wd. still cling'.[2] The conflicts of these Friends,
torn between their desire for baptism and their 'almost
indissoluble'[3] attachment to Quakerism, led to a remarkable
campaign to introduce baptism in the Society, or at least to
make it optional.

The movement began in Kendal, where a hundred members out of three hundred had resigned or lost their membership during the Beacon controversy. In 1837, 'the
Kendalites' sent a proposition on baptism and the Lord's
Supper to Yearly Meeting. It led to hot discussion, but the
proposal was so alien to Quaker traditions that it was returned to its senders, without being minuted in the official
records of Yearly Meeting.[4]

The following year, Yearly Meeting again discussed
baptism, and several Friends defended the practice, but the
Clerk silenced the discussion, and a committee was appointed
to investigate the condition of Friends at Kendal, where some
had been baptized without incurring the usual penalty of
expulsion.[5] Quaker traditions proved stronger than the
anxieties of evangelicals over outward ordinances—anxieties
which affected Friends as eminent as J. J. Gurney.[6]

The Beaconites were at their strongest in 1837, when they
built their chapel, and met in London at the time of Yearly

---

[1] *The Inquirer* (1839), 484ff.

[2] A. R. Barclay to J. J. Gurney, 13 April 1838, *Gurney* MSS, I, 10.

[3] *The Inquirer* (1838), 281.

[4] *The Proceedings of the Yearly Meeting of the Society of Friends ... 1837*, pp. 31–
41. This is a Beaconite reprint, with emendations, of an unofficial report of Yearly
Meeting discussions which appeared in *The Patriot*, at a time when Yearly Meeting
proceedings were a carefully guarded secret.

[5] William Smeal, Account of 1838 Yearly Meeting, pp. 40–3 (MSS in FHL), cf.
*A Quaker Journal Being the Diary and Reminiscences of William Lucas of Hitchin
(1804–61) A Member of the Society of Friends*, ed. G. E. Bryant and G. P. Baker
(London, 1934), vol. i, p. 136.

[6] *Journal*, 2 Aug. 1838.

Meeting, issuing a General Epistle, as if they were a Yearly Meeting. But their movement was destined to be short-lived. In 1844, the year of Crewdson's death, their chapel was sold to the Baptists, only seven years after it was built. Crewdson's death led to the final collapse, but it is clear that the decline had begun earlier: 'those who seceded with him, gradually became united with the Christian churches around them.'[1]

Perhaps the most interesting fact about the movement was this very transience. The author of Crewdson's memoir claims that it was never intended to be permanent, but just a temporary arrangement to meet the needs of the seceders while they were deciding which church to join.[2] This is clearly a *post facto* rationalization; the pages of *The Inquirer* make it clear that they thought they were founding a lasting and expanding church, and any other hypothesis makes it difficult to explain their construction of a £3,000 chapel.[3] It is evident that the schism failed to establish itself on a permanent basis, because the seceders abandoned all the distinctive views and practices of Friends, so that no real differences marked them off from other evangelical churches. But a single church, which never sought to make converts, could not hope to compete with the older denominations, with their wider fellowship, trained ministry, and richer history and literature. For a time, the seceders were held together by loyalty to Crewdson, and to each other. But it was too fragile a basis on which to construct a permanent church.

There is little information about the final religious allegiance of the Friends who resigned, in Manchester and elsewhere. According to one account, '. . . the greater number of them, after wavering about amongst the various sects of Dissenters, finally settled down into sober members of the Evangelical Church of England'.[4] The Manchester dissi-

---

[1] Memoir prefixed to *Glad Tracts*, p. 13, cf. Richard Cockin to Mary Fox, 10 Apr. 1842, printed in *JFHS* (1930), 31.

[2] Memoir prefixed to *Glad Tracts*, p. 13.

[3] *Introductory Remarks* to Beaconite account of 1837 YM, p. 7.

[4] *Quakerism; or The Story of My Life—By a Lady who for Forty Years was a member of the Society of Friends* (Dublin 1851), p. 285. The author of this anonymous work was Sarah Greer, according to *The Eclectic Review* (1851), 609, 618.

dents either became Anglicans or joined various dissenting chapels;[1] one, Isaac Neild, became a Congregationalist lay preacher.[2] Usually, they did not return to Friends, though in 1895, one of the original seceders sought readmission as a Friend, and was granted it immediately, without the usual formality of an interview.[3]

Some of those who left the Society at the time of the Beacon controversy, however, were still Friends enough to feel ill at ease elsewhere. Some joined the Plymouth Brethren, because they retained baptism and the Lord's Supper while rejecting, as Quakers do, a professional ministry. *The Inquirer* printed a number of defences of the Brethren,[4] and Luke Howard was among those who joined them. Occasionally, seceders were so attached to the forms of Quakerism that they did not feel able to join any other church at all. This was the experience of Mary Sewell, the mother of the author of *Black Beauty*. She was baptized at the time of the Beacon controversy, and resigned her membership to avoid expulsion—'It would be difficult to express to you the exceeding pain which this severance cost me.'[5] Her attachment to Friends, and especially to silent meetings was so great, that she never joined another church, though she lived to 1884.

The Beaconite movement had far more impact on English Quakerism than either of the subsequent schisms. This was partly because the numbers involved were greater, and partly because some of the Beaconites were highly respected and influential Friends. Moreover, while the later schisms were the result of views which were held by a small minority, the Beaconites were evangelicals, at a time when evangelicalism had become the accepted creed of Friends. Any Quaker evangelical could look into his own heart, and see a Beaconite. Many sympathized with the seceders, and were

---

[1] cf. the extract on p. 49 above. Their later allegiances are sometimes shown in the *Visitors Reports* on their children, when they resign in later years (*Hardshaw East MM Minutes*, c. 1840–60).

[2] *Manchester Faces and Places*, vol. vi (O.S.), 1895, p. 94.

[3] *Hardshaw East MM Minutes*, vol. viii, p. 362–3.

[4] *The Inquirer* (1839), 343–9, 492–516; 1840, pp. 262–8.

[5] Mrs. Bayly, *The Life and Letters of Mrs. Sewell* (2nd ed., London, 1889), p. 68; cf. pp. 74–5.

forced by their action to consider where their own duty lay. Some future Quaker leaders, such as Robert Charleton and J. B. Braithwaite, came close to resigning at the time. The period of conflict and divided loyalties had a traumatic effect on many such men, intensifying the rigidity with which their own views were held, and creating a fear of ideological discussion and change. In this sense it is possible to say that the Manchester Unitarians, in the 1870s, reaped the whirlwind sown by the Beaconites in the 1830s.

A QUIETIST SCHISM: FRITCHLEY

The Fritchley schism was quite unlike the Beaconite movement, both in the circumstances of its origin and in its subsequent history. Whereas Crewdson was to a large extent forced into schism, the Fritchley separation was the work of a man who aspired to be the leader of an independent religious movement. It created scarcely any stir among Friends, partly because of the small numbers involved, and partly because the quietist and conservative views of its members had already ceased to be influential among Friends.

The originator of the Fritchley schism, John G. Sargeant, was like Crewdson in that he held his views with a convert's fervour. But in Sargeant's case the conversion, which took place in 1838, was from nominal Quakerism to a strict observance of all the regulations which bound Friends at that time—such as the wearing of a collarless coat, the refusal to remove the hat when the usual social proprieties demanded it, and the use of distinctive patterns of speech,—which are discussed more fully in a later chapter of this study. Like some other conservatives, Sargeant suffered from a morbid scrupulosity of conscience—he refused to carry a letter, because it would 'defraud the king of his revenues and customs'.[1] To make matters worse, he lived in France at the time. Since Quakerism was almost unknown there, his obedience to Quaker forms, especially his use of the 'tu' form, exposed him constantly to serious misunderstanding.

[1] *Selections from the Diary and Correspondence of John G. Sargeant* (Newport, 1885), p. 45. The other details about Sargeant come from this source.

Some twenty years later, English Quakers decided to make all these 'peculiarities' optional. Sargeant, who had meanwhile settled in England, was appalled at the decision, remembering his own early struggles and sacrifices to conform to them. His loyalties were alienated from English Quakerism—he was never, in any case, a prominent or influential Friend—and he began to devote his energies to building up the unity of those English conservatives who deplored the recent changes.

The creation of a separatist movement took place gradually. The first stage consisted of a series of conferences, beginning in 1862, attended by some of those who had opposed the liberalizing changes which had been made. These conferences did not commit those attending to schismatic action; indeed some of them were to oppose such a step, in due course. The attendances were small—thirty came in 1864.[1] For most of those who attended, the Conferences were an institutionalized expression of the bonds of friendship which already linked them. In the 1860s, conservative Friends were lonely and scattered figures, suffering from a sense of isolation in their over-whelmingly evangelical meetings. The diaries of Daniel Pickard provide much pathetic evidence of this—his pain, for instance, at his Meeting's long-continued refusal to recognize his ministry.[2] In a typical entry he writes: 'the sense of being so like a stranger in our QMs was greater than usual.'[3] Naturally, conservatives sought some compensation for the trials of their situation in forging closer bonds with the like-minded. But few were thinking of schism, except Sargeant himself.

His intentions were clear as early as 1864, when he went to live in the little village of Fritchley, where he had bought a wood turning business. He established an unofficial meeting there, without, as was customary, seeking the authorization of the appropriate Quaker body: 'As to asking consent to open a meeting here, we are not at the present time feeling easy to do so, and thus show an allegiance to their authority,

---

[1] *Selections from the Diary and Correspondence of John G. Sargeant* (Newport, 1885), p. 133.

[2] He was finally recorded as a minister in 1877 (*The Friend* (1877), 323).

[3] *Journal*, 26 Apr. 1872.

that of the present back-slidden organization.'[1] In 1868, accompanied by two women sympathizers, Sargeant visited America. Here a series of schisms, beginning in New England in 1845, had led to the formation of several small conservative Yearly Meetings. Sargeant visited 'the smaller bodies', and was fired with the determination to found one on similar lines in England—an ambition in which American conservatives encouraged him.[2] His visit created resentment among other Quaker bodies in America, and when he returned to England he was greeted by his fellow conservatives with consternation. He was attacked for his 'undue zeal to promote a separation';[3] it seems clear that his critics were motivated partly by dislike of the prospect of a schism, and partly by annoyance at the extent to which Sargeant had acted on his own initiative.[4]

After two more conferences, in Sept. 1868 and Oct. 1869, the English conservatives agreed to differ. The majority decided to remain Quaker members, but a few followed Sargeant and established an organization of their own, Fritchley General Meeting. The first meeting was held in January 1870: the selection of a small Derbyshire village as the headquarters of the movement, because it was Sargeant's home, shows to what an extent he dominated it. A diary entry by Daniel Pickard, who deplored the schism, describes this inaugural meeting:

A meeting held at Fritchley—called a 'General Meeting' at which more than 20 were present—it is the first of the kind as a distinct and separate community from the Society of Friends at large & professing to stand firm for our primitive principles—I did not feel drawn to it; believing that an undue degree of self importance has got up in the minds of its chief promoters.[5]

Fritchley General Meeting was established as a protest against evangelical theology and the abandonment of many of the 'peculiarities' which had cut Friends off from the wider society. Hardly any records exist which make it

---

[1] *Sargeant Diary and Correspondence*, p. 130.
[2] Especially William Hodgson of Philadelphia.
[3] Daniel Pickard, *Journal*, 14 Sept. 1868.
[4] ibid., 13 Oct. 1868.
[5] ibid., 6 and 7 Jan. 1870.

possible to reconstruct the life of the group, but since it was established as a protest against change it is not surprising that it made no departure from accepted Quaker practices. The Fritchley Friends were to all intents and purposes indistinguishable from an ordinary country Quaker meeting, except that they retained the speech and dress of an earlier day, and did not attend the big periodical gatherings of Friends at Quarterly and Yearly Meetings. They held their own Monthly Meetings, and periodic General Meetings, when sympathizers from a distance would attend. Daniel Pickard visited them from time to time. In 1871 he noted disapprovingly, 'There is I fear, on the part of our friends there, too much of a straining after extraordinary things . . . a studied consistency in outward apparel & appearance.'[1] Later in the same year, after a business quarrel, he made a comment which hints at resentment and restlessness among the younger generation of Fritchley Friends: 'I fear he [one of Sargeant's sons] is not happy in being so tied down as he is and is venting a rebellious spirit in this way.'[2] Pickard's own son, Edward, an eccentric who was destined to vent a rebellious spirit more spectacularly, also visited Fritchley, in the 1890s. He described the movement thus:

There is in Derbyshire a village called Fritchley, known for a settlement of self-styled 'Quakers', who left the 'Larger Body' some 30 years ago. . . . The most noticeable things that they hold by, however, are the so-called 'Quaker' costume (bonnets, coats, &c.) and the sitting on forms together in a seating-house [sic] at stated times . . . there were some amongst them who seemed at that time to be rather more alive to present-day issues and needs . . .[3]

He stated that the Fritchley Friends were quietists: 'They, too, utterly resist being guided by Reason, except in matters of buying and selling, at which they are very sharp.'[4]

This account of the Fritchley Friends at the end of the century mentions both the original points of difference which

---

[1] Daniel Pickard, *Journal*, 27 Jan. 1871.
[2] ibid., 21 June 1871.
[3] Samuel Fox and Edward Pickard, *The Hat Crusade* (Flushing, near Falmouth, 1896–7), vol. ii, p. 128.
[4] ibid., vol. ii, p. 157.

distinguished them from English Quakerism in general—
their retention of the distinguishing externals of the
Quakerism of an earlier day, and their rejection of evangelical
theology. Time was to minimize both these differences. The
Fritchley Friends gave up the peculiarities gradually. A
Friend born in 1883 recalls that as a child she was given a
Quaker bonnet, objected, and was given a sailor suit instead.[1] The last member to wear a Quaker bonnet died in
1933, but the change had begun many years before. It was
not without its attendant stresses—a group of Fritchley
Friends living at Bournbrook, Birmingham, went into
schism in 1906, as a protest against Fritchley's liberalism—
a repetition, on a miniature scale, of the original schism
which cut Fritchley off from English Quakerism.[2]

The theological differences which cut Fritchley off from
the Quakerism of the 1860s became much less important
as evangelicalism declined. The liberals of the 1890s, redis-
covering the virtues of the Quakerism of an earlier day,
regarded Fritchley benevolently, as the standard bearer of
Quaker doctrines during a time of evangelical declension.
As a twentieth-century Friend was to put it, 'small though
they have been in numbers, Fritchley Friends have provided
a useful check to the evangelicalism and worldliness of some
later nineteenth-century Quakerism'.[3]

As the points of difference diminished, the relationship
between Fritchley and English Quakerism improved. When
the schism was established, the Fritchley Friends had very
much the ideology of the chosen remnant. As one of their
early adherents, the aged German J. G. Haymann, put it, 'I
am thankfull [sic] still to say, it was a mercy I was permitted
to mingle with you at Fritchley because it was the only
means of coming out of Babylon.'[4] This spirit of intran-
sigence was still evident in 1875, when Fritchley published

---

[1] This information, and all information given in the rest of this section for which
no source is given, comes from interviews with Mrs. C. Ludlow and Mr. H. Smith
(Sargeant's grandchildren, and the aged Clerk and Assistant Clerk of Fritchley)
and Mrs. E. Davidson (another of Sargeant's grandchildren).

[2] *Fritchley MM Minutes*, 5 Sept. 1906; 2 Apr. 1913; and 1 Sept. 1920. The
schism was too small to survive.

[3] L. Hugh Doncaster, *Quaker Organisation and Business Meetings* (London,
1958), p. 42.

[4] *Fritchley General Meeting Minutes*, 3 November 1870.

a pamphlet claiming that English Friends had 'ceased to uphold the original Faith and Practice of the Society of Friends' and that therefore all their property belonged by right to them![1] But by the late 1890s, the relationship had mellowed considerably. Several Friends paid tribute to the little movement at Yearly Meeting in 1898—one 'hoped that our sympathies might be drawn out to these Friends at Fritchley, who, he believed, were separated from us rather on matters of practice only and not of doctrine'.[2]

One might well ask, why, when the theological and other differences which cut them off from English Friends disappeared, did the Quakers of Fritchley continue to maintain a separate existence? The movement has always been dominated by the descendants of Sargeant—they are, today, almost the only 'Fritchley Friends'.[3] It is clear that they have been influenced by a desire to perpetuate a family tradition, and also, to some extent, by the fictitious importance which its separate organization gives to Fritchley Quakerism.

Any observer who could have compared the first stages of the Beaconite and Fritchley schisms would have been astounded to learn that the former would survive less than ten years, while the latter would not only survive but expand. The Beaconites had more adherents, and a well-developed organization and one would assume that Manchester was a more propitious environment for a new organization than a remote village in Derbyshire. In January 1869, before the establishment of Fritchley General Meeting, Sargeant wrote that only seven Quakers regularly held separatist meetings.[4] Twenty attended the inaugural General Meeting at Fritchley, but it is doubtful if all of these identified themselves with the mvement. The number of Fritchley Friends was so small that a single couple, living elsewhere, constituted a Preparative Meeting, and Meetings were discontinued as families moved elsewhere. But by the

---

[1] *Crowning Evidence that London Yearly Meeting has ceased to uphold the Original Faith and Practice of the Society of Friends;* it is reviewed in *The Monthly Record,* 1875, p. 10.

[2] *The Friend* (1898), 329.

[3] Today, there is only a tiny handful of aged Fritchley Friends, though other Quakers who happen to live near also attend Fritchley Meetings.

[4] *Sargeant Diary and Correspondence,* p. 168.

end of the century, Fritchley had perhaps eighty adherents —how can one explain this survival and slow expansion?

The great weakness of the Beaconites and the Manchester rationalists was that their numbers felt at home in other evangelical churches, and among the Unitarians, respectively. The Fritchley Friends could find a home only in Quakerism; their choice lay between continuing their schism, or returning to the main body. Their ideology of the chosen remnant meant that they were never discouraged by their small size; they saw themselves as a tiny elite, preserving the banner of primitive Quakerism through a time of apostasy.

Throughout the movement's history, most of its members have lived in Fritchley. No branch of the movement has survived permanently elsewhere. This accident of location has had both advantages and disadvantages. It helped foster its sense of identity; there was no other Quaker meeting in the area to challenge members' allegiances. For some, its rural location was an attraction—the village's remoteness, its beautiful situation, readily make it something like a place of pilgrimage. But while its location in some respects strengthened the movement, it placed limits on its expansion. The village was far too small to provide a livelihood for a large number of middle-class Quakers. Members solved the problem in various ways; they lived on private means, or became farmers, or worked elsewhere—in nearby Belper, or in Derby. One worked as far afield as Manchester, spending his weekends in Fritchley. Inevitably, the children of members tended to move elsewhere, in search of work, and to join another Quaker meeting.[1] Early in the twentieth century, the meeting was permanently crippled when forty of its members emigrated to Canada, for economic reasons.[2]

In the nineteenth century, new members were drawn from three sources. Natural increase was important, as were conversions from among people living in the area who felt drawn to Quakerism and were led by geographic accident to adopt it in its Fritchley form. A few went to the lengths of

[1] Details on members' occupations come from interviews.

[2] At first they formed a meeting of their own, but they soon joined the Society of Friends in Canada.

settling in the village in order to be members of Fritchley
General Meeting. The two women Friends who accompanied Sargeant on his first visit to America took this step,
as did several converts to Quakerism, among them H. T.
Wake (1831–1914) and Thomas Davidson (1850–1928).
Davidson was originally a Scottish railway clerk, who
entered a Quaker meeting by chance. He read the journal
of John Wilbur, an American quietist, and felt drawn to
Quakerism in its quietist form. He came to England in
search of the likeminded, and made his home in Fritchley,
becoming the village grocer. In all, Fritchley accepted 17
converts between 1871 and 1883.[1]

Until his death in 1883, Sargeant was the acknowledged
leader of the movement, and his leadership, coupled with
Fritchley's antagonism to the rest of English Quakerism,
fostered its unity. But the reliance on individual judgement,
the concept of the chosen remnant, which produced the
original schism, could easily lead to disagreements within it.
The Bournbrook schism, and Fritchley's quarrel with John
E. Southall, once a leading member of the movement [2] were
partly a manifestation of this tendency, partly the result of
private animosities and ambitions.

Despite its small size and its quietism, Fritchley produced
a disproportionately large number of travelling ministers.
Sargeant himself made ministerial journeys to America,
Norway and France, and many parts of England. Another
Fritchley minister, Jesse Darbyshire, made three visits to
America, and many religious journeys in England. Thomas
Davidson, similarly often travelled in the ministry. One of
the attractions of Fritchley, for its members, was that its small
size invested them, individually, with great responsibility
and influence. They could play a major role in its internal
affairs, and travel as its emissaries, in a way which was possible for relatively few in the wider world of English
Quakerism.

---

[1] *Fritchley General Meeting Minutes, 1871–83.* Unfortunately, they include no
statement of total membership.

[2] Southall, a Cardiff printer, was at one time Clerk of Fritchley General Meeting, but he was silenced as a minister in 1911 and disunited in 1924. (*Fritchley MM
Minutes,* 4 Nov. 1911 and 18 June 1924). cf. Pickard and Fox, *The Hat Crusade,*
vol. i, pp. 20–1 and vol. ii, p. 163.

A UNITARIAN SCHISM:
THE MANCHESTER RATIONALISTS

From time to time in Victorian England, a clergyman holding views which could be variously termed 'unitarian', 'rationalist', or 'free thinking' seceded from one of the established churches, and was followed by his congregation. A number of these small ephemeral churches are described in *Heterodox London*, and Mrs. Ward's *Robert Elsmere* provides an idealized literary reconstruction of one of them. The little congregation, established by the Friends who seceded from Manchester Meeting in 1871, belongs to this genre. The movement was obscure—though it was mentioned in *The Westminster Review*[1]—and short-lived, and, like the Beaconite and Fritchley schisms, largely the result of one man's leadership.

David Duncan was a convert to Quakerism, a Presbyterian minister who adopted the religion of his Quaker wife. The Visitors who interviewed him when he applied for membership in 1852 stated that 'he had been brought under the power of Truth, and at no small sacrifice been made willing to submit thereunto.'[2] He became a merchant and manufacturer, but kept a strong and intelligent interest in the theological movements of the day. It is probable that his opinions changed after he became a Quaker—he cannot have shown any signs of 'rationalist' sympathies when the Monthly Meeting accepted him so readily. Duncan was a born leader, an attractive personality who readily drew disciples—'half worshipped by some who knew him closely'.[3]

As it happened, Manchester Friends had recently opened a Friends Institute, with a library, lectures, and discussions, intended as a social centre for young members in the city. Duncan began to lecture at the Institute—in 1861 he gave a sympathetic introducton to *Essays and Reviews*—and soon attracted supporters. Evangelicals were increasingly alarmed by Duncan's ideas, and the support he attracted, and in 1868 a group of Elders appealed to the Quarterly Meeting to

---

[1] *The Westminster Review* (1875), 327.
[2] *Hardshaw East MM Minutes*, vol. iv, p. 521.
[3] *Manchester City News*, 3 Aug. 1921 (FHL Press Cuttings, VV74); an anonymous article by one who attended Mount Street Meeting from 1867 until 1883.

intervene.[1] A committee was appointed which was conciliatory in intention, and did not condemn Duncan. This was unacceptable to the evangelical party, who appealed to Yearly Meeting. As in the case of Isaac Crewdson, thirty-five years earlier, Yearly Meeting appointed a committee which was to combine the functions of investigator and judge. Inevitably, the committee was dominated by evangelicals. J. B. Braithwaite was the unofficial leader, as Gurney was, during the Beaconite troubles.

The committee conducted what was, in effect, an inquisition. It paid repeated visits to Manchester, following a policy of 'divide and rule' and trying to detach Duncan from his followers. Duncan refused to recant: 'He said that he could not suppress his views; that if he attempted it they would come out at his coat tails.'[2] The case against him was strengthened when he chaired a meeting addressed by Charles Voysey, the founder of the Theistic church. He was disowned, and died, suddenly and prematurely, on the sixth of August 1871, before he had time to appeal against his expulsion.

Although his sudden death, caused by smallpox, was scarcely due to the Monthly Meeting's decision, it lent the halo of martyrdom to his cause, and the unconcealed exultation of the evangelicals hopelessly embittered the situation. Braithwaite, who viewed Duncan as an emissary of Satan, wrote in his diary: 'How wonderful are the ways of Providence! Last year he stood in what appeared to be proud defiance; now laid low in the dust. How clearly may we trace the Hand that has graciously guided and thus far protected our little Society from the inroads of a dangerous scepticism.'[3]

Four days after Duncan's death, eleven of his supporters resigned their membership.[4] Several more resignations followed, but not all his sympathizers took this step—two of

---

[1] The account which follows is based on *The Manchester Friend* (1872), 7, 41, 88, 152; and (1873), 101. Cooper, *The Crisis in Manchester Meeting, passim*, and MS depositions in FHL (Box 9).

[2] J. B. Braithwaite, *Journal*, 20 Apr. 1871.

[3] ibid., 13 Aug. 1871.

[4] Shipley Neave to J. B. Braithwaite, 10 Aug. 1871 (Copy in FHL) Box 9, 4(1).

the most prominent, Charles Thompson, J.P., active in local affairs and in the United Kingdom Alliance, and John Edmondson, whose father invented the patent railway ticket, decided to remain with Friends. Duncan's mantle of leadership was assumed by Joseph Binyon Forster, a partner in a sugar refinery, and the author of a little work on religious liberty. The subsequent history of the schism must be gleaned from the pages of *The Manchester Friend*, which Forster edited for the two years of its existence.

The seceders rented a room on Unitarian premises—in Memorial Hall, in the centre of Manchester, a few yards away from Mount Street Meeting House. After nearly a year, they reported that 42 Friends made it their regular place of worship, and that there was a weekly average of 4–5 visitors, total attendances averaging 30.[1] The meeting is interesting for the way in which it reflects the ideological ideals of the group: the value of freedom of thought, and of free discussion. There was no formal hierarchy of Overseers, Elders, and Ministers, and there was complete liberty of thought and speech. The fear of control, restricting liberty, meant that there was no formal organization at all—the group did not even take a name: 'There is no organisation of any kind; there are neither officers, nor any of the religious "orders" to be found in other Christian societies; hence no name has been adopted.'[2] After Meeting for Worship, which was held on usual Quaker lines, the meeting became an informal discussion group.

In December 1873, when *The Manchester Friend* was ceasing publication, the meeting issued an address, stating that two and a half years had passed since they had formed a separate group 'to speak the thoughts and convictions we entertained which was denied to us within its borders, and for the enjoyment of the privilege of companionship in "unity of spirit" without the limitations imposed upon it by forced identity of opinion on the obscure propositions of theologians'.[3] This address gives the impression of a strongly established and confident body: 'Nothing would

---

[1] *The Manchester Friend* (1872), 99.   [2] ibid.
[3] *The Manchester Friend* (1873), 190.

induce us to return again to the old hedged-in ground"[1]—
but its size made its survival precarious. The very existence
of a meeting with thirty members would be endangered if
two or three families left Manchester, or joined another
religious organization.

After *The Manchester Friend* comes to an end, the subsequent history of the group is shrouded in complete obscurity.
Only one of its members is known to have rejoined Friends
—and that was after the passage of many years.[2] It is probable that the group did not maintain a separate existence for
long, and that its members later joined the Unitarians. One,
Henry Woodhead, was for many years a Unitarian, a member of Upper Brook Street Free Church; '...The Church
was the recognised exponent of reverent and earnest free
thought in Manchester...'[3]

Like the Beaconites, the Manchester rationalists felt that
they had had schism forced upon them. They did not intend
to form a new branch of Quakerism; 'The formation of a
new sect was never contemplated.'[4] Such protestations are
common among sectarians, but in this case it was undoubtedly true. Like the Beaconites, they found their
situation within Quakerism intolerable, but were too attached
to Quaker forms of worship to join another church. Like the
Beaconites, the Manchester dissidents were linked to each
other mainly by kinship and friendship. They did not try to
gain converts, and would in any case have been unlikely to
succeed; and their lack of members meant that their movement was almost inevitably ephemeral.

The history of each of these little movements reflects the
translation of abstract theological ideas into outward practices. The Beaconites laid their primary emphasis on those
evangelical doctrines which they held, of course, in common
with evangelicals of other denominations. They abandoned
the distinctive views of Friends, and established what was,
in effect, a dissenting chapel. But soon they followed their
position to its logical conclusion, and became evangelical

---

[1] *The Manchester Friend* (1873), 190.
[2] *The Annual Monitor* (1914), 183–4.
[3] *The Annual Monitor* (1914), 184.
[4] *The Manchester Friend* (1873), 190.

Anglicans or Dissenters. The Manchester Unitarians were basically committed to the ideal of intellectual liberty. This found expression in an anarchic rejection of all forms of external organization and constraint—they did not even have a name. Their little congregation proved ephemeral, like many other small break-away Unitarian and rationalist churches. Whereas the primary commitment of the Beaconites was to evangelicalism, and of the Manchester Unitarians, to liberty, the Fritchley schism was an attempt to preserve what its adherents saw as the essence of Quakerism—quietism, and the ideal of a Peculiar People. Not only did they not abandon Quaker practices, but, alone of the three schisms, they succeeded in attracting a small but steady trickle of converts. When, after fifty years, their original raison d'être had gone, when they had given up the ideal of a Peculiar People, and quietism seemed no longer in need of defence, the movement was old enough to have the sanction of tradition, and continued under its own momentum.

THE FORCES WHICH FOSTERED UNITY

It would be an error of judgement to exaggerate the importance of these schisms. They were very small, and if one looks at the whole pattern of Victorian Quakerism, and compares it with the divisions of the early Friends, or the waves of Hicksite, quietist, and anti-slavery schisms among American Friends, the most striking thing about it is its relative unity and stability. There were many real challenges to the unity of Victorian Friends. The three schisms which eventuated were the fruit of theological differences, but Friends in the 1850s seriously feared that the temperance question, for instance, would lead to the creation of two separate Yearly Meetings.[1] Moreover some elements in Quakerism definitely encouraged division. The ideal of liberty was enshrined in every aspect of Quakerism—in the equal freedom of all to speak in Meetings for Worship and in business meetings, and in the doctrine of the perceptible guidance of the Spirit, equally enlightening all. In reports of

[1] *The Friend* (1882), 141.

Victorian Quaker debates, we sometimes find Friends who interpreted the doctrine of inspiration to mean the infallibility of whatever they were saying. But it is one of the most striking aspects of Quaker history that on the whole these antinomian tendencies were held in check.

The substantial unity of Friends in the Victorian period can be explained in a number of different ways. Bright attributed it to Quaker virtue: 'Friends are, after all, the most tolerant people on earth, and I verily believe our little Church is the only one that could freely discuss and make great reforms, without schism and something like dissolution.'[1] There were, however, more tangible factors which fostered Quaker unity. Certain of these discouraged both schisms and the resignations of individuals. The intense attachment of members to the Society was compounded of many elements. Quakerism was so different from other denominations; it affected life at so many points—especially before 1860—that to abandon it after a lifetime of sitting through silent meetings, using 'thee' and 'thou', refusing to pay tithes and wearing a collarless coat, was to threaten one's whole sense of identity. Quakers prized length of Quaker descent as a nobleman prizes the antiquity of his titles. Even those who left the Society continued to take pride in their Quaker antecedents. Moreover, in the Victorian period, Quaker membership was difficult to obtain, easy to lose, and correspondingly valued.

The Society of Friends was, in a literal sense, a society of friends and kinsmen. To leave it was to cut oneself off, to some extent, from one's relations and friends, and, very possibly, one's business associates. An interesting exchange of letters on the subject between Quaker cousins, in the late eighteenth century, stresses this. The one planning to resign is warned of 'the many disadvantages with which this step may be pregnant', the threat to 'the enjoyment of an intimate friendship with thy near and numerous Connections'.[2] But he reiterates his determination to leave, 'however vast the Obstacles & great the Disadvantages that this Step may

---

[1] Quoted in Phebe Doncaster, *John Stephenson Rowntree His Life and Work* (London, 1908), pp. 12–13.

[2] John to Bartlett Gurney, 20 Feb. 1785, *Gurney MSS*, II, 211.

bring forth, in the Interests of this World, or . . . the
Friendship & regard of my relations & Friends'.[1]

The education of most Friends at one of a dozen Quaker
boarding-schools reinforced the bonds of kinship with 'old
schoolfellowship'.[2] The periodic gatherings of Friends at
Monthly, Quarterly, and Yearly Meetings meant that an
active member, who attended at least some of these meetings,
came to know the leading members of the Society personally. There was less chance for differences of opinion to
develop into personal hostility. The freedom of all to speak
in meetings meant that all could exercise at least some influence on decisions reached, at every level. The absence of a
professional clergy meant that office was equally open to all;
the enormous number of official appointments of various
kinds meant that responsibility was widely shared among
members—and men naturally identify themselves with an
organization in which they wield even a small amount of
power.

The motives which swayed those who contemplated
schism or resignation but decided to remain in the Society
were naturally varied, but it is safe to assume that they were
usually mixed. J. J. Gurney confided to his diary the reasons
why he did not follow the Beaconites. On the one hand was
a theological consideration—the fear that they gave too little
emphasis to the role of the Spirit.[3] On the other was the
more mundane reflection, that only as a Quaker could he
combine the avocations of minister and banker. In any other
church he would either, as a layman, have to give up his role
as preacher and religious leader, or, as a clergyman, sacrifice many of his 'Secularities'.[4]

The factors which strengthened the unity of Victorian
Friends are various, and it would be difficult to be certain
about their relative importance. But it is clear that the position of those who left the Society, even in the company of
others, was fraught with conflict and difficulty. The situation of those who resigned individually, or were expelled, is
discussed in a later chapter of this book.

[1] Bartlett to John Gurney, 21 Feb. 1785, *Gurney MSS*, II, 28.
[2] *FQE* (1880), 454.
[3] *Journal*, 2 Aug. 1838.   [4] ibid., 1 Aug. 1840.

III

QUAKER ORGANIZATION:—THEORY AND PRACTICE[1]

A STUDY of any organization, religious or otherwise, has two dimensions—the analysis of its formal institutions, and of how they actually work in practice. In other words, an organization has a formal and an informal face, which can bear a greater or a lesser resemblance to each other. In a historical study, time provides a further dimension, because most institutions are in a state of constant change. The organization of a church tends to be regarded by its members as sacrosanct, for obvious reasons. Matthew Arnold complained, 'what are . . . religious organizations but machinery? Now almost every voice in England is accustomed to speak of these things as if they were precious ends in themselves . . .'[2] Quakers were, perhaps, unusually aware of the gulf between the ideals behind actual institutions and their workings in practice—there was no sphere of their corporate life where they were more self-critical.

The organization of the Society of Friends was highly elaborate, and in many respects unique. This chapter is confined to its most important elements, to their theoretical functions, and the way in which theory was translated into reality:

> Between the idea
> And the reality . . .
> Falls the Shadow

MEMBERSHIP

In the nineteenth century, one could become a Quaker in either of two ways—by birth, in the case of the child of two Quaker parents, or by conversion, called 'convincement'.

---

[1] This account of Quaker organization is put in the past tense and refers to the Victorian period only. Some elements have remained constant since then, and some have changed.

[2] Matthew Arnold, *Culture and Anarchy* (Cambridge, 1950 ed.), p. 50.

Membership could be lost through voluntary resignation, or through expulsion, known as 'disownment'. This dimension of Quaker history—exits and entrances—is discussed more fully in the chapter that follows. Here we are concerned only with one aspect—the controversy which was endemic throughout the Victorian period on the rights and wrongs of inherited or 'birthright' membership. Much was written on the subject—the most important contribution was Robert Barclay's *On Membership in the Society of Friends*, published in 1873. Evangelicals tended to oppose birthright membership—it will be recalled that the Beaconites rejected it —claiming that faith cannot be inherited, and that a church should consist only of living members, converted and committed Christians. Some who did not accept these evangelical presuppositions united with them in condemning birthright membership, because of its injustice. It implied a dual standard, for converts had to pass a period of probation, and a trying interview, while the children of Friends enjoyed membership until they rejected it, or forfeited it by a serious offence.

Theological liberals, on the other hand, tended to defend birthright membership. They rejected the evangelical's distinction between the saved and the unconverted, and claimed that there was no way of telling who were 'living' members. They feared that if birthright membership was abolished, a system of theological tests would take its place.[1] Moreover many of them remembered their own phase of religious doubt. Young Friends often passed, they claimed, through a period of doubt or indifference, but retained their membership out of sentiment or inertia and found that their religious life deepened as the years went by. It could do only harm to force them into a premature choice. Of the many points made in John Stephenson Rowntree's *Quakerism Past and Present*, published in 1859, birthright membership is the only one on which he later changed his mind. He had opposed it, but came to believe that a spiritual inheritance is a possession, until renounced or lost.[2]

[1] *The British Friend* (1900), 166–73.

[2] John Stephenson Rowntree, *Quakerism, Past and Present: being an Inquiry into the Causes of its Decline in Great Britain and Ireland* (London, 1859), pp. 112–13; cf. his article in *FQE* 1872, pp. 249–73; and Doncaster, *John Stephenson Rowntree*, p. 15.

The question of birthright membership was introduced at Yearly Meeting in 1899, and fully discussed the following year. The debates attracted a crowded attendance, and many took part, but in the end no change was made. Birthright membership was destined to be a perennial preoccupation of twentieth-century Friends. It was repeatedly modified, and finally abolished in 1959.[1]

Not all who came to Meetings for Worship were Quakers. Anyone could attend, and those who came regularly were formally entered on a list of 'habitual attenders', and special schools, such as Penketh, catered for their children. In the earlier Victorian period, when Quakers were disowned for marrying non-Quakers, many attenders were former members. In the later period, they were largely scholars from Quaker Adult Schools. They could not hold any official position in the Society, be present at business meetings, or contribute to its funds. They were not Quakers, and were, on occasion, reproved if they said that they were.[2]

BUSINESS MEETINGS

The backbone of Quaker organization was to be found in its business meetings, or 'Meetings for Discipline'. These were supplemented by various standing committees, but the Monthly Meeting was the focus of local executive power in the Society, and Yearly Meeting, of central legislative power.

Quaker business meetings can be represented as a pyramid.[3] At the bottom level were the Preparative Meetings, each of which comprised one or several local congregations. A Monthly Meeting covered a larger group of congregations—the number varied—and several Monthly Meetings formed a Quarterly Meeting. The Quarterly Meeting usually covered a county, or group of counties. At the top of the pyramid was London Yearly Meeting, the Parliament of English, Welsh and Scottish Quakerism, which as its name suggests, was held in London once a year. Each meeting guaranteed a minimum attendance for the one above it, by

[1] *Yearly Meeting Proceedings, 1959*, pp. 18–19.
[2] An applicant for membership, in Norwich MM in 1892 was rejected because she claimed she was a Friend, when she was actually an attender.
[3] cf. Fig. I, 'The Structure of Quaker Meetings'.

appointing representatives, but all Quakers were free to attend, and take an active part, and were, indeed, expected to do so, if possible. Fig. 2 shows how a Quaker living in Norwich, for instance, in 1891,[1] was a member of Norwich Preparative Meeting, of a Monthly Meeting, which covered perhaps a third of Norfolk, and of a Quarterly Meeting which covered three counties, as well as of London Yearly Meeting. Until the end of the nineteenth century, women attended a separate, parallel structure of women's meetings, but the men's meeting enjoyed a monopoly of power.

Preparative Meetings were relatively unimportant, and were sometimes not held at all. As their name suggests, they were subsidiary to the Monthly Meeting, and their main function was to appoint Monthly Meeting representatives, and pass on information concerning, for instance, births and burials.

The Monthly Meeting exercised many important executive functions. It decided whether to accept applicants for membership, and whether to expel delinquents. It administered endowments, which sometimes produced incomes of hundreds of pounds, and collected subscriptions for the Quaker central all-purposes fund, misleadingly called the National Stock. It registered births and deaths, and administered the complex regulations governing Quaker marriages. In its turn, it appointed representatives to the meeting above it.

The Quarterly Meeting, which was held four times a year, had, by contrast, few important functions. Its main raison d'être was to act as a channel of communication between its Monthly Meetings and Yearly Meeting, and to appoint representatives to Yearly Meeting. Very rarely, it acted as a court of appeal when a Monthly Meeting's decision was questioned, and still more rarely, it reached sufficient agreement on a proposal for some major change to propose it formally to Yearly Meeting, for debate. In the last two decades of the nineteenth century, some Quarterly Meetings made a conscious adaptation to their lack of real work, and introduced conferences and prepared addresses instead.

---

[1] The boundaries of Meetings were changed occasionally, because of shifts in population.

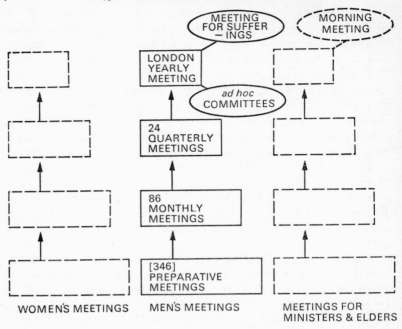

WOMEN'S MEETINGS   MEN'S MEETINGS   MEETINGS FOR
MINISTERS & ELDERS

The numbers of meetings given are for England and Wales in 1851. There is no record
of the number of Preparative meetings, so the number of Particular meetings or Local
congregations (which were usually coterminous with Preparative meetings) is given
instead

Fig. 1   The Structure of Quaker Meetings

Yearly Meeting was the parliament of Quakerism, and
one which every Quaker was free to attend.[1] It discussed the
affairs of the movement as a whole, and debated and decided
proposals to change the rules which governed its corporate
life. Occasionally it acted as a supreme court of appeal
against a sentence of disownment.

In theory, information about the condition of Quakerism
was meant to rise like sap, from one meeting to the next, until
it reached Yearly Meeting, to provide the basis for its deliberations. Many hours' work at Monthly and Quarterly Meetings, in the first half of the nineteenth century, was devoted
to supplying this information, and much of the time of Yearly

[1] A long existing practice to this effect was formally ratified in 1861.

DUBLIN

YEARLY

MEETING

Lancs.&Cheshire QM
Hardshaw East MM

Manchester PM

Norwich MM
Norwich PM

Norfolk Cambs
&Hunts. QM

• Preparative meetings

Monthly meeting boundary

Quarterly meeting boundary

Fig. 2   Two Quaker Meetings in 1891

Meeting was spent listening to it. Unfortunately, the system used was a singularly cumbrous and ineffective one. Each Monthly Meeting had to supply answers to a standardized

questionnaire—the 'Queries'; the Quarterly Meeting
summarized these answers and read them to Yearly Meeting. The method would have worked if it had been confined
to statistics, but most of the queries were better suited to
individual introspection than to a corporate answer. It was
obviously impossible to return an answer, on behalf of an
area the size of Yorkshire, to a question such as 'Are Friends
preserved in love towards one another?' The attempt to
achieve the impossible meant that much of the time of meetings was consumed in tedious debates over fine shades of
language—'It does not appear but that . . .' and so on. A
whole series of such statements, read by Quarterly Meeting
after Quarterly Meeting, wasted Yearly Meeting's time and
had a numbing and confusing effect. Some of the answers
were positively misleading—they listed conversions, but not
resignations, expulsions, or total membership, thus giving a
misleadingly optimistic picture.

The Queries were preserved, despite the recognition of
their ineffectiveness, out of affectionate respect for the *mos
maiorum*. But the system was gradually changed; in 1861, the
systematic collection of statistical data was introduced, and
from 1875 onwards, the practice of answering the Queries
was abolished, except for several quantifiable ones. Later,
Quarterly Meetings began to fill the same function by making
triennial reports on their general condition.

In the early Victorian period, a very important function
of these meetings was a social one. Quarterly and Yearly
Meetings, in particular, were high festivals in the sober
Quaker year, a time of family reunions, of courtships, and of
lavish hospitality. Many young Quakers came to these
gatherings in search of a spouse—Yearly Meeting 'has from
time immemorial served this useful purpose'.[1] The meeting
which regulated the affairs of Ackworth School was very
popular—partly because northern Friends found it more
accessible than London Yearly Meeting, and partly because
of its 'fresh air, beautiful scenery, and greater freedom from
restraint'.[2] These meetings helped unify the Society, and

---

[1] *Diary of William Lucas*, vol. i, p. 21.
[2] *The Friend* (1869), 193. This article by W. C. W[estlake] gives a full account
of the informal attractions of these meetings.

provided a diversion at a time when most conventional amusements were forbidden.

THE DECLINE OF INTEREST IN
BUSINESS MEETINGS

By the end of the 1850s, it was generally recognized that attendance at business meetings had become unattractive to the rank and file membership. Quakers were agreed on the situation, but not on the diagnosis of its cause. It seems clear that the development of the railways was partly responsible. It became possible to attend a distant meeting, transact its business, and return the same day, so that the leisurely gatherings with their attendant festivities, and overnight stay became a thing of the past. Other factors, in the second half of the nineteenth century, contributed to the decline in the social functions of these meetings. As Quakers became more liberal, and permitted more forms of recreation,[1] such gatherings played a smaller part in their lives. After 1860, they could marry non-Quakers, and naturally, if they did so, showed less interest in meetings which only Friends could attend.

In the era before Friends entered politics and local government, many a Quaker with a flair for administration found a real satisfaction in guiding the affairs of Quaker meetings. But as other spheres of action opened to them, the scope of Quaker organization naturally seemed limited.[2] An able man found more interest in the administration of the Board Schools of a big town, with their thousands of children, than in that of Ackworth, with its 300 scholars, and the finances of a city offered more challenge than those of even the best endowed Monthly Meeting.

As the subsidiary attractions of the meetings disappeared, attention naturally focused on their functioning. Friends were often dismayed by what they saw. The time and energy spent answering the Queries was resented, and the system was changed, and the way in which women's meetings[3] and Quarterly Meetings[4] lacked real work seemed an

[1] cf. pp. 155–6 below.   [2] *The Friend* (1873), 276 and (1892), p. 93.
[3] ibid., (1873), 297.   [4] *The Monthly Record* (1881), 153.

abuse—though here change was more difficult and came more slowly.

The abolition of the Queries took away one of the main functions of the Monthly Meeting, and the passage of time gradually eroded another. At the beginning of the Victorian era, the Monthly Meeting shared with the Overseers the duties of an ecclesiastical policeman. In fact, it combined the functions of policeman and judge, investigating the cases of offenders against morality, or against Quaker regulations, and deciding whether to expel them. Even when expulsions were frequent, some were uneasy about this aspect, 'the hand which cuts off or repels . . .'[1] As time passed, expulsion became less frequent, partly because Quaker rules were made less strict, and partly because of a change in the climate of opinion, and a growing distaste for such rigid supervision of church members. Dealing with delinquents came to seem 'intrinsically uninteresting and unedifying . . .'[2] and much of the work which remained was sheer routine—making a record of births and burials, allocating income from endowments to repair a meeting house, and so on. Such routine business was both tedious and also often unduly protracted—in a large meeting it would last three or four hours,[3] and it was always preceded by a meeting for worship. Even to Victorian Quakers, this was 'quite long enough for the flesh and blood of ordinary mortals'.[4] As a result, attendance even at Monthly Meeting tended to be confined to a hard core, except when a matter of unusual interest came up,[5] and members became increasingly reluctant to take office. The decline was relative rather than absolute—there was always a proportion of members who spent much of their leisure time attending meetings and serving on multifarious Quaker committees.

The whole system of governing by business meetings always had an intrinsic injustice, which was minimized by the relative social homogeneity of the movement, until working-class converts began to enter it in appreciable numbers, from the 1870s on. Since members attended these

---

[1] J. J. Gurney, *Journal*, 22 June 1834.
[2] *The Friend* (1871), 181.
[3] ibid. (1857), 91; cf. (1872), 58.   [4] ibid.   [5] ibid. (1879), 153.

meetings at their own expense, they were governed, in effect, by those who could afford the cost of the journey. This was especially true of the higher levels—Quarterly and Yearly Meetings. Attendance at the latter was 'a luxury of the rich or of those who live in London'.[1] The relationship between prosperity and activity in the Society went further than this— only those whose time was largely their own could serve, for instance, on a Yearly Meeting committee, the work of which would continue, with intermissions, for months on end. The wealthy naturally dominated the work of a church with no professional clergy and practically no secretariat. 'From them come the men of leisure, who should be those to stand forward and bear the weight of church affairs.'[2] Quakers themselves were fully aware that the Society tended to be dominated by wealthy men, retired or semi-retired, living near London. An anonymous Friend painted a portrait of one of them in 1830:

Form, (who resides near London . . .) [is known] chiefly on account of his age and respectability. He is almost the father of the yearly meeting. . . . Form, being much at liberty, what with sleeping partnerships, and ostensible retirement from the things of the world, and having grown up in an attachment to all the modes and fashions of Quakerism . . . really devotes a large portion of his time to the society; and living so near town, has something to do with almost all that is officially transacted at head quarters . . .[3]

In the last two decades of the nineteenth century, Quakers became increasingly aware that those who could not afford to travel to meetings were virtually disenfranchized. Sometimes richer Quakers paid the expenses of their poorer fellow members, but it was pointed out that participation in church affairs should not be dependent on haphazard patronage. The suggestion that the expenses of attendance should be paid by the Society was often made, but never seriously entertained.[4] But Friends were troubled by the unequal distribution of power among theoretically equal

[1] *The British Friend* (1897), 125.
[2] Joseph John Fox, *The Society of Friends; an Enquiry into the Causes of its Weakness as a Church* (London, 1859), p. 65.
[3] *The Friends Monthly Magazine* (1830), 682–3.
[4] cf., for instance, *The Friend* (1845), 232.

members, and also by a practical problem—those who had
no say in church policy were naturally reluctant to contribute to its funds.[1] In 1905, as a tardy and inadequate response to the problem, Yearly Meeting was held in Leeds,
instead of London—'To reach the disenfranchised, the
Yearly Meeting must travel.'[2]

QUAKER DEMOCRACY IN PRACTICE

Decisions at Quaker meetings were reached, not by taking
a vote, or informally ascertaining the will of the majority,
but by a unique method called 'taking the sense of the
meeting'. This procedure was intended to avoid majority
tyranny. All present were free to speak to an issue, and when
the discussion was over the Clerk, who combined the duties
of chairman and secretary, would formulate a decision. This
was supposed to reflect, not only the numbers on each side,
but the standing of speakers and the value of their contribution. In this section, an attempt is made to discover how
the system worked, whether the ideal of the full participation of all present was sustained in practice, and how it coped
with extreme and strongly held differences of opinion. The
only Quaker meeting for which sufficiently full records for
such a study exist is the Men's Yearly Meeting.[3]

One cannot ascertain with real precision what proportion
of adult members attended Yearly Meeting, and how many
of these took part in debates. The only information on the
first question comes from the casual estimates of contemporaries. Between 1847 and 1862, five such estimates were
made,[4] ranging from 590 to 1,200–1,500, and averaging

---

[1] cf., for instance, *The Friend* (1856), 177.

[2] *Present Day Papers* (1902), 125.

[3] The analysis which follows is based on the printed accounts of Yearly Meeting
discussions in Quaker periodicals and on manuscript journals of the debates, where
these exist. The subject of this chapter section is discussed more fully in my article,
'Organisation and power in the Society of Friends (1852–9)', *Archives de Sociologie des Religions*, 1965, p. 31ff. This is reprinted in Bryan R. Wilson (ed.) *Patterns
of Sectarianism* (London, 1967), in a revised form. I have obtained more data on
some matters since it was written.

[4] Samuel Alexander, *Account of 1847 Yearly Meeting* (MS in FHL), p. 94; *The
Friend* (1852), 113 (i.e. the number at Yearly Meeting who signed a petition
against the Militia Bill); J. S. Rowntree, *Account of 1854 Yearly Meeting* (MS in
FHL), p. 22; Jonathan Pim to Joseph Rowntree, 26 May 1858 (MS in FHL,

864. In 1862, there were 6,463 male Quakers in England, Scotland, and Wales.[1] If one assumes that the age distribution obtaining in the general population applies to Friends, then in 1862 3,458 male Quakers were of an age to attend.[2] Therefore, rather more than a third of those who were eligible to attend, did so. If, instead of averaging the estimates of attendance, one takes the estimate for 1862 alone, which was 590, then the proportion is much lower—just over a fifth. This agrees with an estimate made in 1878, that a fifth or a sixth of Quaker adults attended one or another of Yearly Meeting's sittings.[3]

A little later, however, a Friend claimed that he counted the attendance at business sittings of Yearly Meeting, and that it was always less than 250.[4] This is much lower than the estimates made between 1847 and 1862. If one accepts the accuracy of both, it can mean one of two things—either, that total attendances declined, despite the improvement of communications, or that while just as many Friends attended some part of Yearly Meeting, few of these attended regularly. In either case, the pattern may reflect a decline of interest in the affairs of the church, or economic changes, a decline in the number of the self-employed. Although the Women's Yearly Meeting was practically powerless, it was far better attended than the men's, presumably because of its members' greater leisure.

Because no vote was taken, the only members who contributed to decisions were those who spoke, and the habitually silent exercised no power at business meetings whatsoever. Over a seven-year period in the 1850s, the average number of speakers at Men's Yearly Meeting was 73—

Temp. Box 93:3, f.28); J. S. Rowntree, *Account of 1862 Yearly Meeting* (MS in FHL), p. 72.

[1] *Tabular Statement*, 1863.

[2] For the age distribution in the general population, cf. B. R. Mitchell and Phyllis Deane, *Abstract of British Historical Statistics* (Cambridge, 1962), p. 12. This number was arrived at by estimating the percentage of the total male population aged 20 and over, and applying it to the total of male Quakers.

[3] *The Friend* (1878), 115. John W. Steel in '*Friendly' Sketches: Essays Illustrative of Quakerism* (London and Darlington, 1876), p. 43, states that 1/15 of the total Quaker membership attended the opening session of Yearly Meeting. The two estimates are not necessarily inconsistent—the second is based on the *total* Quaker population and refers to one sitting only.

[4] *The Friend* (1881), 115.

approximately a twelfth of those attending.[1] There are weaknesses in such an estimate, when our knowledge of total attendance rests on such fragile evidence, and some speakers may be omitted in the records of debates. And a purely quantitative estimate cannot, of course, reflect the varying length and impact of addresses. But it is clear that Yearly Meeting decisions were guided by a small minority of those present.

This impression is strengthened by an analysis of the frequency with which the same individuals spoke. Seven spoke thirty times or more, over the seven-year period studied, fifteen spoke twenty times or more, and forty-eight spoke eight times or more. Josiah Forster, who 'perhaps exercised more influence in the Society than any other man',[2] is recorded as speaking 79 times. An otherwise laudatory memoir notes that 'sometimes his friends grew impatient at the frequency of his remarks.'[3]

Victorian Quakers seem, on the whole, to have accepted the fact that Yearly Meeting decisions were the work of a minority, whose power was symbolically indicated by the fact that they sat near the Clerk's table, the emblem of authority. In 1778, the Friends sitting near the Clerk had been described as 'The Lords Spiritual and Temporal'.[4] A Victorian Friend, looking at the Yearly Meetings of the mid-nineteenth century across the perspective of thirty years, wrote of 'the uprising of the Newer Element and the objections round the Table'.[5] Another referred to 'the principal Friends who take an active part',[6] seemingly unconscious of the contradiction between this state of affairs

---

[1] i.e. of 864, the average of attendance estimates, 1847–62. The speakers were those at Yearly Meeting, 1852–9, inclusive, excluding 1853 for which records are defective. These years were chosen partly because of the importance of the issues discussed, and partly because the records are unusually good—the printed accounts in Quaker periodicals can be supplemented by the detailed MS. accounts of Joseph, John S. and William Rowntree, and Samuel Alexander (in FHL).

[2] William Sturge, *Some Recollections*, p. 52; cf. the relevant stanza of *Quakerieties for 1838*.

[3] *Friends of a Half Century*, p. 117.

[4] James Jenkins, quoted in *London Yearly Meeting during 250 Years* (London, 1919), various contributors, p. 65.

[5] William Beck, MS. letter pasted in front of the bound volume of Samuel Alexander, *Account of 1847 and 1852 YMs* (MSS. in FHL).

[6] J. S. Rowntree, *Account of 1859 Yearly Meeting*, p. 20.

and the egalitarian ideals of Quaker democracy. When a Quaker did ask himself what proportion of those present played an active part, he reached conclusions strikingly similar to those in this study.[1]

It was often claimed that the elite who dominated Yearly Meeting discussions formed a gerontocracy, and that the young were discouraged from taking part.[2] Business, it was claimed, was discharged by 'solid and weighty Friends of some threescore years'.[3] In fact, the average age of speakers of ascertainable age was 55·5 in 1852, and 56·6 in 1859. The average age of the small group who spoke twenty times or more, in the period studied, was 60·7.

The evidence suggests that this domination of the middle aged had given way, to some extent, by the end of the century; that more of those present took part in debates; and that younger Friends felt free to participate. In 1901, Caleb Kemp reflected on this change. He had almost unparalleled opportunities for observation, for he had attended every Yearly Meeting since 1851, and had acted as Clerk for seven years. He stated: 'We had now the expression of the consensus of the Yearly Meeting drawn not merely from the Friends round the table, but from all over the Meeting.'[4]

One problem, which had always existed, was minimized when Quakers expected their discussions to be dominated by a minority—in an assembly of 700 or more, it was impossible for all to speak. When issues which aroused strong feeling were discussed, those who did not have the opportunity to speak, and could not give force to their views by voting, naturally resented their position.[5] The tensions of such a situation, when it occurred, often led to the advocacy of voting procedures.[6] Sometimes Friends tried to

---

[1] *The Friend* (1874), 78. Joseph Hopkins calculated that 70–80 speakers, out of an attendance of 700–800, took part in the 1873 conference on the state of Quakerism.

[2] William Tallack, *Howard Letters and Memories* (London, 1905), p. 214; cf. *The Manchester Friend* (1872), 186.

[3] *The British Friend* (1901), 126.

[4] ibid., 162; cf. p. 126.

[5] cf. *The Friend* (1853), 210–11; (1858), 100; *FQE* (1867), 308; *The British Friend* (1897), 207.

[6] J. Marshall Sturge, in *The British Friend* (1897), 207.

obtain an opportunity to speak by exercising pressure on the Clerk outside the meeting.[1]

Like any deliberative body, Yearly Meeting was at the mercy of irrelevant or eccentric speakers. The Clerk exercised a certain measure of control by his initial selection of speakers. In theory, he could ask a speaker to be silent, but the power was hardly ever exercised. Friends were trained from childhood to sit through protracted and often silent meetings impassively. Therefore, the normal ways in which audiences show their impatience with a tedious or irrelevant speaker were closed to them, and Yearly Meeting would listen with apparently equal attention to the stirring eloquence of a famous minister and the disquisitions of a well-known eccentric or bore. Nevertheless, the dissatisfaction that was felt with the practical workings of Quaker democracy was reflected in the correspondence columns of Quaker periodicals after many a Yearly Meeting.

The respect for minority opinion which made Friends avoid voting procedures meant that they tended to defer decisions on issues where feelings were strongly divided. Some questions were debated for years on end, greatly to the annoyance of the majority party, for fear of acting in defiance of the wishes of the minority. An alternative and increasingly popular way to avoid the burden of decision was to refer a question to a specially appointed autumn conference. Sometimes membership of these was confined to delegates, but usually they were open to all interested, and tended to reproduce the personnel of Yearly Meeting under another name. These conferences would produce recommendations, which Yearly Meeting could accept, reject, or modify. They were sometimes critized, however, for weakening the interest and importance of Yearly Meeting itself.

Friends were agreed that direct divine inspiration was needed to preach a sermon, or to pray. They were divided on whether the same kind of inspiration was necessary to speak at business meetings. In practice, most agreed with the robust common sense of John Bright: 'it cannot require anything in the shape of direct influence from God to decide whether the appointment of *Elder* should be for life, or for

---

[1] *Manchester Conference Proceedings*, p. 16.

a limited period, subject to revision.'[1] But sometimes, especially in the earlier part of the period, speakers in debates would claim to be immediately inspired by the Holy Spirit. 'A convinced Frd was very trying as he laid claim to little short of infallibility.'[2] The difficulty, as critics were not slow to point out,[3] was that the advocates of contending views could not simultaneously be divinely inspired. Friends were forced to decide issues by common-sense criteria, because it was impossible to know in an argument who was inspired. William Allen met with this criticism in an aristocratic home in Switzerland: '"Then", said the Duchess, "how are we to distinguish between the divine influence, and the working of our own imaginations?" I acknowledged that this was the point of difficulty.'[4]

MEETINGS OF MINISTERS AND ELDERS

Parallel to the pyramid of men's meetings, which transacted most of the real business of the Society, were two exactly similar systems: the women's meetings, which are discussed in a later section of this chapter, and the Select Meetings, or Meetings of Ministers and Elders. These were constructed on the same lines, with their Monthly, Quarterly and Yearly Meetings, but differed in their attendance and in the scope of their work from the men's meetings. Select Meetings were attended by both men and women, who held the office of minister or elder,[5] and who in addition, of course, attended the usual business meetings. The Select Meetings answered their own Queries, and were intended to strengthen the state of the ministry, by mutual advice and encouragement. The Yearly Meeting of Ministers and Elders had the important duty of deciding whether to allow ministers who wished to do so to travel abroad in an official capacity. It met

---

[1] John Bright to John Pease, 26 Dec. 1851 (MS. in FHL, Temp. MSS Box 24).

[2] J. S. Rowntree, *Account of 1959 Yearly Meeting*, p. 79.

[3] Robert MacNair, *The Decline of Quakerism: An Enquiry into the Causes which have led to the Present Moral and Numerical Weakness of the Society of Friends* (London, 1860), p. 43.

[4] *Life of William Allen*, vol. ii, p. 302.

[5] The offices of minister, elder and overseer are discussed on pp. 94ff. and 101ff. below.

just before Yearly Meeting—'an assembly of aged and grave persons' with an attendance of perhaps 200–250.[1]

Victorian Quakers always tended to be suspicious of meetings which the rank and file membership could not attend, and many viewed the Select Meetings with 'considerable mistrust and dissatisfaction'.[2] To those not entitled to attend them, the Select Meetings appeared "an assembly isolated in our midst" with the appearance of hierarchical tendency.'[3] The Select Meetings were attended by precisely those 'weighty' Friends who tended to dominate business meetings, and it was an easy step from the recognition of this fact to the claim that they spent their time pre-arranging the decisions of business meetings. Charles Thompson stated in 1871 that 'He was ready to think they were often engaged even in their Meetings in arranging how things could be managed to over-rule the judgment of the body.'[4] Suspicions of this kind led to a proposal, in 1867, to admit overseers to Select Meetings, and revise the lists of ministers and elders from time to time.[5] It was unsuccessful, but dissatisfaction continued, and in 1876 the Select Meetings were reorganized. They were rechristened Meetings on Ministry and Oversight ('M. and O.'), and their membership was expanded to include Overseers and other 'suitable Friends'.[6] Many Friends were disappointed with these changes, as insufficiently radical[7]—they had hoped for the abolition of the eldership altogether—but the system introduced in 1876 was to last, unchanged, for another thirty years. Its subsequent modifications lie beyond the scope of this study.

As their new name suggested, these meetings were intended to fill wide pastoral functions, but it is doubtful whether these were effectively exercised. The right to co-opt 'suitable Friends' was often neglected, and the image which the

---

[1] John S. Rowntree, *A Family Memoir of Joseph Rowntree* (privately printed, 1868), p. 511 (quoting a letter from Joseph Rowntree, dated May 1847).

[2] *The Friend* (1867), 82.

[3] ibid.

[4] Account of an interview with Charles Thompson at Manchester in 1870 (MS. in FHL, Box. 9.6 (3), f.1).

[5] The debate is reported in *The Friend* (1867), 133ff.

[6] ibid. (1876), 144–7. The 'suitable Friends' were to be co-opted by the Meeting—which was still not open to all who wished to attend.

[7] ibid.

Meetings on M. and O. presented to many Quakers is crystallized in a perhaps apocryphal anecdote told by John Wilhelm Rowntree. When a Friend told another that he was not a member of a Meeting on Ministry and Oversight, he is said to have received the reply: 'I should have thought thou was old enough, and rich enough, and dry enough, to be a member of that Meeting!'[1]

STANDING AND AD HOC COMMITTEES

Since Yearly Meeting met only once a year, there was an obvious need for a standing committee to deal with current matters as they arose. This function was filled by the Meeting for Sufferings—its curious title was a relic from the period of Quaker persecution. We know fairly little about the workings of this body and its numerous subcommittees— its beautifully written minute books are a bare record of decisions made and committees appointed, and the reports of its proceedings which began to appear in Quaker periodicals towards the end of the century were almost as brief. It was not an open meeting,—it consisted of ministers and elders, who could attend by virtue of their office, and 'correspondents', who represented the various Quarterly Meetings but did not have to live in them. Until 1857, correspondents were chosen by the elders and overseers of London and Middlesex. This concentration of power, into both a geographic area and a caste of office holders, was resented, and in 1857 the system was changed.[2] But a meeting held in London was inevitably dominated by London Friends. The improvement of communications was to do more to widen the base of its membership than any organizational change, and in the later years of the nineteenth century some wealthy and leisured Friends would travel every month from the provinces to attend its meetings.[3]

For much of the nineteenth century, however, 'country

---

[1] *John Wilhelm Rowntree Essays and Addresses*, p. 168.

[2] According to the new system, elders and ministers could attend as before, and correspondents were selected by the Quarterly Meetings, from a list of names prepared by the MMs of London and Middlesex. (*Yearly Meeting Proceedings*, 1857, p. 28).

[3] *The Friend* (1898), 621. Several well endowed QMs paid their members expenses.

Friends' viewed Meeting for Sufferings with precisely that suspicion with which Select Meetings were regarded by those not entitled to attend them. From their complaints, it appears that they knew even less about the workings of the body than the later historian.[1] In 1855, John Bright made a typical statement of their grievances:

he himself had a great objection to so much power centralising in the body of friends in London. He held all the members of the meeting for sufferings in high respect & would not hear a single thing said against them without endeavouring to answer it but he thought it had a crippling effect upon the country meetings to have all the work done for them.[2]

Various suggestions were made from time to time—that the names of the members of Meeting for Sufferings should be printed,[3] or that it should present more detailed reports to Yearly Meeting on its activities [4]—and a conference on the subject was held, at which London Friends apparently found themselves in collision with country members, desiring change.[5] But geography proved a stronger force than any recommendations. Another kind of inequality was removed in 1897, however, when the first women were admitted to Meeting for Sufferings.[6]

Attendances at Meeting for Sufferings were apparently large, though it is not easy to estimate them exactly. Fifty-one members of Meeting for Sufferings signed the petition against the Militia Bill in 1852, and 131 were present at the first session which included women. The latter was probably an unusually high attendance for a special occasion, but it seems clear that the body was too large for an effective executive committee, and that most of its work was delegated to subcommittees.

Meeting for Sufferings was subordinate to Yearly Meeting; its main actions needed Yearly Meeting's sanction, and

---

[1] *The Friend* (1870), p. 106.
[2] Joseph Rowntree, *Account of 1855 Yearly Meeting*, p. 62.
[3] *The Friend* (1854), 89.
[4] ibid. (1856), 176–8.
[5] *Diary of William Lucas*, II, 500. The demand for change was led by a Quaker from Liskeard, John Allen.
[6] *The Friend* (1898), 366. Slightly over a quarter of those present at the first mixed session were women.

it executed Yearly Meeting's instructions. Inevitably, however, a body meeting at monthly intervals, confronted with a
multiplicity of issues requiring immediate action, acted with
much independence. And since the members of Meeting for
Sufferings were precisely those 'weighty' and knowledge-
able Friends who dominated Yearly Meeting, the chances of
conflict were more apparent than real.

Meeting for Sufferings was of the greatest importance
throughout the nineteenth century. It raised and administered special funds, when directed to do so by Yearly Meeting. It kept an eagle eye on parliamentary proceedings, and
intervened instantly when an issue came up which bore on
Quaker interests. It watched over American ministers in
England, and English ministers abroad. However unrepre-
sentative its constitution, on a multitude of occasions it spoke
and acted for Quakerism, as no other body could.

The exact parallel between the Meetings of Ministers
and Elders and the ordinary business meetings extended to
this body also. The Morning Meeting was the permanent
executive committee of the Yearly Meeting of Ministers and
Elders. When this was not in session, it decided whether to
endorse the proposed journeys of English ministers, who
wished to travel in an official capacity. Until 1861, its duties
included the censorship of books by Friends on Quaker
principles.[1] In 1901, the meeting was given up, and its
work transferred to the Meeting for Sufferings.

Although, from 1833, Meeting for Sufferings was formally recognized as the executive committee of Yearly Meeting, occasionally the latter body appointed an *ad hoc*
committee to undertake a special task. Both the Beaconite
crisis and the Manchester unitarian schism were dealt with
in this way, and occasionally a committee was appointed to
pay a 'pastoral visit in love' to all subordinate meetings.
Considering the importance of their work, their method of
selection was amazingly haphazard. Any individual present
at Yearly Meeting could nominate a member, and nomina-
tions were conventionally never opposed.[2] Thus selection

---

[1] *The Friend* (1861), 144.
[2] cf. *The British Friend* (1893), 223-6, for a quite exceptional case of such
opposition.

for such a committee 'represented the view of *one*, perhaps too partial Friend'.[1] Edward Ash relates how as a young man he became a member of what was to prove perhaps the most significant committee in the history of Victorian Quakerism, through nomination by 'a personal friend of no particular standing in the Society'.[2]

Because of the defects of this system of nomination, a kind of *nolo episcopari* became conventional. Each nominee would object to his appointment, to test the feeling of the meeting as a whole.[3] Like the Select Meetings, and the Meeting for Sufferings, these committees often aroused resentment. The Manchester dissidents called the committee which investigated their case 'a body of men of a highly hierarchical tendency, acting in a judicial character, and so destroying the representative character of our Meetings'.[4] They had, of course, an axe to grind, but such complaints recur in Quaker records.[5]

Standing committees, such as the Home Service Committee or the Friends Service Council have wielded great power in twentieth-century Quakerism, though they have not been without their critics.[6] Two important committees —dealing with home and foreign missions respectively— had nineteenth-century roots.[7] They were technically subordinate to Yearly Meeting, but in fact exercised great independent power, handling incomes measured in thousands of pounds, and controlling scores of full-time workers. Since their work was on lines of which many Friends disapproved, each incurred, inevitably, much criticism as an *imperium in imperio*.[8]

---

[1] *The Friend* (1873), 176–7.

[2] ibid. (1870), 207.

[3] ibid. (1873), 176–7.

[4] *The Manchester Friend* (1872), 112.

[5] e.g. Stephen Perry to Hannah Poulter, 8 Aug. 1867 (MS. in FHL, Portfolio B.27).

[6] Horace Fleming, *The Lighted Mind: The Challenge of Adult Education to Quakerism* (London, 1929), pp. 6–7.

[7] The Home Mission Committee, established in 1882, and the Committee of the Friends Foreign Mission Association, established in 1868. The former was a committee of Yearly Meeting, terminable by it; the latter was in theory an independent organization.

[8] Josiah Forster on the F.F.M.A. (*The Friend* (1869), 129). Exactly the same phrase was to be used of the Home Mission Committee.

THE CLERK

At all these various meetings, the Clerk played a crucial role. He was appointed annually, chosen for his discretion, ability, and general standing. He ran the meeting, decided who should speak to an issue, and crystallized the 'sense of the meeting' in a written minute. He also acted as a secretary, writing up the minutes of each meeting. Although—or perhaps because—the Yearly Meeting Clerks performed their duties under eagle-eyed surveillance, their handling of meetings and the minutes they issued were scarcely ever challenged. The office was not immune from the Quaker habit of self-criticism:

While generally the office has achieved striking success, we dare not say, though we wish we could, that our plan of deciding by a Clerk has never failed, either in recent times or in the past. We have been led to doubt in consequence whether our cherished plan is calculated to stand the strain when a clearly-marked 'Yes' or 'No' issue, which cannot be compromised or delayed, is before a large meeting which is swayed by strong feeling.[1]

Occasionally, a contretemps occurred. At Yearly Meeting, in 1901, the Clerk brought a storm of outraged liberal sentiment on his head when he removed a reference to the Fatherhood of God and the brotherhood of man from a document on peace. But on the whole, the minutes drafted by Yearly Meeting Clerks were seldom questioned—a tribute to the success with which they filled their delicate and demanding office.

In smaller local meetings, where the same Clerk often held office for many years, he was liable to gravitate insensibly from being the servant of the meeting into its director. Some Clerks came to meetings with their minutes already drafted, and responded to fresh suggestions with 'a little deskal irritation'.[2] Where others attended irregularly, the Clerk, with his minute knowledge of the meeting's affairs, naturally came to have a power which was never intended. But in general, the impression one gets of the typical Victorian Clerk is of unwearying diligence, and self-effacing devotion.

[1] *The British Friend* (1895), 101.   [2] ibid. (1894), 222.

MEETINGS FOR WORSHIP AND THE MINISTRY

The typical Victorian meeting-house was 'a square, prim dingy, brick building, belonging to no order of architecture, surrounded generally by a high blind wall.'[1] The room in which meetings for worship were held was completely plain. Ministers and elders sat on a raised platform, facing the rest of the congregation. Anyone, whether a minister or not, was free to preach or pray, but was only expected to do so if he felt a supernatural inspiration. Many meetings were held completely in silence for years on end, and even in meetings well endowed with ministry, the two-hour meeting was always partially spent in silence. The devout Friend was expected to attend three such meetings a week, two on Sunday and one on Wednesday.

The self discipline needed to sit immobile through these meetings can be readily imagined. They fostered the spirit of calm and self-control which was often noted as a Quaker characteristic. Mary Howitt compared women Quakers in meeting with 'images in marble'.[2] The silence of a Quaker meeting often made a profound impression on outsiders, but it was clearly suitable only for an élite. Almost all recollections of a Victorian Quaker childhood mirror the boredom and strain it meant for the young. A youthful member of Goat Lane meeting, Norwich, confided to her diary: 'I have had a bad day. To be sure it is difficult to withstand Earlham Sundays, they are so truly disagreeable. Sometimes I think I will make better use of my time at Goat's, but when I get there, I seldom think of anything else but when it will be over.'[3] Adults sometimes felt the same [4]—for generation after generation, congregations would confess, in response to the relevant Query, 'a little exception in regard to drowzi-ness'.[5]

Converts to Quakerism tended to find the same sort of difficulty as did children. They first presented an acute

[1] *The Spectator*, 25 Aug. 1877, reprinted in *The Monthly Record* (1877), 134–5.

[1] Howitt, *An Autobiography*, vol. i, p. 263.

[2] Louisa Gurney's *Journal*, 1797, quoted in Hare, *The Gurneys of Earlham*, vol. i, p. 68.

[4] *The Spectator*, 25 Aug. 1877, reprinted in *The Monthly Record* (1877), 134.

[5] *Norwich MM Minutes, 1853*, p. 254 (MSS. in Norwich and Norfolk County Record Office).

problem from the 1870s on, when many who attended Quaker Adult Schools were naturally drawn to the religion of their teachers, but could not adjust to the silence or haphazard ministry of Quaker meetings. To meet their needs, services misnamed Mission Meetings were established on the lines of the usual nonconformist service, with prepared addresses, hymn singing and so on. These were held in the evening, and in some areas they came to replace the evening Meeting for Worship altogether. Attendance at these meetings alone did not qualify one for Quaker membership, but many scholars made them their permanent place of worship, and many Quakers, attending them for the scholars' sakes, found that their own ideas about the nature of worship were profoundly modified. Another practice, which was frowned upon, but common, was to attend a Quaker meeting in the morning and another church in the evening, in search of a learned and well-prepared sermon, and the satisfactions of hymn singing and congregational prayer.[1]

By the late nineteenth century, attendance at three meetings a week had become uncommon. Like other denominations, the Quakers found that as transport improved and recreational facilities expanded, church attendances fell; it would be possible to write the history of the decline of sabbatarianism in terms of the invention of the bicycle. Attendance at the Sunday morning meeting throughout Yorkshire was 20 per cent lower in 1904 than on Census Sunday, 1851.[2]

Since all who felt called to do so could speak, and the Spirit notoriously bloweth where it listeth, the Quaker meeting was rich in possibilities of disorder. Eccentric or incongruous ministry was always a problem. All the sermons preached at a Quaker wedding in 1863 dealt either with the Deluge or with 'the opressed [sic] African Race'.[3] The state of the ministry at Bull Street Meeting, Birmingham, was so unsatisfactory in 1867 that outside intervention was needed —'sometimes in some instances what was uttered was not

---

[1] *Hardshaw East MM Minutes, 1891*, p. 334 (MSS. in possession of the Monthly Meeting).

[2] *Yearly Meeting Proceedings, 1905*, p. 142.

[3] [George Price], *Journal*, 7 Feb. 1863 (anonymous MS. Journal in Birmingham University Library).

sence [*sic*]'.[1] Some twenty years later, the same problems recurred in the meeting—'They could not prevail on some Friends there whose utterances were not acceptable to hold their peace'.[2]

On the whole, disturbances were exceptional, and Friends were prepared to accept them as the price they paid for their spontaneous ministry. There were, however, a number of safeguards against abuses, the most effective of which, in the early Victorian period, lay in an extremely exalted view of inspiration. To speak without inspiration, or to be silent when 'a message was given' was regarded as a dreadful trespass—the case of Uzzah, who died for touching the Ark, was often cited as a precedent. But by the later nineteenth century, the high theory of inspiration had declined, and anxiety about totally silent meetings gave way to anxiety about the lack of silence in meetings. There were several causes for this—it was an easy step from Sunday School teaching, or from addressing a Mission Meeting, to preaching at a Meeting for Worship. Many Quakers deplored the change, but were still more alarmed by the readiness of converts drawn from a background of Sunday School teaching and lay preaching to speak at Meetings, in a tenor very different from that of the traditional Quaker sermon. At the opposite pole, men such as John Wilhelm Rowntree weakened the theory of inspiration by insisting on the need for a thorough intellectual training for the ministry, and deploring the poverty of thought which characterized unprepared addresses. As an outsider pointed out, 'unless one is naturally a good extempore speaker, leaning on the Spirit is apt to result in dreary commonplace.'[3] Gradually, the whole character of meetings for worship changed. The protracted silences, broken by highly stylized sermons, professedly under direct inspiration from heaven, were replaced by meetings where many of those present took part, at least occasionally, and a more conversational tone was the norm.

[1] J. B. Braithwaite to Josiah Forster, letter inserted in J. B. Braithwaite, *Journal*, 1865–76 vol., following p. 65.

[2] *The Friend* (1888), 150. For similar troubles in other centres, cf. ibid. (1897), 529; J. B. Braithwaite, *Journal*, 17 Oct. 1869; *Manchester Conference Proceedings*, p. 90.

[3] *The Daily Graphic*, 28 Mar. 1892 (FHL Press Cuttings, BB111).

A special abbreviation was invented to refer to the over-frequent speaker—the P.P.U.—Perpetual Popper Up.[1]

As well as conventional Meetings for Worship, and the so-called Mission Meetings, there was a third genre of Quaker meetings, for which the designation 'mission meeting' would be more appropriate—that is, gatherings for non-Quakers, designed to convert them to Quakerism, or at least to Christianity. Such meetings, called Public Meetings, were traditional in Quakerism. Travelling ministers, in particular, often held them, and the degree of prearrangement necessary was never held to infringe the doctrine of inspiration. Quaker ministry was, however, so stylized, so full of traditional phraseology, that audiences probably had difficulty in understanding it. A critical observer described a meeting held by Elizabeth Fry and J. J. Gurney, two of the most famous Quaker ministers of their time, in 1827: 'Excellent good advice they gave; but the multitude of words employed were only suited to those who are initiated into the manner of Quakerism. To the assembled auditory there, they might as well have spoken Greek.'[2]

In the last quarter of the nineteenth century, a completely different kind of public meeting, on revivalist lines, developed among evangelical Quakers. In 1873, Moody and Sankey paid their first visit to England. Two years later, with uncharacteristic precipitancy,[3] Yearly Meeting gave its approval to what were called General Meetings. At these, a number of evangelicals would gather in a particular area, usually a rural one, for a week of what were in effect revivalist meetings. General Meetings were held only occasionally, but evangelicals such as Jonathan Grubb privately conducted a good deal of work on similar lines. A highly coloured account of one such meeting states: 'One "Mission" in particular, held by a prominent member of the Society of Friends, he well remembers. They were hypnotising the people, singing "Sinner, come home", in a low syren voice, telling the "saved" to bow their heads in

---

[1] Mary Lucy Whiting, *Types of Sunday Evening Meetings and their Respective Values* (Friends Home Mission and Extension Committee Pamphlet, 1908), p. 16.
[2] *Quakerism: or the Story of my Life*, p. 164.
[3] cf. William Pollard in *FQE* (1875), 317.

prayer, and those who wanted to give up their hearts to Christ, to hold up their hands.'[1] This kind of revivalism gradually became discredited in Quaker circles.

Friends had two formal safeguards against disorder and unsuitable ministry in their meetings for worship—the office of Elder, and the practice of officially recognizing or 'recording' ministers. The Elder was an official whose only duty was to encourage promising speakers, and discourage those who were not 'savoury' and 'in the life'; both functions were energetically exercised. The other safeguard lay in elevating speakers of whom the congregation approved into what was, in effect, a caste apart.

The Quaker minister differed from other Quaker officials, such as the Elder, because his appointment implied, not an obligation to perform duties, but the formal recognition of a divinely given power. The ministry among Friends differed from that in other churches in at least four major ways: it was non-professional, it was open to women as well as men, it was held to depend entirely on direct inspiration from heaven, and it implied a right—not always exercised— to travel as an itinerant preacher, with the financial backing of the Society.

The ministry was non-professional in its absence both of training and of remuneration. Any adult was free to preach or pray in meetings for worship. When someone did so frequently, and acceptably, his Monthly Meeting gave him the official status of minister. Once given, it could not be revoked, except in cases of grave delinquency. It not infrequently happened that a Quaker spoke for years as a minister, but because of personal antagonisms in the meeting, or other reasons, was not given the coveted recognition. Inevitably, such a man suffered bitterly under a sense of rejection.

Quaker ministers were never paid for their services—they continued with their ordinary avocations, as bankers, shopkeepers, and so on.

The ministry was open to women, and in the early Victorian period, woman ministers greatly outnumbered men. Men's Yearly Meeting often reflected uneasily on this situation, but for Victorian Quaker women the ministry

---

[1] Fox and Pickard, *The Hat Crusade*, vol. ii, p. 119.

filled an obvious latent function. Like all their middle-class contemporaries, they were 'shut out by the social disabilities of women from any adequate exercise of [their] highest faculties in action on the world without'.[1] The ministry offered a magical escape, for an able woman, from the narrow confines of domesticity. It enabled her to speak in public, and travel abroad, with the approval, indeed the deference, of her co-religionists. Their families often suffered in consequence—it is probably no coincidence that most of the children of famous ministers, such as Anna Braithwaite and Elizabeth Fry, grew up permanently estranged from Quakerism.[2] The business meetings of women were almost powerless, but some women ministers, notably Sarah Lynes Grubb, used their positions in an attempt to sway the real centres of power. A woman minister 'under concern' was free to speak even to Men's Yearly Meeting. Sarah Grubb, and others, made full use of the opportunity.

The theory of direct inspiration had many practical consequences for the Quaker minister. It meant that anyone speaking for the first time in meeting had to grapple with painful doubts and fears, unable to be certain of the reality of his 'call'.[3] Knowing the genuineness of inspiration was always a problem, both for speaker and audience. In the early Victorian period, the problem was partly solved by adopting a highly stereotyped mode of delivery, which was conventionally equated with inspiration. It was characterized by a sing-song intonation, and the use of traditional phrases, usually biblical in origin, such as 'trying the fleece in the wet and the dry'. Some ministers, especially in the early stages of their careers, confined themselves almost entirely to strings of memorized texts.

It is a proof of the sincerity with which the doctrine of inspiration was held, that many ministers ventured into the

[1] John Stuart Mill, *Autobiography*, ed. Harold J. Laski (London, 1924), p. 157.

[2] For Anna Braithwaite's children, cf. *JFHS* (1926), 99. For Elizabeth Fry's children's comment, see [Katherine Fry and Rachel Elizabeth Cresswell], *Memoir of the Life of Elizabeth Fry . . . edited by Two of her Daughters* (2nd ed., London, 1848), vol. i, pp. 499–500; cf. also *Quakerism; or the Story of my Life*, pp. 86–7, and *Journal of Thomas Shillitoe*, vol. i, p. 139.

[3] Grover Kemp, *Journal*, 1823–9 (MSS. in FHL), gives a vivid picture of the doubts and fears of a young minister.

perilous field of mind reading, or 'speaking to states', as it was called. Many claimed to be able to discern the spiritual state of congregations, or of individuals in it. It was particularly common to do so during family visits—an institution which became rarer as the century progressed. A minister who was travelling in an official capacity would often visit individual families, holding a miniature Meeting for Worship with each. J. J. Gurney, recording that he made seventy such visits in a week, stated: 'I find myself almost constantly led on these occasions, (as well as more en masse in the meetings) to speak to particular states—to enter into feeling for almost every individual individually.'[1] It is scarcely surprising that he notes during similar visits, eight years later, 'In an instance or two I was apparently permitted to miss the mark, to my own great humiliation.'[2]

Not all recorded ministers travelled in an official capacity, but all could apply for permission to do so, which was seldom if ever refused. Such journeys ranged in scope from a visit to a few neighbouring villages to a four-year sojourn in America. For local journeys, the approval of the Monthly Meeting was required; journeys abroad needed the sanction of the Yearly Meeting of Ministers and Elders. The cost of the journey outward was defrayed by the Monthly Meeting (or by the Yearly Meeting in the case of journeys abroad), and the minister's maintenance was provided by the meeting visited, though London Yearly Meeting often paid the whole cost of visits to America. Wealthy Friends sometimes defrayed their own expenses, but whether they did so or not, such travels were in practice confined to the unmarried or the prosperous, who could support their families in their absence. These journeys had their obvious attractions, but they were often made at the cost of much discomfort, and personal and financial sacrifice. J. J. Gurney gave up a third of his business profits when he was in America.[3]

As the century progressed, the practice of travelling in the ministry became less common. But the 1890s saw one of the most spectacular cases of itinerant ministry in Quaker

[1] J. J. Gurney, *Journal*, 9 Sept. 1824.
[2] ibid., 9 June 1832.
[3] ibid., 10 Apr. 1837.

history, when Isaac Sharp, born in 1806, embarked on a
series of world wide journeys, to various parts of Europe,
America, the Far East and Australasia: 'The large expenses
of these journeys were borne cheerfully by Friends in England, whose doubts, if they had any, about the wisdom of
such sporadic and discontinuous effort made at such great
cost, were always removed by the conviction of the rightness
of the concerns which from time to time Isaac Sharp brought
before them.'[1] There were occasional complaints at the
expenses of travelling ministers, when they were thought to
be excessive,[2] but on the whole Friends paid substantial
amounts in this way willingly.

Because ministers were in the last analysis self-selected,
and lived wherever inclination or business interests drew
them, they were very unequally distributed among congregations. Some congregations always met in silence, while
others had perhaps half a dozen ministers. In 1868 there
were a hundred meetings without ministry of any kind,
though there was a total of 265 recorded and 400 unrecorded ministers[3] that is, one minister to every twenty
church members (or one recorded minister to every fifty-two
church members)—a far higher proportion than in other
denominations.[4] But the Quaker ministry was so different
from that of other churches that numerical comparisons have
little value; the Quaker minister was essentially a preacher,
not the pastor, counsellor and leader of a congregation.
Pastoral duties were informally shared by the senior and
more devoted members of the meeting, whether they were
ministers or not.

There were difficulties and drawbacks in the recording of
ministers, which led many Quakers to criticize the practice,
from the 1860s on.[5] The essential problem was that there
were no objective criteria for determining the validity of a
speaker's inspiration. Where only one or two Friends spoke

---

[1] *The Christian World*, 25 Mar. 1897.
[2] *The Friend* (1879), 166.   [3] ibid. (1868), 155.
[4] In the same year, the Wesleyans had one minister to every 300 members; in
1870, the Baptists had one minister to every 111·9 members—but these figures do
not include local preachers, probationer ministers and evangelists.
[5] For a summary of the criticisms made, see the report of a Yorkshire Quarterly
Meeting committee on the subject, in *The Friend* (1892), 639.

in meeting, they were recorded without difficulty, if their lives were respectable and their preaching generally acceptable. But when it became customary for many to speak occasionally in meeting, the line of demarcation became difficult to draw. The readiness with which this recognition was accorded differed from Monthly Meeting to Monthly Meeting, and the recognition of one speaker and the overlooking of another inevitably caused resentment. Moreover, once a minister was acknowledged, he tended to feel he had a responsibility to speak, and drift into the practice of preaching habitually in meetings, thus abandoning, unconsciously, the whole theory of immediate inspiration. Once recorded, a minister held his position for life, unless guilty of a grave moral lapse. If his preaching or conduct became unacceptable, the congregation could do little or nothing to remedy the situation. And once they had recognized his inspiration, it was difficult to oppose the specific impulses of that inspiration—to undertake, for instance, extensive journeys.[1]

But the essence of the charge against the practice of recording ministers was its 'incipient clericalism'.[2] It embodied one of the principles of a professional ministry—permanent differential status—and weakened the equality of all members by creating an élite to whom 'deference if not homage' was due. The inequality was heightened by the practice of issuing official 'testimonies'. These were eulogies on the lives and virtues of deceased ministers, read at Yearly Meeting, and subsequently printed. Exemplary and devoted Friends, such as Joseph Sturge, who did not speak in meetings, did not receive this posthumous honour.

Despite the prevalence of discontent, the practice of recording survived well into the twentieth century. It was discussed at Yearly Meeting in 1898 and at a special conference in 1903, but without result. Those who supported recording were often ministers, who valued their own status, and remembered the encouragement they had gained from their acknowledgement. Some feared that if the practice was abandoned, Friends would lose their control

---

[1] *The Friend* (1862), 71–2 and (1897), 140.
[2] Supplement to *The Christian World*, 19 May 1904.

over speakers at meetings. It appears that opposition to recording was strongly localized in a few centres, Reading, Croydon, and Manchester among them.[1] Yet it was sufficiently widespread for the practice to die out gradually. Some Monthly Meetings gave up recording ministers altogether, and some speakers refused the honour when it was proferred. The number of recorded ministers shrank, and the practice was finally abandoned in 1924.

The ideal of the Quaker ministry was always that it should be unpaid and inspirational. In the 1880s, however, a new development took place which was held by many to be a form of the pastoral system. It has been noted that the distribution of ministers among congregations was haphazard. The practice of travelling in the ministry counterbalanced this to some extent, but visits from itinerant ministers were necessarily rare, and there were many areas where meetings were usually silent. In the 1870s, influenced by Moody and Sankey, evangelical Quakers became attracted to revivalism, but many meetings lacked a suitable evangelical Quaker, and work conducted by visitors from outside could only be sporadic. To meet this situation, many evangelicals decided that it was desirable to introduce Home Missioners working on much the same lines as missionaries abroad, with regular financial support, concentrating on full-time religious work.

There was no shortage of youthful volunteers for the work, or of wealthy evangelical businessmen prepared to finance them. The typical Home Missioner settled in a country district, where there was a small Quaker meeting. He devoted all his energies to building up the meeting, winning converts, starting Sunday Schools and Bands of Hope, distributing Bibles and tracts, and so on.[2] He was invariably a strong evangelical, and he fell easily and naturally into the role of a nonconformist minister, preaching regular sermons and exercising pastoral care over the meeting. The first Missioners were financed by private sympathizers, but

---

[1] Supplement to *The Christian World*, 19 May 1904.

[2] One Missioner, Norman Penney, has left very detailed descriptions of his Mission work, at Hawes, 1883–8, and Melksham, 1892–6 (MSS. in FHL). He was in some respects an untypical Missioner, but the record is of great value.

in 1881 a conference was held by those who supported the movement, in an attempt to put it on an official and permanent basis. The Home Mission Committee was established, and succeeded in gaining the grudging approval of Yearly Meeting. The Committee went from strength to strength; by 1893, it controlled forty-three Missioners, and an annual income of £4,537.[1]

No issue in late Victorian Quakerism divided Friends more profoundly than the work of the Home Missioners. The divisions at Yearly Meeting were reflected in the fact that the first Home Mission Committee was appointed only for a year. Thereafter, for over a decade, it was reappointed annually,[2] and on each occasion there was bitter dispute over the reappointment. Many Friends opposed it, on theological and on personal grounds. At the theological level, it was seen as a first step in the direction of a professional ministry. At the personal level, the situation was exacerbated by the character of the Missioners themselves. All were young, many were converts to Quakerism, all were extreme evangelicals. They tended to be of working-class origin—if they had been of independent means, the vexed question of financial support would never have arisen. They were often anathema to long established communities of well-to-do, conservative, birthright Friends. As J. S. Rowntree told Yearly Meeting frankly: 'there were not many of them engaged in this work who were blessed with much wealth or learning. . . . He believed that a good deal of the criticism which had been passed upon some of the things that had been done by the workers was due to their having offended the tastes of some in the Society.[3]

To the evangelicals who supported the work, all objections were frivolous compared with the pressing and paramount duty of saving souls. They thought that it was monstrous that a man could only undertake full time evangelical work if he was wealthy, or became a foreign missionary. They resented their critics bitterly, and pointed to the

---

[1] *The Friend* (1893), 366.
[2] In 1889 it was appointed for three years, and in 1892, for one year. In 1893, it was reconstituted on a representative basis.
[3] *The British Friend* (1893), 176.

Missioners' 'Hundreds of conversions',[1] their palpable and incontestable zeal and good will.

The era of the Home Missioner was brief; it lasted perhaps thirty years. It came to an end, not through a sudden conflict or reversal of policy, but through an imperceptible change of attitude, the decline of evangelicalism, and the revival of interest in early Quakerism. It happened gradually; fewer and fewer new Missionaries were appointed, and existing ones drifted into other activities. The decline of the movement lies beyond the time span of this book, but one can discern a symptom of change in 1906, when the Committee's name was changed to the Home Mission and Extension Committee,[2] and Missioners were encouraged to become the organizers of religious activities over a large geographic area, rather than the pastors of a single congregation.

ELDERS AND OVERSEERS

As well as the ministry, there was one other kind of permanent personal status in Quakerism, the office of Elder, which was open to both men and women. The formal duty of the Elder was to supervise the ministry, proferring advice, encouragement, and discouragement, as seemed appropriate. The Eldership was an honourable diginity, given, for life, to those senior and respected Friends who could not become ministers, as they did not speak in Meetings for Worship: 'The Eldership used to be looked on as a " status " to be acquired by Friends not " ministers ", who through social position and a comfortable income had " weight " in the Society—in fact, as a kind of spiritual Peerage.'[3] The Eldership did not escape the perennial Victorian Quaker tendency to fear the formation of an élite. Many advocated re-appointing Elders periodically,[4] or, more radically, abolishing the office altogether, but like the recording of ministers, the institution proved stronger than its critics.

[1] *The Friend* (1892), 310.
[2] ibid., (1906), 360–1.
[3] Edward Grubb, *Eldership a Definite Service* (printed for Yearly Meeting of Elders, 1934, no place of publication given), p. 2.
[4] This was the subject of QM propositions from Lancashire (1850) and Suffolk (1868).

Overseers were re-appointed periodically. Like the ministry and the Eldership, the office was open to men and women equally, but its duties were less agreeable and it was less honorific. Each Monthly Meeting had a number of Overseers—one Quaker in twenty was an overseer in 1871 —who were essentially disciplinarians and detectives. They investigated infringements of Quaker rules, or cases of moral delinquency, reproving the culprit, or, if the case was sufficiently serious, reporting it to the Monthly Meeting. Frequently the Visitors appointed by the Monthly Meeting to report on delinquents were also the Overseers who investigated the case in the first place.[1] Offenders often complained bitterly that a handful of Friends combined the functions of accuser, jury, and judge.[2] As the disciplinary functions of Quaker meetings declined and Quaker regulations became less stringent, the importance of the work of the Overseers shrank accordingly.

FINANCE AND SALARIED STAFF

The central fund of the Society of Friends, the National Stock, was collected once a year in the Preparative Meetings, which passed the totals on, via the intermediate levels, to Yearly Meeting. In theory, Yearly Meeting directed how much should be raised, but this was little more than a pious aspiration. The money was collected from individuals— Quakers usually avoided weekly collections at Meeting for Worship, in case outsiders, attending casually, got the impression that ministers were paid for their services. The Collection Books for the component meetings of Bristol Monthly Meeting have been preserved[3]—they show that in 1863, for instance, 91 out of a total of 380 members (including many children) contributed to the National

[1] For the role of Visitors, and a fuller discussion of the treatment of delinquents, see pp. 118ff. below.

[2] William Rathbone, *A Memoir of the Proceedings of the Society called Quakers, belonging to the Monthly Meeting of Hardshaw, in Lancashire, in the case of the Author of a Publication entitled A Narrative of Events etc* (Liverpool, 1805), p. 29; *Quakerism; or the Story of my Life*, pp. 396–7.

[3] MSS. in Bristol Archives Office. The total number of members in the MM at that time is to be found on the flyleaf of another MS. deposited in the Bristol Archives Office, 'A List of the Members of Bristol Monthly Meeting'.

Stock. Contributions, which were carefully recorded, ranged from £20 to 5s., but were usually under a pound.

The disadvantage of this system—which also applied to the printed subscription lists which were standard practice in Victorian charities—was that it exposed the largesse of the rich and the humble contribution of the poor to the public eye. Sometimes, to save trouble, rich Friends raised the whole amount among themselves, and did not ask poorer members to contribute at all.[1] The objectionable discrimination which this implied led George Cadbury to introduce weekly collections in the meeting at Bournville—and to make his own contribution in small coins.[2]

There is evidence that there was some difficulty in raising subscriptions for the National Stock. Country members tended to be vague about the uses to which it was put. One told Yearly Meeting, 'Many would, he felt sure, be very glad of subscribing if they were told more distinctly what the term really meant.'[3] It had less appeal than charities, or foreign missions,[4] and some Quakers objected to a general purposes fund on principle, either sincerely, or as 'a cloak for covetousness'.[5] The amount raised varied from district to district—in 1898 one Friend pointed out, with some acerbity, that Devon and Cornwall gave 3s. 1d. per head, while Lancashire and Cheshire produced only 1s. 2d. per head![6]

Until the very end of the nineteenth century, the National Stock always showed a comfortable surplus, an unusual situation for religious and charitable organizations.[7] This was essentially because the outlay was so small, for there were no ministerial salaries to be paid, and practically no paid staff. There was little demand for new buildings—the

---

[1] *Norwich MM Minutes 1858*, p. 572; *The Friend* (1871), 129; *The British Friend* (1907), 172.

[2] A. G. Gardiner, *Life of George Cadbury* (London, 1923), p. 187.

[3] *The Friend* (1871), 129.

[4] ibid. (1872), 165.

[5] ibid., i.e. they disapproved of one or more of the uses to which it was put, or they could not know in advance what its uses were.

[6] *The British Friend* (1898), 162.

[7] cf. Samuel Fothergill, *Essay on the Society of Friends: Being an Inquiry into the Causes of their Diminished Influence and Numbers, with suggestions for a Remedy* (London, 1859), p. 144.

1851 religious census had shown that the Quakers had the amplest accommodation, in relation to their numbers, of any denomination in England.[1] Population shifts meant that some meeting houses were of little use, but the Society expanded so slowly that new ones were seldom required.

The uses to which this central fund was put varied little throughout the Victorian period. In 1839–40, to take a sample year, there was an income of £5,028,[2] mainly drawn from subscriptions. If we except a special non-recurring item,[3] the main charges were £906 for printing Quaker books, which would have been largely recouped in sales, and the expenses of travelling ministers, £392. £85 went on the needs of the little communities of Quakers on the Continent, and varying small sums were spent on rates, taxes, repairs, stationery, the printing of official documents, and incidentals. £69 was paid to 'sundry Annuitants' and £63 to the 'National Poor'. Only £210 was paid in salaries.

The balance sheet for 1889–90 shows that the income is much smaller (£3,415) and expenditure also is lower (£2,309). The annuitants and 'National Poor' have disappeared, and much less is spent on publishing books and papers. The costs of travelling ministers have fallen slightly, but much more is spent on salaries—£700. By 1910, the amount spent on salaries was destined to rise to £1,757. But on the whole, the two balance sheets are strikingly similar.

But the National Stock was only one element in the Quaker financial scheme. Money was raised by subscription, in similar fashion, to defray the expenses of Quaker boarding schools, and considerable sums were raised and spent locally. The minutes of Hardshaw East Monthly Meeting, for instance, in 1852 and 1853, show that although it was the best endowed meeting in England, it found it necessary to raise money by subscription for the National Stock, for the local Quaker school, at Penketh, for the national Quaker

---

[1] *Sketches of the Religious Denominations of the Present Day . . . and The Census, comprising the number of each Denomination abridged from the Official Report made by Horace Mann, Esq.* (London, 1854), pp. 72 and 92.

[2] The balance sheets, before 1857, are to be found in the manuscript volumes of *YM Minutes* (in FHL); after that date, they appear in the printed *Yearly Meeting Proceedings*. Sums of money are given to the nearest pound, in this chapter section.

[3] The inspection of Quaker registers.

school at Ackworth, for the poor of the meeting, for the
Meeting's running expenses, for a special educational fund
and for the Negro and Aborigines Fund.[1] In a single year,
£561 was raised for these purposes.

Quaker endowments provided an income of £27,426 in
1876,[2] which was very unequally divided among the various
meetings. They were often, however, small, with incomes
which did not repay the labour of administration. Some
were tied to eccentric purposes, or purposes which time had
made so, like the fund for repairing the saddles of Friends
attending Yearly Meeting. Poorly endowed meetings often
envied the blessings of their richer neighbours, but Quaker
endowments in general presented a confusing, if not chaotic,
picture. Many Quakers demanded the re-allocation of trust
income, but little was done in this sphere in the Victorian
period.

But other forms of official Quaker expenditure were a
bagatelle compared with the Quaker community's annual
outlay on home and foreign missions, and philanthropy. In
1897 Quaker subscriptions and donations to official Quaker
bodies included the following:[3]

National Stock	£ 1,493
Friends Foreign Mission Association	£10,524
Friends Syrian Mission	£ 1,515
Home Mission Committee	£ 3,207
Ackworth School	£ 1,046
Friends Temperance Union	£ 174
Total	£17,959

This does not include subscriptions to the Friends First Day
School Association, The Friends Tract Association, or the
Bedford Institute,[4] or the response of Quakers to international crises, and *ad hoc* appeals, which in 1897–8
included:

[1] *Hardshaw East MM Minutes*, 1852, pp. 434–530 and 1853, pp. 530– end of vol.
xiv, and vol. xv, pp. 1–79.

[2] According to *The Friend* (1876), 212 (quoting a parliamentary return). In *The
Friend* (1863), 139, the figure is given as £17,000, *per annum.*

[3] Tabulated in round figures by Edward Grubb, in *The Friend* (1898), 661.

[4] A Quaker religious and educational centre in Whitechapel, supported by
Friends throughout England.

Armenian Relief Fund	£17,400
Pemba Mission	£ 5,800
Indian Famine Fund	£ 8,400
the Dukhobortski	£ 1,300

and much of the £37,265 raised for the Russian Famine Fund.[1] Nor does it include the sums which Quakers, as individuals, subscribed to many local and national charitable societies. Many of the societies which had relied most heavily on Quaker financial support, such as the Peace Society and the Anti-Slavery Society, were in decline by this time, but Quaker names still figure prominently on the balance sheets of many charities. It is clear that the Quaker community's expenditure on home and foreign missions, and on philanthropy, was more than equivalent to its savings through its lack of a salaried ministry and secretariat.

Indeed by the 1890s, Quaker commitments had proliferated to such an extent that they placed a real burden on a small church. One country Quaker published an energetic protest against the burden which was placed on local meetings by repeated appeals from London: 'We in the country, whose interest is naturally not so much excited in the last new scheme, are expected to do our share. . . . All the same, something must go to London, so that the amount sent by our meeting may present a decent appearance.'[2] Many of these societies struggled on from year to year with a deficit, tided over by advances from a wealthy and devoted treasurer —James Hack Tuke did this for the Friends' Foreign Mission Association for years on end.

Victorian Quakerism was almost completely lacking in salaried staff. London Yearly Meeting had only one paid official—the Recording Clerk. His office had an apparent connection with longevity, for only four men held the position between 1811 and 1917.[3] Yorkshire Quarterly Meeting

[1] Tabulated in round figures in John Dymond Crosfield, *The Straw on the Camel's Back, or the Financial Pressure exercised from Devonshire House on the Members of the Society of Friends* (no publisher or date, [1898]), p. 4. Interim reports on these appeals are to be found in Quaker periodicals.

[2] Crosfield, *The Straw on the Camel's Back*, p. 9.

[3] William Manley (1811–44); James Bowden (1844–57); Charles Hoyland (1858–90) and Isaac Sharp (1890–1917; not, of course, the travelling minister of that name).

paid a small honorarium to a Transcribing Clerk, and many local meetings made informal arrangements with humble Friends to write up their voluminous minutes, for a small fee.[1] All other clerical and administrative duties were performed by Quaker members, in their leisure time, without payment.

In the 1890s, large Quaker organizations such as the F.F.D.S.A. and the Home Mission Committee found that they could no longer function in this way, as their duties became more onerous, and prosperous and leisured Friends became more difficult to find. They began to employ 'a small number of concerned Friends . . . as salaried staff, usually in inadequate and overcrowded quarters and at very small salaries'.[2] Perhaps the most striking change which has taken place in Quaker organization this century has been the rapid expansion of salaried staff, a change not unaccompanied with misgivings: 'The growth of a large official staff at Friends' House also raises the question as to whether the Society which has rejected the authority of a professional ministry is placing too much responsibility for initiative in the hands of a centralised body of administrators.'[3]

THE POSITION OF WOMEN

The equality of men and women in Quakerism was more apparent than real, but the powers open to women were so large compared with their restricted role in other religious —or, for that matter, secular—organizations in Victorian England, that they deserve to be regarded as one of the most striking elements in Quaker organization.

Their distinctive dress, their freedom to preach and pray in public, their eminence in philanthropy, and their reputation for domestic virtues,[4] meant that Quaker women made a great impression on contemporaries. Several writers claimed that the wider role given to the Quaker woman

---

[1] cf. *Norwich MM Minutes, 1869*, p. 383, and 1870, p. 436.

[2] T. Edmund Harvey, 'Looking Back', *JFHS* (1953), 56.

[3] Fleming, *The Lighted Mind*, pp. 5–6.

[4] Frances Power Cobbe, 'The Final Cause of Woman', in *Woman's Work and Woman's Culture: A Series of Essays*, ed. Josephine E. Butler (London, 1869), p. 25n.

explained her eminence in philanthropy.[1] During the London School Board elections of 1879, *The Spectator* advised voters to select 'Quakeresses in all but their creed'.[2]

In fact, the equality of women extended only to their freedom to hold certain offices, of which that of minister was the most important. This was, indeed, of great significance—it is difficult to imagine any other early Victorian context where the silver eloquence of Elizabeth Fry could ever have found expression. One has only to think of the aged Sarah Grubb, haranguing Men's Yearly Meeting in the early 1830s on the evils of evangelicalism, to realize what power the ministry gave to women of eloquence and strong personality. Perhaps unconsciously, many Victorian women ministers used the concept of inspiration to manipulate their masculine environment.[3] But until the end of the nineteenth century, all important decisions, both at the local and at the national level, were made without any reference to the opinions of the women's meetings at all.

The only real function of Women's Yearly Meeting was to issue an epistle, and the only function of its subordinate meetings was to read it. It is true that the lower meetings answered the Queries, but since the men's meetings answered for both men and women, and only Men's Yearly Meeting was able to put this information to practical use, the process was farcical, and was recognized as such.

In the early Victorian period, women apparently felt little discontent with their situation. They enjoyed the social aspect of meetings, and, for the rest, saw them as opportunities for edification, where they preached each other sermons. But by the early 1870s, they no longer took the subordination of women for granted. John Bright's daughter deplored 'the separation of the body into two parts, one which legislates, and another which, while amenable to any penalties in the power of the Society to impose, has no part in the conduct of its business'.[4] Another woman Friend com-

---

[1] Letter from Lucretia Mott, dated 20 April 1869, printed ibid., p. xlv. cf. Thomas Clarkson, *A Portraiture of Quakerism* (3 vols., 2nd ed., London, 1807), vol. iii, 295–6.

[2] *The Friend* (1880), 102.

[3] cf. pp. 24 and 95 above.

[4] *The Friend* (1873), 203.

plained, 'We . . . retire into a second meeting which we know is to be filled either with a play of business, a heavy stillness, or a continued exercise of the morning's feeling.'[1] But over twenty years were to elapse before the position of women was changed. In 1896, Men's Yearly Meeting decided that women formed an integral part of Quaker organization, that they should be able to serve on the Meeting for Sufferings, and that the most important issues at Yearly Meeting should be debated in joint sittings of men and women. Women's Yearly Meeting retained a separate existence for another ten years. Gradually, in different parts of the country, local business meetings adopted joint sittings of men and women—the change was already under way in the early eighties.[2] At the same time, the ancient Quaker custom whereby men and women sat on opposite sides of the room at Meeting for Worship fell into desuetude.

Was the relatively large scope open to Quaker women mirrored in greater freedom in the other relations of life? The question is impossible to answer, for the reality was as diverse as human relationships themselves. But one suspects that dominant figures such as Sarah Grubb and Elizabeth Fry were quite exceptional, and that many Victorian Quaker men shared the authoritarianism of the great Liberal, John Bright:

He could worship what he called charming women, but he could *never* bear women to assert themselves. . . . He did not think his sisters had a right to think for themselves with regard to any offer of marriage. . . . He once told me that daughters had no right to have the money their father had left them if it would be of use to their brothers in business.[3]

The evidence suggests that many Quaker women would have agreed with him.[4]

At almost every point, Quaker organization differed profoundly from that of other churches. It is impossible to write

[1] *The Friend* (1873), p. 227.
[2] ibid (1883), 159.
[3] Priscilla McLaren to Helen Clark, 8 Apr. 1893, quoted in John Vincent, *The Formation of the Liberal Party 1857–1868* (London, 1966), p. 210.
[4] cf. the correspondence in *The Friend* (1873), 226–8, for different attitudes, among Quaker women, to the rights and role of women.

about Friends without using a large number of words such as 'disownment', 'convincement', and 'Queries', which are either peculiar to Quakerism or have a distinctive meaning in the Quaker context. Most of the important elements in Victorian Quaker organization, have seventeenth-century roots, but it did not spring Minerva-like from the brain of George Fox or from the early Friends. It was in a continual state of flux, changing in obedience to inward and outward pressures and influences. The system was highly complex, and not always fully understood by Victorian Friends themselves. Each of the facets of Quaker organization which has been analysed here was significant for the life of the body, but there is one facet which has such far-reaching ramifications that it is worth studying separately. This aspect, that of conversions, expulsions and resignations, forms the subject of the next chapter.

IV

EXITS AND ENTRANCES

THE extent of a church's membership is determined partly by demographic factors, such as family size, and partly by the numbers who join and leave it. The demographic characteristics of Victorian Quakerism are briefly discussed in a later chapter of this book. This chapter deals first with the general pattern of Quaker membership figures in the nineteenth century, and secondly, in some detail, with recruitment to the body, and expulsions and resignations from it.

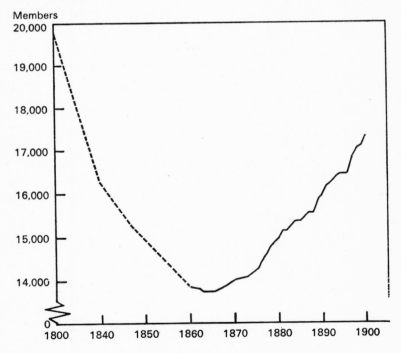

Fig. 3   Membership of London Yearly Meeting 1800–1900

THE PATTERN OF MEMBERSHIP FIGURES

The English Quakers first began to compile and publish their membership totals and statistics of recruitment, resignations and expulsions in 1861, when they managed to overcome their misgivings about King David's punishment for numbering the people of Israel.[1] These anxieties, incidentally, were not peculiar to Quakers; they were shared by Congregationalists, when they first began to publish annual membership figures, nearly forty years later.[2] Before 1861, we have reliable membership figures for 1840 and 1847, when two unofficial Quaker censuses were conducted under the supervision of Samuel Tuke. For the earlier part of the century, we have a number of contemporary estimates, and the calculations, based on all available statistics, made by John Stephenson Rowntree in 1859.[3]

After carefully considering all the available evidence, Rowntree estimated that there were 60,000 Quakers in England and Wales in 1680.[4] The decline in membership numbers which took place in the eighteenth century and which was partly due to emigration, does not concern us here—by 1800, the number of English and Welsh Quakers had fallen to perhaps 19,800.[5] Forty years later, when the first actual enumeration was made, it had sunk still further, to 16,227. The first official Quaker returns, made in 1861, showed a total of 13,859 for the previous year.[6] In the first sixty years of the nineteenth century, membership totals had fallen by no less than 30 per cent. Small wonder that the formal deliberations of Quakers in the fifties were haunted by the consciousness of their decline. It was so much a truism that an anonymous donor made it the subject of an essay contest, which attracted 150 entries.

[1] cf. *II Samuel* 24, and *I Chronicles* 21.

[2] *The Congregational Year Book, 1899*, pp. ii–iii.

[3] For his prize-winning essay, *Quakerism Past and Present*, he used nation-wide Quaker statistics of births, deaths, marriages and recruitment, and assembled statistics of emigration, resignations and expulsions for a smaller sample area.

[4] ibid., pp. 68–73.

[5] ibid., p. 87.

[6] All Quaker statistics for the period after 1861, for which no other source is given, come from the Tabular Statement presented annually to Yearly Meeting, and printed with its *Proceedings*, and in Quaker periodicals. They are perhaps the most reliable of all nineteenth century denominational statistics.

In the 1860s the decline at last begins to level out, and membership figures show an increase for every year after 1864. Victorian Quakers were naturally heartened by the change, but the apparent expansion was deceptive. Between 1871 and 1901, their membership totals rose by 24·5 per cent. But in the same period, the population of England and Wales expanded by 43 per cent, so that in terms of the proportion they formed of the total population—the only real criterion—they were still declining. To see Quaker membership figures in perspective, we need to compare them with trends in other denominations, over the same period. Such comparisons are difficult to make—some denominations, such as the Congregationalists and the Unitarians, did not publish membership figures at all. Those which did so varied considerably from the Society of Friends in size, and often in social composition—and their membership figures were of course, affected by crises and schisms peculiar to each movement. But when these qualifications are borne in mind, it is interesting to note that in the same period—1871–1901—the Wesleyan Methodists expanded by 31 per cent, the Methodist New Connection (a church of comparable size to the Quakers) by 41·3 per cent and the Baptists, (whose loose organization made their statistics self-confessedly inaccurate), by 36·6 per cent.[1] All these churches were expanding more slowly than the general population—but the Quakers the most slowly of all.

Although the Quakers declined throughout the century when viewed relative to population growth, in absolute terms their membership statistics exhibit a very striking and unusual pattern, which is shown in Fig. 3—steady decline until the middle 1860s, and then equally steady expansion. This pattern must be explained either by demographic changes (which are discussed later in this study), by emigration, or by the changing ratio between recruitment and resignations and expulsions. Between 1800 and 1860, the

[1] Wesleyan Methodists statistics used here and subsequently in this book come from the *Minutes of Conference*, New Connection statistics from the *Minutes of Conference of the Methodist New Connection*, and Baptist figures from *The Baptist Handbook* for the relevant year; The Baptist and Methodist New Connection statistics are for England only.

English Quakers lost perhaps 700 members by emigration.[1]
Part of the remaining loss was due to the fact that deaths
outnumbered births, but the most important contributory
factor was the way in which losses through resignations and
expulsions greatly outstripped gains through recruitment.
Rowntree estimated the discrepancy at 2,400.[2]

We cannot descibe the ratio between losses and recruitment in the years before 1860 with any great precision, as

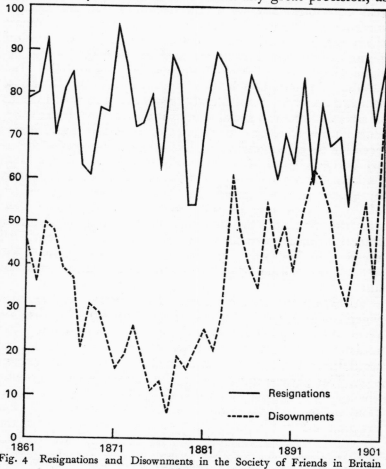

Fig. 4   Resignations and Disownments in the Society of Friends in Britain
1861–1901

[1] Rowntree, *Quakerism Past and Present*, p. 86.   [2] ibid., p. 88.

Friends only compiled statistics of recruitment.[1] But the
available evidence makes the pattern abundantly clear. Until
1860, expulsions or disownments greatly outnumbered admissions of new members. The main reason for this was that
Quakers unfailingly expelled every member who married a
non-Quaker—perhaps between a quarter and a third of all
who married at all.[2] Some of these joined other churches;
others continued to attend meeting, but without enjoying
the privileges of membership. In 1852, the numbers of the
latter group were estimated—probably over-generously—
at over 9,000, 'a body principally separated through the
stringency of our rules respecting marriage'.[3] It was estimated that only 8 per cent of these were ever restored to
membership.[4] It is not surprising that Rowntree exclaimed
that history did not yield a comparable instance of 'so
deliberate an act of suicide on the part of a church'.[5] In
1860, the regulation was changed, and the change was
immediately mirrored in membership trends. For the rest
of the century, recruitment outstrips losses through expulsions and resignations. From 1860 on, the total numbers
of resignations and expulsions are so small that we cannot
read too much significance into their year by year fluctuations.[6] But two elements emerge clearly: resignations
always outnumber expulsions, and the numbers of expulsions decline throughout the sixties, reach their lowest
average in the seventies, and rise again in the eighties and
nineties.

This pattern is confirmed by other evidence. In the
middle years of the nineteenth century, the strict super-
visory control which the Society exercised over its members

[1] These were not given in the Minutes of Yearly Meeting—they must be compiled from the original MSS. returns made by Quarterly Meetings, bound in
bundles of *Yearly Meeting Papers*, in FHL. The statistics on which Fig. 5 was
based, for the years before 1861, were compiled in this way. Figures of expulsions
and resignations can only be gained by going through the minutes books of
individual Monthly Meetings. I did this in the case of the two Meetings discussed
in detail below; local Quakers compiled such data for Rowntree in ten Meetings.

[2] Rowntree, *Quakerism Past and Present*, p. 156.

[3] *The Friend* (1852), 90.

[4] ibid. (1857), 95.

[5] Rowntree, *Quakerism Past and Present*, p. 156.

[6] These are charted in Fig. 4.

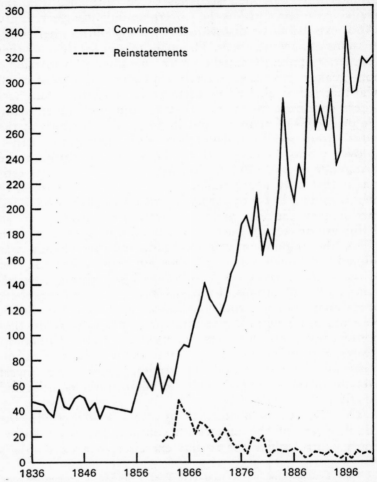

Fig. 5   Convincements and Reinstatements in the Society of Friends in Britain
1836–1901

was declining.[1] Friends became increasingly reluctant to
expel members for financial failure, or for infringements of
Quaker regulations, and the penalty was more and more

---

[1] This paragraph is based on the practice of the two large Meetings studied in
detail later in this chapter.

confined to grave offences. But in the eighties, while this greater leniency continued, many meetings became more concerned about their nominal members. These had often been left in peace, provided they lived a respectable life, but it now became customary to conduct periodic purges of membership lists, and remove those who never came to meetings and showed little prospect of doing so.

Recruitment figures, in striking contrast to resignations and expulsions, rise very markedly in the last forty years of the century. Between 1840 and 1849, the average annual number of converts was 44·8. Between 1880 and 1889, it was 223·8. Undoubtedly the most important single contributing factor was the expansion of the Quaker Sunday School movement,[1] bringing many working-class children and adults into close contact with Friends.

The rate of turnover among Friends was low. In 1882, for instance, the number of new recruits admitted equalled 1·1 per cent of their total numbers;[2] their losses through resignation or expulsion, 0·72 per cent. Unfortunately we have no truly comparable data for other denominations, because their procedures varied so greatly. In 1882, the first year in which they published such data, the Wesleyans' new members equalled 14·1 per cent of their total membership —but this includes the children of members, who were not received into membership until they grew up, whereas Quaker children became members automatically at birth. The Wesleyans' totals of those who lost their membership, other than through death or a change of residence, came to 6·4 per cent of the whole in the same year—but these figures must be treated with the greatest caution, and are probably not truly comparable with Quaker data at all. All that can be said is that the rate of turnover in the Society of Friends was probably lower than that of the larger denominations.[3]

[1] For which, see Ch. 9 below.

[2] The totals of new members and former members who were reinstated have been added together in working out this percentage.

[3] Quaker statistics of losses 1887–96 were compared with those of the various branches of Methodism for the same period, in *The Friend* (1898), 190–1. It was concluded that Quaker losses were much lower.

RECRUITMENT, EXPULSIONS AND RESIGNATIONS

The study of those who join a church and those who leave it is a particularly neglected dimension of religious history. The reasons for this are not difficult to ascertain. Statistics in this field are hard to come by, and even when they exist as plentifully as they do for the Society of Friends, taken by themselves they form only the visible part of the iceberg. A study of recruitment, for example, tells us much about a church's image of itself, and its relationship to outsiders. Does it welcome new recruits and accept them readily, or does it view them with reserve and put them on probation? What tests, if any, are applied to prospective members? What sections of society are they drawn from, and what elements in a church's image attracts them in the first place? Conversely, a study of expulsions tells us much about the relationship between the church in its corporate capacity and its component members. Does it keep a close watch over their lives and expel delinquents, as the Victorian Quakers did? Or does it, like the Anglican church, contain a large proportion of nominal members?

Statistics alone can reveal little of the answers to these questions. The student of contemporary religious movements can obtain information from converts by interviews— though this particular aspect has been relatively little studied—but this approach is, of course, not open to the historian. But the historian of Victorian Quakerism has access to a kind of source material which is perhaps unique, for Friends made, and in some cases preserved, what are, in effect, miniature case histories of all who entered and left the movement—the 'Visitors' Reports'.

When anyone wished to become a member of the Society, or to resign his membership, he sent notification to the local Monthly Meeting.[1] The Meeting appointed two of its number as Visitors to interview him and report. The same procedure was used when the Meeting learnt of a case of delinquency among its members, and was considering whether to expel the culprit. The Visitors presented a writ-

---

[1] Either formally by a letter, or informally, by giving a message to someone who would attend the Meeting.

ten report to the Monthly Meeting, which reached a decision on the case, usually on the basis of the report. These reports were preserved in some meetings, either pasted into bulky volumes called Guard Books, or transcribed into the Monthly Meeting minute books.

In the pages that follow, an attempt is made to examine the processes of recruitment, resignation and expulsion in two large and probably fairly typical Monthly Meetings.[1] The Meetings chosen were those centring on Norwich and Manchester. Each included a number of smaller towns as well.[2] Their geographic boundaries are shown in Fig. 2.

The Visitors' Reports have many inadequacies as source material. The amount of information they give varies greatly, and they were clearly supplemented verbally. They were used as the basis of a detailed analysis, simply because they provide the only systematic source of information on a major and neglected aspect of religious history.

TWO CASE STUDIES: INTRODUCTION

Both Monthly Meetings studied here were dominated by a large urban meeting [3]—Goat Lane, Norwich and Mount Street, Manchester, respectively—the seventeenth and tenth largest Quaker congregations in England, in 1904.[4] The

[1] To ascertain which Meetings preserved these records, a circular letter was sent to every Monthly Meeting in England. The range of choice was restricted— many had destroyed these reports, sometimes in quite recent years, and a few still regarded them as confidential. Only fairly large Meetings had a sufficiently large turnover to merit studying. To see whether the two Meetings chosen were typical, a London meeting's records were examined as well—the only differences were what one might expect—more cases of financial failure, and greater geographic mobility of members.

[2] Norwich MM's records are deposited in Norwich and Norfolk Record Office. The records of Hardshaw East MM are still in the MM's possession, and were consulted in Mount Street Meeting House, Manchester, by special permission. These Meetings were chosen partly because of their importance in Victorian Quaker history; the latter is untypical in one respect—it was the scene of two schisms, described in Chapter II above. But losses occasioned by these schisms are readily recognizable.

[3] The census of attendances, printed in *Yearly Meeting Proceedings, 1905*, pp. 195ff., shows that in 1904, Norwich had 113 present at the morning service, the rest of the MM 38, and Manchester had 136 present, the rest of the MM, excluding the boarding school children at Penketh, 142.

[4] ibid., p. 21.

cities in which they were situated presented a striking contrast, both in size and in their social and economic composition.

Though Manchester Meeting was large by Quaker standards, it was minuscule in relation to the huge industrial city which surrounded it—'this great meeting at Manchester, with its 400 members scattered about, and sometimes almost concealed from view among a population of over 400,000'.[1] The cotton industry created Victorian Manchester, with its teeming working-class population, its factories and warehouses, its dramatic contrasts of wealth and poverty. It was a visible symbol of capitalist achievement—'rightly understood, Manchester is as great a human achievement as Athens.'[2] The cost of this achievement, in poverty and misery, was mirrored in the works of observers as various as Mrs. Gaskell, Engels and de Toqueville: '*ici est l'esclave, là le maître: là les richesses de quelques-uns: ici, la misère du plus grand nombre.*'[3] In this polarized society, the Manchester Quakers were a well-known, respected, and prosperous community of manufacturers, merchants, retailers, and professional men,[4] the social composition of which changed little throughout the century.

Norwich, on the other hand, was only a fifth the size of Manchester.[5] Its population increased so slowly in the nineteenth century that it seemed like decline—a consequence of its economic stagnation, and recurrent unemployment. By the end of the eighteenth century, it had lost its traditional pre-eminence in textile manufacture to the great industrial cities of the north. In December 1853, Harriet Martineau described 'the extinction of the celebrity of ancient Norwich, in regard both to its material and intellec-

---

[1] *The Friend* (1873), 336.

[2] Disraeli, *Coningsby*, Book IV, Chap. 1.

[3] Alexis de Toqueville, *Voyage en Angleterre et en Irlande de 1835*, p. 81, in *Voyages en Angleterre, Irlande, Suisse et Algerie* (ed. J. B. Mayer and André Jardin, Paris, 1957).

[4] cf. J. T. Slugg, *Reminiscences of Manchester Fifty Years Ago* (Manchester and London, 1881), pp. 183–6; *The Manchester City News*, 4 Feb. 1905 and 11 Feb. 1905 (FHL Press Cuttings, CC 73–4) and 3 Aug. 1921 (FHL Press Cuttings, VV 74). cf. Katherine Chorley, *Manchester Made Them* (London, 1950), p. 123.

[5] At the time of the 1861 census, when Norwich had 74,891 and Manchester 378,000 inhabitants.

tual productions. Its bombazine manufacture has gone to Yorkshire, and its literary fame to the four winds.'[1]

Until the middle years of the nineteenth century, Norwich was a famous centre of wealthy and patrician Quakerism. Visiting ministers, such as William Savery and Thomas Shillitoe, thundered against its wealth and ostentation—'the gayest meeting of Friends I ever sat in'.[2] Joseph John Gurney and William Forster, two of the most famous Quaker ministers of their time, were Norwich Friends. But in the decades following Gurney's death in 1847, the social composition of the meeting changed entirely. Many Friends resigned or were expelled—it was well known that wealthy families, in time, tended to gravitate to the Established Church—and others left Norwich. In 1838, Goat Lane, Norwich, had 150 members. Fifty years later, not one of these or their descendants were members of the meeting— except for one man, who had been recently restored to membership.[3] Crabb Robinson noted the same phenomenon among the Norwich Unitarians, in 1832: 'Went with Mottram to Octagon, Congregation very small—splendour of the old Octagon is gone—many families are dead or have left N is the explanation given, but why no new ones?'[4] The Norwich Quakers were replenished by a stream of working-class converts, drawn mainly from the Adult Schools. In 1902 the Meeting pointed out the change this had effected, in a plaintive reply to an appeal for funds: 'We are well aware that these visits [from Home Mission workers] entail expense; but the "well-to-do" Friends have departed from this District and our Monthly Meeting is almost entirely composed of those "who are doing their utmost" to "maintain themselves and their families in an honorable independence".'[5] By 1914, of a total of 191 members, 97 were converts, and 31 converts' children, 'mostly of the Artisan class'.[6]

[1] Harriet Martineau, *Biographical Sketches 1852–1868* (2nd ed., London, 1869), p. 336.

[2] *Journal of William Savery*, p. 278 (1798); cf. *Journal of Thomas Shillitoe*, vol. i, 38 (1794).

[3] *Norwich MM Minutes, 1888*, pp. 286–7.

[4] Quoted in R. K. Webb, *Harriet Martineau, A Radical Victorian* (London, 1960), p. 56.

[5] *Norwich MM Minutes, May 1902*, minute 12 (n.p.).

[6] ibid., Aug. 1914 (Triennial Report).

The records of these two very different Monthly Meetings, supplemented by information from other sources, form the basis of the analysis which follows.

Applicants for Membership in Norwich and Manchester

In this section, five main questions are considered—how did applicants come into contact with Quakerism, what Churches, if any, were they drawn from, what elements in Quakerism attracted them, what was their social and economic background, and what kind of reception did they meet with?

Most applicants came into contact with Friends in one of two ways—through some kind of family relationship, or through the Quaker Sunday Schools for adults and children, known as First Day Schools.

A large number of applicants—72 per cent of those whose previous religious affiliation was stated—had been brought up as Friends from childhood, or joined because they were married to or hoped to marry a Quaker, or through the influence of Quaker friends or employers. Many applicants for membership differed only technically from birthright Friends. This fact reflects the formalities surrounding birthright membership—there was a large class of men and women who had been brought up as Friends but for one of a number of technical reasons were not members.[1] One such applicant told the Visitors: 'She has never attended anywhere else. She believes in Christ as her personal Saviour, and trusts they will accept her as she is the only one of the whole family not a Friend.[2] Another stated 'she felt as if she had belonged to Friends all her life nearly.'[3] A third and not untypical example was a woman who was received into

---

[1] Only the child of two Quakers was a Friend by birthright, though where a married couple were admitted into membership their children could be admitted as minors. The class of those who were brought up as Friends, but were not members, included the children of habitual attenders who never sought membership, of convert couples who did not seek membership for their children, and of families where only one parent was a Friend.

[2] *Norwich MM Minutes, July 1908*, minute 2 (n.p.).

[3] ibid., *Aug. 1906*, minute 4 (n.p.).

membership in 1900, at the age of 59. Her grandfather had been a Friend who was expelled for marrying a non-member, but he retained his Quaker views and imbued his children with them. Her mother had been attached to Quakerism, though not a member. The applicant had attended meetings regularly until her marriage, and subsequently as often as possible.[1]

Cases of applicants who were not really converts to Quakerism at all, but simply sought a change of technical status, from lifelong attender to member, were almost certainly more common than the Reports reveal.

Marriages between Quakers and non-Quakers very often led to a conversion to the Society, or a resignation from it. The views of Friends on matters such as baptism were so different from those of other churches that it was probably difficult for a Quaker to live in happy marriage with a fervent Christian of another persuasion. Applications for membership which resulted from marriage with a Quaker were more frequent than the Reports reveal. This kind of application, however, only becomes common after 1860, for before that date all Quakers who married non-members were expelled, a procedure which tended to alienate the couple. But the odd case did occur—in 1855, a woman resigned after thirty years as a Friend admitting that she had joined only to please her husband, 'an arrangement which she consented to, rather than desired, more as a matter of convenience than of conviction'. After the death of her husband, she returned to her original allegiance.[2]

Of those applicants who came from a non-Quaker background, probably the majority, after 1870, were brought into contact with Friends through the First Day Schools. These were intended for the poor; they sought to evangelize non-Christians, but very often had the effect of weaning Christians from their original denominational allegiance. For the others, Quakerism was the only form of Christianity of which they had first-hand knowledge. Their adoption of Quakerism was in a sense an accident—had they

[1] *Hardshaw East MM Minutes*, vol. ii, p. 120.
[2] Ibid., vol. v, p. 162.

attended Wesleyan schools, they would have become Wesleyans. Since the scholars tended to come from a lower social class than most Friends, and were unaccustomed to distinctive Quaker practices, such as silent meetings, their admission posed many problems. The attitude of Friends to First Day Scholars, and the various solutions evolved to meet the difficulties that arose, are discussed later in this book. But it should be noted that many applications immediately traceable to a Quaker upbringing were ultimately due to the Adult Schools—if a man became an enthusiastic Adult Scholar, he would encourage his wife to do likewise, send his children to Quaker Sunday Schools, and bring them up as Quakers.

The Reports frequently omit to state that an applicant had come to Friends via the schools, and the Mission Meetings associated with them. Applicants were usually known personally to most of those present—it was unnecessary to write down facts which were well known to all. But Norwich Meeting itself declared that the schools were its 'chief feeder'.[1] The Norwich Adult School was established in 1869, and William White, writing in 1886, made special mention of Norwich as an Adult School which had produced many recruits to Quakerism.[2] Most Norwich applicants came to Quaker membership via membership of an intermediate body, the Gospel Band. This was established after 1876, and had died a natural death by 1895, for all its members had joined Friends, or become regular attenders.[3] The Manchester Adult School was established in 1860,[4] and grew rapidly by distributing relief during the cotton famine. Probably fewer of its members became Quakers than did so in Norwich, but between 1890 and 1897 at least eight out

[1] *Norwich MM Minutes, August 1914,* minute 6 (n.p.). A. Eddington, who came to Norwich in 1869, gave similar evidence (Joan Platt, *The Quakers in Norwich* (from materials compiled by A. J. Eddington, Norwich, 1926), p. 27).

[2] [William] White, *The Development of the Sunday School System in the Direction of Adult Instruction* (paper read to the Autumnal Convention of the Sunday School Union, 1886).

[3] *Proceedings of Manchester Conference, 1895,* p. 103. The precise date of the Gospel Band's Foundation is uncertain.

[4] *The Friend* (1862), 60. Two different dates, the first incorrect and the second correct, are given in G. Currie Martin, *The Adult School Movement Its Origin and Development* (London, 1924), pp. 99, 112.

of 51 recruits came from the Adult Schools and the Mission Meetings.

What churches, if any, were applicants drawn from? Many, as has been noted, had been brought up as Quakers, or had attended Quaker meetings or Mission Meetings for a very long period. For the rest, previous church allegiance is given fairly infrequently. Applicants who had not belonged to any church at all seem to have been relatively rare. The most commonly mentioned previous allegiance is Anglicanism—this reflects the numerical strength of the Established Church,[1] and the tendency of the uncommitted to describe themselves as Anglican. Converts from the various branches of Methodism, and from the Congregationalists and Baptists, taken together, outnumber those from Anglicanism. They tend to display certain common characteristics, which go far to explain their decision to become Quakers.

Such applicants had often played an active part in the affairs of the church to which they had previously belonged. This tendency had been pointed out in 1859: 'their proselytes are ALMOST INVARIABLY persons who, in connection with other bodies, have already attained to a considerable degree of Christian experience'.[2] The applicants in Hardshaw East Monthly Meeting, between 1861 and 1900, included six Sunday School teachers, two local preachers and two who were active in social work—this is by no means a complete list, and after 1901 the trend intensifies to a remarkable extent.[3]

One of the attractions of Dissent in general was the scope it offered for lay action: 'they have more offices, deaconships and visitors and tract distributors. This is an attraction to small shopkeepers and mechanics, who find they are looked

---

[1] On Census Sunday, 1851, the Anglicans returned 26,656 out of a total of 57,803 church attendances in Manchester, and 15,087 out of 31,369 in Norwich.

[2] Samuel Fothergill, *Essay on the Society of Friends: Being an Inquiry into the causes of their diminished influence and numbers, with suggestions for a Remedy* (London, 1859), p. 56.

[3] Applicants for membership in *Hardshaw East MM Minutes, 1901–19*, include 24 Sunday School teachers, 4 local preachers, 4 active in unspecified social or mission work, 2 prospective foreign missionaries, and 6 active either in War Victims' Relief, the Christian Endeavour Movement, or in writing for Quaker periodicals.

upon as somebody in the congregation.'[1] It is not difficult
to understand the attraction of Quakerism, with its exclusively lay organization and its open ministry, to this nonconformist élite. As one Norwich Quaker convert put it, 'that is
what we working people want if we join a Church: we want
something to do.'[2] Norwich Quakers had a conscious policy
of feeding the zeal of converts by giving them work and
responsibility.[3] But in many Quaker meetings, the scope
offered converts was more apparent than real. Despite its
multifarious offices and committees, Quaker organization
was dominated by senior and birthright Friends.[4] And
many Quakers found the enthusiasm with which former
nonconformists took part in public preaching and prayer so
distasteful that they actually expressed a preference for converts from a non-Christian background.[5]

Nonconformists who were active as lay preachers, or as
teachers in Quaker or non-Quaker Sunday Schools, were
sometimes led to reject the whole concept of a professional
ministry. A Congregationalist couple who were admitted to
the Society declared that it was their Adult School work
which had made them 'see beyond being fed by a one-man
ministry'.[6] Sometimes 'feeling dissatisfied with the clergyman'[7] was elaborated into a rejection of the whole concept
of a professional clergy. Of course, personal animosities of
one sort or another underlay a certain proportion both of
exits and of entrances. A minute recording the resignations
of a father and three daughters in Hardshaw East in 1848
expressed the wish 'that they may witness an increase of that
Christian Charity which "hopeth all things" & "thinketh
no evil".'[8]

A change of residence sometimes led to a change of church

---

[1] Quoted in E. R. Wickham, *Church and People in an Industrial City* (London,
1957), p. 116.
[2] *Birmingham F.F.D.S.A. Conference Proceedings, 1890*, p. 66.
[3] ibid, p. 186.
[4] *The Monthly Record* (1879), 184, complains that converts are precluded from
active work. cf. Oliver Morland, *William White A Brother of Men* (London, 1903),
pp. 139–40.
[5] *The Friend* (1891), p. 144.
[6] *Norwich MM Minutes, July 1908*, minute 1 (n.p.).
[7] *Hardshaw East MM Minutes*, vol. vi, p. 16.
[8] ibid., vol. iv, p. 192.

adherence—Pickering has noted the same phenomenon in his study of church membership in two contemporary English towns.[1] This was especially true of Manchester—those who had been church members in their home towns, felt free to experiment in the anonymity of a great city. Sometimes they attended a Quaker meeting out of curiosity, liked it, and attended regularly; the change, under these circumstances, involved no painful breach with former church associates. Conversely, young Quakers who came to live in Manchester sometimes drifted away from the Society. A young man, expelled in 1852, was a case in point: 'it appears to us that this practice [i.e. of attending church] had gained on him more through his non-intercourse with Friends than through doctrinal considerations.'[2]

Some applicants for membership give the impression of being strongly inner-directed [3] and self-reliant, and of trusting their own judgement, and welcoming the silence of meeting. Sometimes this independence led to a restless progress from denomination to denomination—it was often claimed that the rate of expulsions and resignations was higher among converts than among birthright Friends.[4] Sometimes these applicants had developed strong views on war, oaths, or the sacraments before coming into contact with Friends—one even claimed he had used 'thee' and 'thou' independently.[5] Another 'was attracted to Friends because he already disapproved of oaths and the payment of church rates'.[6]

What aspects of Quakerism attracted new recruits? Several of these elements have been mentioned already: the attraction of a purely lay organization to members of the nonconformist élite, and the perennial appeal of a church with no clergy, creed, or set form of service to some individuals of both a religious and markedly independent cast of mind. Applicants naturally explain their desire to join the Society in doctrinal and religious terms—phrases such as

[1] 'Religious movements of Church members in two working-class towns in England', *Archives de Sociologie des Religions*, 1961, p. 139.
[2] *Hardshaw East MM Minutes*, vol. iv, p. 503.
[3] cf. *The British Friend* (1899), p. 313.
[4] *FQE* (1872), 267–8.
[5] *Hardship East M.M. Minutes*, Vol. IV, pp. 116–7.
[6] *Norwich MM Minutes, 1845*, pp. 294–5.

'purity of worship', 'simplicity of worship', and so on, are often used. Some, especially among the First Day School scholars, were drawn to Quakerism by admiration for an individual Friend, especially, for a beloved teacher. The Quaker reputation for philanthropy attracted some—one applicant stated that he had always admired 'their social work among the poor and afflicted'.[1] Another stated that he was drawn to Quakerism less by doctrinal considerations than by 'the life of the members and his appreciation of their mode of worship'.[2]

But membership of the Society in the nineteenth century offered advantages of a more tangible nature. At the lowest economic level, the very poor could not but be conscious of the financial support which the Society gave its indigent members. This was a formal obligation of Monthly Meetings until 1860, and an invariable practice for many years later.[3] It is likely that poor relief prevented more applications than it encouraged—Monthly Meetings inevitably were reluctant to accept members who were likely to be a drain on their resources, and prospective applicants were keenly aware of the interpretation which could be placed on their motives: 'attenders . . . say they are treated as though they came for the money.'[4] But the advantages of membership went beyond this. The children of members were educated at boarding schools with a graduated scale of fees, depending on the income of the parent. Where necessary, even these fees were paid in part or wholly by the Monthly Meeting to which the family belonged. (The incomes of the schools were supplemented by subscriptions and endowments.) Thus the children of the poor received a middle-class education, and rose inevitably in the social and economic scale—'by elevating all into the middle classes, Friends have lost the poor.'[5] George Cadbury claimed that many fathers of large families had adopted the peculiarities of Friends with the sole object of educating their children.[6] And even those who were unlikely to need poor relief, or a

[1] *Hardshaw East MM Minutes*, vol. xii, p. 194, and Guard Book.
[2] ibid., vol. ix, p. 202.
[3] *Norwich MM Minutes, 1873*, pp. 542–4; also June 1905, minute 9 (n.p.).
[4] *The Friend* (1873), 327.   [5] ibid., 328.
[6] Gardiner, *Life of George Cadbury*, pp. 181–2.

subsidized education for their children, could well have ulterior motives in applying for membership. Joining any church, in the Victorian era, conferred respectability. This was doubly true of the Quakers, with their prosperous middle-class image, and their reputation for philanthropy. An aspiring business man found himself with a network of commercial contacts, and a ready-made reputation for integrity. 'It is an advantage, and no slight one either, to be a member of a Society so highly esteemed and respected.'[1] It would be absurd to claim that the typical application for membership was based on economic calculation, but it would be unrealistic to ignore an element of which Victorian Quakers themselves were keenly aware. Where high profession and economic interest coincide, it is folly to speculate on a man's motives. But it is clear that if a man was hesitating as to whether to apply for membership—or resign the membership he already possessed—the prospects of benefits in store might tip the balance.

The Visitors' Reports shed little light on the social and economic class of applicants. Norwich declared in 1914 that they were 'mostly of the Artisan class',[2] but in both Monthly Meetings, in the Victorian period, it is exceptional to find an applicant's occupation stated. Our knowledge of this subject must be gleaned from the generalizations made by contemporary Friends.

Until the 1860s, Friends tend to lament the absence of the poor from their meetings. But the tide was turning— William White stated in 1863 that the poor had joined 'to a certain extent' and that he had shaken hands with new members who were blacksmiths, carpenters and so on.[3] In the last thirty years of the century, it was generally accepted among Friends that most applicants were working-class, and had come to the Society via the Adult Schools. 'The accession had been chiefly in the large towns, from amongst the labouring population of the North of England.'[4] This was a truism among late Victorian Friends—though many viewed the phenomenon with dismay—but it leaves us with

---

[1] *The British Friend* (1880), 19.
[2] *Norwich MM Minutes, August 1914,* minute 6 (n.p.).
[3] *The Friend* (1863), 179.   [4] ibid. (1879), 158.

a problem. If it is true that most accessions were from the working class—and there seems no reason to doubt it—how can we explain the continuing middle-class image of the Society, and its predominantly middle-class composition, as far as it can be ascertained?[1] Several explanations suggest themselves—either accessions were too few to alter the social composition of the body, or Quaker educational facilities rapidly lifted working-class families into the middle class, or working-class applicants were already on the verge of the middle class.

All three elements seem to have been present. Although many converts were 'the poor of this world' from the vantage point of a Quaker manufacturer, they belonged to the so-called respectable working class, the word 'respectable', as Miall pointed out with indignation, being 'a term we employ with exclusive reference to whereabouts in the social scale'.[2] An aged Birmingham Quaker, recalling Adult School applicants, writes, 'I would think that the majority of those who joined were already merging into the middle class.'[3] In 1899, John Wilhelm Rowntree stated that Adult Scholars 'are not "poor", as a rule, but mainly belong to the comfortable artizan class'. [4]

What was the atttitude of Friends towards prospective new members? A considerable measure of caution in accepting new recruits was built into Quaker formal procedures. An applicant was invariably expected to attend meetings for worship regularly for at least several years, before sending in his application at all. Once the application was made, an interview followed, which many found a severe ordeal. Then they waited for the next Monthly Meeting to meet and reach a decision. Sometimes the delay extended for months, if the Meeting was heavily burdened with business, or could not reach agreement. And there was always the chance that an application might be rejected: it is not surprising that many men and women attended Quaker meetings for a lifetime, but never applied for membership. The minutes of meetings, of course, leave much unrevealed; sometimes

[1] cf. pp. 171ff., below.
[2] Quoted in Wickham, *Church and People*, p. 119.
[3] *Correspondence.*   [4] *Present Day Papers*, vol. ii, Apr. 1899, p. 24, n.

attenders were invited to apply, sometimes they were discouraged, intentionally or unintentionally. A blacksmith
complained in 1874, 'it seemed almost as though the
Quakers had practically put up a placard, "No blacksmiths
need apply".'[1]

Generally, an applicant was expected to have attended
meetings regularly, to be of respectable life, and to state his
agreement with the distinctive teachings of Friends on matters such as war, oaths and the sacraments. In Norwich, an
evangelical-type declaration of faith was standard practice—
most Reports make some such statement as 'He realises
that he is redeemed through the atonement of our Lord
Jesus Christ.'[2] In the Society as a whole, many evangelicals
claimed that a confession of faith should be a pre-requisite of
membership. A writer in *The Friend* in 1871 asked, 'Ought
we to endeavour to ascertain if the applicant is a converted
person?'[3]

Since there were no formal criteria governing admissions,
the readiness with which applications were granted differed
considerably from region to region. 'In some meetings new
members are freely admitted, and as freely dissevered, others
are so cautious that . . . it is no surprise to have heard the
hope expressed that it will not be so hard to enter the kingdom of Heaven as the Quaker fold!'[4]

There is abundant evidence that many Friends were
reluctant to admit new members at all, especially if they
came to the Society via the Adult Schools. Until the middle
years of the century, this suspicion probably extended to all
applicants, regardless of their social background. Meetings
would hesitate,

for no reason whatever, except some idea that '*enough of the Friend*'
has not been exhibited, or because some influential member 'does not
know much of the individual,' or because another is afraid of a
'Methodistical spirit', of 'creaturely activity', or, more strange than
all, 'because four or five have recently been admitted, and there is
danger of going too fast'.[5]

---

[1] *The Friend* (1874), 249.
[2] *Norwich MM Minutes, June 1906*, minute 2 (n.p.).
[3] *The Friend* (1871), 250.   [4] *The British Friend* (1897), 49.
[5] *The Friend* (1864), 254.

Whatever the reasons given for this reluctance, it is clear that it was rooted in the fact that Victorian Quakerism consisted largely of a number of inter-related families, claiming generations of Quaker ancestry. The difficulty was much greater when the applicant was, like most Adult Scholars, of working-class background. A speaker at a conference of Quaker Sunday School teachers stated it with brutal frankness: 'Do you wish to invite chimney sweepers, costermongers, or even blacksmiths, to dinner on Firstday? Do you intend to give their sons and daughters a boarding school education?'.[1] These social barriers—which many Friends acknowledged, though usually less frankly—should not afford matter for an indictment against Victorian Quakerism. They simply meant that the social divisions found in society at large were mirrored in the little world of Quakerism, as in other churches, where they were symbolized by the practice of pew rental. A Friend born at the end of the nineteenth century writes: 'Adult School members were looked upon as "different" & also, to some extent as inferior, by "born Friends"—though of course superficial friendship was maintained. . . . It is easy for anyone who is a hereditary Friend for generations (my ancestors date back to the time of George Fox) to feel that any "received" Friend is "different", because heredity *is* a power in one's life.'[2] These prejudices were not universal—some Sunday School teachers rejoiced to see their pupils join the Society—but they were very widespread in the last three decades of the century, and Quaker records refer to them repeatedly.

We can obtain a rough index of the readiness with which applicants were received by estimating, first the number of Adult Scholars who became Friends, and secondly the number of applications which were rejected. Although applicants from the schools loom large in an analysis of applicants,

---

[1] *The Monthly Record* (1870), 140.

[2] *Corresp.* The present writer published a letter in *The Friend* in 1964, asking elderly Friends for their recollections of the reception given to Adult Scholars applying for membership. 31 replies were received of which 28 expressed an opinion on the matter in question. 12 stated that prejudice and antagonism existed, and 16 (11 of which were from former applicants) stated that such attenders and applicants were welcomed.

only a very small proportion of scholars ever became Friends. In 1865, for instance, the Quaker Sunday School for children in Manchester had 205 members (who were compelled to attend meeting for worship). The Men's Adult School had 150 members, and the women's branch 40—a total of 395 individuals under Quaker influence in a single year.[1] Yet between 1861 and 1880, there were only 77 successful applicants for membership in the whole Monthly Meeting[2]—and many of these were not former scholars.

The number of applications which were rejected was fairly low—1 in 16, in Hardshaw East, between 1841 and 1919, and 1 in 12, in Norwich, between 1841 and 1900. It seems likely that unsuitable individuals were informally discouraged from applying at all. But it is remarkable that the Reports seldom state an adequate—or any—reason for rejecting applicants, though Monthly Meetings did not hesitate to transcribe every detail of a case of expulsion, the ins and outs of a bankruptcy, or any case of embezzlement. Manchester rejected six applicants between 1861 and 1880. Two of these had attended Quaker meetings since childhood. The length of attendance for the other four was 12 years, 14 years, 40 years, and 50 years. In two cases, no reason for rejection is given. Of the others, one lacks 'tenderness and openness of spirit', one lacks a clear knowledge of Quaker principles, one lacks a sense of spiritual need, and the fourth fails to attend mid-week meetings (at a time when they are falling into desuetude). Either there were more substantial reasons for rejection, which were given verbally, or prospective applicants were expected to attain a much higher standard than birthright members. In the absence of more conclusive evidence, it is impossible to know.

To sum up, admission to the Society of Friends was difficult to obtain in the nineteenth century. To some extent this reflects a concept of the Society as a Peculiar People, a religious élite, cut off from the rest of society, and suspicious of outsiders. It reflects the importance of bonds of kinship and friendship among Quakers, strengthening their reluctance to admit strangers. The problem was intensified when

---

[1] *The Friend* (1865), 81.
[2] Excluding children admitted on their parents' application.

the Quakers took up Sunday School work on a large scale, and for the first time large numbers of working-class men and women were brought into close contact with Quakerism. A predominantly middle-class church naturally had an ambivalent attitude to large numbers of working-class recruits.

The Expulsion of Members in Norwich and Manchester

As the study of recruitment sheds light on the relationship between Quakerism and the rest of society, so a study of expulsions tells us much about the relationship between the corporate church and its individual members. The difference between resignations and expulsions (called disownments) was often more apparent than real. Some members resigned to avoid the ignominy of expulsion, and frequently the same situation could lead to either a resignation or a disownment. Thus, if a Quaker joined another church, he was expected to resign his Quaker membership. If, as often happened, he neglected to do so, he was expelled.

The records of expulsions are much fuller than those of resignations. The reason for this is obvious. If an individual resigned, the responsibility was his own, not the Monthly Meeting's. But when a Meeting expelled one of its members, it was taking a grave step. Since the right of appeal existed, there was always the possibility that it would have to justify its action. So while every detail of an expulsion is carefully noted, the Meeting's minutes often contain only the bare mention of a resignation. Moreover, it is often difficult to discern the real reason for a resignation, even where a fuller account is given. Naturally enough, those resigning tended to explain their action in religious and doctrinal terms, as a conversion to the principles of another church, yet the evidence makes it clear that other factors often existed.

The general pattern of Quaker disownments and resignations presents a striking paradox. On the one hand, the rate of loss in this way was very low—apparently much lower than in the various branches of Methodism.[1] On the other

[1] cf. p. 117 above.

hand, Quakers expelled their members with a readiness which was shared by few denominations, not only for moral lapses, but for breaches of Quaker regulations.

It is not difficult to see why the rates of loss were low. A low recruitment rate and a low leakage rate tend to go together. The very fact that Quaker membership was difficult to acquire and easy to lose made it a privilege, not to be lightly discarded. Friends often complained that worldly and nominal members still clung to their membership.[1] For a birthright Quaker to leave the Society meant a painful breach with family traditions, relatives, and friends. Moreover, Quaker beliefs and modes of worship were so different from those of other denominations that to attend and join another church meant a radical change, whereas it was relatively easy for a Wesleyan, for instance, to feel at home among the Congregationalists, and members of the major nonconformist denominations often changed their allegiance readily, out of considerations of convenience, or through the appeal of a popular preacher.[2]

The readiness with which Quakers expelled their members showed that they viewed themselves as a spiritual élite. The ideal of an all-embracing church, where the tares and the wheat grew together, had no placed in their philosophy.

In practice, members were expelled for two kinds of transgression—either for offences such as immorality, dishonesty, or habitual drunkenness; or for acts which were condemned, not as morally culpable, but as breaches of Quaker regulations. Until 1860 all Quakers who married non-members were expelled. Marriage with a first cousin, and bankruptcy, were also occasions for expulsion, though here the severity with which the rule was applied varied, and practice became more liberal as the century progressed. Non-attendance of meetings was the cause of many expulsions, though again, practice varied. Quakers were not permitted to pay church rates or tithes, but there were ways of evading the prohibition, and it seldom, if ever, led to

---

[1] Fox, *The Society of Friends*, p. 46. cf. *The British Friend* (1880), 92.

[2] The factors which made Friends reluctant to leave the Society are discussed more fully on pp. 65–67 above.

expulsion.[1] Quaker pacifism did not become an important cause of loss of members until the First World War.[2]

Until 1860, more members were expelled for marrying a non-Quaker than for any other cause: it occasioned well over a third of all expulsions in one of the Meetings studied, and over half in the other. In both Meetings, the new regulation passed in 1860, permitting such marriages, led to a dramatic drop in the number of disownments. The significance of this prohibition, and the campaign which led to its change, are discussed elsewhere in this study.[3]

The expulsion of bankrupts was justified by the theory that bankruptcy was a form of dishonesty, since it defrauded creditors. Cynics sometimes claimed that the practice was rooted in the fear that those who failed would claim poor relief from the Meeting, but the main motivating force behind it was probably the desire to safeguard Friends' reputation for prudence and integrity in business. In theory, each case was judged on its own merits, and only culpable bankrupts were expelled. But many Quakers, throughout the nineteenth century, felt uneasy about the justice of the whole procedure. It sometimes happened that 'the parties concerned belong to the same Meeting', so that a man was judged by his creditors.[4] Even when such palpable injustice was excluded, all who failed in business had to submit to a detailed Quaker investigation into their business records and private expenditure. Often a man's misfortune became his crime; many were expelled for failures which were due to bad luck, fluctuations in trade, or simple errors of judgement. Even those who escaped disownment lost all their standing in the sect. Despite her Europe-wide reputation as a philanthropist, and the great wealth and standing of her family, Elizabeth Fry had difficulty in gaining admission for her son to a patrician Quaker school, because of her husband's business failure. As the century progressed the proportion of bankrupts who were disowned diminished

---

[1] Doncaster, *John Stephenson Rowntree*, p. 13.

[2] Quakers who joined the forces in the First World War were not disowned, but many resigned.

[3] cf. pp. 115, above, and pp. 146–7 and 158–9 below.

[4] Anne Reckitt's diary, quoted in Major Desmond Chapman-Huston, *Sir James Reckitt a Memoir* (London, 1927), p. 65.

steadily, as the injustice of the policy became more widely recognized.

Non-attendance of meetings was a common cause of disownment in Manchester Meeting. Very often, perhaps usually, the phrase refers, not to simple indifference, but to the practice of attending Church or Chapel. It seems that practice in regard to members who were lax in attending, but had not joined another church, varied considerably. At every period in the nineteenth century, there was a considerable residue of nominal members who were left undisturbed—John Wilhelm Rowntree claimed that they were so numerous that membership lists were a mockery.[1] *The Friend* had lamented in 1864 that 'Individuals are retained from year to year in nominal membership, who manifest no disposition to attend our meetings for worship, or to identify themselves with us in any way.'[2] But some of these were expelled: in 1848 a Quaker was disowned because 'on First Days, when in Manchester, he frequently went into the Country'[3]—surely the most understandable of all imaginable trespasses. Later in the century, the Meeting showed a greater interest in the factors behind non-attendance. In 1878, a committee which visited non-attenders reported: 'They found the religious circumstances of those whom they visited very various. In some cases family influence or distance from Meeting appeared to be the hindering cause in others there seemed to be a complete alienation from our Society & an identification with some other religious body.'[4] From time to time, in the last two decades of the nineteenth century, the Meeting purged its membership lists, trying to distinguish between those whose non-attendance was due to circumstances, and the indifferent. A report in 1900 stated:

The reasons given for non-attendance were many and varied. We have been impressed with the difficulties connected with the attendance at a city meeting house. Some Friends who live at a distance and come into town for business desire to be free from travelling on one day of the week; others look at the expense incurred in travelling, while the mothers of little children are often closely occupied with home duties.

[1] *Present Day Papers*, vol. v, (1902), p. 383.   [2] *The Friend* (1864), p. 210.
[3] *Hardshaw East MM Minutes*, vol. iv, p. 158.   [4] ibid., vol. vii, p. 440.

... Occasionally Friends whom we have visited have frankly told us that their interest in our Society has waned, some of them at times attending other places of worship.[1]

In 1910, the Meeting analysed 80 cases of irregular attendance—12 were due to difficulties of access, 30 to other engagements, such as Sunday School work, 33 to 'Temperament', and 5 to personal antagonisms.[2]

One of the most striking aspects of the pattern of expulsions is the steep decline in the number of grave offences, such as dishonesty, drunkenness and immorality. In Hardshaw East, the total number of these declined from 35 in 1841–60, to 15 in 1861–80, to 4 in the last two decades of the century. The smaller Meeting at Norwich, with its very low total number of disownments, does not show a similar pattern, but there are parallels elsewhere. Between 1801 and 1850, in Witham Monthly Meeting, in Essex, there were 80 disownments, which included 16 cases of immorality, 5 of drunkenness, 1 of felony, and 1 of assault.[3] Fifty-four Quakers were disowned for immorality in a London Meeting between 1803 and 1853.[4]

The total number of grave offences is always low in relation to the total number of members, but it appears to decline as the century progresses. This is certainly not due to the greater leniency of Monthly Meetings, which never extended to embezzlement or seduction. One is left with the paradox that as Quakers became less strict, and conformed more to the mores of society as a whole, they were guilty of fewer offences. Yet this does seem to be the case. In 1879, a well-known Friend told Yearly Meeting that when the present state of affairs was compared with the 'infidelity, and even immorality' formerly found among London Friends, there was cause for encouragement.[5] In the earlier part of the period, it is quite common for the records of local meetings to contain accounts of black sheep, scions of respectable Quaker families, whose careers nearly always end in emigration to Australia or America.

---

[1] *Hardshaw East MM Minutes*, vol. x, pp. 440–1.   [2] ibid., vol. xii, pp. 114–5.
[3] *Temp. Box* 93/4: f.21 (MS. in FHL).
[4] ibid. f.22 (Devonshire House Monthly Meeting). Similar data for other Meetings is given in *Temp. Box.* 93/3 and *Temp. Box.* 93/4, unnumbered sheet between ff.43 and 44.   [5] *The Friend* (1879), 156.

Such details appear in striking contrast to the Quakers' pious and respectable image. Where the evidence is so fragile, one can offer only a tentative explanation—that the extreme strictness of early Victorian Quakerism produced, on occasion, an extreme reaction. Some of the case histories in the Minute Books give this impression, and Quakers themselves sometimes claimed that this was so.

Many of the Quakers who were expelled, especially for financial failure or 'marriage out', were placed in a position of great difficulty. Frequently, their religious views were unchanged. They had either to make a considerable adjustment to the practices of another church, or swallow the humiliation of their expulsion and continue to attend Quaker meetings, or give up church attendance altogether. John Bright wrote in 1851 that 'Friends are peculiarly unfortunate if from any cause they leave the Society—their training in it has done much to make it almost impossible for them to join any other Body.'[1] The relationship between Friends and their expelled members depended on the nature of the offence, and on the attitude of the individual himself. But it is not surprising that many of those who were expelled, alienated from Friends but unable to join another church, fell into religious indifference. In 1872, a Monthly Meeting decided to visit all of its former members who had been disowned over the past thirty years—a total of 87, 47 of whom had been expelled for marrying non-Quakers. Only 24 could be traced. Of these, 13 never read the Bible, and 11 went to no place of worship.[2]

The whole process of expulsion was often bitterly resented by those who were its victims.[3] A Victorian Quaker was under minute surveillance by his co-religionists from the moment when his birth note was entered in the Minute Books until the time when his Meeting, with equal precision, recorded the details of his burial. Paradoxically, the way in which power was distributed among members, with all able

---

[1] John Bright to John Pease, 26 Dec. 1851, *Temp. Box* 24 (MS. in FHL).

[2] *The Friend* (1872), 124. The Meeting was Dorking, Horsham and Guildford. It is not clear whether the 13 who do not read the Bible include the 11 who attend no place of worship, but it seems probable.

[3] One of the strongest expressions of this is to be found in Sarah Greer's anonymously published *Quakerism: or the Story of My Life*.

to attend meetings, restricted their personal freedom. The behaviour of each was speedily known to all, and any delinquency was certain to be observed and dealt with.

Once a member was 'under dealing', he had no freedom of action. Refusal to submit to the Visitors' investigation was to incur certain expulsion, but the Minute Books contain several amusing—or pathetic—instances, where the delinquent's desire to avoid an interview was matched by the Visitors' zeal to effect it. In 1854, after the exercise of much ingenuity on both sides, a woman was expelled for, among other things, 'frustrating the endeavours of friends to extend to her that Christian Oversight which our Discipline enjoins'.[1] In 1846 an illuminating passage records the sequel to repeated attempts to interview a delinquent who had stated his unwillingness to be interviewed: 'we have recently been informed by one of the familey [sic] that he has absented himself from home and business to prevent our meeting with him.'[2]

The aspect which aroused most resentment was the way in which a Meeting discussed and decided a case in the absence of the accused. He had no opportunity to defend himself—he could only put his viewpoint to the Visitors, and hope that they would represent his views adequately.[3] Sometimes the resentment at an expulsion, especially for business failure, was so great that whole families resigned in protest.[4] A delinquent lost status in the Society, not only for himself but for his relatives as well. When Elizabeth Fry's daughter, Rachel, married a non-Quaker, her paramount, almost her only concern was whether 'the many things that may be said or thought respecting it may in the view of society cast a cloud over me & over my services'.[5]

The readiness with which they expelled their members, despite their declining numbers, shows the Quakers' essential disregard for numerical strength, their desire to preserve their public reputation at all costs, their view, often expressed

---

[1] *Hardshaw East MM Minutes,* vol. v, p. 119.

[2] ibid., vol. iv, pp. 31–3.

[3] Anne Reckitt's diary, quoted in Chapman-Huston, *Sir James Reckitt A Memoir,* pp. 65–6.   [4] ibid.

[5] *Journal,* 16 May 1822 (1820–22 vol., in Norfolk and Norwich Record Office). 'Society' means the Society of Friends.

explicitly, that Quakerism was not a creed for the average man, but for a spiritual élite. A study of expulsion procedures shows, with startling clarity, the power of the corporate church *vis-à-vis* its members. It is a paradox that a church whose polity was rooted in the ideal of freedom—the freedom of all to participate in decisions—exercised a degree of surveillance over the lives of its adherents for which there were few parallels on the Victorian denominational scene.[1]

The Resignation of Membership in Norwich and Manchester

Factors which produced conversions to Quakerism often led to resignations from it—the influence of a marriage partner, personal antagonisms, a change of residence, a restless desire for experiment and change. Just as many apparent cases of conversions were really technical changes of status, when a lifelong attender became a member, many resignations, like many cases of expulsion for non-attendance of meetings, were simply the formal recognition of a long-standing state of affairs. When a married couple resigned or were expelled, their children retained their Quaker membership. Very frequently, such children were brought up as members of another denomination, yet were technically Quakers. When they grew up, they resigned a membership which had no meaning for them, or alternatively were expelled.

Naturally enough, those who resigned their membership tended to explain their action in religious terms, as a positive preference for the teachings and practices of another church. The Visitors' Reports give us little real information about resignations, beyond the fact, which other sources confirm, that those who left the Society often became Anglicans. Those who left for religious reasons were usually influenced by doubts about the sacraments, especially baptism, or by dislike of the silence and haphazard ministry of Meetings for Worship. In these circumstances, the Anglican church, with its stress on the sacraments and its liturgy, had an obvious appeal. A man who resigned in Manchester in 1915

[1] The Brethren were perhaps the nearest to Friends, in this respect.

was speaking for generations of ex-Quakers when he said: 'I have felt that, on the whole, the spiritual help to be de- rived from ordered & liturgical services, together with the glorious musical praises to God, & the hearing of the Bible read through once or more times every year far & away excelled the deadening, chilling (to me) silence of most Friends Meetings for worship.'[1]

But the change from Quakerism to Anglicanism was often the product of social factors. It was a truism among Friends, as among Dissenters in general, that their wealthiest members tended to gravitate to the Established Church, and whole families were eventually lost in this way. Even when the disabilities of Quakers had disappeared, and a man could remain a Friend and aspire to parliament, and even a title, and send his sons to public school and university, the Establishment continued to exert its pull. A Congregation- alist put it succinctly, 'Beyond any doubt, what the Estab- lishment confers upon her sons is, in a word, *status*.'[2] The history of a branch of the Pease family illustrates the process. Joseph Pease, the first Quaker M.P., was a zealous Friend who became a minister in his later years. His son, Joseph Whitwell Pease, remained a Friend, but he became a baronet, moved from Darlington to a country-house, and was in most respects indistinguishable from the landed gentry among whom he lived. Joseph Whitwell's son, Alfred, also an M.P., wrote several books on hunting, and lived the life of a landed gentleman until the family fortunes collapsed in 1902. The outbreak of the First World War ended his allegiance to Quakerism, which had always been tenuous. Both his sons fought in the war, and the younger was killed in 1916. Other patrician Quaker families under- went a similar evolution.

Deciding whether to accept applications and resignations, and to expel delinquents, was among the most important duties of Monthly Meetings, a matter to which they devoted a great deal of time and thought. Yet it is a facet of Quaker history which hardly appears in most Quaker records—the

[1] Letter pasted into *Hardshaw East Guard Book* (1912–30 vol. n.p.), 7 Feb. 1915.
[2] E. Paxton Hood, *Thomas Binney: His Mind Life and Opinions, Doctrinal, Denominational, Devotional, and Practical* (London, 1874), p. 222.

periodicals, the reports of conferences, the scores of biographies. With a handful of eminent exceptions, converts seldom played a conspicuous part on the Victorian Quaker stage, and those who left the Society drop out of its records as abruptly and completely as if they had ceased to exist. Yet exits and entrances were full of significance, not only for the individuals directly affected, but cumulatively for the little church they joined or left. And although the inadequacies of the records make study of the subject difficult, it is impossible to understand Victorian Quakerism without considering why men joined it, and under what circumstances, and for what reasons they came to leave it.

V

THE GROWTH OF
'CONFORMITY TO THE WORLD'

A T the beginning of the nineteenth century, Thomas
Clarkson wrote his *Portraiture of Quakerism*, a book
based on nearly twenty years' intimate association
with Friends. It was essentially a detailed analysis of the
many ways in which they differed from the rest of society:
'The Quakers, as every-body knows, differ, more than even
many foreigners do, from their own countrymen. They adopt
a singular mode of language. Their domestic customs are
peculiar. . . . They are distinguished from all the other
islanders by their dress. The differences are great and
striking.'[1] If Clarkson could have observed the same church
a hundred years later, he would have found that the outward
signs which had distinguished Friends as a race apart, a
Peculiar People, had disappeared, and that they were out-
wardly much the same as other Englishmen of the day. They
had adopted that 'conformity to the World' against which
generations of Quaker prophets had warned. This chapter
discusses the 'peculiarities' of Friends, and how they came
to be abandoned.

The restrictions which Quakers imposed on themselves
in, for instance, the year of Victoria's accession, fall into
three categories. The first consisted of those formulae of
behaviour which were peculiar to Quakers, and which,
whatever their original purpose may have been, acted
essentially as barricades, separating Friends from the rest of
the society in which they lived. The second category
affected Friends' relationship with the state; it concerned a set of grievances of which some, but not all, were
common to other Dissenters. The third consisted of restrictions upon consumption, which limited the recreations
Friends were permitted to enjoy; many of these prohibi-

[1] Clarkson, *A Portraiture of Quakerism*, vol. i, pp. ii–iii.

tions can be found equally in other Victorian evangelical groups.

THE MACHINERY OF ISOLATION

Of those formulae of behaviour which hedged Friends from 'the World', the most important were their distinctive patterns of dress and speech, and their rule forbidding marriage with non-members. The details of Quaker costume varied from period to period. When Victoria came to the throne, a Quaker man was distinguished by his collarless coat and broad brimmed hat, a woman by her 'Quaker bonnet' and choice of plain unornamented clothes in dark colours. The most striking elements in Quaker speech were their use of the second person singular pronoun, which had otherwise become archaic, and their avoidance of the conventional names for weekdays and months, and of all honorary forms of address, such as 'Mister' or 'Sir'. The details of speech patterns differed from one region to another; 'thee' was often used instead of 'thou', and expressions such as 'thee is' and 'thee are' distressed grammatical purists.[1] 'First Day' and 'First Month' replaced 'Sunday' and 'January', and an orthodox Quaker letter began, 'Dear Friend, Robert Peel'. Men were forbidden to remove their hats as a sign of respect, even in contexts where the custom was otherwise invariable. No Quaker could wear mourning, or mark the graves of the dead in any way whatsoever. The regulations governing dress and speech were known collectively as 'plainness', or 'peculiarity', and will be referred to in this way, for brevity's sake, for the rest of this chapter.

The uses of peculiarity were obvious. It strengthened the Society's sense of identity enormously; Quakers recognized each other instantly, and so did the rest of English society. *Punch* always depicted John Bright in Quaker dress, though he abandoned it soon after entering public life. It was not optional—it was formally required in the official Quaker handbook, the *Book of Discipline*. Applicants for membership who did not adopt it were rejected, whatever the excellences

---

[1] *The Friends Monthly Magazine* (1830), 185–6; *The Essayist and Friends' Review* (1893), 29–30.

of their character.[1] But the actual practice of Friends varied considerably. The two poles of possible behaviour were known as 'gay Friends' and 'very plain Friends'. 'Gay Friends' were very unlikely to be chosen for office; they were subjected to continual hints and reproofs, both formally and informally. But they were not expelled, though most 'gay Friends' came to find their position uncomfortably ambiguous, and opted either for Anglicanism or for a stricter form of Quakerism. When Elizabeth Fry was a child, she and her brothers and sisters were 'a set of dashing young people, dressing in gay riding habits and scarlet boots'.[2] All became either plain Friends or Anglicans. Quakers who adopted the externals of their sect after a period of laxity, often did so after great spiritual struggles. It is recorded of an eighteenth-century member of the Lloyd family, who had been 'a young man of gaiety . . . a companion of Lords and Ladies', that when he was converted, and had his Quaker costume brought to him, 'he felt as if they had brought him his coffin.'[3] Because his dress was a symbol of the sincerity of a Quaker's religion, it tended to be a central preoccupation of Quaker families. 'Parents and Children anxious, thoughtful, fretting one another whether there is to be a collar or no collar, a bow or not a bow, a cap or not a cap. . . .'[4]

The prohibition of marriage with non-Quakers—or 'marriage out', in Quaker terminology—was often justified by the biblical injunction against being yoked with unbelievers. It reflected Friends' traditional concept of themselves as a Peculiar People. Later, when evangelicalism became dominant among them, they came to recognize the extent of their basic agreement with other evangelical Christians and to have doubts about the applicability of Paul's injunction. Meanwhile, until 1860, it was, as was noted in the last chapter, the most important cause of the decline of the Society. Yet while it reduced its membership, it immensely

---

[1] There is a striking case of this in *Hardshaw East MM Minutes*, vol. iv, pp. 302–3.

[2] *Harriet Martineau's Autobiography with Memorials by Maria Weston Chapman* (London, 1877), vol. i, p. 301.

[3] Samuel Lloyd, *The Lloyds of Birmingham with Some Account of the Founding of Lloyd's Bank* (Birmingham and London, 1907), pp. 102–3.

[4] Louisa Hoare to Joseph John Gurney, 18 July 1832 (*Gurney MSS.*, I, 282).

strengthened its internal cohesiveness. Generations
pulsory endogamy meant that Quaker families were
to each other by repeated links of almost unbelieval
plexity. But the ruling, like the one which expell
cousins who married each other, forced out members who
would otherwise have remained devout Quakers for a lifetime, and caused a painful crisis in many a Quaker family.
Joseph John Gurney wrote pathetically, when his son was
expelled for breaking the marriage rules, 'my heavens as well
as earth have been strangely shaken'.[1]

These various rules had certain elements in common.
They acted as a hedge between Friends and the rest of
society; they were not optional, and therefore could only be
abandoned by a corporate decision of the church. At the
same time, they did not affect Quakers *qua* citizens, and so
lay completely in their own hands; Friends did not need to
wait for an Act of Parliament.[2]

QUAKERS AND THE STATE

The next category of behaviour in which Quakers differed from other Englishmen concerned their relationship
with the state. Some of their problems were peculiar to
Friends, while others were common to Dissent in general.

When Victoria came to the throne, the worst grievances of
Dissent had already been remedied. Quakers had not shared
all these grievances—the legality of their marriages had
been recognized since 1753, but other Dissenters had to
wait until 1836 for the right to marry in their own chapels.
The fact that Dissenters could only be buried with Anglican
rites in parish churchyards, and were, on occasion, refused
such burial at all, was not a problem for Friends, who were
amply provided with their own burial grounds. Like other
Dissenters, they could not enter the older English universities, but few of them wished to. The rare Friend who
studied law or medicine went to London or Edinburgh. The

---

[1] *Journal*, 27 July 1846.
[2] When Quakers changed their marriage regulations in 1860 and 1872, the law
recognizing the legality of their marriages had to be changed, but the matter was
of no interest to any but Quakers, and the change was secured without difficulty.

burning grievance which Quakers and other nonconformists shared, and which was not remedied until 1868, was their liability to pay church rates. Like other nonconformists, Friends bitterly resented the demand to contribute to the expenses of the Established Church. Their resentment was probably exacerbated by the fact that the rate was not levied if a majority of parishioners decided against it, so that a succession of bitter local contests kept the matter continually before them. Quakers petitioned repeatedly against church rates, and on occasion took an active part in local contests. But their opposition went in one respect further than that of other nonconformists: they refused to pay them at all. Instead, they followed a policy of passive resistance, and permitted part of their goods to be confiscated.

Distraint in lieu of payment of church rates was a perpetual source of annoyance to Victorian Friends. Sometimes the goods taken were much more valuable than the rate demanded. Many, however, discovered a *modus vivendi*, either leaving the sum demanded in a conspicuous position, or buying back the goods taken for the exact sum which was required[1]—practices which, needless to say, were officially frowned upon.

The second sphere in which Quakers refused to conform to the demands of the state concerned tithe rent charge. As with church rates, Quakers were expected to refuse payment, and suffer distraint of their goods instead. But whereas all Victorian Quakers were agreed that church rates were an illegitimate demand which should be resisted, they were profoundly divided on the 'inextricable & interminable'[2] question of tithe rent charge.

The Quakers' refusal to pay tithes had its origins in their objections to a 'hireling ministry'. It is *a priori* surprising, that when their views on this did not change, they were deeply divided on the justice of tithe rent charge, for nearly forty years. The debate began when the Tithe Commutation

---

[1] *Quakerism: or the Story of My Life*, pp. 223–8. This source is often unreliable, but here the detailed account rings true, and is confirmed by complaints of Friends against the practice.

[2] Thomas Pease's description, quoted in J. S. Rowntree, *Account of 1854 YM*, p. 46.

Act of 1836 was passed. This did not affect the essential character of tithes, but converted them into a fixed charge on land, payable to the ecclesiastical owner of the tithes, or to a lay impropriator as the case might be. It would be wearisome to enter into the tortuous details of Yearly Meeting debates on the subject, and the arguments adduced for and against payment. Briefly, those who advocated payment stated that since the fact that land was subject to tithe was taken into account in determining its price (or the rent payable by a tenant), to withhold it was dishonest.[1] They claimed that they were not responsible for the use to which the money was put, any more than they were responsible for the way in which taxes paid in wartime were used. Those who opposed payment pointed out that the commutation of tithes had not changed their essential nature. They were still used to finance a church of which Friends disapproved. Alternatively, if paid to a layman, they were an unjust imposition, for nothing was given in return. Sentiment, respect for the sufferings of the past, and a fear of seeming to lower standards played a large part. In 1865, a Friend pointed out that the number of pounds lost the previous year through distraint in lieu of tithe was less than the number of Quaker men and women imprisoned under Charles II, often for refusing to pay ecclesiastical demands.[2]

In 1851, after years of procrastination, Yearly Meeting pronounced on the tithe question. The commutation of tithes had not altered their nature, but leniency was recommended to those who thought differently.[3] The equivocal verdict fanned controversy. It was generally agreed that where tithe rent charge was paid to a layman, it did not affect Friends' testimonies, and in 1855 payment to lay impropriators was permitted. But the tithe question proved to be one in which the practice of Friends moved more rapidly than their official policy. Continual complaints were made of the 'increasing disposition to pay tithes'.[4] It was pointed out that 'A law that is generally ignored, or infringed without reproof, is practically no law at all.'[5] In 1873 Yearly Meet-

---

[1] For a clear exposition, see *The Friend* (1866), 14ff.
[2] *The Friend* (1865), 121.   [3] ibid. (1851), 106; also (1856), 147.
[4] *The Friend* (1863), 95.   [5] *FQE* (1871), 291.

ing removed the relevant prohibition, bringing its formal ruling into accord with the practice of members.[1]

The remaining sphere in which the Quakers' beliefs affected their attitude as citizens, concerned their opposition to all war.[2] Yet the pacifism of Victorian Friends had much less practical impact on their lives than did their refusal to pay church rates. They were theoretically liable to be drawn for the militia, but the militia was so small that it was practically a volunteer force, and the ballot was seldom drawn. Friends played an active part in the successful agitation against the Militia Bills of 1846 and 1848. When a Militia Bill finally became law in 1852, it did not have the effect they had feared, because of the growth of volunteer rifle clubs. From 1860 on, the Militia Ballot Act was suspended annually. Occasionally a rate was levied to cover the expenses of the militia. Friends could not pay this, and had their goods distrained instead; but this was a bagatelle compared with church rates.

Whenever their peace testimony has impinged directly on the lives of Friends, there have always been some who have abandoned it. During the Napoleonic wars, a number of Quaker ship-owners were disowned for arming their ships, or chartering them to the government for military purposes.[3] No Friend publicly defended the Crimean War[4]—though some deplored the publicity which a Quaker peace mission to the Tsar attracted—but many held their views silently.

One frequently finds instances of Victorian Friends doubting the abstract rightness of Quaker pacifism, or of uncertainty about its implications. During the Chartist disturbances in the forties, Friends were divided about whether they could serve as special constables.[5] Some disregarded their scruples, and did so. Samuel Fothergill, writing soon after the Crimean War, stated that many active Quakers

---

[1] The Friend (1873), 223.

[2] The history of Quaker pacifism has two dimensions—(1) the history of the official attitudes of the church, and how it affected the conduct of members, and (2) the way in which some members tried to diffuse peace principles in society as a whole, by joining voluntary societies. The first aspect is discussed in this chapter, the second in that dealing with philanthropy.

[3] The Friend (1858), 121; Anne Ogden Boyce, Records of a Quaker Family: The Richardsons of Cleveland (London, 1889), pp. 118–19.

[4] The Friend (1900), 337.   [5] The Friend (1848), 87, 91, 132.

would justify war in private conversation. [1] In the same year—
1859—an anonymous letter to *The Friend* pointed out that
it was easy to be a pacifist in a secure and well-guarded state:
'It therefore becomes us, at the present day . . . to speak
with diffidence, as never having really had our principles put
to the test.'[2] Such a test could only come when the national
security of Britain was involved. When the crisis came, in
the First World War, not all Quakers could share the
optimism of the Victorian Friend who explained to *The
Times* about 'a Providence whose outstretched hand has so
long, so seriously, and so manifestly been exerted in order
to maintain Britain as the foremost instrument for diffusing
civilisation . . . throughout the world'.[3]

The Boer War, at the end of Victoria's reign, laid bare
the potential divisions among Friends on the peace issue.
The Quaker president of the Peace Society, Sir Joseph
Whitwell Pease, gave oblique support in public speeches to
the government's policy,[4] and another eminent Friend,
Thomas Hodgkin, wrote that Britain was the lamb and
Kruger the wolf, and that 'if all war is absolutely condemned
under all circumstances by the Sermon on the Mount,
Business . . . is equally condemned.'[5] The official reaction of
Friends was tardy and inadequate. Meeting for Sufferings
contented itself with reissuing a truncated version of an appeal
for peace which had been published during the Crimean
War;[6] John Wilhelm Rowntree mourned that it was 'so
feeble'.[7] It was not until Yearly Meeting met, some nine
months after the war began, that after much disapproving
comment on the divisions of Friends on the matter, a fuller
statement on the war appeared. *Reynold's Newspaper* commented acidly that 'the sect is no longer to be regarded as a
strenuous and united peace organization.'[8]

---

[1] Fothergill, *Essay on the Society of Friends*, p. 180.
[2] *The Friend* (1859), 208–9.
[3] William Tallack, in *The Times*, 19 Jan. 1894 (*FHL Press Cuttings*, BB 24). A
third of all men Friends of military age enlisted in the armed forces during the
First World War (statistics are given in *The Friend* (1922), 782).
[4] *Reynolds' Newspaper*, 18 Mar. 1900.
[5] Louise Creighton, *Life and Letters of Thomas Hodgkin* (London, 1917), pp.
240–1.
[6] *The Friend* (1900), 19.   [7] *Present Day Papers*, vol. iii, 1900, p. 115.
[8] *Reynold's Newspaper*, 18 Mar. 1900.

Quaker 'distinguishing views', then, affected their relationship to the state in three[1] main ways—their passive resistance to church rates, to tithes, and to military requirements of every kind. The first problem came to an end in 1868, when church rates ceased to be compulsory. The second was solved by a gradual change of attitude among Friends themselves. The third was of little practical significance to Victorian Friends. Most of them accepted pacifism unquestioningly, as part of the apparatus of an inherited creed. But the challenge of the Boer War showed how far they were from unanimity on the issue. The First World War was to drive many Quakers out of the Society altogether, as they recognized that pacifism was, for them, simply an inherited dogma, not a matter of personal conviction. For others, pacifism became a living faith under the challenge, and they became conscientious objectors. Some went to prison, and a few, even, came within appreciable distance of a firing-squad.

QUAKER PURITANISM

The third kind of limitation which Quakerism imposed on the lives of its members involved a large number of restrictions on consumption and on recreation. We can group them under a word which has been used in many different ways—puritanism. Quaker puritanism must be understood in two contexts. Many of the restrictions Quakers imposed on themselves were a living tradition, from the time of Fox. Yet we can find similar prohibitions among Anglican evangelicals, and in other nonconformist churches.

It is difficult to trace the outlines of early Victorian Quaker puritanism with any great precision. Many of the prohibitions which surrounded them were informal and could be disregarded without risking expulsion. Practice differed from family to family and from period to period.

In theory, Quakers were supposed to apply the principle of plainness to their houses as well as their persons. But practice varied widely. A true Quaker puritan wrote in 1817:

---

[1] Their refusal to swear oaths had little practical importance, since their right to affirm was amply provided for.

I have been almost ready to blush for some, at whose houses I have been, where pier-glasses with a profusion of gilt carving and ornament about them, delicately papered rooms with rich borders, damask table-cloths curiously worked and figures extremely fine, expensive cut glass, and gay carpets of many colours, are neither spared nor scrupled at.[1]

Rich Quakers such as Joseph John Gurney trod a delicate balance between their desire for a standard of living commensurate with their wealth, and their fear of offending their co-religionists. In 1844, Gurney confided to his diary, 'We are stepping a little forward in the way of clearing our delightful mansion, of those things which may be stumbling blocks to others—to wit, the looking glasses.'[2]

The orthodox Quaker home, in the early nineteenth century, contained no pictures or portraits. Clarkson noted that in the many Quaker homes he had visited, the only pictures he had ever seen were a painting of a slave ship, or of William Penn's treaty with the Indians, or a plan of Ackworth school.[3] Yet even here there were exceptions, such as the Quaker artist, Samuel Lucas of Hitchin (1805–1870)—a minor talent, yet with an authentic passion for his calling—'If I had been born without hands, I must none the less have painted with my feet.'[4]

All Quakers condemned gambling, throughout the nineteenth century. 'Vain sports', usually interpreted as field sports, were officially forbidden, but some young Friends loved hunting, and were not entirely without defenders: '"I have great sympathy", said Joseph Pease, "and I am not ashamed to own it, with those of my young Friends who justify themselves in pursuing field sports. I remember when I did likewise."'[5] Strict Quakers never went to the theatre—no great privation, when one considers the state of the Victorian stage. They did not learn music, and shunned singing and dancing, even in the family circle. One

[1] John Barclay, in a letter quoted in *Barclay Letters and Papers*, pp. 100ff. cf. *Journal of Thomas Shillitoe*, vol. i, p. 210.

[2] *Journal*, 8 July 1844.

[3] *A Portraiture of Quakerism*, vol. i, pp. 292–4.

[4] Reginald L. Hine, *Hitchin Worthies Four Centuries of English Life* (London, 1932), p. 221.

[5] At Yearly Meeting in 1856. *The Friend* (1856), 97.

finds occasional exceptions in wealthy families of 'gay Friends', but an early Victorian Quaker who showed an interest in the arts would have been regarded as an anomaly, both by his co-religionists and by outsiders. Imaginative literature was condemned. In 1818 William Allen counselled a young Frenchman to 'Be careful not to read books of an immoral tendency, as novels, romances, &c . . . they are poison to the mind.'[1] In 1857, an account of the virtues of a deceased minister mentioned novel reading as the chief vice of her unconverted youth.[2]

The spirit in which these various activities were condemned and the fidelity with which they were avoided varied considerably. Some, perhaps a majority, took it for granted that music, hunting and so on were 'unQuakerly'. They accepted the prohibitions unquestioningly, as a necessary part of their creed. Strenuous evangelicals, such as William Allen, objected to the arts essentially as trivial, a distraction from the great concerns of life, the soul's eternal salvation and 'the groans of suffering humanity'.[3] Puritanism was less a set of detailed regulations than an attitude of mind, crystallized in Allen's account of a visit to Killarney: 'We went round Turk Lake, the scenery of which is also delightful, but with all I did not feel in my element, and seemed to be doing no good; I had, indeed, a little serious conversation with the boatmen, and read them a paper on Temperance.'[4] For others, the tradition of Quaker puritanism involved them in painful conflict with their natural tastes. Francis Place described it vividly: 'I have known some who loved Paintings, and Engravings, and Statuary and Music, and Dancing and Singing,—and would if they had dared have gone to the play-houses. Two of these used occasionally and by stealth to indulge a little, and one who frequently came to me would sit for an hour or two to hear the children practice on the Piano Forte.'[5]

Puritanism was not, of course, peculiar to Friends. One can find exactly the same sentiments about novel reading,

---

[1] *Life of William Allen*, vol. i, p. 337.   [2] *The Friend* (1857), 99.
[3] For a discussion of the fine arts in these terms, see *The Friend* (1844), 275.
[4] *Life of William Allen*, vol. iii, p. 239.
[5] B.M.Add.MSS. 27823 (Place Papers), f.61.

the theatre, dancing, and gambling among the Congregationalists of the same period.[1] Almost every word of G. W. E. Russell's description of 'Aloofness from the world' among the evangelical Anglicans of his childhood[2] is equally applicable to Friends. Indeed, a rigorous code of behaviour was one of the outstanding characteristics of society, or more precisely, of middle-class society,[3] at the time. It is the best known face of 'Victorianism', a phase in the history of morals and manners as yet too little analysed and understood.[4]

Yet by the 1840s, the characteristic outlines of Quaker puritanism are already beginning to disappear. It is difficult to plot the transformation precisely, but Quaker debates of the 1860s and 1870s contain many jeremiads against the change, which was almost complete by the 1880s. To a large extent, it was a manifestation of that more general change taking place among Friends, from a Peculiar People to one denomination among others, which has already been discussed in other contexts in this book. Yet one finds parallels in other churches—the Congregationalists experienced much the same development.[5]

The change which took place among Friends was not, of course, uniform, since it depended, not on the church's corporate decision, but on a slow modification of the views of hundreds of individuals and families. One can only note landmarks on the way. One of the most rapid and complete changes concerned their attitude to music. When William Sturge (born in 1820) had his children taught music, he was one of the first Bristol Friends to do so, and was called to account by the Overseers.[6] By the 1870s, music was sufficiently acceptable for many Friends to advocate its teaching in Quaker boarding-schools. 'The Ackworth piano', once

---

[1] R. Tudur Jones, *Congregationalism in England 1662–1962* (London, 1962), p. 231.

[2] George W. E. Russell, *A Short History of the Evangelical Movement* (London, 1915), pp. 132–4.

[3] And of the occasional family of evangelical aristocrats, and of a minority of the working class, such as the Primitive Methodists.

[4] The best analysis is Maurice J. Quinlan, *Victorian Prelude. A History of English Manners 1700–1830* (New York, 1941).

[5] Jones, *Congregationalism in England*, pp. 290–2.

[6] Sturge, *Some Recollections*, p. 47.

acquired, became a symbol, over which much ink was spilt. The gradual acceptance of novel reading was sometimes attributed by Friends to the influence of *Uncle Tom's Cabin*[1] —undoubtedly an oversimplification. One letter to *The Friend* in 1869 used capital letters to express the writer's alarm at the growth of 'the practice of DANCING' among Friends.[2] Soon afterwards, another writer stated that the practice of playing cards in the family circle was a likely prelude to 'a life of dissipation'.[3] At the same time, the practice of wearing mourning,[4] and of attending the theatre,[5] grew among Friends. These changes did not take place without opposition. One evangelical told Yearly Meeting in 1880 that the effect of novel reading on the spirit was like that of alcohol on the body—meaning, of course, that both were equally bad.[6] The change taking place among Friends did not go unnoticed by contemporaries. In 1875, *The Westminster Review* declared, with some exaggeration:

Influential Quakers—'weighty Friends'—are the owners of the choicest paintings, which are exhibited to the world after the costliest entertainments, amidst the melody of operatic performances. In the hunting-field, in the ball-room, at the whist-table, some of the very best performers of our acquaintance are gentlemen who are to be found every Sunday sitting under their hats . . . waiting for divine illumination.[7]

But while the traditional forms of puritanism were disappearing, two new ones, alien to the Quakerism of an earlier day, took their place—teetotalism and sabbatarianism. Quakers played an important role in the temperance movement. Although teetotalism never became universal among them, it came close, in the later years of the nineteenth century, to an official creed. The changing attitude of Friends to teetotalism and their support of the various branches of the temperance movement are described in some detail later on.

Sabbatarianism had no place in earlier Quaker traditions. On the contrary, they strongly opposed the idea—'we know

---

[1] *The Monthly Record* (1873), 58.   [2] *The Friend* (1869), 282.
[3] *The Friend* (1869), pp. 292–3.   [4] ibid. (1879), 245.
[5] ibid. (1880), 143.   [6] ibid., p. 142.
[7] *The Westminster Review* (1875), 319.

no moral obligation . . . to keep the first day of the week more than any other.'[1] But in the Victorian period, they absorbed a considerable measure of sabbatarianism from other churches. An interesting confrontation of the old and the new Quaker viewpoints appeared in the short-lived *Friends' Monthly Magazine* in 1830, when one writer defended the sanctity of the Sabbath, and another affirmed the traditional Quaker viewpoint.[2] The sabbatarianism of Victorian Friends found expression in their personal behaviour, in their rigid exclusion of secular occupations on Sunday.[3] But it was modified by Quaker tradition; Quakers seldom shared the scruples of other Sunday School teachers about teaching writing on Sunday, for instance. Nor did they participate in the aggressive sabbatarianism which crusaded for restrictive legislation, as did the Anglican dominated Lord's Day Observance Society.[4] Joseph Sturge resigned from the board of directors of the London and Birmingham railway in protest against their policy of Sunday travel, but declared himself opposed to Sunday legislation.[5]

Most Friends would have agreed with him, partly out of respect for Quaker tradition, partly from dislike of the state's encroachment into the religious sphere. As *The Friend* observed in another connection, 'We are not of those who believe that public morality can be materially promoted by legislative enactments.'[6]

Changes in the forms of Quaker puritanism took place silently and invisibly. One scarcely ever finds the old and the new in articulate confrontation—simply the odd reference from Friends who deplore or welcome the process of change. In the sphere of those restrictions which affected Friends' relation to the state, the problem of church rates was ended

---

[1] Barclay, *Apology*, p. 250.

[2] *The Friends' Monthly Magazine* (1830), 612–13, and 663.

[3] cf. Hare, *The Gurneys of Earlham*, I, 90; *Life of William Allen*, III, 118; Janet Whitney, *Geraldine S. Cadbury 1865–1941, A Biography* (London, 1948), pp. 24–5; T. Edmund Harvey, 'Looking Back', *JFHS* (1953), 51.

[4] The best account of the sabbatarian movement in general, is George Mark Ellis, 'The Evangelicals and the Sunday Question 1830–1860: Organized Sabbatarianism as an Aspect of the Evangelical Movement' (Harvard Univ. Ph.D. thesis, 1951).

[5] Henry Richard, *Memoirs of Joseph Sturge* (London, 1864), pp. 250–5.

[6] *The Friend* (1850), 73.

by government action. There were many debates among Friends on tithe rent charge, but they hinged largely round technicalities. It is only those regulations which were discussed first in this chapter, concerning marriage, dress, and speech, which were changed by the corporate decision of the church. The debates which preceded these decisions crystallize the forces of change, and the forces of conservatism.

THE FORCES OF CONSERVATISM AND THE FORCES OF CHANGE

All the important decisions which had the effect of lessening the differences between Friends and the rest of English society were taken in the 1850s. The first step was in 1850, when the old prohibition against erecting gravestones was removed. Sentiment and convenience alike dictated the change. In a sense, the debates preceding the decision form a comic prelude to the more important discussions later in the decade. The lengthy and anxious attention which Yearly Meeting gave to questions such as whether gravestones should be perpendicular or horizontal was both amusing and pathetic. It is the classic instance of a preoccupation with trivialities which sometimes characterized Victorian Quakerism, which Lord Chief Justice Edward Fry described as producing 'a chasm in my feelings between myself and systematic Quakerism which I have never got over'.[1]

In 1856, a far more important change came up for discussion, when Yorkshire Quarterly Meeting introduced a proposal that Quakers should be allowed to marry non-members. The originating spirit behind the move was Joseph Rowntree, a York master grocer, whose son and namesake was to found the famous cocoa firm. The proposal had a stormy history. After an abortive attempt to reject it on procedural grounds, and a vehement debate, it was postponed to the following year—the classic Quaker solution to differences of opinion. In 1857, there was another impassioned discussion—'the most animated Quaker assembly I had witnessed'.[2] In 1858, the matter was debated again, and

[1] Quoted in Agnes Fry, *A Memoir of the Right Honourable Sir Edward Fry, G.C.B. etc. 1827–1918* (Oxford, 1921), p. 168.

[2] Joseph Rowntree, *Account of 1857 Yearly Meeting* (MS. in FHL), p. 41.

then referred to a conference composed of Quarterly Meeting representatives and members of Meeting for Sufferings. The conference reported in favour of the change, and the Yearly Meeting of 1859 decided accordingly. It came into effect when the parliamentary statute dealing with Quaker marriages had received the necessary emendation.

The proposal to make peculiarity of dress and speech optional[1] had a very similar history. It was introduced in 1857, not by a Quarterly Meeting, but by a private individual, the Birmingham corn factor, radical, and philanthropist, Joseph Sturge. Again attempts were made to avoid discussion on procedural grounds, but the day was carried by the popularity of the proposal, and the great prestige of Sturge himself, then nearing the end of a lifetime of remarkable charitable endeavour. But though the Meeting was prepared to discuss the proposal, it was not prepared to adopt it. It was referred to the conference dealing with the marriage question, which in due course reported in its favour. Sturge died a few days before the decisive Yearly Meeting of 1859 met—the advocates of change did not scruple to invoke 'his sweet spirit'.[2] A large majority agreed with the proposal, but there were sufficient dissentients to make its adoption difficult. A way out was found,[3] and peculiarity of dress and speech finally became optional in 1860.

Other changes were also debated in these years. Some dealt with questions of organization, such as the composition of Meeting for Sufferings, or the administration of poor relief. Some were rejected or left undecided—the proposals to allow first cousin marriages, and to permit the payment of tithe rent charge and the use of unstamped receipts.[4] But none of the other questions discussed were as pregnant with

[1] Technically, it was a proposal to abolish the second part of the Fourth Query concerning 'plainness of speech, behaviour and apparel'.

[2] J. S. Rowntree, *Account of 1859 Yearly Meeting* (MS. in FHL), p. 77.

[3] A committee had been appointed to discuss the general revision of the Queries. The question of the Fourth Query was left to this committee, which duly reported in favour of change.

[4] The law requiring receipts to be stamped was obsolete and disregarded. Friends insisted on the use of the stamp, to avoid 'defrauding the king of his customs, duties and excise'. The ruling led Quaker businessmen into many practical difficulties.

consequences for Quaker history as the debates on marriage with non-Quakers, and on peculiarity. They crystallize the attitudes underlying two very different periods of Quakerism. The argument used, when disentangled from a mass of repetition, technicalities, and Quaker rhetoric, make articulate the conscious theory supporting two contrasting social attitudes.[1]

The debates reveal an intellectual difficulty which was endemic in Quakerism. Where is the ultimate authority in religious matters to be found? Conservatives appealed to Quaker tradition, and to the writings of the early Friends. 'B. Braithwaite . . . hesitated in true conservative spirit to change what was 100 years old.'[2] But many evangelicals, such as the temperance leader Samuel Bowley, took a different view: 'the fact of early friends or of any persons having suffered for principles was no test of their truth.'[3] They claimed that the only authority lay in scripture, and that any regulation which was not clearly in accord with the letter or spirit of scripture was *ipso facto* invalid. Since the Yearly Meetings of the fifties were dominated by evangelicals, the debate on whether to permit first cousin marriages hinged largely round the precedent of the daughters of Zelophedad.[4] Since scriptural precepts were binding on all Christians, whether Quakers or not, and precepts which were not scriptural were invalid, this theory had the implication of weakening the authority of the church over its members. In fact, appeals for liberty were made repeatedly during the discussions of these years. In 1859, a speaker made incidental use of the expression 'a corporate conscience',[5] and sparked off a significant exchange on the liberty of the church member, and its relationship to the authority of the church. The Clerk, in a statement which won general acceptance, opted for the individualist viewpoint: 'each

---

[1] These debates are briefly discussed, in a more generalized and theoretical context, in my article 'From Sect to Denomination in English Quakerism', *The British Journal of Sociology*, 1964, p. 207, reprinted in revised form in *Patterns of Sectarianism* (ed. B. R. Wilson), London, 1967.

[2] William Rowntree, *Account of 1859 Yearly Meeting* (MS. in FHL), n.p.

[3] Joseph Rowntree, *Account of 1858 Yearly Meeting* (MS. in FHL), p. 41.

[4] *Numbers*, 36:11–12. The other precedents were the marriages of Jacob (*Genesis* 29) and the daughters of Eleazar (1 *Chronicles* 23:22).

[5] J. S. Rowntree, *Account of 1859 Yearly Meeting*, p. 89.

member is primarily responsible to Christ and not to the Church.'[1]

Many of those who opposed change were evangelicals, but all quietists were also, in this context, conservative. Their reverence for the teachings of the early Friends and their distrust of change made their standpoint plain. But had the conservative viewpoint depended on the support of the small group of quietists, it would have been very quickly defeated. The most influential opponents of change were evangelicals, who stated their case in other terms.

The opponents of change enjoyed an important dialectic advantage. They were defending the more strict and difficult position, so it was easy to represent their opponents as lowerers of standards, shrinking from the rigours of true religion. They repeatedly used the biblical metaphor of the broad and the narrow way, and profited by a semantic confusion, in the various meanings of the term 'the World'. 'The World' could either refer objectively to society in general, or be used in the pejorative—and biblical-sense, as in 'the World, the Flesh and the Devil'.

We find the expression in the debates of these years repeatedly: 'Some were apprehensive that the Society of Frds, would become assimilated more & more to other denominations, and even to the World.'[2] Sometimes the opponents of change denounced the proposals in almost apocalyptical terms: 'he in solemn tone was willing to leave the judgment with God . . . those on the other side would perhaps at no distant period be scattered and swept away.'[3] One of the difficulties was that while plain dress was required of Friends, all zealous members did in fact wear it, so that it was easy to represent peculiarity as the cause, rather than the consequence, of religious fervour.

One of the strongest forces against change was sentiment, the reluctance of middle-aged Friends to abandon a manner of speech and dress which they and their ancestors had adhered to for a life-time. Since plainness was the most

---

[1] J. S. Rowntree, *Account of 1859 Yearly Meeting*, p. 89.
[2] John S. Rowntree, *Account of 1862 Yearly Meeting*, p. 23.
[3] William Rowntree, *Account of 1859 Yearly Meeting*, n.p.

obvious distinguishing sign of a Quaker, many felt that to abandon it was to threaten the separate identity of the society. 'If the costume went he tho't or feared the Sty. would gradually be merged in the World at large.'[1]

It was clear that the abandonment of peculiarity and of the prohibition on intermarriage would bring Quakerism much closer to other denominations. Many feared this result, clinging to the ideal of a Peculiar People. Others, especially evangelicals, rejoiced at the prospect. As Samuel Bowley put it, since 'we differed from other Xtian bodies containing good & spiritually minded men, he thought we should see how far we could unite with these not how far we could differ'.[2] A Quaker's view of marriage with non-members obviously depended on whether he viewed other Christians as 'will worshippers', or as evangelical brethren, following a slightly different path to God.

The most commonly used and effective argument against change, applicable especially to debates on peculiarity, was a utilitarian one, summed up in the repeated use of the metaphor of a hedge. Peculiarity, by making the religion of a Friend immediately apparent, protected him from many temptations. The answer to this, however, was obvious: 'A hedge, if it keeps in those that are on one side, will as effectually keep out those who are at the other.'[3]

It was generally accepted that the original reasons behind the peculiarities and the marriage rules had lost their validity. Few claimed that marriage with a non-Quaker (which necessarily took place outside the Meeting House) implied a recognition of a 'hireling ministry', that 'you' was a flattering form of address, or that 'Wednesday' implied homage to pagan gods. It was recognized that the distinctive dress of a Quaker—which originated in a refusal to follow the dictates of fashion—had evolved into a uniform, which did not exemplify the virtue of simplicity any more than did the uniform of an ecclesiastic or a policeman. Therefore, conservatives defended their case in terms of utility, tradition, or asceticism.

[1] J. S. Rowntree, *Account of 1859 Yearly Meeting*, p. 72.
[2] Joseph Rowntree, *Account of 1858 Yearly Meeting*, p. 42.
[3] Fothergill, *Essay on the Society of Friends*, p. 159.

The advocates of change were motivated primarily by their anxiety at the declining condition of the Society. The rule which expelled every Quaker who 'married out' led to a fatal drain of otherwise unexceptionable members. And it affected membership trends in other ways, since many, forced to choose their marriage partner from within a restricted circle, did not marry at all.[1] Joseph Rowntree assembled a mass of statistical evidence on the relationship between Quaker marriage regulations and the acknowledged decline in membership[2]—a strikingly original approach, in the Quaker context of the time. The opponents of change did not deny that membership was declining; they replied either that this did not matter, since Friends were 'a chosen remnant', or that it was due, not to the strictness of the rules which bound Friends, but to the laxity with which they were obeyed: 'Our numerical decrease! Whence does it arise? From unfaithfulness; from forsaking the Fountain of living water.'[3]

Plainness of speech and dress had a less obvious impact on membership trends, but those who attacked it did so for similar reasons. They claimed that the peculiarities often alienated young Friends from the Society. They discouraged prospective recruits from applying for membership: 'many persons outside tho't the costume an integral part of Quakerism, regarded it as absurd & asked no further as to our principles.'[4] To the advocates of change, peculiarity of dress and speech were obsolete survivals retained in unthinking conservatism, in blatant contradiction with the ancient Quaker emphasis on the non-necessity of outward forms in religion. They sometimes referred to the Pharisees' tithes of mint and cummin, as a parallel.

The advocates of change were, of course, victorious. What were the implications of their victory for Quakerism?

---

[1] Fothergill, *An Essay on the Society of Friends*, p. 172; Rowntree, *Quakerism Past and Present*, pp. 157–8.

[2] J. R[owntree], *Statements connected with the Marriage Regulations of the Society of Friends* (Privately printed, 1858). The original data he collected survives in manuscript in FHL (*Temp. Box* 93/4).

[3] *The British Friend* (1854), 162.

[4] J. S. Rowntree, *Account of 1859 Yearly Meeting*, pp. 72–3.

THE CONSEQUENCES OF CHANGE

As both parties had foretold, the changes of the fifties brought Quakerism much closer to other denominations. They dovetailed with other earlier and later changes in Quakerism which had the same effect—the adoption of evangelical theology, the extension of Quaker Sunday Schools, their entry into the field first of foreign and then of Home Missions, their increasing role in political life. By the eighties, half of all Friends who married were marrying non-Quakers.[1] Quakerism inevitably became less of an exclusive family network. Of course a legislative change did not immediately alter the habits, especially the speech habits, of a lifetime, but plain dress and speech were gradually eroded in the years after 1860. S. G. Hobson recalled his parents' adoption of modern dress, in the eighties, as an event which 'shook the family to its depths', adding that they continued to use the traditional Quaker language until they died.[2] Yet all such changes were relative. The importance of kinship, the sense of isolation from 'the World', though modified, continued to exist. To take an illustration from the sphere of language, the Quakers officially abandoned their distinctive patterns of speech. Yet they continued to use many words and phrases peculiar to Friends and scarcely intelligible to others. Two letters to *The Friend* in 1877 complained of this: that Friends spread concerns, wound up concerns, were introduced into deep baptism, gathered up the sense of the meeting, were largely engaged, and so on.[3] Until the end of the Victorian period and beyond, they continued to employ a private language, yet were scarcely aware of the fact.

In the later Victorian period, Friends sometimes feared that by abandoning their outward distinguishing marks they had endangered their sense of corporate identity. They felt that they had moved so close to other denominations that they had little which was distinctively Quaker left. John Wilhelm Rowntree was to make this point repeatedly, as part of his appeal for the abandonment of evangelicalism and the return to the older more distinctively Quaker the-

[1] *The Friend* (1885), 145.
[2] S. G. Hobson, *Pilgrim to the Left, Memoirs of a Modern Revolutionist* (London, 1938), p. 17.   [3] *The Friend* (1877), 302-3.

ology of the Light Within. 'A small body like the Society of Friends, which has with almost dramatic suddenness broken down its social barriers and mingled with the world after a century of aloofness, must have very clear convictions if it is not to lose its identity.'[1] Such Friends, writing at the end of the century, recognized that the Society had passed through a period of revolutionary change. Their attitude to it was often ambivalent—self-congratulation at escape from trammels which they regarded as unnecessary, with a certain admixture of nostalgia for the self-sufficiency and internal cohesion of the Quakerism of an earlier time.

[1] *Present Day Papers* (Sept. 1899), 20.

PART TWO

The Quakers and Society

VI

THE ECONOMIC AND DEMOGRAPHIC STRUCTURE OF QUAKERISM

THE detailed study of demography or of economic history lies outside the usual scope of the historian of religious movements. Usually, religious historians rely on the generalizations made by contemporaries, outside or within the movement, about its social and economic structure. When such generalizations are numerous and consistent, they are unlikely to be wrong, and all the available evidence points to the overwhelmingly middle-class structure of Dissent in general, and of Quakerism in particular. As *The Eclectic Review* stated in 1857, 'The various dissenting denominations derive their chief strength from the trading and manufacturing classes.'[1] Quakers constantly made such generalizations about themselves. *The Friend* was voicing a truism in 1851 when it stated, 'Belonging as we do, almost entirely to the middle class—nearly all engaged in business of some kind—all well educated.'[2] In 1863 the total annual income of English Friends was estimated at between two and three million pounds:[3] that is, £182 for every Quaker man, woman and child in London Yearly Meeting,[4] at a time when the average wage was

[1] *The Eclectic Review* (1857), part ii, p. 250.
[2] *The Friend* (1851), 32.   [3] ibid. (1863), 208.
[4] i.e. taking two and a half million as the estimate. Income was not, of course, thus equally distributed.

approximately £50 per annum. Benevolence and prosperity were the two main ingredients in the popular image of a Quaker: 'In the eyes of half our countrymen of the present day, the first characteristic suggested by the name Quaker, is *Philanthropist*—a good-hearted, placid, rich man, whose profession is to do good.'[1]

DEMOGRAPHIC CHARACTERISTICS

Quakers considered that their economic and social composition was so self-evident that it needed little investigation. They were, however, deeply interested in their demographic trends and their relationship to those of society as a whole, and from time to time Victorian Friends of an actuarial cast of mind analysed the available statistics with much care and acumen. Both the analyses and the data they are based on must be studied with discrimination—there are a number of built-in biases in Quaker 'vital statistics'[2]—but a few broad conclusions emerge with clarity. Women outnumbered men, to a greater extent than in the general population. Friends attributed the disparity to the fact that men emigrated and resigned their membership more often, and were more frequently expelled.[3] The way in which Quaker statistics of births, marriages and deaths were compiled makes them difficult to use in a demographic analysis, but it appears that throughout the nineteenth century, the death rate outstripped the birth rate. This in its turn was due to the fact that Friends married less frequently, and later, than the general population—'our marriages are rather late

---

[1] Thomas Hancock, *The Peculium; an Endeavour to throw light on some of the Causes of the Decline of the Society of Friends, especially in regard to its original claim of being the Peculiar People of God* (London, 1859), p. 55.

[2] Studies of the age structure of the Quaker population at death were based on the *Annual Monitor*, which appeared annually, and attempted to record all Quaker deaths—but the deaths of infants were often omitted. Quaker marriage statistics apply only to marriages between two Quakers, and leave out the many marriages with non-Quakers. Birth statistics omit the progeny of such marriages. Analyses of the age structure of the Society were also affected by the practice of admitting children as minors.

[3] John Thurnam, *Observations and Essays on the Statistics of Insanity* (London, 1845), Appendix II, 'Contributions to the Statistics of the Society of Friends', pp. xix–xx.

and prudent, our families not large.'[1] In the first half of the century, the low incidence of marriage was due as much as anything to the regulation forbidding marriage with non-Quakers. Later, the tendency to defer marriage or to avoid it altogether was largely a manifestation of the middle-class virtue of prudence.[2] Quaker writers repeatedly deplored this phenomenon, and it was even mentioned in the Yearly Meeting Epistle for 1869.

The high life-expectancy of Friends reflected their predominantly middle-class composition. In the 1850s, the average age at death among Friends was over fifty-three[3]— nearly double that of the general population.[4] In 1869, it was fifty-five.[5] By 1878, it had risen again slightly, to 55.5 —while that of the general population was thirty-three.[6] Clearly, Friends' longevity reflected their high standard of living—though a writer in *The Alliance News*, mindful of the spread of temperance views among them, preferred to attribute it to teetotalism.[7]

It was sometimes claimed that generations of inbreeding had had an adverse effect on Friends—in particular, that the incidence of insanity among them was unusually high.[8] The relatively high number of Quakers at the York Retreat, an asylum run by and for Friends, partly reflects their outstanding record in the treatment of the insane, so that Quaker families were prepared to commit relatives who would in other circumstances have been kept at home. But even when this circumstance is taken into account, Friends usually admitted the high insanity rate among their members, and attributed it to generations of intermarriage.

GEOGRAPHIC DISTRIBUTION

If one studies the distribution of Quakerism as it is revealed in the 1851 religious census, and in the census of

[1] J. W. Graham in *The Spectator*, 16 June 1900 (FHL *Press Cuttings*, BB 43).
[2] cf. J. A. Banks, *Prosperity and Parenthood* (London, 1954). cf. *The Friend* (1871), 241; *The British Friend* (1895), 278.
[3] *The Friend* (1858), 12 and (1859), 23.   [4] ibid. (1858), 12.
[5] ibid. (1869), 38.   [6] ibid. (1878), 185.   [7] Reprinted ibid. (1885), 44.
[8] *The Globe*, 22 Nov. 1844 (article summarized in *The Friend* (1845), 28); Thurnam, *op. cit.*, Essay III, 'On the Liability to Insanity in the Society of Friends' pp. 169ff.; *The Friend* (1874), 180 and (1883) pp. 149 and 201.

attendance which Friends themselves conducted in 1904, it is clear that it changed relatively little in the intervening years, though, of course, individual meetings expanded or declined. The various meetings in and around London formed the largest single concentration. Birmingham, and, in 1851, Bristol, were the next most important centres south of the Mersey, but the greatest concentration of large Quaker meetings was to be found in the big industrial cities of Lancashire and the West Riding of Yorkshire. Quakerism was almost entirely absent from Wales and Monmouthshire. In 1851 and in 1904, most Friends were members of large meetings in big industrial cities, though Quakerism was also strongly entrenched, through historical circumstances, in a few smaller cities and towns such as Norwich, Banbury, and Kendal.

It is clear, however, that a map of the distribution of Quaker mirrors, to a large extent, that of the general population. The concentration in London reflected its enormous size, rather than any special proclivity of Friends for life in the metropolis. In order to find where Friends were most strongly concentrated, it was necessary to consider the proportion they formed of the total population in different areas. The map on page 170 (Fig. 6) shows what proportion the Quakers formed of the total population in the various counties of England and Wales in 1851.[1]

When considered in this way, a rather different picture emerges. Quakers were relatively numerous throughout the North of England—especially in the North and West Ridings of Yorkshire, and in Cumberland and Westmorland. Further south, there was another area of strong concentration in Gloucestershire, Oxfordshire, and Warwickshire—this reflected the presence of the large meetings at Bristol and Birmingham, and the smaller but still important meetings at Banbury, Oxford, Chipping Norton, Cirencester,

---

[1] The attendance at morning meeting for worship and the total population of each county form the basis of this map. Attendance at the morning meeting for worship is the best available guide—many Friends neglected to attend the evening meeting. The distribution of meeting houses and the provision of seating accommodation is of little value as a guide. Many meeting houses in country areas were deserted, or almost empty.

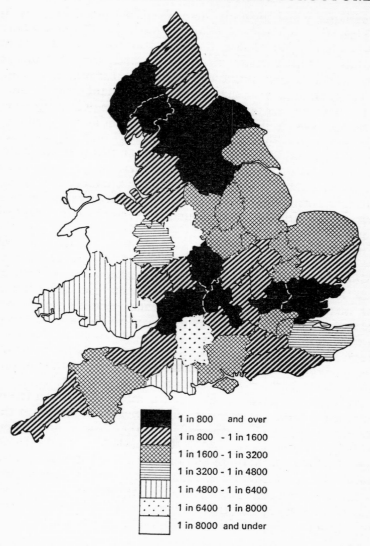

1 in 800   and over

1 in 800   - 1 in 1600

1 in 1600 - 1 in 3200

1 in 3200 - 1 in 4800

1 in 4800 - 1 in 6400

1 in 6400   1 in 8000

1 in 8000 and under

Fig. 6   The distribution of the Society of Friends in 1851 proportionate to the general population

Axbridge, and Wells, and several Quaker boarding-schools. The remaining area of relatively great Quaker concentration was to be found in two of the Home Counties, Essex, and

Hertfordshire. With the exception of Wales and Monmouthshire, where there were hardly any Friends at all, they were relatively evenly distributed. There did not seem to be any very obvious reason for many regional variations—why there were so few Quakers in Kent, for instance, in contradistinction to the rest of the Home Counties. The most important difference seems to be less between one county and another than between urban and rural areas—nearly all the Quakers in Hampshire lived in Southampton, nearly all the Warwickshire Quakers in Birmingham, and so on. The absence of Quakers in Dorset reflects as much as anything the county's rural character.

ECONOMIC AND SOCIAL COMPOSITION

If we accept the generalizations Friends made about themselves, they were predominantly middle-class, and mainly engaged in trade. There is no reason to doubt their own evaluation, but it seemed desirable to do further research into the matter for two reasons. First, the terms Quakers used, such as 'in trade' are inevitably vague and imprecise. Secondly, there is quantifiable evidence on which to verify their claims.

The only systematic evidence, on a national scale, about the social and economic composition of the Society—apart from the oblique evidence provided by demographic data—is to be found in a set of large manuscript volumes in Friends House: the Digests of Births, Marriages, and Deaths. They usually list the occupation of the individual concerned (of the father, in the case of births). For this analysis, records of deaths have been used,[1] for death, unlike marriage and parenthood, is universal, and the peculiarities of Quaker membership rules make their marriage and birth records very incomplete.

[1] These records include non-members who were buried in the Quaker way (marked N.M. in the Digests). Since local meetings exercised their discretion in allowing non-members burial in Quaker graveyards, and there was nothing in a Quaker burial to attract a non-Quaker, it is likely that these were attenders of long standing, Quakers in all but name, and have been included in this analysis accordingly. They are fairly numerous in 1840–1 and probably consisted mainly of Quakers who had been disowned for marrying out but continued to attend. Later they became much fewer.

It is generally agreed that occupation is the most important single determinant of social class.[1] Yet the analysis of occupational data is beset with difficulties. In the absence of other information, the bare statement of an individual's occupation often tells us little about his social and economic position. As the Registrar-General complained in 1911, 'The farmer for instance may farm 10 acres or 1,000, and the draper or iron-puddler may be the head of a large establishment or his lowest paid assistant or labourer.'[2]

In addition to this problem, to which there is no very obvious solution, the question of the organizing principle to be used in assigning occupations to social classes presents many difficulties. The Registrar-General did not begin to classify occupations into social classes until 1911. When he did so, the results were unsatisfactory, since some of the categories used were estimates of social class, while others were determined by the nature of the industry.[3] Moreover too little distinction was made between the levels of employment in any given industry. More recent classifications, such as that made by Glass and his collaborators, have the disadvantage that some nineteenth-century occupations have become obsolete, while the social prestige of others has changed. Thus the clerk has fallen from Class I in the 1911 Census, to Class III in later Censuses, to Class V in the seven-fold Glass classification. In the face of these difficulties, the system which has been adopted is that used by Charlotte Erickson in her study of steel and hosiery manufacturers[4]— to use the simplified four-fold classification of the Glass study, and to print a detailed breakdown of the relevant occupations in an Appendix.

An analysis of the occupations of the Quakers who died in 1840 and 1841, in 1870 and 1871, and in 1900 and 1901, strikingly confirms the Quakers' continuing image of themselves as a predominantly middle-class body. At each period, the members of Class I—the 'gentlemen', bankers, mer-

---

[1] *Social Mobility in Britain*, ed. D. V. Glass (London, 1954), pp. 5–6 and 30.

[2] *Seventy-Fourth Annual Report of the Registrar-General of Births, Deaths, and Marriages in England and Wales*, 1911, p. xli.

[3] ibid. xl–xli and Table 28A, pp. 73–87.

[4] Charlotte Erickson, *British Industrialists: Steel and Hosiery 1850–1950* (Cambridge, 1959), pp. 230–2.

chants, farmers, and professional men—form roughly half of the total. Class II—retailers, independent craftsmen, foremen and clerks—is always the second largest. The relative and absolute position of Class III remains stable throughout the period. It consists largely of a great variety of skilled or semi-skilled workers, some of whom were doubtless self-employed and so belong in fact to Social Class II. Most of these were not factory workers, but worked at traditional skilled crafts in small workshops. Some belonged to the so-called labour aristocracy. This group has not been subdivided further, because of the inadequacy of the data, and the difficulty of this kind of classification.[1] Class IV consists of a small but not negligible group of unskilled labourers. They form slightly more than one-fourteenth of the total in 1840–1, rather less than one-thirteenth in 1900–1.

The social structure of Quakerism, as revealed in this analysis, is precisely opposite to that of the general population. 'The labouring classes' were frequently estimated at 70 per cent of the total population in Victorian England.[2] In the Society of Friends, the largest single group was Class I. But although the analysis confirms the generalizations made by Friends themselves, it reveals the existence of Quaker cloggers, cordwainers, dry-wallers, stockingers, bricklayers, and agricultural labourers, whose existence is scarcely hinted at in any other form of Quaker record. They lacked the leisure and means to attend Quaker meetings, especially the more important ones, held at a distance. They did not share the enthusiasm of the typical Victorian middle-class Friend for appearing in print. Their theological opinions, if they had any, are forgotten. They were necessarily the recipients rather than the distributors of the philanthropists' bounty. And if a history of Quakerism becomes, inevitably, a history of middle-class Quakerism, this simply reflects a problem common to all social histories —the difficulty of resurrecting the largely unrecorded lives of the inarticulate poor.

[1] cf. E. J. Hobsbawn, *Labouring Men* (London, 1964), Chap. 15.
[2] B. Seebohm Rowntree, *Poverty A Study of Town Life*, 2nd ed. (London, 1902), p. 26n.1.

The fact that Classes III and IV were just as strong in 1840–1 as they were in 1900, after half a century of Adult School work, suggests a question. If there was always a stratum of Friends 'in humble life', why was it so often stated, as a barrier to the admission of working-class Adult School converts, that Friends formed a socially homogeneous middle-class group? The explanation seems fairly clear. On the one hand, members of Classes III and IV were always in a minority. On the other, Friends naturally tended to identify the Society with its more prosperous and so more active members. This gulf between rich and poor Friends—of which there is a great deal of evidence[1]—simply means that the unifying effect of belonging to a small and exclusive church was not sufficient to counteract the social divisions of the day. A character in a Victorian novel recognized the same class-structure in a Congregationalist chapel: 'all in the way of business, except just the poor folks, as is all very well in their place, and never interferes with nothing, and don't count'.[2]

The analysis of the occupations listed in records of deaths sheds some light on the changing occupational structure of the group. Two generalizations were made repeatedly by contemporary Quakers: that there was a widespread tendency among them to abandon agriculture, and that, towards the end of the century, fewer engaged in retail trade and more were to be found in the professions. The complaint that they were being forced out of agriculture by the tithes problem was endemic among eighteenth- and nineteenth-century Friends. The advocates of the payment of tithe rent charge liked to paint idyllic pictures of the spiritual blessings of rural life, but the claim that an ever diminishing number of Friends were farmers was often made outside the context of controversy,[3] and is repeated by modern historians.[4] Yet

---

[1] Logan Pearsall Smith, *Unforgotten Years*, pp. 118–19; *The Friends Monthly Magazine* (1831), 379 and 511; *The Friend* (1864), 44.

[2] Mrs. Oliphant, *Salem Chapel* (New Edition, Blackwoods, Edinburgh and London, n.d.), p. 10.

[3] e.g. in *The Friend* (1847), 15–16 and (1866), 105.

[4] Arthur Raistrick, *Quakers in Science and Industry* (London, 1950), pp. 53–4 and Paul H. Emden, *Quakers in Commerce: A Record of Business Achievement* (London, 1939), p. 14.

the analysis of deaths records shows the continuing strength of agriculture. Farmers formed the largest single group in Class I in 1840–1, and, in the two later periods, only the amorphous category of 'gentlemen' is larger. This picture is confirmed by a study of a predominantly rural area, such as Banbury Monthly Meeting.[1] Far more Friends were engaged in trade than in agriculture. Probably more would have engaged in agriculture had it not been for the continual irritant of tithes. But although Quakerism was predominantly urban, there was evidently a larger stratum of Quaker farmers than the generalizations of Friends themselves suggest.

The second generalization which was often made was that the number of retail traders was declining, and that an increasing number of Quakers was to be found in the professions. A correspondent in *The Friend* claimed in 1891 that:

'the Society has clearly discerned that retail trade is not what it was fifty years ago, and many of its members now find useful employment in law, medicine, engineering, and other pursuits.'[2]

Some years later, a manufacturer reflected on the changed social composition of Yearly Meeting, dominated not by businessmen and their relations but by 'masters and mistresses of Schools, heads and headesses of Summer Schools, Secretaries of Missions and Settlements, etc., etc.'.[3] The analysis of the occupations listed in records of deaths shows the strength of retail trade in the earlier period. In 1840–1, the thirty-nine retailers form the largest single occupational group; they include sixteen grocers, and twelve drapers. In 1880 the occupations chosen by boys leaving Quaker schools over the previous ten years was analysed; a third went into retail trade.[4] By 1900–1 the number of retailers had fallen to almost half the 1840–1 total, but the total membership of Class II has increased slightly. The difference was made up by clerks, overseers and commercial travellers, who, perhaps, represent the élite of the Adult

[1] cf. pp. 178–9 below.   [2] *The Friend* (1891), 55.
[3] J. N. Richardson in 1914, quoted in Charlotte Fell Smith, *James Nicholson Richardson of Bessbrook* (London, 1925), p. 163.
[4] *The Friend* (1880), 168.

Schools, and their children. But the group of professional men had not increased proportionately. Sixteen Quaker professional men died in 1840–1, and ten in 1900–1. But the numbers involved are small, and in any case records of deaths tend to represent the occupational structure of an earlier time. In the absence of more evidence, it would be unwise to be dogmatic.

Any analysis of the occupational structure of the Society must take into consideration the structure of occupational prestige among Friends themselves. This was certainly rather different from that current in society in general, though of course it changed from period to period, and was on the whole assumed rather than explicitly stated. Wealth was the key to occupational prestige among Quakers. All nineteenth-century accounts of the Society, whether made from within or without, stressed the zeal and aptitude of its members for the accumulation of wealth. Clarkson, writing at the beginning of the century, stated that Quakers regarded wealth as the main source of prestige, since other forms of status were forbidden them: 'Men, generally speaking, love consequence. Now the Quakers though they have consequence in their own Society, have none in the world. They can neither be legislators nor magistrates. They can take no titles to distinguish them. . . . But riches give all men consequence.'[1]

At the summit of the Quaker hierarchy were not hereditary and titled landowners, but a closely interrelated network of wealthy bankers, merchants and manufacturers. The norm, for a Victorian Quaker, was to be 'in trade'. Many Quaker retailers were men of considerable ability, prosperity, and standing in their local communities. Master grocers, drapers, millers, and corn dealers—such men saw themselves as middle-class, and as, in a sense, the backbone of Quakerism, since it was realized that the very rich were very often attracted to Anglicanism. In the analysis which had just been made, retailers and self-employed craftsmen are grouped together in Class II, yet there was a great gulf between, for instance, a Quaker shoemaker, working on his own, and a master grocer with half a dozen shop-assistants

[1] *A Portraiture of Quakerism*, vol. iii, p. 256.

and apprentices, and several domestic servants, who travelled to London once a year for Yearly Meeting. The elder
Joseph Rowntree, typical of such men, was offered the
mayoralty of York. School-teaching was regarded with
relative disfavour—Friends repeatedly complained at Yearly
Meeting that Quaker schools were inadequately staffed,
and recognized that it was because teachers were poorly
paid. In the early Victorian period, Quaker men became
teachers out of a rare sense of vocation, or because they
lacked the talents or opportunities for business. Brewing
was a popular occupation among Friends until the temperance movement developed,[1] and there were so many Quaker
corn dealers and millers that they were sometimes popularly
blamed for periodic corn shortages. Robert Howard, discussing these charges at the end of the eighteenth century,
attributed the popularity of milling to the attractiveness of
rural life, and stated that Quakers controlled a tenth of the
corn trade at Uxbridge.[2]

Data on occupations alone, unsupplemented by other
evidence, is very unsatisfactory, and the difficulty of classi-
fying occupations has been complained of by whoever
attempts it. To take an illustration from the marriage
registers, where, unlike death records, the same individual
can appear repeatedly, Stafford Allen is variously described
as a drug-grinder, a manufacturing chemist, and a gentleman. Had he been described simply as 'drug-grinder' one
would not have surmised that he was educated in the classics
under private tutors, was addicted to field-sports, and was a
successful manufacturer and noted philanthropist. To estimate an individual's economic condition with precision,
more information is needed: in particular, the number of his
employees, if any, and the number of his domestic servants,
if any. The latter point is a very useful guide to social class.
In 1889, Seebohm Rowntree estimated that 29 per cent of
the population kept a resident domestic servant, and made
this the line of demarcation between the middle and working
classes.[3]

---

[1] *FQE* (1907), 205.
[2] *A Few Remarks on Corn and Quakers* (2nd ed., London, 1800), p. 17.
[3] B. Seebohm Rowntree, *Poverty, A Study of Town Life*, pp. 14 and 26 n.1.

This kind of detailed information cannot be obtained from the Digests of births, deaths, and marriages. The most valuable supplementary source is to be found in the enumerators' manuscript books of census returns, from 1851 on; but since this material is topographically arranged it is necessary to know the precise addresses of the individuals sought. In the absence of this information, searching census returns for a group as small and dispersed as the Quakers presents many difficulties.[1] Nevertheless, a study was made of the social and economic composition of the Society in two contrasting areas: the city of Bristol, and Banbury Monthly Meeting, which embraced the country town of Banbury and its surrounding villages. It was based on local membership lists, trade directories, census returns, and references in local memoirs and histories.[2]

Banbury was a small country town throughout the nineteenth century. It had a population of 6,427 in 1831, just over double this at the end of the century. In 1837, there were 161 Quakers in Banbury and the surrounding villages. The Quaker community in Banbury itself displayed considerable social homogeneity. Joseph John Gurney visited the town in 1829, and described it in a letter: 'In the *country* friends are reduced & scattered. *Here* they are an increasing & very comfortable Society and it has been *pleasant* to become acquainted with them. We seem to me to flourish better in the middle class than among those below them.'[3] The most prominent element in the economic life of the Quaker community was Gilletts' Bank. It went under various names, throughout the nineteenth century, but was

---

[1] A complete list of Banbury Monthly Meeting members for 1851 was available. But it did not give precise addresses, only general addresses, such as 'Banbury', which sometimes proved wrong, and not all could be traced. In Bristol, a membership list, with addresses, was available for 1864. Some of the addresses proved inaccurate for the 1861 Census, and in any case tracing the relevant portions of the unindexed 1861 Census returns presented so much difficulty that only a fifth could be indentified, and it was necessary to rely on trade directories and on occupational data given in the membership lists.

[2] *Bristol MM Membership List, 1864–1924*, in Bristol Archives, Bristol. *Banbury MM Membership List, 1837–[1859]* in Oxford County Record Office, Oxford. There is a later membership list, rough and imprecise, in the safe at Banbury Meeting House. Census returns are in the Public Record Office—H.O. 107/1733 and 1734 (Banbury 1851) and R.G.9/1712ff. (Bristol, 1861).

[3] Joseph John Gurney to Joseph Gurney, 28 Apr. 1829 (*Gurney MSS.* III, 508).

dominated by the Quaker, Joseph Ashby Gillett, from 1823 until his death in 1853, and subsequently by his sons.[1] For the rest, Banbury Quakers were mainly prosperous retailers, with one, or occasionally two, resident domestic servants, and a varying number of assistants and apprentices. There was also a rapidly changing population of Quaker apprentices, shopmen, and commercial travellers. The Quaker community in Banbury in 1851 included five grocers (or grocers' widows), two bakers, a druggist, a bookseller, a retired farmer, and a miller, and their families, as well as the wife of an attorney who played a prominent part in local affairs but does not figure on membership lists and was presumably disowned. Samuel Beesley, who died in 1843, was a baker who produced Banbury cakes on a large scale—he sold 139,500 in 1840.[2] John Head, and subsequently his son, Joseph John, were well-known clothiers and woolcombers with a number of employees.[3] There were also several representatives of 'the poor', who required help from the Monthly Meeting from time to time: a shoemaker with a large family, a servant at Grimsbury, a widow described in the Census returns as 'supported by Friends'.

In the surrounding countryside, the Quaker community showed less social homogeneity. There were several large farming families whose various members had holdings ranging from fifty to a hundred acres and employed perhaps five labourers apiece, on the average. We find a Quaker timber merchant, and several Quaker grocers and druggists, as well as a scattering of Friends 'in humble life'—self-employed craftsmen, without domestic servants or other assistants; agricultural labourers and domestic servants. With their families, they and similar Friends in Banbury formed perhaps a tenth of the members of the Monthly Meeting.

In 1861, Bristol Monthly Meeting was coterminous with the city and its suburbs. It had 385 members; the population of Bristol was 154,000. Predictably, its extremes of

[1] For a full account of this bank, see Audrey M. Taylor, *Gilletts Bankers at Banbury and Oxford* (Oxford, 1964).

[2] Alfred Beesley, *The History of Banbury: Including Copious Historical and Antiquarian Notices of the Neighbourhood* (London, 1841), pp. 568–9.

[3] George Herbert, *Shoemaker's Window: Recollections of a Midland Town before the Railway Age* (ed. Christiana S. Cheney, Oxford, 1948), pp. 45, 99 and 101.

wealth and of poverty were much greater than in Banbury and its environs. An account published in 1851 describes it in these terms: 'the Bristol Meeting was divided into three sets: the high Friends, or the rich and well born; the rich and low born, and the poor.'[1] In this context, 'low born' probably means *nouveau riche*; the line of demarcation between the first and second classes, if it existed, is unimportant. Many Bristol Friends were men of considerable wealth. Their numbers included George Thomas, 'the philanthropist and merchant prince'[2] and his brothers, and the wealthy rentier, Robert Charleton, noted for his 'princely liberality in giving'.[3] Albert and Theodore Fry were among the owners of the Bristol Wagon Works, which had over 150 employees at the time of the 1861 Census, and between eight and nine-hundred twenty years later.[4] Another branch of the Fry family owned the chocolate factory. At the time of the 1861 Census, it had only fifty employees, but it expanded enormously under the direction of the third Joseph Storrs Fry (1826–1913), and employed over 5,000 workers at his death.[5] These were only the best known representatives of a large phalanx of Quaker merchants and manufacturers. Most of them lived in villas in the patrician suburbs of Clifton and Durdham Downs, and employed two or more domestic servants. The life of one of these families —that of the land surveyor William Sturge (who employed four domestic servants)—has been recreated in some detail in the recollections of his daughter.[6] Many of these Quakers were 'gentlemen'; they figure in trade directories,[7] without any occupations being listed. But the trade directories for the sixties also listed Quaker solicitors, stockbrokers, account-

---

[1] *Quakerism: or, the Story of My Life*, p. 231.

[2] Richard Tangye, *The Growth of a Great Industry. 'One and All' An Autobiography of Richard Tangye of the Cornwall Works, Birmingham* (London, 1889), p. 45.

[3] A Note by J. S. Fry, in Anna F. Fox, *Memoir of Robert Charleton, Compiled Chiefly from his Letters* (London, 1873), p. 179n.

[4] *Work in Bristol. A Series of Sketches of the Chief Manufacturies in the City* (reprinted from *The Bristol Times and Mirror*, Bristol, 1883), p. 47.

[5] Agnes Fry, *A Memoir of Sir Edward Fry*, pp. 37–8.

[6] M. Carta Sturge, *Some Little Quakers in their Nursery* (London, 1929).

[7] 'General List of Names of the Gentry, Merchants, Professors & Tradesmen of Bristol', *Mathew's Annual Directory for the City and County of Bristol, including Clifton, Bedminister, and Surrounding Villages*.

ants and property dealers, manufacturers of cement, watches, umbrellas, soda water and shoe lasts, wholesale grocers, tea dealers and stationers, flour dealers, leather factors, millers, and tallow chandlers. The number of their employees and the scale of their establishments varied, but they were, on the whole, wealthy and well-known men. It is difficult to estimate the number in this class exactly; in several cases, entries in membership lists and trade directories cannot be identified with each other with certainty, and the total number varies considerably, depending on whether adult sons are counted separately or not. But of those male Quakers who are listed as separate householders in 1864, at least fifty-one belonged to this favoured class. To their number should be added their frequently large families, and a number of women householders, either spinsters or widows, described in the census returns as fundholders or landed proprietors, living in wealthy suburbs, and employing domestic servants.

Although Friends' per capita income was probably higher than that of any other denomination in Bristol, not all, of course, were merchants and manufacturers. At the other end of the social scale were the inhabitants of the Friends' Asylum, New Street, where, until 1866, indigent members lived rent free. Between these two extremes, were a few small retailers and skilled artisans. But they were in a minority. 236 out of 385 members of the Monthly Meeting belonged to Social Class I in 1864.

It is clear that there was a considerable difference in the social composition of the two areas studied. The Bristol Quaker community contained many families of considerable wealth. The Friends of Banbury and its environs were, on the whole, lower in the economic scale, a society of prosperous retailers and farmers. Both meetings contained some artisan members, and a few were really indigent. The two case studies made confirm the impression gained from an analysis of Quaker occupations. The Society on the whole was middle class, and much richer than a sample of the general population. But it included a stratum of Friends 'in humble life', who did not play any prominent part in Quaker activities.

THE GREAT QUAKER MERCHANTS, FINANCIERS, AND INDUSTRIALISTS

A study of the economic composition of Victorian Quakerism cannot be concerned exclusively with the typical. It is well known that in the eighteenth and nineteenth centuries many Quaker families[1] rose to great wealth. They included the Peases, with their far flung industrial empire, the Gurneys, Lloyds, and Barclays in banking, Allen and Hanbury in pharmacy, Hornimans in tea packaging, Reckitts in blue and starch, Clarks of Street in shoe manufacture, Huntley and Palmer in biscuit making, Crosfields of Warrington in soap making, Bryant and May in match manufacture, and the three cocoa and chocolate firms of Rowntrees, Cadburys, and Frys—and the list is very far from being exhaustive. The Quakers are mentioned in every discussion of the relationship between puritanism and business success, and several books and articles have been exclusively devoted to Quakers in industry.[2]

The only way to ascertain whether Quakers were in fact disproportionately successful in business and finance would be to establish a criterion of economic success, in terms of which quantifiable and comparable data could be gathered, and to compare the numbers of Quakers who succeeded in terms of it with the numbers in other denominations who do likewise. In fact, such a comparison is impossible: the data for it does not exist. But in view of the small size of the Society and the large number of Quaker firms whose names have become household words, there is little doubt that they achieved outstanding success out of all proportion to their numbers.

Systematic information in the sphere of Quaker business history is very hard to come by. Existing studies of the subject tend to be biographical and anecdotal in their approach. And while there are many biographies of Quaker businessmen, there are very few analytical histories of individual Quaker firms. The debate on the relationship between

---

[1] Many wealthy Quaker families, such as the Barclays, Hoares, Harbords, and Lloyds, left the Society, wholly or in some branches, during or before the reign of Victoria.

[2] Emden, *op. cit.*, and Raistrick, *op. cit.* Short accounts of well-known Quaker firms have appeared in *JFHS* at various times.

religion and capitalism belongs to the province of economic history. Nevertheless, it is impossible to write of Victorian Quakerism without at least a mention of the great Quaker industrialists and financiers, and without a few reflections on the reasons for their success.

Quakers themselves tended to explain their success in terms of puritan qualities of character, especially industry and frugality. 'The training of Friends', said Mr. Cadbury, 'gave them the qualities most likely to lead to success in business. They were taught self-denial, rigid abstinence from all luxury and self-indulgence.'[1] Cadbury attributed his success in business to iron parsimony in his early years,[2] and Joseph Storrs Fry practised a lifelong asceticism which was essentially a matter of temperament.[3] Yet frugality alone never established any large fortune,[4] and insofar as conspicuous business success is attributable to traits of character at all, it is equally due to ruthlessness, willingness to take risks, energy, imagination, and ambition—qualities which have very little to do with religion, and are certainly not the prerogative of any denomination.

In the heyday of Quaker puritanism, both Friends and outsiders often remarked on the fact that Friends' rejection of many of the pleasures and ambitions of their society allowed them to direct their energies more single-mindedly to the pursuit of wealth. There may be a grain of truth in this analysis, but although Quaker puritanism prohibited certain activities, such as dancing and singing, many 'gay' Quakers paid little regard to such prohibitions, and even strict members found plenty of permitted avenues of expenditure. Joseph John Gurney, the outstanding Quaker religious leader of his time, confided to his diary that his private expenditure amounted to £4,000 a year.[5]

A more important factor was that Victorian Quakerism sanctioned and indeed encouraged the pursuit of wealth. As in any Christian church at any time, there are plenty of

---

[1] *The British Monthly* (May 1901), 300 (FHL *Press Cuttings*, BB 199).
[2] Gardiner, *Life of George Cadbury*, p. 23.
[3] *The Annual Monitor* (1914), 70.
[4] On this point cf. Kurt Samuelsson, *Religion and Economic Action* (Stockholm, 1961), pp. 83–7.
[5] *Journal*, 8 July 1821. In addition to this he intended to save £2,000 a year.

warnings against the spiritual dangers of riches; it is a recurrent theme in Yearly Meeting epistles. But in practice, wealthy Friends dominated the affairs of the Society. The rich philanthropist who could afford to figure largely on subscription lists was held up as an example, and the bankrupt was punished with expulsion. The less fortunate complained bitterly that 'whatever else we do or do not, I suspect that if we do not succeed in providing for ourselves and our families reputably, we shall only be lightly esteemed in the Church;... the poor man's wisdom is very apt to be despised, and ... to *get rich* is *one* important part towards "a good degree" in the Society.'[1] But respect for riches was not, of course, peculiar to Friends. As a Sheffield physician put it in 1843, 'the concentrated feeling of the present age is the adoration of wealth.'[2]

In any case, it is abundantly clear that the success of those who rise to great wealth must be explained, not in terms of their individual traits of character or motivation (though naturally the wealthy, in *post facto* interpretations of their success, explain it as a triumph of character) but in terms of the external framework of the opportunities available to them, and of the prevailing economic and social conditions.[3]

One of the most important of these conditions was the solid structure of Quaker prosperity. Rags to riches stories are as rare in Quakerism as elsewhere. Most of the great Quaker entrepreneurs were sons of a small manufacturer or well-to-do tradesman. Joseph Storrs Fry, Joseph Rowntree, and George Cadbury took existing businesses and transformed them, partly with the aid of inherited capital. The great financier, Samuel Gurney, who died worth £800,000, was the son of a rich man. Alexander's Discount Company was established by William Alexander (1769–1819), but expanded tremendously under his son, George William. Isaac Reckitt founded the blue and starch business which became a household word under the leadership of his son, James.

Many Quaker families progressed steadily, over a period

---

[1] *The Friend* (1844), 277.
[2] Quoted in E. R. Wickham, *Church and People in an Industrial City*, p. 93.
[3] cf. Samuelsson, *op. cit.*, pp. 70, 78–9, and 81ff. C. Wright Mills, *The Power Elite* (2nd printing, New York, 1959), pp. 96–7.

of two or three generations, from moderate prosperity to great wealth. Edward Pease (1711–1785) established a wool-combing and wool-dealing business in Darlington. His son, Joseph, continued the business, and like many in a similar position, extended into small-scale banking. Edward, his son, through acumen, luck, or a combination of the two, attained wealth and celebrity by sponsoring the Stockton to Darlington railway. His son, Joseph, the first Quaker M.P., and his brother Henry, expanded the family's railway interests, acquired collieries and ironstone mines, and in effect founded the city of Middlesbrough. Joseph's son, Joseph Whitwell, who became a baronet, further expanded the family's enormous network of textile, banking, iron, coal, and railway interests.

Even for those who lacked the advantages of inherited wealth, a start in business, and opportunities to borrow capital, came fairly easily. W. E. Forster attained the economic success which made his later political career possible through the backing of the brothers Samuel and Joseph John Gurney. He was distantly related to them by marriage, but they were motivated mainly by esteem for his father, a noted minister, and by confidence in his own character.[1] William White was a convert to Quakerism, the son of a Wesleyan upholsterer. With Quaker help, he purchased a bookshop. He concentrated mainly on printing, and the foundation of his prosperity was laid by an order for labels from the Quaker firm of Huntley and Palmer. In his turn, he gave free office space to a young Cornishman who was destined to achieve much greater business success—to Richard Tangye,[2] who, with his brothers, founded a great engineering firm. Mathias, writing of late eighteenth-century Quaker brewers, stresses this aspect:

the picture of a religious ethic acting directly upon the individual over-simplifies the direct impact of ideas upon events, by ignoring the opportunities and strength given by the fact of community amongst the faithful . . . The world of the religious-cum-kinship group provided an environment of mutual trust and confidence within which a

1 Samuel to Joseph John Gurney, 30 Sept. 1840 (*Gurney MSS.* II, 433).
2 He was not a Friend, but his father was a convert to Quakerism and he was educated at a Quaker school and taught there for a time.

private 'invisible hand' could accommodate the advantages of each member with the benefit of all.[1]

Sutton, in his study of the Clarks of Street, reaches very similar conclusions.[2]

Many successful Victorian Quaker entrepreneurs flourished partly because of factors outside their own control. Quaker tea dealers and cocoa manufacturers profited by the decline in the national consumption of alcohol. Both they and manufacturers of other articles for domestic consumption, such as shoes, soap, biscuits, and other foodstuffs, profited by the steady expansion of the home market through a rapidly growing population and rising standards of living.

It is clear that these factors help explain the success of the great Quaker financiers and industrialists. But they did not, of course, guarantee it. Samuel Gurney's bank, Overend and Gurney, crashed with far-reaching consequences ten years after his death. *The Friend* gave special mention to the event, because of 'the connection of so many of our members—as shareholders or depositors, and of some of them as directors —with the above company'.[3] Gurney's brother-in-law, Joseph Fry, the husband of the famous philanthropist, Elizabeth Fry, failed in business in the 1820s. The Peases' bank failed in 1903. George Cadbury's father-in-law, the stockbroker John Taylor, ended his career in bankruptcy. William White's business failed in his old age. And the records of any city Meeting are full of examples of Quakers who failed in business; who, despite the advantage of the Quaker 'invisible hand', succumbed to bad luck, bad judgement, or a mixture of the two.

CONCLUSION

All the available evidence points to the fact that Victorian Friends were a predominantly middle-class group. This is reflected in their occupational structure, and in their high

---

[1] Peter Mathias, *The Brewing Industry in England, 1700—1830* (Cambridge, 1959), p. 289.
[2] George Barry Sutton, 'Shoemakers of Somerset: A History of C. & J. Clark, 1833–1903' (*Nottingham University M.A. thesis*, 1959), Chapter 8, *passim*.
[3] *The Friend* (1867), 66.

life-expectancy. Yet there was also a stratum of Friends 'in humble life', who do not figure prominently in Quaker affairs, and whose existence tends in consequence to be overlooked. But although the average Friend was middle-class, a prosperous master tradesman, perhaps, there was also a glittering superstructure of great industrialists and financiers, who have attracted much attention through the relevance of their example to the debate on the relationship between religion and capitalism. The reasons for their success lie outside the scope of religious history and the major preoccupations of this book, but the available evidence suggests that it is attributable less to specifically puritan traits of character than to the prosperity and internal cohesion of the Quaker community.

VII

QUAKERS IN POLITICS

Both individually and in their corporate capacity, Quakers touched on political life at many points. Some of these aspects—such as their work in local government—can only be mentioned briefly in a study of this kind. This chapter analyses the political quietism of early Victorian Friends, its relationship to their actual practice, and the way in which it was first challenged and then definitively abandoned. It discusses Friends' allegiance, first to the Whigs and later to the Liberal Party, their attitude to 'Political Dissent', and the part they played severally in politics, both in and out of Parliament.

THE ERA OF POLITICAL QUIETISM

The records of eighteenth- and early nineteenth-century Quakerism are full of examples of 'The ancient circumspect care of Friends with regard to Politics, and the exciting circumstances of General Elections'.[1] Quaker ministers denounced politics in unmeasured and frequently amusing terms,[2] and Yearly Meeting epistles—the official voice of English Quakerism—repeated the cautions.[3] Clarkson noted that

Politics, which generally engross a good deal of attention, and which afford an inexhaustible fund of matter for conversation to a great part of the inhabitants of the island, are seldom introduced, and, if introduced, very tenderly handled in general among this Society. I have seen aged Quakers gently reprove others of tenderer years . . . for having started them.[4]

What did the prohibition mean in practice? To those who took it seriously—probably a majority in the early nine-

---

[1] Pickard, *An Expostulation*, p. 37.   [2] cf. *Letters of Sarah Grubb*, p. 283.
[3] YM Epistle, 1818.   [4] *A Portraiture of Quakerism*, vol. i, pp. 365–6.

teenth century—all interest in politics, political discussions, even the study of political reports in newspapers, were forbidden. William Howitt was rebuked in the 1830s for using the word 'Radical' in conversation.[1] But the practice of Friends was far from uniform. Some took part in local government, and because they defined their work as nonpolitical, they escaped censure. Birmingham, for instance, was governed by Street Commissioners from 1769 until the city's incorporation in 1838. Some Friends were among their number[2]—one of them, Richard Tapper Cadbury, became a Commissioner in 1822 and was chairman of the body from 1838 until its dissolution in 1851. Quakers as unimpeachable as William Allen, the elder Joseph Rowntree, and Joseph John Gurney flung themselves into local elections, on behalf of the candidates of their choice.[3] The last named was deeply attracted by the idea of standing for parliament, and went through great mental conflicts on the subject.[4] Macaulay's defeat in the Edinburgh election in 1847 was attributed to the opposition of Friends[5]—which perhaps sheds light on his unsympathetic treatment of William Penn! But the tolerance afforded to members who dabbled in elections was limited, and depended a good deal on the complexion of their politics. The Quakers who aided Wilberforce's return for Yorkshire in 1812 were in a very different situation from the occasional Quaker radical, such as Joseph Metford, who was silenced as a minister in 1834 because his 'strong political bias' was inconsistent with 'the peaceful quiescent spirit of a minister of the Gospel'.[6]

The quietist rejection of politics, then, was never com-

[1] Mary Howitt, *An Autobiography*, vol. i, p. 260.

[2] Maurice H. Bailey, 'The Contribution of Quakers to Some Aspects of Local Government in Birmingham 1828–1902' (*Birmingham University M.A. thesis*, 1952), pp. 20–1.

[3] *Life of William Allen*, I, 179; Swift, Joseph John Gurney, Chapter V, *passim*; *Parl. Papers, 1835*, X, pp. 224ff.

[4] *Journal*, 6, 19, and 21 Jan. 1833; 14 Mar. 1833.

[5] *The Friend* (1877), 272 (a letter from James Clark, who obtained his information from Charles Sturge, who contributed £50 to Macaulay's opponent).

[6] His daughter's account of the affair, written in 1878, is printed in *JFHS* (1928), 45ff. For a contemporary account, with details of his offences, see T[homas] R[obson]'s Ac[coun]t of a Western Journey, with His Beloved Wife—1833, 7 Oct. 1833 (MS. in FHL).

pletely consistent or uniform. And paradoxically, it was
never held to apply to the Society's repeated attempts to
influence Parliament, as a powerful and remarkably successful pressure group. Quakers organized themselves for
political agitation very early in their history—their highly
centralized organization made this relatively easy, and the
inconveniences which their refusal to take oaths, for instance,
subjected them to, gave them a powerful motive for seeking
legislative changes. In the nineteenth century, it was
generally recognized that they were powerful and effective
allies in any agitation—Cobden's correspondence repeatedly
evidences his awareness of this.[1]

A special committee of the Meeting for Sufferings kept
a careful watch on parliamentary proceedings, to see when
issues came up which affected the interests of Friends.
They took action, not only over such issues, which
were fairly rare, in the nineteenth century, but also over
matters which affected the general interests of Dissent, or
the principles of Friends—especially concerning war—
or philanthropic concerns on which they were generally
agreed.

The modes of political action open to them were various.
Petitioning was very popular among Victorian Friends. It
was more important then than now, one of the main ways in
which extra-parliamentary opinion was brought to bear upon
the House. Yet Friends probably tended to over-estimate its
effectiveness: a touching passage in the journal of a Scottish
Friend who was active in the anti-slavery agitation records
his disillusion when he saw how cavalierly the petitions
which had been collected with such labour were received by
the House.[2] When matters arose which Friends considered
particularly important, they campaigned on two additional
fronts—exerting pressure on M.P.s from the constituencies,
and sending deputations to the ministers in power. The
combination of influential local Friends and the wealthy
merchants and financiers who dominated Meeting for Suffering was a telling one. As Cobden observed, 'They have a

---

[1] J. A. Hobson, *Richard Cobden. The International Man* (London, 1918), pp. 80–1,
122–3; see also p. 246, below.

[2] William Smeal, *Account of 1838 YM* (MS. in FHL).

good deal of influence over the City moneyed interest which has the ear of the government.'[1]

Much Quaker political activity, especially when it took the form of petitioning, was rather perfunctory. When they petitioned against an aggressive foreign policy, for instance, they did so essentially as a gesture, to relieve their own consciences, rather than in the hopes of swaying the government. Yet from time to time an issue arose which they regarded as of great importance, and they immediately swung into powerful and effective action. An analysis of the corporate political action of the Society in the decade 1840–50 provides many illustrations of the different types of issue which confronted Friends.[2]

Some petitions, deputations and declarations, were essentially gestures, with little prospect of practical effect. To this category belong the Friends' 1848 petition against capital punishment,[3] and their address to Queen Victoria on the evils of slavery, which was later presented to other European sovereigns and the government of the United States.[4] Probably, their petitions against Church Rates should be similarly regarded.[5] Sometimes they petitioned parliament or sent a deputation to the government against a specific grievance, such as the payment of Poor Law chaplains out of the rates,[6] or financial exactions made in connection with distraints,[7] or their inclusion in the provisions of a bill to regulate charitable trusts.[8] But only two issues aroused them to a powerful nation-wide agitation—the educational clauses of the 1843 factory bill, and the militia bills of 1846 and 1848.[9]

The political activity of Friends, both in the quietist era and after it, had another aspect which, if not peculiar to the Society was at least especially characteristic of it—the

---

[1] B.M.Add.MSS. 43653 (Cobden Papers), f. 17: Cobden to Ashworth, 12 Apr. 1842.

[2] The account which follows is based on the MS. minutes of Meeting for Sufferings. Unfortunately the minutes of the parliamentary committee of the Meeting for Sufferings are missing for the period 1799–1890.

[3] *Meeting for Sufferings Minutes, 4 February and 3 March 1848.*

[4] ibid., *12 March and 8 June 1849.*

[5] ibid., *2 April 1841 and 1 February 1850.*

[6] ibid., 15 March 1841.   [7] ibid., 16 May 1845.   [8] ibid., 30 June 1845.

[9] ibid., 29 Mar., 5 Apr., 7 Apr., and 19 May 1843; 7 Jan. and 3 Mar. 1848.

practice of seeking interviews with 'the Great' in general, and royalty in particular. The theory behind this was that the enlightened ruler was an incomparable power for good in society, both through the power of his example, and through his ability to make beneficial changes. But the assumption that the formal ruler of a nation also monopolized effective power was often unjustified, and it is difficult to avoid the conclusion that much of the Victorian Quaker penchant for the company of 'the Great of this World' was sheer snobbery. The sight of William Allen, arranging the finances of the father of the future Queen Victoria; of Elizabeth Fry, entertaining the King of Prussia to lunch; of Christine Alsop, 'a welcome visitor in the Royal nursery', did not make a favourable impression on contemporaries. *The Eclectic Review*, in an otherwise favourable account of Elizabeth Fry, stated that 'Her weakness was that of her generation, the idolatry of rank, wealth, and title.'[1] Cobden said with reference to Sturge, whom he admired and loved, 'The only fault I find with our "Friends" is their inveterate propensity to run after Emperors & kings.'[2]

The most spectacular example of this kind of attempt to exercise influence through personal contact with rulers was the expedition made by Joseph Sturge, Henry Pease, and Robert Charleton to St. Petersburg, on the eve of the Crimean War. Cobden deplored the venture: 'I rather think you overrate the effect of deputations to crowned heads. "Friends" have been charged with being too fond of keeping company with the "great". . . . If a party of Friends were *now* to set off on a visit to Nicholas, it might I think expose them to the charge of seeking their own glorification.'[3] The mission was abortive, and the ridicule it received in the press, led many Friends to deplore it.[4] Yet the practice of addressing 'the Great' continued, and two years later, Cobden was again giving similar advice.[5]

The success of Friends in obtaining the ear of royalty

[1] *The Eclectic Review* (May 1848), 542.
[2] B.M.Add.MSS. 43664 (*Cobden Papers*), f.54v: Cobden to Parkes, 3 Nov. 1856.
[3] B.M.Add.MSS. 43722 (*Sturge Papers*), ff.8–8v: Cobden to Sturge, 3 Jan. 1854. cf. ff.10–11v.
[4] *The Times*, 21 Feb. 1854. J. S. Rowntree, *Account of 1854 YM*, pp. 47–8.
[5] Add.MSS. 43722, ff.109v–10.

bears striking witness to their standing and prestige. And whatever the implications of their attitude to royalty and nobility, it was one that was almost universal in pious and philanthropic circles of the time. It was well known that philanthropies tended to flourish in direct proportion to the eminence of their titular—and titled—patrons. Dickens satirized this tendency in *Our Mutual Friend*.[1]

Even those Quakers who were most adamant about separation from 'the World' hardly ever thought of condemning deputations to rulers, petitioning, and lobbying, or even viewed them as political. It was left for an alderman of York to ask Yearly Meeting whether a religious body should fling itself so enthusiastically into political agitation.[2]

POLITICAL QUIETISM CHALLENGED

Until perhaps the early 1830s, the Society's attitude to politics was essentially paradoxical. It formed an exceptionally effective and well organized pressure group, yet officially deplored interest and activity in elections and party politics. But during the next twenty years, Quaker attitudes to politics were transformed. The old pressure-group activity continued, but the distrust of elections and party politics was completely abandoned by all but a few conservatives and eccentrics. It was one of the most rapid and complete reversals of attitude in Quaker history. On one hand, it was a manifestation of that change which forms a central theme of this study, by which Friends grew closer to the society in which they lived. On the other, it reflected changes in Dissent in general. The Wesleyan Methodists gradually modified their traditional Tory quietism, and the Congregationalists underwent a similar change of attitude. Contemporaries, with much justice, saw the 1832 Reform Act as the charter of Dissent.[3] Quakers, like other Dissenters, moved out of the political wilderness they had inhabited

---

[1] Book I, Ch. XVII (i.e. the letter which Boffin receives from the Duke of Linseed).

[2] Joseph Rowntree. J. S. Rowntree, *Account of 1854 YM*, p. 73.

[3] Raymond, G. Cowherd, *The Politics of English Dissent* (London, 1959), p. 85.

so long, and became an increasingly effective voice in English parliamentary politics.

The challenge to Quaker political quietism had four main aspects—the entry of Friends into local government; their entry into parliament; their changing attitude towards Quaker radicals such as Bright and Sturge; and their relationship to 'Political Dissent'.

Although Quakers were sometimes Poor Law Guardians, or members of various *ad hoc* bodies such as the Birmingham Street Commissioners, they were, like other Dissenters, cut off from most municipal and other offices by the Test and Corporation Acts.[1] In 1828, the Acts were repealed in so far as they applied to dissenters, after a powerful agitation in which Quakers played no part. But the road to office was still closed to them, for the declaration required by the new Act, and subsequently by clause 50 of the Municipal Corporations Act, was unacceptable to Quaker consciences. In 1830 a Quaker stated: 'those who are fond of putting extreme cases whereon to found an "*argumentum ad absurdum*" may amuse themselves by imagining a "Quaker"—Privy-Counsellor, a Sheriff, a Mayor, or an Alderman.'[2] Acts passed in 1837 and 1838 modified the declaration to a formula acceptable to Friends, and a bitter conflict on the propriety of taking office immediately ensued. It was the only occasion on which the Society had to make a formal decision on the relationship between its principles and political action. A majority, apparently, thought Friends should not take office—'I think if the meeting had been polled, nearly nine out of ten would have decided that no friend could honestly take the declaration.'[3] In the end, Yearly Meeting issued an equivocal, but on the whole discouraging minute on the subject.[4] For years, opinion and practice varied. The matter was complicated by the fact

---

[1] It is often claimed that these acts were nullified, in practice, before their repeal, by their periodic suspension, as well as by the practice of occasional conformity. But cf. Manning, *The Protestant Dissenting Deputies*, pp. 3, 217, 221; A. C. Whitby, 'Matthew Arnold and the Noncomformists' (*Oxford University B.Litt. thesis*, 1954), p. 148.

[2] *The Friends Monthly Magazine* (1830), 391.

[3] John Southall, at 1838 YM, *JFHS* (1921), 89–90.

[4] *YM Minutes, 1838*, vol. xxv, pp. 188ff. (MS. in FHL).

that some of the duties of mayors and magistrates, such as calling out the militia, were impossible for Friends, and that members of a church which forbade the payment of tithes and church rates were in an equivocal position when they promised not to disturb the Established Church in the 'Possession of any Rights or Privileges'. Edward Smith of Sheffield declined office because of the declaration; Joseph Sturge accepted it but refused the declaration; the elder Joseph Rowntree became an alderman but refused the mayoralty. Time was on the side of those Quakers who took office. In some cities, such as Birmingham and Darlington, they were destined to play a part quite disproportionate to their small numbers.[1] In the nature of things, only a few Friends could hope to enter parliament. But by the later decades of the nineteenth century, service as a Poor Law Guardian, J.P., or borough councillor had become characteristic of the prosperous and 'weighty' Friend. Indeed, some feared that the Society would lose the services of its natural leaders in consequence: 'The Society of Friends cannot spare to public affairs all its men of leisure, high principle, and intellectual ability.'[2]

In 1833, Joseph Pease entered parliament as member for the newly created constituency of South Durham. The only legal obstacle in his path—the oath required of members on taking their seats—was readily removed, and he was permitted to make an affirmation. The entry of the first Quaker into parliament is an obvious landmark, yet its significance is perhaps more apparent than real. It created curiously little furore among Friends, except in his immediate circle.[3] There were several reasons for this. The novelty of his position was disguised by the fact that the patrician Quaker circles to which he belonged had already furnished a number of M.P.s, such as Hudson Gurney—all of whom, however, had previously left the Society. To a Gurney, the salient fact about the 1837 election was that Pease was the only relative left in parliament: 'What shall we do for franks—is the cry

---

[1] Bailey, *op. cit., passim;* Steel, *'Friendly' Sketches,* pp. 93–4.
[2] *The Friend* (1880), 54.
[3] *The Diaries of Edward Pease The Father of English Railways,* ed. Alfred E. Pease (London, 1907), p. 65.

of *all*.'[1] In general, the wealth and standing of Pease's
family, his own unimpeachable orthodoxy, and perhaps not
least, his inconspicuous career in the House, disarmed
potential Quaker critics. 'Mr. Pease ... one of the most
useful, though not one of the most shining, members of the
House',[2] who travelled from London to Durham to attend
a Quarterly Meeting, never provided a focus for debate on
the rights and wrongs of political action.

This focus was to be provided by the more dramatic
political careers of Joseph Sturge and John Bright. Sturge
never succeeded in entering parliament, but his role in
radical politics horrified Friends in the 1830s and 1840s.
He first took part in politics in 1832, as an active supporter
of the Birmingham Political Union—he and a few other
like-minded Friends were publicly rebuked by a co-
religionist in the columns of the *Birmingham Gazette*.[3]
Sturge held no office in the Society, and so was less vulner-
able than Joseph Metford, the minister who was silenced for
his radicalism. In any case, his work in the anti-slavery
movement and later, on behalf of the partially emancipated
slaves of the West Indies, outweighed his radical sins in
many Quaker eyes. Worse was to come, however. In 1841,
he founded the Complete Suffrage Union, in a probably
foredoomed attempt to unite Chartists and middle-class
radicals behind a programme acceptable to both. Inevitably,
many Friends found this difficult to distinguish from 'the
mad & wicked conduct of some of the Chartists'.[4] He was
subjected for a time to near-persecution,[5] and at the Yearly
Meeting of 1843 felt it necessary to justify his activities,
'which have caused great dissatisfaction to his friends'.[6]

In that year, another Quaker radical, John Bright, entered
parliament for the first time. His growing prominence in the
Anti-Corn Law League coupled with his unconventional
demeanour and outspokenness at Quaker gatherings led

---

[1] Anna Gurney to Joseph John Gurney, 15 Aug. 1837 (*Gurney MSS*. III, 2).
[2] *Random Recollections of the House of Commons, from the year 1830 to the close of
1835 ... by one of No Party* (London, 1836), p. 289.
[3] Richard, *Memoirs of Joseph Sturge*, p. 69.
[4] B.M.Add.MSS. 43723 (Sturge Papers), f.1: Sturge to Bright, 28 May 1842.
[5] Richard, *op. cit.*, p. 330.
[6] *Diary of William Lucas*, vol. ii, p. 312.

many to distrust him.[1] Friends often approved of the aims of the League but deplored its methods,[2] and the disapproval of many of his fellow Quakers in the early years of his public life left lasting scars. Many years later, Bright was invited to become an Elder, but declined the offer in a touching *retractatio*, on the grounds that his political career had disqualified him.

The presence of both Bright and Sturge at the Yearly Meeting of 1843 led the senior Friends who drafted the Yearly Meeting epistle to reflect on the dangers of 'political associations'.[3] One veteran philanthropist stated that 'The political meetings of the day are a Snare of the adversary . . ..'[4] The epistle which was issued urged Friends to remain 'quiet in the land' provoking Bright to a passionate defence of his own position.

In a very few years, this kind of quietism had become a historical curiosity. The Complete Suffrage Union failed, and the League was canonized by success and the prosperous years that followed. Sturge the radical was overshadowed by Sturge the philanthropist, and when he died in 1859, the Yearly Meeting assembled at that time was grief-stricken. Bright won the respect of his co-religionists by his courageous opposition to the Crimean War, and long before his death he had become a revered and 'weighty' Friend.

Until the 1830s, the corporate interests of Dissent were represented by the Protestant Society and the Protestant Dissenting Deputies—moderates, who sought to obtain redress from specific grievances, and who gained their greatest success in the repeal of the Test and Corporation Acts, in so far as they applied to Dissenters. The Deputies continued their work throughout the nineteenth century and beyond. Friends co-operated with them on occasion, when their own interests were affected, but on the whole they remained aloof from their agitations, preferring to conduct their own campaigns to gain their own ends—a policy

---

[1] Boyce, *The Richardsons of Cleveland*, p. 209.
[2] *The Anti-Corn Law Circular*, 19 Nov. 1840; *The Diaries of Edward Pease* p. 195.
[3] Josiah Forster, *Account of 1843 YM*, ff.9ff.   [4] ibid., f.11.

which has earned them a sharp rebuke from the Deputies' historian.[1]

In the 1830s, Dissenters became more vocal and aggressive in their claims, and a number of ephemeral societies were formed. It was not until 1843, however, that a challenge occurred which temporarily welded them into an effective political unity. In 1843 Graham introduced his factory bill, which would, *inter alia*, have established a network of factory schools under the supervision of the Established Church. Dissenters were outraged at the proposal, and a campaign ensued in which Quakers took an active part: Bright ruefully compared their relative indifference to the Anti-Corn Law League with their zeal in this cause: 'all attending a public meeting, making speeches, moving resolutions, promoting agitation, leaving their sweet retirement . . . for the tumult of political strife.'[2] Friends petitioned Parliament against the proposals. On this as on other matters, however, they were not unanimous: one Quaker diarist wrote some years later that 'every attempt at a national scheme is barked down by our *drab* republicans, the philanthropic Fungi which prove more the rottenness than the vitality of Quakerism.'[3]

One man, the Congregationalist minister Edward Miall, aspired to transform the zeal which had been inspired by a specific issue into a permanent movement. He was destined to become the prophet of Political Dissent. He hoped to divert Dissenters from *ad hoc* agitations on specific grievances to a general campaign on a matter of broad principle, against the Establishment of the Church of England. His writings reveal much the same view of society as those of the Anti-Corn Law League leaders. He identifies aristocracy, privilege, and the Establishment; he resents the social inferiority of Dissenters, and longs to arouse their sense of corporate identity and pride of class, and make them a real power in the land. In 1844 the British Anti-State Church

[1] Bernard Lord Manning, *The Protestant Dissenting Deputies*, ed. Ormerod Greenwood (Cambridge, 1952), pp. 213–14.

[2] George Macaulay Trevelyan, *The Life of John Bright* (London, 1925), pp. 105–106. The passage refers to the Peases of Darlington.

[3] *Diary of William Lucas*, vol. ii, p. 463.

Association was founded, better known by its later name, the Liberation Society.

Predictably, Friends were always divided in their attitude towards the Liberation Society. So, for that matter, were all other Dissenting denominations. The core of Miall's support came from Congregationalists and Baptists—but the hostility with which many Congregationalists viewed him was an exact parallel to the hostility of many Quakers to Bright and Sturge. Both Bright and Sturge were warm supporters of Miall. Miall's son was to dedicate his biography of his father to the former, who wrote of the Established Church as 'that overgrown and monstrous abuse . . . a *wen* upon the head'.[1] Sturge played an active part at the Liberation Society's inaugural conference,[2] and his nephew, Charles Gilpin, M.P. for Northampton from 1859–65, was an active member of its central council.[3] The Quaker philanthropist, Joseph Cooper, was so prominent in the movement that it was said 'his house was the cradle of the Liberation Society'.[4] Yet many Quakers opposed the movement, partly from a dislike for trenchant militancy—the legacy of generations of quietism—and partly from the feeling that more was to be gained by cultivating the friendship of the powers that be. Cobden's acid comment on Samuel Gurney, in another connection, is relevant here: 'you must never expect to see him in the public arena upon any question which does not pass current with *The Times* and its readers, or have the sanction of the Prince, or a Bishop.'[5] In 1863 a Friend actually pubished a pamphlet condemning the disestablishment movement, 'with the approval of some of the leading Friends of the meeting'.[6] When Miall introduced his disestablishment motion in the Commons in 1871, Bright and his brother-in-law, the banker-novelist E. A. Leatham, supported him, but the other Quakers in parliament, William Fowler, Edmund Backhouse, Jonathan Pim, and Joseph Whitwell Pease, abstained,[7] to the disgust of some, but not

[1] Trevelyan, *The Life of John Bright*, p. 201.
[2] Arthur Miall, *Life of Edward Miall Formerly Member of Parliament for Rochdale and Bradford (London, 1884)*, p. 257.
[3] ibid., p. 130.   [4] *The Annual Monitor* (1883), 148.
[5] Hobson, *Richard Cobden The International Man*, p. 62.
[6] *The Friend* (1863), 95.   [7] *Hansard*, 3rd series. ccvi (1871), 572–3.

all, of their co-religionists.[1] Both Pim and Francis Bassett,
who entered parliament in 1872, were actively opposed to
disestablishment.[2]

On the whole, then, Quakers played little part in the
history of 'Political Dissent'. Many disliked the militancy
of the Liberation Society, and they tended to prefer to conduct their own agitations on specific and limited issues.

THE PARTY ALLEGIANCES OF FRIENDS

Overwhelmingly, though not universally, Friends supported first the Whigs and later the Liberal Party. In this
they were typical of nonconformists generally. The alliance
was rooted in the consciousness of benefits received. As *The
Eclectic Review* put it in 1844, 'To the Whigs, as a party, the
dissenters of England owe much. Whatever we have wrung
from the intolerance and bigotry arrayed against us, has
been by their help.'[3] They looked first to the Whigs, and
later to the Liberal Party, for favourable legislation. The
hope was often disappointed, and the alliance was sometimes subjected to severe strains—most notably by the 1870
Education Act—but until Home Rule split the Liberal
Party, a Tory Dissenter seemed a contradiction in terms. In
1871 the Quaker member for Huddersfield described the
Liberals as 'a party of Dissenters' and Dissent as 'the
strength and marrow of the Liberal Party'.[4] Nearly forty
years later, *The British Weekly* stated, 'we do not know what
the Liberal Party is, if it is not a Nonconformist party.'[5]

Most Quakers, like John Bright, took their political
allegiance for granted—'In fact, I could not be otherwise
than Liberal.'[6] No Quaker sat on the Tory benches until the
Home Rule crisis, though some ex-Quakers, such as the
Fair Trade advocates W. F. Ecroyd and S. S. Lloyd, did so.
Quaker periodicals were unashamedly partisan, and the
occasional Quaker Tory, such as Joseph Sturge's father, or

[1] *The Friend* (1871), 147, 166 and 194–5.
[2] *The Manchester Friend* (1872), 121.
[3] *The Eclectic Review* (1844), ii, 344–5.
[4] *Hansard*, 3rd ser. ccvi (1871), 546 and 548.
[5] Quoted in '*Nonconformity and Politics*' by a *Nonconformist Minister* (London,
1909), p. 111.   [6] Trevelyan, *The Life of John Bright*, p. 19.

the banker Joseph Ashby Gillett, was generally felt to be in a paradoxical position.[1]

The Home Rule crisis divided Friends, both in Parliament and outside it. When the Commons voted on the second reading of the Home Rule bill, in 1886, in the division which brought down Gladstone's government, Quakers were to be found in both lobbies. Bright and his second son, William Leatham, and the cousins Lewis and Theodore Fry, took opposite sides. The Peases in general followed Gladstone, but Arthur Pease was a Unionist.[2] Outside the House, most Friends were Gladstonian Liberals, but a minority feared that the Irish Quakers would be victimized by a Catholic majority, and bitterly reproached the Quaker advocates of Home Rule for their 'betrayal' of their brethren.[3] *The Friend* called the Irish question 'a sore in our corporate life which is a source of great weakness'.[4] For the first time, the partisanship of Quaker periodicals became open to criticism. When *The British Friend* described the 1895 election as a victory for the drink seller and the ecclesiastic, its editor earned an energetic rebuke.[5]

After 1886 there were Friends on both sides of the House. Most followed Gladstone, but Bright and his eldest son, John Albert, Lewis Fry, Arthur Pease and the Ulster manufacturer, J. N. Richardson, became Unionists. As Robert Spence Watson, the Quaker president of the Liberation Federation, complained bitterly, in time Liberal Unionists tended to become indistinguishable from conservatives.[6] John W. Wilson entered parliament as a Unionist for North Worcestershire in 1895, but later crossed the floor over tariff reform. Only one Quaker, Frank Leverton Harris, Richardson's son-in-law, entered parliament as a Conservative during Victoria's reign. In 1914 both he and the only other Conservative Quaker M.P., Alfred Bigland, were

[1] cf. the stanza on Gillett in *Quakerieties for 1838, by An Embryo 'Harvest Man'* (London, 1838), p. 7.

[2] *Hansard*, 3rd ser. cccvi (1886), 1240–5.

[3] Cf. Creighton, *Life and Letters of Thomas Hodgkin*, pp. 162–3; *The Friend* (1886), 141.

[4] *The Friend* (1890), 29; cf. (1887), 2.

[5] *The British Friend* (1896), 150 and 207; cf. *The Friend* (1898), 59–60.

[6] Robert Spence Watson, *The National Liberal Federation from its commencement to the General Election of 1906* (London, 1907), p. 57.

destined to abandon the pacifism of their church and give
zealous support to the war effort.

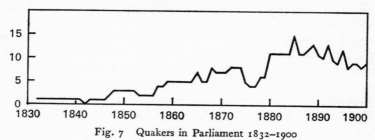

Fig. 7   Quakers in Parliament 1832–1900

QUAKERS IN PARLIAMENT [1]

The Quakers who sat in Victoria's parliaments do not
form a group susceptible of accurate statistical analysis. The
problem is essentially one of definition. M.P.s who remained
Quakers were outnumbered by ex-members, the most
eminent of whom was W. E. Forster, who lost his membership for marrying Matthew Arnold's sister. These ex-
Quakers included those who lost their membership before,
during, and after their parliamentary career; those who, like
Forster lost it for a technical trespass; and those who, like
Sir Robert N. Fowler, resigned through a specific preference
for another church. Quaker members of parliament showed
equally little homogeneity. Some, like Bright's nephew,
Walter S. B. McLaren, were nominal Friends.[2] For others,
Quakerism was the primary commitment of their lives. And
how shall we classify a man like Henry J. Wilson, the
Sheffield cutlery manufacturer who, though not a Quaker,
habitually attended Meeting for Worship and acted with
Friends in many reforming agitations.[3] Very often, the line
of demarcation between Quakers and ex-Quakers is more
apparent than real. The latter frequently continued to
identify themselves with Friends, to a greater or lesser

[1] The account which follows is based on biographies, where they exist, obituaries,
and standard works of reference such as *Dod's Parliamentary Companion*, as well as
Hansard and division lists.   [2] *The Annual Monitor* (1913), 86.

[3] W. S. Fowler, *A Study in Radicalism and Dissent. The Life and Times of Henry
Joseph Wilson 1833–1914* (London, 1961), p. 24; *The Friend* (1912), 393 and 1914,
pp. 501–2.

extent,[1] and the former often experienced a tension between their Quaker heritage and their secular environment.

But although Quaker M.P.s formed a group which was blurred and shifting at the edge, it was readily recognizable, and had a number of clear characteristics. The graph facing this page shows how the numbers of Quakers in parliament climbed steadily throughout the period. There was only a single Quaker in parliament, in the first ten years of Victoria's reign. There were two or three in the next decade, five to ten in the sixties and seventies, and ten to fifteen between 1880 and 1895, when the numbers begin to drop again. Altogether, thirty-three Quakers entered parliament during the Victorian period.[2]

Only one of these men—John Bright—left a real mark on the politics of his time. Even he never attained offices higher than the Presidency of the Board of Trade and the 'useless place of Chancellor of the Duchy . . .'[3] and his tenure of office added no lustre to his reputation. The typical Quaker M.P. was not a career politician but a wealthy businessman who entered parliament in middle age. Very frequently, he had spent his life in the constituency he represented—generations of Peases represented various Durham constituencies, and both George Palmer and his eldest son were alderman, Mayor, and M.P. for Reading. J. W. Wilson lived far from his constituents, but relied on the influence of his friend and fellow-Quaker, George Cadbury, to return him for 'N. Worcester where C[adbury']s influence predominates'.[4] Quaker M.P.s tended to enter parliament out of social rather than political ambition—they were Arnold's 'industrialists in search of gentility'.[5] Several,

---

[1] This view, expressed by an ex-Quaker M.P., is quoted in Agnes Fry, *A Memoir of Sir Edward Fry*, p. 13. cf. *The Friend* (1869), 205.

[2] Counting as Friends those who are described as such in *The Friend* (1904), 818 and 832, but excluding one case where *The Friend's* classification is clearly inaccurate.

[3] Bright's own description—some years before he held the office. Bright to J. B. Smith, 28 Oct. 1865 (volume of Bright–Smith correspondence in Manchester City Library), f.52.

[4] B.M.Add.M.S. 41215 (Campbell-Bannerman Papers), f.148v.: Herbert Gladstone to Campbell-Bannerman, 19 Nov. 1899.

[5] Matthew Arnold, *Culture and Anarchy* (first published 1869; Cambridge, 1950), p. 210.

such as Joshua Rowntree and the younger Samuel Gurney, were basically philanthropists, who entered parliament in much the spirit in which they would have accepted office in a charitable society. Neither Thomas Fowell Buxton nor W. E. Forster was a Friend, though both were closely linked with the Society. Each searched his own heart to examine his motives in entering parliament, and discovered a mixture of altruism and political ambition.[1] But the typical Quaker M.P. came closer to Cobden's satirical description: 'our popular constituencies . . . have for the last ten years been falling into the way of returning some rich capitalist or contractor—a man past the middle age, of no political antecedents, and whose only ambition in going to Parliament is social position.'[2]

Once in Parliament, they tended to become conscientious but obscure backbenchers, diligent in attending debates and committees, occasionally holding a minor office. The obscurity of most Quaker M.P.s may be due to the chance fact that a small group of men did not happen to include anyone of real political ambition and ability, except Bright. Bright claimed that Quakerism was a barrier to office, and there was some truth in the contention. Although his wealth and respectability might secure the Quaker industrialist a seat in parliament, he was not a member of the traditional ruling class. Probably, the degree of his social assimilation to his parliamentary environment was in inverse proportion to his identification with Quakerism. Joseph Pease claimed that he was victimized,[3] and Bright complained, before he was given office, 'I am an "outsider" and a "pariah" among politicians, and therefore cannot be thought of';[4] but there were factors other than Quakerism to account for this. Probably, a Quaker was at some disadvantage in competing for the highest prizes. None happened

---

[1] Charles Buxton, *Memoirs of Sir Thomas Fowell Buxton, Bart.* (2nd ed. London, 1849), p. 87. T. Wemyss Reid, *Life of the Right Honourable William Edward Forster* (London, 1888), vol. i, p. 89.

[2] Cobden to Richard, 12 Feb. 1864, quoted in Hobson, *Richard Cobden The International Man*, p. 328.

[3] *Hansard*, 3rd ser. xvi (1833), 687.

[4] Bright to J. B. Smith, 28 Oct. 1865 (Bright–Smith correspondence, Manchester Library), f.52.

to have the blazing ability and ambition which enabled Disraeli to break into the charmed circle.

The Quakers in parliament never voted as a bloc—they prided themselves on their independence. Their lack of agreement on Disestablishment and Home Rule has been noted, and they showed a similar lack of unanimity on temperance legislation.[1] Technically pacifists, they on occasion supported specific wars—Joseph Pease voted for the war with China in 1840.[2] Most were Free Traders, but Joseph Pease, despite the attacks of his Free Trade co-religionists, was a protectionist.[3] Even clusters of Quaker relatives refused to vote as a bloc: 'The Peases must surely form the largest family party in the House. . . . Such a contingent would be well worth securing for any cause or ism if families voted *en bloc*; it is well known, however, that they carefully eschew anything like uniformity of opinion and action.'[4]

Quakers in parliament were much more actively identified with philanthropic movements and reforming agitations than were the general run of back-benchers. The Presidency of the Peace Society was practically hereditary in the Pease family, being held successively by Joseph Pease, his brother Henry, and his son Joseph Whitwell—all of whom were M.P.s. The last named was also President of the Anti-Opium Society. The younger Samuel Gurney, who represented Penrhyn and Falmouth from 1857 to 1868, took an active part in the relief of the distress caused by the Franco-Prussian War, and held office in a multitude of societies, including the British and Foreign Schools Society, the Peace Society, the Anti-Slavery Society and the Aborigines Protection Society.

A description from an observer whose interests lay far beyond the little world of Quakerism mirrors the philanthropic, slightly eccentric image of the Quaker M.P.: 'When I came home the Slavery subject was on a footing with the C.M.S. or the Anti-opiumists, etc. It was a *fad*

---

[1] *The Friend* (1864), 159.
[2] *Hansard*, 3rd ser. liii (1840), 954. cf. George Crosfield, *Account of 1840 YM*. ff.2–2v. (MS. in FHL, Portfolio 21/40).
[3] *Hansard* 3rd ser. xviii (1833), 974–5; cf. p. 243ff, below.
[4] *The Echo* (1 Aug. 1897), FHL *Press Cuttings* BB 34.

represented in the House by a small set of Quaker faddists. When they spoke the House emptied.'[1]

Quaker M.P.s often acted as the parliamentary spokesman for a number of good causes. Joseph Pease acted as parliamentary spokesman for the R.S.P.C.A. in the 1830s.[2] Joseph Whitwell Pease, Joshua Rowntree, and J. E. Ellis and the near-Quaker J. H. Wilson were among the most prominent opponents of the opium trade with China, though another Friend, Arthur Pease, earned the obloquy of his co-religionists by supporting the majority on the Opium Commission of 1895.[3] Rowntree and Ellis, who were brothers-in-law, were energetic opponents of the Boer War, and advocates of better relations with Germany, in the years before the First World War. Quakers were among the most persistent opponents of capital punishment,[4] and Josephine Butler's agitation against the Contagious Diseases Acts relied heavily on the parliamentary advocacy of Friends such as William Fowler.[5] Of course, not all their work in parliament was so altruistic. Bright and Joseph Pease, factory owners both, had an unhappy record on the limitation of factory hours.[6] J. E. Ellis, a colliery owner, earned a vote of no confidence from his miner constituents for his failure to support a Miners' Bill,[7] and J. W. Pease's opposition to a proposed railway out of regard for his own railway interests was cited by T. H. S. Escott to prove his thesis that the Commons is 'chiefly composed of economic interests'.[8]

The outstanding social characteristics of Quaker M.P.s as a group were their degree of interrelatedness and their prosperity. Some of them came from families of almost proverbial wealth—the Judge in *Trial by Jury* uses the simile,

[1] F. J. to E. Lugard, 3 June 1894 (typed extract), Lugard Papers, Rhodes House, Oxford, M.S.Br.Emp.57, f.106v.

[2] Edward G. Fairholme and Wellesley Pain, *A Century of Work for Animals. The History of the R.S.P.C.A. 1824–1934* (London, 1934), pp. 71–4.

[3] *The British Friend* (1898), 271–2.

[4] William Tallack, *Howard Letters and Memories* (London, 1905), pp, 138 and 147.

[5] 1880 Annual Report, *The Friends Association for abolishing the State Regulation of Vice*.   [6] cf. p. 246ff below.

[7] Arthur Tilney Bassett, *The Life of the Right Honourable John Edward Ellis M.P.* (London, 1914), pp. 102–3.

[8] Quoted in John F. Glaser, *Nonconformity and Liberalism, 1868–1885. A Study in English Party History* (Harvard Univ. Ph.D. thesis, 1948), p. 523.

At length I became as rich as the Gurneys.

The Quakers in parliament were a phalanx of factory and colliery owners, and company directors, plus several successful lawyers, such as J. F. B. Firth. Indeed the only Quaker in parliament in relatively modest circumstances was Joshua Rowntree, a Scarborough solicitor. The large number of ex-Quakers in parliament reflects the tendency of the very wealthy to leave Quakerism, which was discussed earlier in this study. Indeed the expense of a parliamentary career made a fair degree of prosperity indispensable. Bright claimed that he spent £500 a year 'in the performance of my duties as a member of Parlt. & in the expenses incurred by it.'[1] It necessitated a second residence in London, and protracted absences from business; and the cost of elections themselves remained high far into the nineteenth century. In 1880, the *average* costs of a parliamentary candidate were over £3,100 for a county and over £1,200 for a borough.[2] Ambitious men who lacked inherited wealth, such as T. F. Buxton and W. E. Forster, had to establish themselves in business before embarking on a political career. Small wonder that those Quakers who entered parliament were drawn from the economic élite of the Society, which an American described as 'a world of Barclays and Gurneys and other rich English Quaker families which like a Quaker Versailles, holy and yet splendid, shone for us across the Atlantic with a kind of glory'.[3]

The extraordinary degree of interrelatedness of Quaker M.P.s was partly the consequence of their wealth. Compelled to marry Quakers until 1860, and frequently disposed to do so afterwards, they naturally sought their wives from among their social and economic peers. This meant that the small group of very wealthy Quaker families became linked, in the course of several generations, by increasingly numerous and complex bonds of intermarriage. Eight members of the Pease family sat in Victoria's parliaments, and they were linked by their own or their kinsmen's marriages to Gurneys,

[1] B.M.Add.MSS. 43723 (Sturge Papers), f.19: Bright to Sturge, 18 Apr. 1853.
[2] H. J. Hanham, *Elections and Party Management. Politics in the time of Disraeli* (London, 1959), p. 251.
[3] Logan Pearsall Smith, *Unforgotten Years*, pp. 15–16.

Frys, Backhouses, and Buxtons to a much greater number of M.P.s. John Bright was not a member of this patrician inner circle, but with him in parliament sat his brother, his sons, three brothers-in-law[1] and a nephew. His niece, Kate Lucas, married J. P. Thomasson, M.P. These genealogical details are illustrative only, and the links of kinship between Quaker members of parliament could be traced much further. The normal interrelatedness of Victorian Quakers is intensified in this context, for a father or uncle in parliament naturally turned a man's thoughts towards a political career—as 'Uncle Buxton' influenced the young W. E. Forster.

OTHER QUAKERS IN POLITICS

Some Quakers who never entered parliament at all made a more important contribution to the political life of their time than the run of Quaker backbenchers. Joseph Sturge's role in the radical politics of the 1840s is a case in point, as is the career of Robert Spence Watson in the National Liberal Federation. The latter refused to stand for parliament, believing that he could do more good from a standpoint of disinterestedness[2] and many aspects of his policy resulted from a conscious attempt to translate Quaker ideals of church polity into the secular sphere.[3] A contemporary described the Liberal Federation as 'an attempt to form a political church without a creed, and without a bishop, and without a synod'.[4] In the early twentieth century, Seebohm Rowntree, who rose to fame through his study of poverty in York, exercised an influence over the counsels of the Liberal party which was wholly incommensurate with his public reputation. Quakers exercised power in another way, however, in a chapter of political history which is no less important for the extreme obscurity which surrounds it—the influence of the very wealthy, who made major contributions to party funds.

[1] i.e. W. H. and E. A. Leatham, the brothers of his second wife, and Duncan McLaren, the husband of his sister, Priscilla.
[2] Percy Corder, *The Life of Robert Spence Watson* (London, 1914), 201–2.
[3] *Manchester Conference Proceedings*, p. 139.
[4] A. W. W. Dale, *The Life of R. W. Dale of Birmingham* (London, 1898), p. 422.

The full story of the great Quaker industrialists' relationship with the Liberal Party will probably never be known.[1] This chapter section concentrates on the political activities of the most important of them, George Cadbury.[2] Like Joseph Rowntree, Cadbury embarked on experiments in housing and employees' welfare that had oblique implications for politics. Sometimes he acted in a way calculated to affect legislation directly—as in the sweated trades exhibition he sponsored in 1906, or his financial backing of the National Old Age Pensions League. The aspects which aroused the anger of his opponents, however, were his widespread purchase of newspapers and his secret financial backing both of individuals and of organizations.

His newspaper purchases began with the acquisition of four Birmingham papers in 1891. He had at that time no thought of acquiring a national paper, and would probably not have done so had it not been for the challenge of the Boer War. At Lloyd George's instigation, he acquired an interest in *The Daily News* and later took over the paper completely, though it involved him in continual anxiety and financial loss. Both this and subsequent newspaper purchases, like the comparable acquisitions of the Rowntree trust, were undoubtedly motivated by the sincere, if self-confident and paternalistic, humanitarianism which was the guiding principle of his life. His political opponents noted with alarm the power resting in the hands of two cocoa manufacturers, and their identification of the cause of humanitarian reform with the fortunes of the Liberal Party. In 1907, Bonar Law complained in the Commons: 'It was unreasonable and unfair that the large fortunes made out of the protection of this industry should be used, as they were used, to subsidise newspapers (loud cheers) and to help to

[1] I am grateful to Professor H. J. Hanham for his help on this matter. He informs me that the various records relevant to Liberal Party management shed no light on the subject. I searched the remaining Cadbury papers at the Bournville Cocoa Works without success—most of the papers used by Gardiner in his biography of George Cadbury were later destroyed. Mr Peter Rowntree informs me that scarcely any of Joseph Rowntree's papers survive.

[2] Cadbury's main period of political influence was 1900–14, but he is studied in this chapter because of his intrinsic importance, and because far more material on his political activities came to light than in the case of any other Quaker industrialists.

finance members of Parliament, whose whole influence was used to prevent other people from getting precisely the same advantage.'[1] His explanation of Cadbury's political interests —the desire to prevent Free Trade in cocoa—misses the mark, but there is much evidence that Cadbury gave considerable sums both to the Liberal Party and to individuals within it.

Gardiner, who worked in the closest association with Cadbury for many years, stated that 'He contributed freely to the party funds, especially during the period when T. E. Ellis was Chief Whip'[2]—that is, from 1894–9 and that he gave financial support to individual politicians who required it.[3] In 1909, Cadbury was asked to deny the frequently made charge that he had given £20,000 to the Liberal Party.[4] He did deny it—though his choice of language suggests that the denial was evasive, to say the least—but admitted that 'I have supported certain candidatures in which I have been interested'.[5] He helped Ignatius Lincoln in this way,[6] and paid half Jesse Herbert's salary when he was Political Secretary to the Chief Whip.[7]

Cadbury's role as *eminence grise* meant that he was subjected to many different kinds of attack. He was accused of hypocrisy—for publishing betting news while supporting the Anti-Gambling League—and of trying to buy his way to a peerage, though in fact, he repeatedly declined proferred honours. A more serious charge was that he turned a blind eye to the sources of his cocoa, which was grown under conditions of virtual slavery—a criticism which led to a famous libel case.[8] But the heart of the case against him was that he exercised great and irresponsible political power. His donations inevitably led to the almost unconscious assumption of influence. Thus, when he gave a sorely needed £500 to the funds of the I.L.P., he attempted to use the

---

[1] *The Times,* 15 May 1907.   [2] Gardiner, *Life of George Cadbury,* p. 61.
[3] ibid., p. 109.   [4] *The Times,* 6 Oct. 1909.   [5] ibid., 7 Oct. 1909.
[6] Information from Professor H. J. Hanham.
[7] B.M.Add.MS. 41215 (Campbell-Bannerman Papers), f.148: Herbert Gladstone to Campbell-Bannerman, 19 Nov. 1899.
[8] Cadbury *v.* Standard Newspapers. Cadbury was awarded a farthing's damages, but the verdict, influenced by a brilliant defence by Sir Edward Carson, was probably unjust to him.

vantage point this gave him to prevent the I.L.P. from split-
ting the Liberal vote.[1]

Cadbury believed that the extent of his power was justified
by the excellence of his intentions. He was a philanthropist
who saw the limitations of private benevolence, and used his
wealth to attempt to sway state action, to bring about, on a
national scale, measures such as old age pensions which he
had already introduced in his little kingdom at Bournville.
An interesting exchange of letters between Campbell-
Bannerman and Herbert Gladstone in 1899 show the way
in which he was regarded by professional politicians. The
former, about to visit Birmingham, sent Gladstone an urgent
appeal for information: 'I have an invitn. from Mr. George
Cadbury . . . it wd. be convenient if I was told something
about him.'[2] The Chief Whip at once replied with this
vignette: 'His great absorptions are better conditions of life
for the working classes, & religion. He hates political
humbug & has no sympathy with 'irreligiousness'—Ask
him about his own work people whom he has brought out
into a model village away from B[irming]ham.'[3]

The relationship of Victorian Friends to politics is a subject
with a remarkable number of facets—the Society's activity
as a pressure group, its rapid abandonment of its rejection of
party politics, its relationship to 'Political Dissent', the entry
of Friends into local and national politics, and the influence
exercised by some Quaker party advisers and political patrons
who never entered parliament. Yet their most important
contribution to the society in which they lived was probably
made not in politics at all, but in philanthropy.

---

[1] B.M.Add.MS. 46058 (Herbert Gladstone Papers), f.129. Cadbury to Herbert
Gladstone, 8 Oct. 1900.

[2] B.M.Add.MS. 45987 (Herbert Gladstone Papers), f.42: Campbell-Bannerman
to Herbert Gladstone, 17 Nov. 1899.

[3] B.M.Add.MS. 41215, ff.148v.–149, Herbert Gladstone to Campbell-Bannerman, 19 Nov. 1899.

VIII

QUAKERS AND PHILANTHROPY

THE world of Victorian philanthropy, with its host of competing, and often conflicting agencies, was one of chaotic vitality. Nor is it easy to find a working definition of philanthropy to act as a guiding principle through the confusion. Owen, in his massive study of the subject, confined his attention to work which was humanitarian in the twentieth-century sense of the word, and which was accompanied by substantial donations of money.[1] The first limitation, at least, would have been meaningless to the Victorians, who made little distinction between work for men's bodies and work for their souls: the Anti-Corn Law agitators searched their Bibles for texts about the scarcity of bread,[2] and a movement as overtly other-worldly as the Lord's Day Observance Society buttressed itself with humanitarian arguments. The only adequate definition is some such tautology as that of the eighteenth-century nonjuror, who wrote that charity is 'doing good to the souls and bodies of men'.[3]

There can be no doubt that the part played by Quakers on the philanthropic scene was wholly disproportionate to their limited numbers. The innumerable tributes paid by contemporaries are borne out by the large number of Quaker names on lists of officers of charitable societies and on their subscription lists, both at the local and at the national level. Only a minority of the Quaker community was active in this way, but the members of this minority, drawn from its more prosperous strata, were likely to be active in half a dozen societies or more. Thus the names of three Friends, Joseph Ashby Gillett, Henry Beesley and

[1] David Owen, *English Philanthropy 1660–1960* (London, 1965), p. 1.
[2] The biblical texts which appeared regularly on the front page of the *Anti-Bread-Tax Circular*.
[3] Quoted in M. G. Jones, *The Charity School Movement A Study of Eighteenth Century Puritanism in Action* (new edition, London and Edinburgh, 1964), p. 3.

James Cadbury, recur repeatedly in the charitable annals of Banbury. Local philanthropy was more important than that at a national level in terms of the numbers of Friends actively involved, but their efforts in support of a multitude of local schools, hospitals, coal-clubs and soup-kitchens must await the attention of the local historian.

The Quaker reputation for philanthropy rested partly on the munificence of a few very wealthy men, partly upon the efforts of a class of prosperous and unusually energetic businessmen who helped control the destinies of a number of large charitable societies and, in effect, made a second career out of philanthropy. The men of the first class were frequently of great business ability, devoting their earlier years to the accumulation of wealth, their later ones to dispensing it, often under the veil of great secrecy. Richard Reynolds was a striking example in the early nineteenth century; in Victorian England, their numbers included Joseph Storrs Fry,[1] William Wilson of Bradford,[2] George Sturge[3] and the tea magnate, John Horniman.[4]

Some members of the second class have won enduring fame. William Allen was their outstanding representative until his death in 1847, and Joseph Sturge, until his death in 1859. Such men are remembered primarily as originators and organizers of philanthropic movements, but their work was accompanied by large money contributions. William Allen devoted most of his considerable financial resources to his agricultural settlement at Lindfield.[5] The extent of Joseph Sturge's munificence astonished Cobden, who asked him if he had found the widow's cruse.[6]

THE WELL-SPRINGS OF PHILANTHROPY

One cannot discuss Quaker philanthropy without considering the motives which lay behind it, and, in particular, the factors which made Friends pre-eminent in this field. Victorian biographers took it for granted that the good

---

[1] *The Annual Monitor* (1914), 63ff.   [2] *The Friend* (1850), 57–8.
[3] ibid. (1888), 123–4; M. Carta Sturge, *Some Little Quakers in their Nursery*, p. 109–10.   [4] Details of his will in *The Daily Telegraph*, 26 Dec. 1893.
[5] *Diary of William Lucas*, vol. ii, p. 331.
[6] B.M.Add.MS. 43723 (Sturge Papers), f.243: Cobden to Sturge, 20 May 1857.

works of philanthropists sprang from the religion they professed—'By their fruits ye shall know them.' Recent students of philanthropy—partly in reaction against Victorian hagiography—have tended to go to the other extreme, and emphasize its latent functions.[1] The truth probably lies somewhere in between. Religion alone does not explain philanthropy, for at every period there have been many Christians who were not philanthropists. Moreover, it is abundantly clear that Victorian charities offered many this-worldly satisfactions to their supporters. Yet it would be absurd to study philanthropy in isolation from a religion which makes the corporal works of mercy the pre-requisite of salvation. In particular, there is a clear nexus between philanthropy and evangelicalism.

Until the 1850s or later, Friends were not unanimous about the value of philanthropy. Some retained the social ideals of quietism, even when they were no longer personally quietists—the concept of a Peculiar People, avoiding contact with other denominations, the distrust of external action, which could distract a man from the inward condition of his soul. All the prominent Victorian Quaker philanthropists were evangelicals. They read their Bibles daily, noting their warnings about the spiritual perils of riches, and the necessity of charity. Evangelicalism tended to produce great earnestness in her children, a vivid consciousness of the eternal reward to be won or lost, a desire to do those good works which signify the possession of saving grace. Indeed the wealthy tended to see alms-giving as a kind of supernatural insurance. Samuel Gurney was congratulated for being 'by some peculiar fortune fitted for pleasant traffic *here*, and certain also of a good market above'.[2]

For the wealthy, philanthropy also filled a psychological function. It assuaged their guilt at a gulf between rich and poor which was at once far more extreme than anything in our society, and more evidently mirrored in differences of

[1] Owen, *op. cit.*, pp. 164ff.; Margaret B. Simey, *Charitable Effort in Liverpool in the Nineteenth Century* (Liverpool, 1951), pp. 55–8 and 62–4; Brian Harrison, 'Philanthropy and the Victorians', *Victorian Studies*, June 1966, pp. 357ff.

[2] Mrs. Thomas Geldart, *Memorials of Samuel Gurney* (London, 1857), pp. 26–7.

dress, diet, housing and style of life. They felt that the generous use of wealth justified them in the possession of it —'they would feel uneasy in the enjoyment of plenty and comfort . . . if they felt that they refused assistance to any who demanded it at their hands.'[1]

Much of the weakness of Victorian philanthropy sprang from this subjective orientation. Too often, it was geared to the psychological or spiritual needs of the donor, rather than to considerations of practical efficacy. Numerous societies with similar aims competed with each other and divided the available support. Bright and Cobden attacked the Peace Society for advocating peace on grounds and in ways which had no chance of winning general acceptance.[2] The United Kingdom Alliance wasted its great resources pursuing the chimera of local option, instead of supporting attainable measures of reform, such as Bruce's 1871 Licensing Bill. The anti-vivisectionists went into schism over this very issue—the ideal versus the attainable.[3] One Quaker philanthropist, with more self-awareness than was usual among his kind, analysed the way in which charities tended to become self-perpetuating vested interests, their support becoming a substitute for the search for effective remedies for social evils: 'all this machinery, itself, may absorb our thoughts and energies, and distract them from the real plodding work, the actual struggle with evil.'[4]

The most common criticism levelled at Victorian philanthropists was their love of recognition and praise. The very structure of a Victorian philanthropy, with its phalanx of honorary Vice-Presidents, its host of offices, and its printed subscription lists, encouraged the charitable to seek the bubble reputation. Critics as diverse as *The Times* and Francis Place attributed Quaker philanthropy to 'a love of distinction, which they can in no other way indulge'.[5] In the early nineteenth century, when most conventional avenues to distinction were closed to a Quaker, philanthropy formed what was in effect a world of its own, with its own titles and

---

[1] *The Friend* (1847), 5.   [2] Cf. pp. 219ff below.

[3] *Life of Frances Power Cobbe as told by Herself* (London, 1904), pp. 689ff.

[4] J. S. Fry, in *The Friend* (1860), 27.

[5] B.M.Add.MS. 27823 (Place Papers), ff.60-1, memorandum dated Dec. 1827, based on observations made in 1813-15; *The Times*, 30 Aug. 1838, p. 4.

distinctions.[1] Moreover, the reputations made in this way often extended far beyond Exeter Hall—as witness the Europe-wide renown of Elizabeth Fry. In these circumstances, some admixture of motives was perhaps inevitable— yet some of the most munificent Quaker philanthropists, such as Richard Reynolds, went to extraordinary lengths to keep their benefactions secret.

Many Quakers probably cared less for their reputations in society at large than for their standing in their own community. Although some prophets warned against the implications of philanthropy, in the little world of mid-Victorian Quakerism the figures to whom most honour was paid were the minister 'in good esteem' and the philanthropist. Indeed the less fortunate sometimes complained that the honour which was paid to the munificent was, by definition, out of reach of the 'struggling lower-middles'.[2] The wealthy, indeed, had often little choice in the matter. Especially after the advent of penny postage, they were deluged with requests from the advocates of assorted good causes.[3] Quakers knew each others' financial position fairly exactly, and their gifts to philanthropy were detailed in printed Annual Reports. The rich could not ignore the demands made upon them if they hoped to retain their standing in the Quaker community.

By the mid-nineteenth century, philanthropy was a hereditary duty in many prosperous Quaker families. It was noted in the 1860s that many of the Quakers who were active among the poor of Spitalfields were the descendants and namesakes of the founders of the Spitalfields Soup Society, in 1797.[4] The letters in the Gurney collection[5] show how members of the family—including some who are not remembered as philanthropists—took it for granted that in a bad year it was their duty to help the poor of Norwich.

Many Victorian philanthropists undoubtedly enjoyed their work. Long before she became famous, Elizabeth Fry, then Gurney, discovered the emotional satisfaction of charity—'There is a sort of luxury in giving way to the

[1] cf. a perceptive analysis in *The Saturday Review* (3 May 1856), 2.

[2] *The British Friend* (1898), 61.   [3] *FQE* (1869), 166.

[4] William Tallack, *Peter Bedford, The Spitalfields Philanthropist* (London, 1865), pp. 23–4.   [5] In FHL.

feelings. I love to feel for the sorrows of others.'[1] It is no coincidence that the single, the childless, and the widowed figured prominently in Quaker philanthropy. Thus, of the most prominent figures in the First Day School movement, William White and Joseph Storrs Fry were bachelors, and Joseph Sturge was a childless widower for much of his adult life. Many philanthropists, such as Sturge, possessed a restless vitality which did not find sufficient outlet in even a demanding business career.[2] Two years before her death, staying bored and restless at Sandgate, Elizabeth Fry complained, 'I think a place so remarkably void of objects does not suit my active mind . . . there is a danger of depending on active occupation for comfort and even for a certain degree of diversion.'[3]

Women of ability often found in charity the satisfaction they would have found, at a later date, in a career. It utilized their talents, and filled an often superabundant leisure—this was especially true of Quaker women, to whom, for much of the century, many conventional middle-class pursuits, such as music and painting, were closed. There was a literal truth in the pious aspiration of a Yearly Meeting Advice: 'The best recreation of a Christian is the relief of distress.'[4]

The Quaker reputation for philanthropy, like the comparable reputation of the Unitarians, rested largely on the fact that, as a wealthy community, they were able to render very considerable services to whatever causes they favoured. The philanthropist was necessarily prosperous; the generosity of the poor to each other has existed in every age, but has never been called philanthropy.

Factors other than their wealth, such as their prestige and immense respectability, made the Quakers valuable allies in any agitation. Their support did much to confer respectability on the teetotal movement, in its early stages, and on the agitation against the Contagious Diseases Acts. The strong links of kinship and friendship which bound them meant

---

[1] *Journal*, 16 May 1797; cf. 18 June 1798.
[2] B.M.Add.MS. 43664 (Cobden Papers), f.55v: Cobden to Parkes, 3 Nov. 1856.
[3] *Journal*, undated entry, 1843 (1843-5 volume, p. 27).
[4] *Book of Extracts*, 1834, p. 44.

that a Quaker could write to fellow-members, who were probably also relatives, in every part of England and gain their support for a good cause. The regular gatherings of Friends at Monthly, Quarterly, and Yearly Meetings, meant that the advocates of, for instance, teetotalism, had ample opportunity to spread their views. And the tradition of itinerant ministry could easily embrace the platform lecturers who were so important in the spread of any Victorian movement. The son of a Quaker Leeds philanthropist remembered from his childhood the succession of

visiting Friends who were sometimes not entertaining to be entertained, hospitality to be provided for people who had lately appeared or would shortly appear on a platform, from which they would address solid Yorkshire Nonconformists on Opium, on Gambling, on the iniquities of the Trade (which should be controlled), on the blessings of Free Trade (which should not be controlled), on Peace, on Social Purity, on Foreign Missions.[1]

To reflect on the springs of philanthropy is not, of course, to deny the value of its contribution. Similarly, it seems pointless to judge the philanthropist because he worked within the intellectual context of his time, and took social inequality for granted—as Cole does, when he criticizes Sturge because he attacked the manifestations of social evils, instead of their causes—whatever that may mean.[2] In 1878 *The Friend* stated that 'The palpable evils afflicting humanity in any part of the earth, are the topics that most closely occupy the thoughts of Friends everywhere.'[3] It was a proud boast, and probably one which no other denominational paper could have made with equal justice. To contemporaries, this was the chief glory of the Quakers. For that matter, it is so still.

One cannot discuss philanthropy very profitably in the abstract, as if it were a single coherent entity. Yet Victorian charities, seeking the same, or not infrequently diametrically opposed objects, existed in incredible profusion, and simply to list them, in a directory such as Sampson Low's *The Charities of London*, or Loch's *Charities' Register and*

[1] William Fryer Harvey, *We Were Seven* (London, 1936), p. 3.
[2] G. D. H. Cole, *Chartist Portraits* (London, 1941), p. 186.
[3] *The Friend* (1878), 3.

Digest, fills a substantial volume. The account which follows, of the role of Friends in specific charities, is necessarily short and selective. It is not difficult to ascertain which movements they supported most generally: they listed them from time to time,[1] and the most popular recur in biographies and obituaries. Considerations of space have led to the exclusion of some important movements, in which Quakers played a considerable role, such as the R.S.P.C.A.,[2] the anti-opium movement, and the anti-vivisection movement; Friends came close to supporting the last-mentioned officially.[3] Similarly, there is no account of Friends' generous corporate response to international crises, such as the Irish famine. But the movements discussed in the pages that follow were probably those which were most important to Victorian Friends.

THE PEACE MOVEMENT

The peace movement is rather different from others in which Friends were interested, for they were bound to support it, in theory at least, by virtue of their very Quakerism. Their attitude to pacifism, in so far as it affected their personal conduct, was discussed in an earlier chapter. This chapter section discusses their efforts to spread peace principles in society generally.

The key criticism which was always levelled at the peace movement, in its various branches and phases, was its lack of realism. This was implicit in the situation: a few thousand Quakers, allied with the like-minded from other denominations, were unlikely to exercise any real influence on international politics. Not all made the attempt. Only a minority of Friends were actively involved in pacifist movements, and few of the outstanding Victorian pacifists were Friends.

The history of the Victorian peace movement has a number of facets. It produced a number of theoretical justifications of pacifism—one of the best known was written some years earlier by a Quaker, Jonathan Dymond—and innumerable blueprints for arbitration systems or world

---

[1] *The Friend* (1843), 64; (1846), 8; (1851), 139 and (1858), 127.
[2] Fairholme and Pain. *A Century of Work for Animals*, pp. 69, 71–4. *The Friend* (1850), 57.   [3] *Yearly Meeting Proceedings, 1889*, p. 22.

government. The details of these utopias, however, are of less interest than the practical efforts made by various peace societies to diffuse pacifist principles.

Sometimes the Society of Friends acted in an official capacity, as when, in 1841, Meeting for Sufferings printed a declaration on the evils of war,[1] or when three Friends visited the Tsar of Russia in an effort to avert the Crimean War. Friends themselves realized that the very fact that pacifism was an official tenet of their church made it more difficult for them to spread it among others. In general, those who felt a strong personal commitment to pacifism were not content with supporting the official policy of their church on the matter, but also chose to act through other channels.

The Peace Society was founded in 1816, at the close of the Napoleonic wars. It was one of a number of benevolent societies which originated at an informal meeting at William Allen's home, though the initiative came partly from another Quaker, the Welsh iron-founder, Joseph Tregelles Price.[2] But non-Quakers were present, and it was never to be an exclusively Quaker enterprise. It was essentially a propagandist body. In its early years, its operations were confined to circulating pacifist literature—'The object of the Society shall be to print and circulate Tracts.'[3] Indeed, it bore a strong family resemblance to the Friends' Tract Society. Gradually it extended its scope to include lectures and public meetings, and it presented its first parliamentary petition in 1841. But its objectives were always educational, and the means at its disposal painfully inadequate for the vastness of its task. It took the so-called 'high' pacifist position, condemning war, not on humanitarian or economic grounds, but as contrary to Christianity. It was realized that this limited its appeal, but its members tended to pride themselves on their refusal to seek a broader basis.[4]

Support of the Peace Society tended to go hand in hand with a number of other sympathies—these well illustrate that interrelatedness of philanthropic interests which forms

[1] *Meeting for Sufferings Minutes, 6 November 1840, 30 April 1841, and 24 January 1842* (MSS. in FHL).
[2] *Life of William Allen*, I, 224; *The Herald of Peace* (1855) 212.
[3] *Objects, Rules etc* (n.d., [1845]), p. 2, Rule 2.
[4] *The Herald of Peace* (1840), 117; cf. (1854), 6–7.

a recurrent theme of this chapter. Opposition to duelling and to capital punishment were almost official tenets.[1] In the 1830s it supported the anti-slavery movement,[2] and in the 1870s, the anti-opium movement,[3] and the agitation against the Contagious Diseases Acts.[4] The resolution of the First General Peace Convention in 1843 included one on temperance,[5] and a speaker at the 1841 Annual General Meeting apparently disturbed no one when he launched into an attack on 'the accursed Bread Monopoly'.[6]

The link between pacifism and the Anti-Corn Law League was particularly strong. Many supporters of the League saw Free Trade as the key to international peace, and speeches at Peace Society meetings often showed precisely the same social orientation as the League, the same hatred of aristocracy and privilege. One speaker rejoiced that the Peace Society did not embrace 'the landgraves of the day—the coronetted barbarians of the age'.[7]

For the first thirty years of its existence, the Peace Society made little impact on public opinion. It is doubtful if it seriously sought to do so; its members paid their subscriptions and distributed their tracts essentially as a personal gesture. From perhaps 1846 until the Crimean War broke out in 1854, the peace movement in England underwent a revival. It was dominated in those years by four men, Cobden, Elihu Burritt, and the Quakers Bright and Sturge. The revival was partly due to the success of the anti-Corn Law agitation. Victorian agitations tended to be each others' heirs, and the success of the League freed energies for the peace movement. Dymond had hoped that the success of the anti-slavery movement would have this effect.[8] The challenge of the Militia Bills of 1846 and 1848 also aroused pacifists, and one cannot ignore the curious impact of Elihu Burritt.

1 *The Herald of Peace* (1838), 2, 137 and 187–8; (1841), 261ff.
2 ibid. (1838), 2–3.   3 *Peace Society Annual Report, 1877*, pp. 25–6.
4 *Peace Society Annual Report, 1870*, pp. 17–18.
5 *The Herald of Peace* (1843), 397.   6 Ibid. (1841), 328–9.
7 ibid. (1841), 328. cf. [Jonathan Dymond] *An Enquiry into the Accordancy of War with the Principles of Christianity, and an Examination of the Philosophical Reasoning by which it is defended* (London, 1823), pp. 11–13.
8 Charles William Dymond, *Memoir Letters and Poems of Jonathan Dymond with Bibliographical Supplements* (privately printed, 1911), p. 53.

Burritt, who was not a Friend, was an American black-smith, a remarkable autodidact who rose to prominence in the peace and anti-slavery movements. He came to England in 1846 at the invitation of a Quaker and spent much of the next decade here, founding several new pacifist organizations, the Olive Leaf Circles and the League of Brotherhood. The Peace Congresses of 1848–53 were his idea. He associated so much with Friends that he began using 'thee' in his correspondence. He was rather an unlikely figure to be *persona grata* among Victorian Quakers, and the welcome many of them gave him probably reflects the poverty of the English peace movement at that time. To others, however, he was an impractical visionary[1]—they shared Cobden's scepticism[2] about the lasting value of his work.

Joseph Sturge was a dominant figure in the English pacifist movement in the years before the Crimean War. Henry Richard was in an excellent position to assess his role, for he became secretary of the Peace Society in 1848, and dominated its fortunes until his death forty years later. He wrote of Sturge, 'around no one's personal history could the [Peace] movement be made to revolve with greater propriety. . . . For he was to a large extent its animating spirit.'[3] Sturge devoted financial support and his remarkable energy to all forms of peace work. He helped finance Burritt's projects,[4] was president of the Peace Society at his death, and played a major role in the peace congress movement.[5] On two occasions, he attempted to avert war by his personal intervention,[6] and was with difficulty dissuaded from going to India at the time of the Mutiny. His visits to the great made him an easy butt for criticism, but for Sturge, action was a moral imperative. He could not be content to further the cause of peace by tract distribution.

Sturge was an orthodox Quaker pacifist, holding that war

[1] *The Friend* (1846), 215. The support he received from many English Friends is mirrored in the collection of his correspondence in FHL.
[2] Hobson, *op. cit.*, pp. 71–2.
[3] Richard, *Memoirs of Joseph Sturge*, p. 428.
[4] *The Bond of Brotherhood* (June 1859), 162.
[5] Richard, *op. cit.*, pp. 429–30.
[6] cf. p. 192 above. The other occasion was the Schleswig-Holstein dispute in 1850.

is contrary to God's will under every circumstance. Cobden
and Bright were pacifists of a very different kind. Bright
wrote at the time of the Indian Mutiny, 'I have never
advocated the extreme peace principle, the non-resistance
principle in public, or in private. I don't know whether I
could logically maintain it.'[1] Bright's opposition to war rested
partly on humanitarian grounds, given classic expression in
his Crimean War speeches, and partly on economic grounds.
His genuine distress at the human cost of the Crimean
campaign did not make him any less sensitive to its effect on
commerce.[2] As Cobden put it, '. . . all good things pull
together. Free trade, peace, financial reform, equitable taxation, all are co-operating towards a common object.'[3]

Both Bright and Cobden criticized the Peace Society for
building its pacifism on too narrow a basis, and for the
essential impracticality of its approach. 'I dislike working
at an impossible cause, or by an impossible method.'[4] Their
attitude to the 'high' pacifism of the Peace Society and of
the Society of Friends was ambivalent. On the one hand,
Cobden dissociated himself from them in public, fearing to
have his arbitration proposals and non-interventionist
foreign policy branded as the idealism of fanatics, or the
peculiar doctrine of a sect. He made the distinction carefully
when introducing his arbitration resolution in 1849: 'There
were at present two movements going on in this country.'[5]
But he realized that any work for peace rested heavily on
Quaker support. He told Sturge, 'There is no vitality in
the movement excepting that which springs from your
religious body.'[6] And it was the orthodox pacifists, Burritt
and Richard, who stumped the country whipping up support for his resolutions.[7]

Although their peace views rested on a less exalted basis

[1] M.B.Add.MS. 43723 (Sturge Papers), f.85v–6: Bright to Sturge, 24 Sept.
1857.
[2] Bright to J. B. Smith, 31 Dec. 1855 (Bright–Smith correspondence in Manchester City Library).   [3] Richard, op. cit., p. 424.
[4] B.M.Add.MS. 43845 (Sturge Papers), f.51: Bright to Sturge, 11 Oct. 1857.
cf. Joseph Rowntree, Account of 1855 Yearly Meeting, pp. 69–71.
[5] Hansard, 3rd ser. cvi (1849), 118.
[6] B.M.Add.MS. 43656 (Cobden Papers), f.153: Cobden to Sturge, 10 Aug. 1849.
[7] Elihu Burritt, Ten Minute Talks on all sorts of topics, with Autobiography of the
Author (London, 1874), p. 25. cf. The Herald of Peace 1856, p. 65.

than those of the Peace Society, both Cobden and Bright made a more effective contribution to the cause. They sacrificed their great popularity by their opposition to the Crimean War, and Cobden, in particular, from the dissolution of the League until his death, devoted his best energies to the cause of international peace. During the war, in order to give a more effective voice to the peace party, Cobden and Sturge established *The Morning Star*, with financial help from rich Quakers such as Edward Backhouse, and Joseph and Henry Pease.[1] Its first editor was the secretary of the Peace Society, but when it appeared in danger of turning into a second *Herald of Peace*, Bright's brother-in-law, Samuel Lucas, became editor.[2]

In retrospect, the years 1846–54 were to seem the Indian summer of Victorian pacifism. Its supporters noted the failure of the first two militia bills, the relative success of Cobden's motion in favour of arbitration, and the series of spectacular peace congresses. In 1853, a new edition of Grotius' *The Law of War and Peace* came out, in response to the growing popularity of the peace movement.[3] But the Crimean War was destined to crush English pacifism for a decade. The peace congresses disappeared for a generation, and the futility of the hopes of 1846–54 were made all too clear by the events of 1854–6.

The next sign of vitality in the English peace movement came, not from the middle-class, Quaker-dominated Peace Society, but from a very different social context. In 1870 Randal Cremer established the Workmen's Peace Committee, destined to become the Workmen's Peace Association, and later the International Arbitration League. Cremer was originally a carpenter, though he was to become an M.P. and Nobel Prize winner. He had been a leading member of the Reform League, and Edmond Beales, the President of the Reform League, presided over the new organization from its inception until his death. The International Arbitration League was a labour organization, non-

---

[1] B.M.Add.MS. 43722 (Sturge Papers) f.83v: Sturge to Cobden, 27 Sept. 1855.
[2] Charles S. Miall, *Henry Richard, M.P. A Biography* (London, 1889), pp. 113–18.
[3] Christina Phelps, *The Anglo-American Peace Movement in the Mid-Nineteenth Century* (New York, 1930), p. 31.

religious and class-orientated, and closely linked with similar movements on the Continent. The Peace Society, however, regarded it benevolently, seeing it as a working-class auxiliary to itself.[1] It gave it financial support, as did a number of individual Friends, such as John Horniman, George Palmer, and Richard and George Cadbury.[2]

When yet another peace organization was founded in 1882, again by a non-Quaker, the Peace Society was less enthusiastic. It commented on Hodgson Pratt's International Arbitration and Peace Association reproachfully— 'We cannot but deeply deprecate any effort tending to divide the resources and energies of the Friends of Peace.'[3] But a few years later it was paying Pratt the ultimate compliment of comparison with Joseph Sturge.[4] The Peace Society had come to see itself as the venerable father-figure of English pacifism.

The Peace Society itself underwent something of a revival in the 1870s. Largely in consequence of the passage of Richard's arbitration resolution in the Commons in 1873, all English pacifist societies came to concentrate mainly on advocating arbitration.[5] Many who saw little point in the constant reiteration of abstract sentiments in favour of peace —which, in the abstract, never found a serious opponent— were prepared to support a concrete policy with some chance of success.[6] But from the eighties onwards, the Peace Society was in decline. New movements, such as the Inter-Parliamentary Union and the series of congresses beginning in 1889, captured the imagination and offered greater chances of success. The Peace Society's income declined steadily in the nineties and there were constant complaints of lack of funds, despite a large legacy from John Horniman. The Annual Reports of the nineties show the Society's old lack of realism; despite their constant mention of financial difficulties, there is the old optimism about the progress of the cause of peace, and the Peace Society's contribution towards it.[7]

1 *Peace Society Annual Reports, 1875*, p. 14; *1877*, pp. 19–20; *1880*, p. 8.
2 Howard Evans, *Sir Randal Cremer His Life and Work* (London, 1909), p. 86.
3 *The Herald of Peace* (1880), 134.   4 ibid. (1889), 167.
5 *Peace Society Annual Report, 1875*, pp. 19–20.   6 ibid.
7 e.g. *Peace Society Annual Report, 1890–1*, pp. 5–6.

Only a few of the leading Victorian pacifists were Quakers at all. Their role was to provide a solid core of prosperous and reliable supporters—'We are nothing without the "Friends"'.[1] Their views were respected even by those normally hostile to pacifism—*The Quarterly Review*, in a sarcastic account of the Paris Peace Congress, paid them tribute: 'we greatly respect that sober brotherhood.'[2] Until the 1850s, Friends were the main subscribers to the Peace Society,[3] but did not support it as enthusiastically as many wished,[4] and Annual General Meetings were dominated by clergymen. It seems that some Friends were fearful of compromising the purity of their peace principles, while those who did support it were careful to avoid giving the impression that it was a Quaker organization. But later, Quaker domination became increasingly apparent. The secretary, Henry Richard, was a Congregationalist, but the President was always a Friend after Sturge's term of office. In 1870 two out of five Vice-Presidents, at least twelve out of eighteen General Committee members, and over a third of Executive Committee members were Friends.[5] They continued to provide the bulk of its financial support; all but one of those who subscribed £25 or over in 1885–6 were Friends, or closely connected with them. But support of the Peace Society did not necessarily indicate a strong personal commitment to pacifism. It was practically a hereditary obligation in some prosperous Quaker families. And on the whole, Friends played little part in other Victorian peace organizations.

From the late eighties on, the Society of Friends began to take a stronger interest in pacifism in its official capacity. The immediate occasion of its awakened interest was a conference on peace and arbitration held concurrently with the Richmond conference on doctrine in 1887. After the English delegates returned home, a network of Quaker committees was set up to discuss the dissemination of peace ideals, which culminated in the holding of an inter-church

---

[1] Cobden to Richard, 17 Oct. 1853, in Hobson, *Richard Cobden: The International Man*, p. 105.   [2] *The Quarterley Review* (1849), 470.
[3] *The Irish Friend* (1841), 105.
[4] *The Annual Monitor* (1841), 125 and 143–4. *The Herald of Peace* (1840), 121.
[5] *Peace Society, Annual Report, 1870.*

conference.[1] A number of individual Friends, such as Joseph Gundry Alexander,[2] Joshua Rowntree, and John Edward Ellis were prominent in the peace congress movement, or other forms of pacifist activity. Probably peace, the Adult Schools and the opium question were the causes closest to the hearts of Quaker philanthropists in the closing years of the nineteenth century.

THE ANTI-SLAVERY MOVEMENT

The great age of the anti-slavery movement ended in 1833. The abolition of negro slavery in the British empire in that year radically changed its nature. Previously, it had sought the abolition of slavery within the empire by means of exerting pressure on the government at Westminster. Abolitionists were often divided about the best means to employ, but never about their aim. Indeed one of the great attractions of the anti-slavery movement was that there could scarcely be two opinions about the evils of plantation slavery. It was one of those polarized issues so beloved of reformers, and, in the complexity of human affairs, so difficult to find. After 1833, however, issues relating to slavery became more complex, and abolitionists themselves were often divided. The movement was to be conducted on two fronts.

The first of these was its attack on slavery in countries outside the British empire. This goal could not, of course, be attained within the context of British politics, so that abolitionists rather resembled the Peace Society in the disparity between the magnitude of their aims, and the limited means at their disposal. The means they adopted, indeed, were similar: the publication of books, tracts and articles, correspondence with the like-minded in other countries, and periodic international gatherings.

The second aspect, which forms the theme of this chapter section, was the attitude of abolitionists to issues in British politics which had a bearing on slavery. After 1833 the

---

[1] *Peace Society, Annual Report, 1893–4*, p. 8.

[2] For details of his work in the International Law Association and the Peace Congress movement, see Horace G. Alexander, *Joseph Gundry Alexander* (London n.d. [1920]), pp. 40ff. and 174ff.

most important of these were the so-called apprenticeship system which replaced slavery in the West Indies, Buxton's Niger expedition, the sugar duties, and the West African squadron. Each of these issues was to create profound divisions among the opponents of slavery. The pages which follow analyse the way in which Quakers threaded their way through these troubled waters, and how the anti-slavery movement forms a theme in counterpoint with the Free Trade and peace movements.

The apprenticeship system, which in practice varied little from slavery, had been introduced, with the approval of many philanthropists, to bridge the transition from slavery to freedom in the West Indies. In March 1835 the government appointed a Select Committee to investigate reports of abuses which were already filtering back to England. The Committee, in effect, supported the system while deploring the abuses. Among the many who felt dissatisfied with the verdict, Joseph Sturge translated dissatisfaction into action. In the company of another Friend, he sailed for the West Indies in 1837 to see and report for himself. This was not his first venture into anti-slavery work—he had been an active supporter of the Agency Committee, the radical wing of the abolitionist movement—but it was his opposition to the apprenticeship system which made him the national leader of the movement.

When he returned to England, Sturge published *The West Indies in 1837*, which had a considerable impact on public opinion. He established a new organization, to conduct an agitation similar to that of 1833—the Central Emancipation Committee. The chain of events which followed is well known. A snap division in a thin House resolved in favour of the immediate abolition of the apprenticeship system. The decision was later reversed, but meanwhile the colonial legislatures, noting the way the wind was blowing, had decided to end a system for which they had never had any great enthusiasm, and which was destined to come to an end soon, in any case.[1] Inevitably, Sturge gained the credit in abolitionist eyes, just as the League gained the

---

[1] This account is based on W. L. Burn, *Emancipation and Apprenticeship in the British West Indies* (London, 1937).

credit for the abolition of the Corn Laws. The actual workings of the system were apparently less reprehensible than they seemed to Sturge. He saw it, like every other issue, as a simple confrontation of the forces of good and evil.

The interests of the emancipated slaves remained close to Sturge's heart and the hearts of Friends in general. The Society of Friends contributed £400 towards the debts of the Central Emancipation Committee.[1] In 1838, Yearly Meeting decided to raise a special fund for the benefit of 'the African race'.[2] As the Negroes and Aborigines Fund, this was raised regularly from 1846 on. Much of it went in grants for educational purposes in the West Indies—grants accompanied by 'a considerable supply of Friends Books and Tracts'.[3]

Sturge did not rest on his achievements, but immediately turned to the creation of a new British and Foreign Anti-Slavery Society, in 1839. Although he held no position in it for several years,[4] he was to guide its policy. Quakers were overwhelmingly dominant in the new Society. The London banker, George W. Alexander, was its indefatigable treasurer, and fourteen out of twenty-seven committee members were Friends.[5] As a result of Quaker influence, the Society was explicitly pacifist from the beginning, a policy full of unforeseen consequences.

The next important development was the Niger expedition of 1841. It was the brain-child of the veteran abolitionist Thomas Fowell Buxton, who was not a Friend, though closely linked with the Society. He believed that Britain's efforts to suppress the slave trade by policing the coast of West Africa with a squadron had proved ineffective, and proposed to cut the slave trade off at its roots by supplanting it with other forms of commerce in the interior. The plan was not new, but it rapidly gained influential supporters and government sponsorship. Sturge and his supporters were critical of the scheme though they did not oppose it openly. The arms which the expedition carried offended their

---

[1] *Meeting for Sufferings Minutes, 7 February 1840.*   [2] ibid., *4 June 1838.*
[3] For the various uses to which the Fund was put, ibid., *11 May 1842.*
[4] When Corresponding Members were introduced in 1843, he became one. [*British and Foreign*] *Anti-Slavery Society Annual Report,* 1844, p. 7.
[5] ibid., 1840.

pacifism,[1] and Sturge, at least, feared that despite the piety of its promoters the scheme might result in 'the same infamous conquest of Africa as has taken place in India'.[2] *The Anti-Slavery Reporter* practically ignored the project,[3] and the only prominent Quaker in the Anti-Slavery Society to support it was Samuel Gurney. Gurney was Buxton's brother-in-law, and a less scrupulous pacifist than many of his fellow-members of the Peace Society.[4] In the event, the expedition, ravaged by sickness, was a disaster.

Between 1840 and 1846, the main issue which confronted and divided British abolitionists was the sugar tariff. West Indian sugar was protected on the British market by high tariffs, a relic from the mercantilist era. Since West Indian sugar was more expensive to produce than Cuban and Brazilian, and was in any case inadequate in quantity, English sugar was much dearer than that sold on the continent. The sugar duties would doubtless have gone the way of other tariffs repealed in Peel's budgets had it not been for the fact that the emancipation of the West Indian slaves had converted them into what was, in effect, a subsidy to free labour.

The issue was to divide not only public opinion in general, but also the anti-slavery party, for in the 1840s Free Trade was more important than slavery to many reformers. Arguments, humanitarian and otherwise, could be marshalled on both sides. To Sturge, himself a convinced Free Trader, the proposal to remove the sugar tariffs was a proposal to subsidize slavery. To increase the demand for the slave-grown sugar of Cuba and Brazil was to increase the demand for slaves, and encourage the slave trade. The sufferings of the English poor, who could not afford to buy sugar at all, were not to be compared with those of the unhappy victims of the Middle Passage.

[1] Samuel to J. J. Gurney, 30 Sept. 1840 (*Gurney MSS.* II, 433). Samuel Gurney to Sturge, 24 Oct. 1840 (Anti-Slavery Society MSS. in Rhodes House, Oxford), C 110, f.22.

[2] Sturge to Beaumont, 25 Apr. 1842 (Rhodes House MSS.), C.110, f.95.

[3] Its only reference was to print a letter on the subject from Lord John Russell, without comment.

[4] B.M.Add.MS. 50131 (Sturge Papers), f.217v: Cobden to Sturge, 21 Oct. 1850. Cobden to Richard, 5 Jan. 1850, quoted in Hobson, *Richard Cobden the International Man,* p. 62.

The opponents of the sugar tariffs used the same blend of economic and humanitarian arguments that they used against the Corn Laws—not surprisingly, for they were, on the whole, the same men. Manufacturers had a direct interest in their repeal. The less the English consumer spent on food, the more he could spend on manufactured goods, or, alternatively, the less he needed to receive in wages. Moreover, they were fascinated by the vast potential market in Brazil, which needed to export sugar to England before she could afford to import her cotton goods. Why should they sacrifice the prospect so that England might act as the moral conscience of the world?

To these considerations they added, like all Victorian controversialists, an arsenal of moral and humanitarian arguments. It was often claimed that abolitionists were more sensitive to the sufferings of the distant negro than to those of the English labouring poor. This argument was popular with the poor themselves. Chartists broke up an Anti-Slavery meeting at Norwich, urging the Gurneys to remember the slaves at home.[1] *The Times* pointed out that Joseph Pease's concern for slaves contrasted oddly with the fate of 'the wretched little beings who are toiling from morning to night among the wheels of his own machinery'.[2] Bright's zeal for Free Trade turned him into something very like an apologist for slavery, an episode which Trevelyan, his biographer, entirely ignores, though he dwells on his anti-slavery rhetoric at the time of the American civil war. He agreed with the view that the diet of the English poor was more important than the claims of 'a distant and barbarous people'.[3] He opposed a bill to prevent the investment of British capital in the slave trade,[4] called Palmerston's interest in slavery 'a benevolent crotchet',[5] and showed a passionate interest in trade with Brazil,[6] promising that

[1] B.M. Egerton MS. 3675, Part I, ff.144–6v: Katherine Fry to Mrs. Pelly, 19 November 1840. cf. *The Anti-Slavery Reporter*, 1840, p. 296.

[2] *The Times*, 30 Aug. 1838.

[3] Hutt's phrase. *Hansard*, 3rd ser. lxxxi (1845), 1158. cf. ibid., 1844, lxxiii. 660 and B.M.Add.MS. 43845 (Sturge Papers), ff.12–15v: Bright to Sturge, 1 Sept. 1843.   [4] *Hansard*, 3rd ser. lxxi (1845), 940–1.

[5] ibid., civ. (1849), 787.

[6] ibid., 3rd ser. lxxiii (1844), 659ff. cf. Harvey to Sturge 4 June 1840 (Rhodes House MSS.) C.110, f.23.

17—V.Q.

'anti-slavery notions would not be a hinderance in the way of any Gentleman who came forward in favour of Free-trade opinions'.[1] Some leading Quakers, such as Ashworth, shared his views,[2] but when he claimed to speak for Friends in general he overstated his case.[3] But it was left for Peel to point out the strange discrepancy between Bright's speeches and the Quaker anti-slavery traditions of the past.[4]

The issue divided the Anti-Slavery Society to the point of schism. Its London Committee decided to oppose any change in the tariffs, and exerted pressure on the government to this effect. They were at once deluged with letters from their branches in the provinces, 'generally, but not universally, differing from them'.[5] The 1843 anti-slavery convention showed itself profoundly divided over the issue, and came to no decision.[6] A small group of Free Traders, irrevocably opposed to the Committee, seceded from the Society and circularized its members with attacks on its policy.[7] At the 1844 General Meeting, both sides stated their viewpoint acrimoniously. Some days later, a thinly attended special meeting, apparently dominated by Quakers,[8] confirmed the Committee's policy, but these divisions fatally weakened the Anti-Slavery Society's public image, and gave a valuable weapon to the Free Trade party.[9]

In the event, the sugar tariffs fell with the Corn Laws, as Free Traders had long predicted. The immediate result was to subsidize the slave trade; when the news reached Havana, it was illuminated in celebration. J. J. Gurney wrote prophetically to his daughter: 'I have felt the *pain* of being beaten on the Sugar question, & greatly fear that blood & tears will flow abundantly in consequence.'[10]

These divisions among the anti-slavery party, and among Friends, outlived the differential tariffs. In 1848 Yearly Meeting refused to accept the recommendation of Meeting

---

[1] *Hansard*, 3rd ser. lxxiii (1844), 660.
[2] B.M.Add.MS. 43653 (Cobden Papers), f.1: Ashworth to Cobden, 9 May 1841.   [3] *Hansard*, 3rd ser. lxxi (1843), 940.
[4] ibid. lxxiii (1844), 679.
[5] *The Anti-Slavery Reporter* (1841), p. 105. cf. p. 113.
[6] ibid. (1843), 103–6.   [7] ibid. (1844), 53–4.
[8] *The Friend* (1844), 131.   [9] *Hansard*, 3rd ser. lxxiii (1844), 660; cf. 655.
[10] Gurney to Anna Backhouse, 4 Aug. 1846 (*Gurney MSS.*, III, 885).

for Sufferings that it should petition parliament against
Cuban and Brazilian sugar. As late as 1853 a correspondent
referred to the bitterness of these divisions among Friends:
'I would not, if I could avoid it, have anti-slavery Friends
and pro-slavery Friends making slavery or its opposite the
bond of Christian fellowship'.[1]

The only course of action left for Sturge and his supporters was personal abstension from slave-grown produce.
This was no novelty: William Allen had abstained from
sugar for forty-three years, for this reason. Those who used
free labour produce did not seriously hope to end slavery in
this way, any more than those who subscribed to the Peace
Society expected to put an end to war. In both cases, what
was sought was personal exemption from complicity in a
known evil. The question of whether Friends should use
slave-grown produce was to prove a subject of strong contention in the Society, producing lengthy controversies in
the correspondence columns of *The Friend*.

The remaining issue in the forties which related to slavery
concerned the naval squadron which Britain maintained to
police the coast of West Africa against slavers: Buxton, as
part of his justification of the Niger expedition, had attacked
the squadron as ineffective. The Anti-Slavery Society took
the same line. In 1846 it memorialized Russell on the subject, stating that not only did the squadron fail to attain its
object, but actually increased the hardships of the captives,
since slavers were built for speed, not for stowage.[2] It
recommended that the government should instead exert
pressure on the Spanish colonies and Brazil, bound by treaty
to suppress the trade. This attitude was due largely to the
pacifism of the Quakers who dominated it: the Peace Society
petitioned against the squadron at the same time.[3] But many
abolitionists were appalled at their policy. Sir George
Stephen, the veteran of the Agency Committee, called it a
'grievous mistake',[4] and *The Patriot* claimed that 'they have
bestowed their influence in favour of a movement directly

---

1 Joseph Rowntree to Josiah Forster, 23 Aug. 1853, quoted in John S. Rowntree, *A Family Memoir of Joseph Rowntree*, p. 574.
2 *The Anti-Slavery Reporter* (1846), 169–72.
3 *The Herald of Peace* (1845), 288.
4 Stephen, *Anti-slavery Recollections*, 210.

opposed to the principles of the very party whose social name they have usurped.'[1]

Unfortunately, this well-meaning attack on the squadron coincided with another, which was very differently motivated. Between 1845 and 1850, William Hutt, M.P. for Gateshead, launched a series of similar attacks in the Commons. He was indifferent, to say the least, to the fate of the slave trade's victims, but opposed the squadron on grounds of economy. The conventions of public life demanded that he should support his case by arguments of a more elevated kind. Paradoxically, he derived them from the Anti-Slavery Society. The Society felt uneasy about this ally and the association soon broke down. The Anti-Slavery Society claimed that the government should force Brazil and Cuba to co-operate by threatening to re-impose the differential sugar tariffs, proposals which were anathema to Hutt, a convinced Free Trader. By 1848 the Society was attacking Hutt: 'The Committee ... dare not balance, in the same scales, the profits of merchants and manufacturers, against the liberty, the civilisation and the happiness of their fellow-men.'[2]

In the event, Hutt's campaign failed, and the squadron soon achieved resounding success. In 1850 it moved into Brazilian waters, and after some hesitation the Brazilian government decided to co-operate with it. By 1853, the Brazilian slave trade was virtually extinct.

From the 1850s, the Anti-Slavery Society was in a state of decline. It was in some ways comparable to the Peace Society, but, unlike the Peace Society, the movement had known better days. It was its misfortune that all the issues in British politics in the 1840s which affected slavery were issues on which abolitionist opinion was deeply divided. From the 1850s on, the arena of anti-slavery action lay elsewhere. The English society could do little to oppose slavery in the United States, or in Brazil and the Spanish colonies. Occasionally an issue arose over which it could take action, such as the prosecution of Governor Eyre, but essentially it

---

[1] Quoted in *The Anti-Slavery Reporter* (1849), 184.
[2] ibid. (1848), 92. For criticisms of the Committee, ibid. (1849), 184–5.

was living on the memory of more glorious days. Its support came mainly from Friends, in a traditional and largely sentimental association. In 1883 it described itself as 'a small and earnest body' but admitted that 'to most of the world it has practically ceased to exist'.[1]

The consciousness of the role they had played in earlier phases of the anti-slavery agitation largely determined the continuing official interest of Friends in the movement. A special committee of Meeting for Sufferings dealt with Negroes and Aborigines, and a fund was raised regularly for their benefit. By a donation of £800 it bestowed its official blessing on the Anti-Slavery Society.[2] In the Quaker tradition of deputations to crowned heads, it memorialized Victoria on the subject in 1849,[3] and later William Forster carried the document to various European rulers and to America. At the very end of the century, however, the Society found a more effective expression for what the Meeting for Sufferings called its 'heritage of changeless opposition to slavery', when a Quaker industrial mission was established among the slaves of Pemba, who were liberated in 1897.

THE TEMPERANCE MOVEMENT

Both peace and opposition to slavery were official pre-occupations of Friends. They were the aspects of Quaker philanthropy which were most indelibly associated with their image, and which brought them most fame. Their role in the temperance movement is less well-known, yet it was probably of greater practical significance. The complexity of temperance history, with its numerous competing organizations, makes it difficult to summarize in a short space. It seems, however, that the temperance movement, and the role of Quakers in it, can be divided into four phases. The first, in the 1830s, condemned only the consumption of spirits. The second, which began in the 1830s, made teetotalism obligatory. The third phase began with the estab-

[1] *The Friend* (1883), 81.
[2] *Meeting for Sufferings Minutes, 3 December 1841.*
[3] cf. p. 191 above.

lishment of the United Kingdom Alliance, in 1853. The U.K.A. hoped that local option would be introduced by government action. It did not insist on teetotalism from its supporters, and for the next twenty years the temperance movement was divided into two camps—the supporters of the U.K.A. and the 'moral suasionists' who relied on individual conversions to teetotalism. In the fourth and final phase, from the 1870s on, the U.K.A.'s lack of success disillusioned many of its supporters. The forms of temperance work diversified and the number of abstainers in the churches—and in the Society of Friends—increased; but the apocalyptic zeal which characterized the early temperance reformers faded.

The British and Foreign Temperance Society, often called the Moderation Society, was founded in 1831. It required abstention from spirits only, and was an eminently respectable body, favoured by 'Lords, Bishops, Squires & Philanthropists of that class who decline personal sacrifice', as a critic put it.[1] Quakers were strong supporters, both as subscribers and as office holders;[2] their support probably involved little, if any, change in their personal habits. With near unanimity, the Yearly Meetings of 1830 and 1835 passed recommendations against the consumption and manufacture of spirits.[3]

The teetotal phase of the temperance movement began in a very different social context, led by the so-called labour aristocrats of the north of England. In 1832 the Seven Men of Preston took the teetotal pledge, under the leadership of the weaver turned cheese-factor, Joseph Livesey. The movement spread through the work of itinerant working-class lecturers, and several national societies were established.

It was during this first phase of the teetotal movement, when it was led by working class and often extreme advocates, that the Quakers played a singularly important role.

---

[1] *The Dunlop Papers*, vol. i, *Autobiography of John Dunlop* (privately printed, 1932), p. 119.

[2] *The Friends Monthly Magazine* (1831), 472; *British and Foreign Temperance Society Annual Reports*.

[3] There are no adequate extant reports of the discussions at either of these YMs, but an account of a debate on the subject at the 1833 YM shows near unanimity—*JFHS* (1919), 73.

A number of wealthy and influential Quaker philanthropists were among its earliest middle-class adherents, and provided the financial backing and the respectability which it otherwise lacked. They included Robert Charleton, Joseph Eaton, and the Thomas brothers, all of Bristol, Samuel Bowly of Gloucester, and John Cadbury of Birmingham, who was converted by Livesey's famous Malt Liquor Lecture.

How can this early and enthusiastic support be explained? The first Quaker converts to teetotalism[1] were already active philanthropists. They believed that drink was a cause, if not the only cause, of poverty and crime, and felt that it was unjust to deprive the poor of one of the few compensations of their lives, when they were unwilling to follow suit.[2] They used the words of Paul, beloved of Quaker teetotalers throughout the century: 'If meat make my brother to offend, I will eat no flesh while the world standeth.'[3] Since Friends were already accustomed to a fair degree of puritanism,[4] and were used to running counter to the customs of society in many respects, they were less affected than other middle-class men by the obstacles involved—dislike of singularity, dislike of asceticism, dislike of losing face by association with proletarian enthusiasts.

Whatever their motives, their services to the first phase of teetotalism were immense, and Livesey paid them generous tribute. He singled out among others, Eaton, who left £15,000 to the cause, and William Wilson, who was rumoured to purchase temperance tracts for free distribution by the half million.[5] One of the early itinerant lecturers, Thomas Whittaker, wrote an autobiography which is full of references to Friends: 'They were at one time almost the only people who had got a decent home, who gave us habitation.'[6]

---

[1] In earlier periods there were, of course, individual Quaker teetotalers, but they did not form part of a general movement.

[2] The address to the Society of Friends by teetotal Friends, in *The Friend* (1843), 242. Samuel Bowly, 'Temperance Experiences', *The Western Temperance Herald*, 1 February 1871, p. 19.

[3] ibid.   [4] cf. pp. 152ff. above.

[5] *The Staunch Teetotaler* (1867), 185.

[6] Thomas Whittaker, *Life's Battles in Temperance Armour* (London, 1884), p. 89; cf. pp. 159ff.

The value of their support inevitably meant that they wielded considerable influence over the fortunes of the movement. As the Scottish temperance pioneer, John Dunlop, wrote in 1847, 'As members of the Society of "Friends" form the most of our small monied constituency, their aid is quite requisite.'[1] An example of this power occurred in the late thirties, when the temperance movement was split over whether teetotalers should be allowed to offer alcohol to guests—a conflict with obvious class implications, since only the prosperous were likely to be embarrassed by the problem. By dint of redirecting their financial support, the Quakers succeeded in re-uniting the warring branches to form the National Temperance Society.[2] In the twenty years that followed, teetotal principles spread rapidly among Friends. But although a majority were to become total abstainers, in the course of the century, teetotalism was never compulsory, or universal. One has, therefore, two separate phenomena to explain—why did teetotalism spread so rapidly in the Society, and why did a substantial minority resist it?

In the late thirties and early forties, Friends were sharply divided as to the value of the teetotal movement. *The Irish Friend* complained that some readers attacked its excessive zeal in this direction, and others its apathy.[3] But the evidence suggests that the number of Quaker teetotalers increased steadily, decade by decade. The movement was strongest among Friends from the north and west, and weakest in London.[4]

As has been noted in other connections, Quakerism, with its periodic gatherings and close personal ties, was singularly well adapted to the spread of a philanthropic enthusiasm. A single Quaker who was widely loved and esteemed could exercise incalculable influence among his fellow members. But the greatest strength of the movement, in a Quaker context, was its plane of moral elevation. Teetotalers urged their brethren to follow a path of self sacrifice for the benefit

[1] *The Dunlop Papers*, vol. i, p. 308.
[2] ibid., pp. 197–8, 320.
[3] *The Irish Friend* (1840), 4.
[4] *The Friend* (1856), 185; William Rowntree, *Account of* 1856 YM, p. 66; *The Monthly Record* (1876), 42.

of others. There was little their opponents could do beyond discussing the wedding at Cana, and whether Timothy took wine or grape juice for his stomach's sake. Some religious leaders, J. J. Gurney among them, apparently adopted total abstinence less out of personal conviction than from a fear of weakening their influence. Three entries in Gurney's journals tell their own story. In 1837 he records his victory over alcohol; in 1842 he writes that he has been an abstainer for over a month; and in 1843 he proudly notes the completion of three teetotal months.[1] His sister, Elizabeth Fry, never became a teetotaler, but was clearly uneasy about her failure to do so. Another philanthropist, Daniel Pryor Hack, became a teetotaler at the age of seventy.[2]

Teetotalers exercised great pressure on their co-religionists. The evidence suggests that from the fifties on, in some regions at least, non-abstainers were in a minority and very much on the defensive. Complaints were made that teetotalism was a prerequisite for office[3] and that non-abstaining ministers were coerced in this direction.[4] Much later, a non-abstaining Quaker, trying to explain the astonishing spread of teetotalism in the Society, attributed it to the difficulty of withstanding men of strong convictions who took their stand on high moral principle:

We must all have met with Friends who, to judge at least by their language, and by their looks when the subject is mentioned, include the drinking of a glass of wine among the catalogue of deadly sins. The rapid growth of the movement amongst Friends may be due partly to the fear of running counter to this strong opinion, and also to a laudable desire not to offend the consciences of ultra-abstainers.[5]

But a substantial minority remained unaffected by these pressures. They were less vocal than the teetotalers, but occasionally aired their views in the columns of *The Friend*, using some such pseudonym as 'Moderation' and bringing the wrath of half a dozen temperance enthusiasts on their heads in the next issue. A sympathetic teetotaler wrote of their reluctance 'to break with the long-established usages

---

1 *Journal*, 14 April 1837; 21 November 1842; 21 January 1843.
2 *Friends of a Half Century*, p. 186.   3 *The Friend* (1850), 221-2.
4 ibid. (1851), 71.   5 *FQE* (1907), 202.

of life—to be singular unless from an adequate motive—to make the rule of the weak the law of all . . . jealousy of the curtailment of religious liberty'.[1] But for those who aspired to join the élite of the society, such considerations weighed less than the esteem of their co-religionists.

The rapid spread of the temperance movement among Friends placed Quaker brewers and wine merchants in a position of great difficulty. As early as 1839, William Lucas noted that he was under pressure to give up his brewery.[2] This was to become a familiar dilemma of Quaker brewers, constantly exhorted in public and private to become tanners. A few, such as the Lucases, had enough independence of mind to retain both their breweries and their Quakerism. But others, such as Samuel Bowly's brother, Edward, abandoned Quakerism,[3] while some changed their avocation, either out of real conviction or in response to continual pressure.

Although speeches by temperance enthusiasts, in the movement's early stages, tended to cause alarm and offence at Yearly Meeting,[4] as the century progressed, Yearly Meeting debates on the subject showed a surprising degree of unanimity on the subject. A few extremists thought that teetotalism should be compulsory, but most influential leaders had no desire for it to become a rock of division. Men such as Bowly had taken an active part in campaigning for the relaxation of Quaker discipline in other spheres, and they had no desire to forge new fetters. They sought only gestures of official approval, to which most non-abstainers had no objection. In 1860 Yearly Meeting advised its members against the 'improper' use of alcohol. The original adjective, changed after protests, was 'unnecessary'. In 1864 it stated that it viewed the efforts of temperance workers 'with cordial satisfaction'. In 1874 those who were engaged in the manufacture of intoxicating drinks were urged in kindly and moderate terms to change their trade if possible. In 1896 Friends were exhorted 'to prayerfully consider' whether they should become teetotalers.

---

[1] The Friend (1875), 82.   [2] Diary of William Lucas, vol. i, p. 160.
[3] Maria Taylor, Memorials of Samuel Bowly (Gloucester 1884), pp. 6–7.
[4] Robert Barclay to J. J. Gurney, 16 June 1838 (Gurney MSS.) (I, 23).

In the years between the decline of the anti-spirits movement in the 1830s, and the formation of the United Kingdom Alliance in 1853, the temperance movement was
synonymous with teetotalism. It was this aspect which was
to affect the life of the Society of Friends most closely. But
after 1853, the temperance world, and the Quaker temperance world within it was split into two camps, the prohibitionists and the moral suasionists.

The U.K.A. was inspired by the Maine Law, or, more
precisely, by early and misleading reports of the spectacular
success of the Maine Law. Its first aim was prohibition, but
this was soon modified to local option. At first, teetotalers
welcomed it, but later, many became sharply critical. They
objected to the fact that it did not insist on teetotalism from
its supporters, to the impracticality and unwillingness to
compromise which often characterized its policies, and to the
whole concept of a teetotalism arbitrarily imposed from
above. Temperance legislation could only be effective if it
corresponded to the wishes of the public. A change in the
climate of opinion was the first essential, and this could only
be achieved through 'moral suasion'. Nevertheless, in its
early stages, the U.K.A. was the focusing point for great
hopes.

The U.K.A. was founded by a Quaker, Nathaniel Card,
but since he died three years later he exercised relatively
little influence over its fortunes. Most Quaker temperance
leaders welcomed the new movement.[1] The role of Quakers
in the movement was most important in its early years,
when its subscription lists were full of Quaker names, its
annual reports full of grateful tributes to Quaker supporters.
In 1863–4, Bristol contributed £106. 9s. 0d. to the movement.
£100 of it came from two Quakers.[2] Quaker periodicals
backed it from the beginning; the Alliance Annual Report
for 1866–7 described them, doubtless with no pun intended,
as 'true and courageous friends'.[3] In 1881, the U.K.A. was
described as 'an organisation which owes its existence very

---

[1] *The U.K.A. Annual Reports 1853–73*, make special mention of, among others,
Edward Thomas, Richard Barrett, Joseph Eaton, Joseph Sturge, Robert Charleton, Cyrus Clark, John Priestman, Charles Pease, Joseph Thorp and Samuel
Bowly.
[2] *U.K.A. Annual Report, 1863–4*, pp. 22ff.   [3] ibid., *1866–7*, p. 13.

largely to the zealous labours and munificent contributions of members of the Society of Friends.'[1]

But even in the early years of the Alliance, Quaker opinion was sharply divided about its value. Some, such as John Taylor, welcomed it initially but later became its opponents. Prohibitionists and moral suasionists clashed at Quaker temperance gatherings[2] and in the correspondence columns of *The Friend*.[3] Most of the U.K.A.'s influential Quaker supporters were already middle-aged when the movement was founded. By the 1870s many of them were dead, and they were not replaced by another generation of equally zealous and affluent Quaker supporters.[4] Many, perhaps most, Quaker temperance enthusiasts became disillusioned with the U.K.A., especially by its lack of realism. A few were still wedded to the cause; the Quaker John Hilton was the Alliance's parliamentary agent at the turn of the century.

From perhaps the 1870s we can date the fourth and last phase of the Victorian temperance movement. It was characterized by a change which has often been described as a change from sect to denomination in religious movements. The first generation of temperance reformers felt that they had discovered the fulcrum to change the world. Their optimism, their joyful pugnacity, fed on opposition, but were blunted by decades of hope deferred.[5] It was a paradox of which Friends were well aware that while zeal for the temperance movement declined, the forms of temperance work diversified, and the number of Quaker teetotalers increased, swelled by those brought up as such from infancy. From the middle eighties onwards, Quaker periodicals scarcely mention temperance.

Just as religious movements need to attract adult converts in their early years, but later tend to rely on natural increase and education, Quaker temperance efforts came to centre round Bands of Hope for children, and similar organizations for their Adult Scholars. Teetotalism was strongly encour-

---

[1] *The British Friend* (1881), 305.   [2] *The Friend* (1860), 225.
[3] ibid. (1858), 178–9, 206–7; (1865), 248–9; (1866), 10–11, 34–6, 55–8, 76–8, 95–6.   [4] cf. *The British Friend* (1881), 305.
[5] Joseph Livesey in *The Western Temperance Herald* (1 July 1868), 100; Robert Charleton in ibid. (1 January 1871), 5.

aged among these scholars, and practically a *sine qua non* for their teachers.[1] Many Friends became active in establishing coffee carts, and later, coffee houses, in the belated recognition that 'cold and want of home comforts' were the chief allies of the public house.[2] A few joined the Good Templars —a teetotal version of freemasonry—though others disliked the movement.[3] At the end of the nineteenth century, the Quaker cocoa manufacturer, Joseph Rowntree, created a stir by a series of books advocating the Gothenberg system, that is, the municipal ownership of public houses.

As well as the simple passage of time, other factors helped to diminish interest in the temperance movement, among Friends as among others. Perhaps the most important was the decline of drunkenness in society generally. Another was the repeated failure of attempts to influence legislation. In 1899 a Friend spoke of 'just coming to the close of a long period of discouragement and disappointment, the result partly of real and partly of imaginary defeat'.[4] Moreover, a change was taking place in social thinking. 'Drink' no longer seemed satisfactory as a blanket explanation for all social evils. To young Quakers much preoccupied with the magnitude and complexity of 'the Social Problem', traditional temperance advocacy seemed reactionary, a wilful refusal to think. An epigram became current to the effect that whereas drink was commonly regarded as stimulant, to Quakers it was a soporific.[5]

FREE TRADE AND FACTORY LEGISLATION

It has already been noted that philanthropy was not the fruit of pure and uncomplicated benevolence, but often sprang from very mixed motives. No movement exemplified this admixture more strikingly than the Anti-Corn Law League. It could be variously regarded as a political movement, the instrument of an economic pressure group, or as a philanthropy, and indeed it was all three. Where a man's

---

[1] *Proceedings of FFDSA Dublin Conference, 1870*, pp. 41–59.
[2] *The Monthly Record* (1875), 73; cf. pp. 60 and 74.
[3] ibid. (1873), 43, 52–4.   [4] *The British Friend* (1899), 179.
[5] *The Ploughshare* (1916), 290.

economic interests and his philanthropic pursuits coincide, we cannot know which predominates. The most that can be said is that many elements are present. This was clearly true of the League, and true, though to a lesser extent and less obviously, of many other charitable movements as well.

Many of the Quaker manufacturers who supported the League did so out of economic self-interest. Bright recognized this element clearly—in 1842, when he was trying to raise a number of subscriptions of £500 each, he pointed out that they would be a good investment, even if the cause of repeal was speeded by only six months. The accuracy of their economic diagnosis has been questioned, but to Leaguers of the time it seemed self-evident truth. They believed that the unrestricted import of corn would aid exports, by giving other countries greater purchasing power. It would expand the home market, by making the purchasing power of wages greater. Chartist critics feared that cheap food would provide an excuse for low wages, but the Leaguers always repudiated this inference.

Like the Liberation Society and the Peace Society, the League derived much of its strength from its class ideology. It appealed to manufacturers' pride of class, their feeling that they needed no protection themselves, and would not concede it to others. It focused the nonconformist's ancient resentment against the Established Church, the aristocracy, and privileged, all of which he readily identified with each other. The repeal of the Corn Laws would strike a blow against aristocratic landlords and tithing clergy. As the Quaker Ashworth put it, in a letter to Cobden, '. . . what I admire most, is the *animus*, thy never-to-be-forgiven audacity of venturing upon the Citadel of Monopoly, and bearding the Aristocratic and Sacerdotal Power by which it is backed.'[1] This element of class animosity became nakedly apparent when the Leaguers turned to attacking the Game Laws, in 1845.

But the peculiar charm of the League, to Bright and many others, was the fact that to support it could be regarded as philanthropic as well as an investment. The manufacturer

[1] B.M.Add.MS. 43653 (Cobden Papers), f.6v.–7: Ashworth to Cobden, 21 Sept. 1841.

could look to future economic benefits and feel a glow of
righteousness into the bargain. Indeed, in the literature of
the League, Free Trade is often depicted as a panacea for all
social evils, '. . . a measure which would go further than any
other that could be proposed to feed the hungry, to clothe
the naked, and . . . to enlighten the ignorant.'[1] The fact that
the philanthropic element went hand in hand with economic
self-interest does not mean that it was therefore insincere.
The League's leaders repeatedly referred to the blessing
cheap bread would bring to the poor, in their private letters
to each other, and there is no reason to doubt their sincerity.
Sometimes, however, they deliberately exploited the philanthropic appeal of the League in a bid for wider support.
Ashworth wrote to Cobden that it was desirable to secure
the backing of philanthropists. He made the curious suggestion that if the term 'Free Trade' seemed too mercenary
to Exeter Hall, it could be rechristened 'Free Intercourse'.[2]

A further attraction of the League, in Quaker eyes, was
its association with the peace movement. William Allen
stated the theory clearly, in 1836: 'The real Christian is a
Citizen of the World, and considers every man as a brother
. . . [God] has so distributed his gifts according to the
peculiarities of climate and local circumstances, as to render
an interchange of commodities between the inhabitants of
remote regions a mutual benefit.'[3] Cobden, on occasion,
emphasized the pacifist implications of Free Trade for the
benefit of potential Quaker supporters,[4] but his own devotion to peace was unquestionable. He wrote to Sturge, when
Repeal had been achieved, that the best consequence was
that 'the whole civilized world will become *quakers* in the
practice of peace.'[5] When Sturge was looking for subscribers to the Peace fund, he advised him to use Anti-Corn
Law subscription lists.[6]

Most Friends supported the aims of the League, though

---

[1] *The Anti-Corn Law League Circular* (25 June 1839), n.p.
[2] B.M.Add.MS. 43653 (Cobden Papers), ff.19–19v: Ashworth to Cobden 14
April 1842.   [3] *The Lindfield Reporter* (1836), 361.
[4] B.M.Add.MS. 43653 (Cobden Papers), f.14v: Cobden to Ashworth, 12 April
1842
[5] B.M.Add.MS. 43656 (Cobden Papers), f.13v: Cobden to Sturge, 26 March
1846.   [6] ibid. f.79v: Cobden to Sturge, 29 Nov., 1848.

not necessarily its methods. Quaker periodicals, which rigidly excluded politics in the thirties and forties, made an exception for Free Trade, on the grounds that it was a philanthropic question.[1] Of the 'ABC' of the League, Ashworth and Bright were Friends. Sturge was another zealous supporter, subscribing £100 a year or more,[2] until his sympathies became estranged over the sugar question. Other prominent and prosperous Friends, such as Edward Smith of Sheffield and George Thomas of Bristol, were pillars of the League in their respective localities.[3] In general, the core of Quaker support came from among the manufacturers of the north. Cobden was always urging his Quaker sympathizers to widen the basis of support among Friends, and in particular to enlist the wealthy and influential Quakers of London: 'Persecute Alexander and the Lombard Street people.'[4] A League newspaper wrote that Joseph Pease's advocacy of protection was an anomaly, 'indebted as our cause is to the great body of the Society of Friends'.[5]

The philanthropic protestations of the Leaguers, and of the Quakers among them, have always seemed to have a hollow ring in the light of their hostility or indifference to Shaftesbury's attempts to limit the working-hours of factory children.

From 1833 to 1841, Joseph Pease was the only Quaker in parliament. In 1843, Bright succeeded to this position of lonely eminence. Both were hostile to attempts to limit the hours of factory children.[6] Bright called Fielden's Ten Hour Bill 'one of the worst measures ever passed in the shape of an Act of the Legislature',[7] and Shaftesbury recalled, 'Bright was ever my most malignant opponent'.[8]

---

[1] *The Quarterly Magazine and Review Chiefly Designed for the Society of Friends* (1832), 175ff; *The Lindfield Reporter* (1836), 361–5; *The Irish Friend* (1842), 24–5.
[2] Richard, *Memoirs of Joseph Sturge*, p. 277.
[3] B.M.Add.MS. 43653 (Cobden Papers), ff.76–77v: Smith to Ashworth, 4 Nov. 1845. ibid. 43649 (Cobden Papers) f.7: Cobden to Bright, 2 June 1841.
[4] B.M.Add.MS. 43649 (Cobden Papers), f.7: Cobden to Bright, 2 June 1841.
[5] *The Anti-Corn Law League Circular* (19 November 1840); cf. 22 Oct. 1840 and 25 Mar. 1841.
[6] *Hansard*, 3rd ser., 1833, xix.906–7; 1839 xlviii.1084; 1844, lxxiii, 1132ff; 1847, lxxxix, 1148.   [7] ibid., 1847, lxxix.1148.
[8] Quoted in J. T. Ward, *The Factory Movement 1830–1855* (London, 1962), pp. 411–12.

Edmund Ashworth, another prominent Quaker Leaguer, admitted to employing under-age children.[1] When the Ten Hour Bill finally passed, in 1847, both Bright and Ashworth tried to defeat its intentions, in their own factories, by means of a shift system.[2]

Pease, Bright and the Ashworths did not necessarily speak for English Quakerism, but the evidence suggests that their attitude was fairly representative of it. In 1833 it was noted in Bradford that Friends had contributed £1,000 to the anti-slavery movement and £3 to the factory movement.[3] Shaftesbury claimed that their hostility to himself and his work verged on persecution.[4] The picture is not one of unrelieved blackness. In 1832 a Quaker periodical expressed warm sympathy for the factory movement,[5] and William Allen and the ex-Quaker Samuel Hoare were office-holders in the short-lived Society for the Improvement of the Condition of the Factory Children which was founded in the same year. But the Society achieved little— it is not mentioned in the three massive volumes of Allen's official biography—and Oastler blamed its failure on the machinations of a Quaker.[6] No Quaker played a prominent part in the agitation for the limitation of factory hours. Where they appear in its history at all, it is almost always as its inveterate opponents.

It is not the task of the historian to judge the past, though it is difficult and perhaps undesirable for him to avoid taking some sort of stand in relation to its moral and humanitarian issues. But it seems to the present writer that the hostility of many Quakers to factory reform does not mean that they were hypocrites in their philanthropic efforts, or that they were insincere when they spoke of the blessings that cheap bread would bring to the poor. Men such as Bright naturally absorbed the ideals and assumptions current in the class and period to which they belonged. Liberty was paramount among these ideals, and they could not necessarily be expected to see that it was farcical when applied to the rela-

---

[1] Ward, *op cit.*, p. 171.   [2] ibid., pp. 357–8.   [3] ibid., p. 109.
[4] Quoted in J. L. Hammond and Barbara Hammond, *Lord Shaftesbury* (London, 1923), p. 108.   [5] *The Quarterly Magazine and Review* (1832), 284.
[6] Ward, *op. cit.*, p. 63.

tionship between factory owner and operative, any more than they could have shared Engels's view of the intrinsic injustice of the social structure in which they lived. Even reformers are usually aware of only a few of the many abuses of the society in which they live. It is as unrealistic to see Quaker philanthropy as the product of self-interest and hypocrisy as it is to view it simply as that spirit of benevolence which provides the *deus ex machina* in so many of Dickens's novels.

PRISONS AND CAPITAL PUNISHMENT

Friends' reputation in this sphere was created largely before and after the Victorian period, by Elizabeth Fry, who became a legend in her own lifetime, and by some notable twentieth-century Quaker penal reformers. Nevertheless, both penal reform and opposition to capital punishment are so associated with the Quaker image that a brief account of their Victorian history seems desirable. Yet they were much less important than the other movements discussed in this chapter, whether measured by the numbers of Friends involved, or by the importance they attached to them. Moreover, the records of many of the societies which did exist are defective and meagre.

When Victoria came to the throne, Elizabeth Fry was an ageing celebrity, with only six years of active life ahead of her.[1] Her work had had two main aspects—prison visiting and penal policy. In 1816, she had begun making regular visits to Newgate. In due course, she did much to reform the chaotic conditions of the women's prison there. Subsequently, she encouraged the formation of committees of middle-class women in other centres to undertake similar work. These various committees were united in a nation-wide organization—the British Ladies Society. In her later years she used the prestige and experience she had gained at Newgate to give weight to her practical recommendations on prison policy, and in particular, to oppose the system of

---

[1] Her last illness began in 1843 and she died in 1845. She is discussed very briefly in this study because she has already received much attention from biographers, and because her main work belongs to an earlier period.

solitary confinement, which was currently becoming fashionable.

Naturally enough, in the establishment of committees for prison visiting, she relied heavily on the support of her fellow Quakers. The first committee of twelve formed to supervise the Newgate prisoners included eleven Quakers,[1] and she made use of her Quaker contacts in starting similar work in other centres. A young woman Friend attended a London meeting on prison discipline in 1821 and observed, 'it was very largely attended and seemed almost like an adjournment of the Yearly Meeting, so many Friends.'[2] Interest in prisons was not the prerogative of woman Friends. There were a number of Quaker men on the committee of the Society for the Improvement of Prison Discipline which was established in 1818, but it achieved little.

The work of these committees of woman visitors continued, and was always linked with Quakerism. In 1856 it was stated that 'A Friend established it, [i.e. the British Ladies Society,] Friends are still amongst the most active members of the Committee.'[3] Very few records of this work exist, apart from that at Newgate. But the Society was small, in comparison with other Victorian charitable movements—there were only seventeen committees in Great Britain in 1827[4]—and the paucity of references to it in Quaker records suggest that very few were actively involved.

The Howard Association, which was founded in 1866, was concerned not with prison visiting but with penal policy. From its beginning until his retirement in 1901, its Quaker secretary, William Tallack, was the brain and voice of the movement. He was not a member of the wealthy Quaker circles which provided so many philanthropists, but a relatively poor man who moved from school teaching to the paid secretaryship, first of a capital punishment society, and sub-

---

[1] Thomas Fowell Buxton, *An Inquiry whether Crime and Misery are Produced or Prevented by our Present System of Prison Discipline* (6th ed., London, 1818), p. 134.

[2] Quoted in Emma Gibbins, *Records of the Gibbins Family, also a Few Reminiscences of Emma J. Gibbins and Letters and Papers related to the Bevington Family* (Privately Printed, 1911), p. 111.

[3] *The Friend* (1856), 164.

[4] *Sketch of the Origin and Results of Ladies' Prison Associations, with Hints for the Formation of Local Associations* (London, 1827), p. 20.

sequently of the Howard Association. He was something of an eccentric, and *persona non grata* in some Quaker circles, but his devotion to the cause he served was unquestionable.

If Tallack was the voice of the Association, Quaker philanthropists of the traditional type provided the purse. The original backing came from a group of prosperous Stoke Newington Friends, including the manufacturer, Stafford Allen, and the surgeon, Joseph John Fox. Soon it enjoyed the support of many eminent Friends, including a phalanx of M.P.s and the philanthropists Robert Alsop, Edmund Sturge and Samuel Gurney.[1] John Bright, who was a patron of the Association, told Yearly Meeting that there was no charitable movement which better deserved the support of Friends.[2]

It is not necessary here to analyse Tallack's views of penal reform.[3] He was, *inter alia*, an advocate of solitary confinement—the system which Elizabeth Fry had fought—and of 'reformatory and economic labour'. His ideas remained essentially unchanged during the forty-five years in which he spoke for the Association, and time inevitably turned him from a reformer into a reactionary. To prison reformers of the nineties, such as Salt, the founder of the Humanitarian League, Tallack laid too much stress on deterrence and too little on rehabilitation. Salt wrote that 'Mr. Tallack was a reactionist; he belonged to an antiquated school of thought, quite out of sympathy with the new style of prison reform.'[4]

Though this was not among its official tenets, Tallack and most of the Association's supporters opposed capital punishment. This was typical of Friends in general—in this respect they anticipated the social conscience of the rest of society by well over a hundred years. They provided the core of support for a succession of small and short-lived anti-capital punishment societies. The first of these, founded at a

[1] The names of office holders are to be found in successive *Annual Reports*. For Tallack's comments on the role of individuals, see his *Howard Letters and Memories*, Chapter 2, 'A Committee of Pleasant Colleagues', *passim*.

[2] *The Friend* (1873), 133.

[3] A typical summary can be found in *The Howard Association Annual Report*, 1872, pp. 3–5. His ideas are discussed in Gordon Rose, *The Struggle for Penal Reform The Howard League and its Predecessors* (London, 1961), pp. 21–5 and Chapter 3 *passim*.

[4] Henry S. Salt, *Seventy Years Among Savages* (London, 1921), p. 142.

meeting at William Allen's home in 1808,[1] sought to lessen the number of capital offences. Subsequent societies, such as that formed by Allen's partner, Barry, some twenty years later,[2] sought to abolish them altogether. This second society was backed by some of the most eminent Quaker philanthropists of the day,[3] but throughout its existence of perhaps thirty years it suffered from want of adequate support and financial backing. In 1863 yet another society was founded, by a group which included Tallack and the M.P. Charles Gilpin, but it suffered like its predecessors from financial inanition[4] and after 1866 its supporters channelled their energies into the Howard Association.

The weakness of these successive societies which were founded and supported largely by Friends does not mean that they were indifferent to capital punishment. Rather, they were disinclined to spend much money or energy in pursuit of a goal which seemed unattainable. But Quaker and ex-Quaker M.P.s supported the cause in parliament,[5] and by a number of addresses and petitions against capital punishment, the Society of Friends showed itself officially opposed to it. Before one such petition, in 1856, a debate took place of which, by chance, very full reports survive. Opinion was overwhelmingly in favour of a petition, but three leading evangelicals opposed it, on the ground that the inviolability of human life was not a scriptural doctrine.[6] They brought a storm of outraged protest on their heads. One of those present claimed 'that there were minds of a certain cast . . . who had dwelt (as it were) so long in the shadow of Mount Sinai that they could not see the teachings of the Mount of Olives with the clearness with which many babes in Christ could see them.'[7]

Subsequent history makes Friends' early stand on capital punishment of especial interest, but capital punishment and penal reform never really captured the imagination of Victorian Friends in general, or received the degree of enthu-

---

1 *The Philanthropist* (1815), 223; *Life of William Allen*, vol. i, p. 104.
2 *The Friend* (1864), 102–3.
3 *The Friends Monthly Magazine* (1830), 359.
4 *The Friends and Capital Punishment* (1883), p. 2. (This anonymous brochure is certainly by Tallack.)   5 Tallack, *Howard Letters and Memories*, p. 47.
6 *The Friend* (1856), 100.   7 ibid.

siastic support which they gave, for instance, to the temperance movement.

'SOCIAL PURITY'

Most of the reforming agitations to which Victorian Friends were deeply committed were established before 1860. In the seventies and early eighties, however, one of their chief preoccupations was the campaign against the Contagious Diseases Acts of 1864 and 1866. Quaker periodicals referred to it repeatedly, under the euphemism 'Social Purity', though usually in such guarded terms that it would be difficult to understand, in the absence of supplementary information, what the agitation was about.

The Contagious Diseases Acts were intended to safeguard public health along lines which had been long familiar on the Continent. They applied to certain military districts only, and established a special corps of non-uniformed police with the task of registering prostitutes, who were subjected to periodic medical examinations. Suspected prostitutes were liable to arrest and compulsory examination. The Acts aroused little interest at the time, for their implications were not at first realized, but a manifesto which appeared in the press at the beginning of 1870 heralded the beginning of a nation-wide agitation, under the leadership of Josephine Butler, a clergyman's wife. The Quakers were destined to be among her earliest and most influential supporters, playing a role not dissimilar to the one they filled in the first stages of the teetotal movement.

When the well-known inhibitions of the Victorians are remembered—which, the history of the agitation suggests, may have been over-emphasized—it is surprising that respectable middle-class Quaker philanthropists should have sprung to the defence of the civic liberties of prostitutes. The system was obviously open to abuse—the literature of the movement is full of stories of innocent servant girls who leap into the sea to avoid examination. It is clear, however, that the agitators were concerned less with the abuses to which the Contagious Diseases Acts could lead than with the principles they were thought to embody.

For Josephine Butler, the central grievance was the differential treatment of men and women. The Acts dealt with
an evil in which both men and women were by definition
equally involved, but only women suffered their penalties.
She saw them as a manifestation of that subordination of
women to men which she had long resented in other spheres,
for they safeguarded the vices of men through the humiliation of women. This was probably the aspect which appealed
most strongly to her women Quaker supporters. From time
to time, letters lamenting the inequality of the sexes appeared
in Quaker periodicals,[1] and some of the signatories of the
manifesto of 1 January 1870 were, like John Bright's sisters,
actively interested in the question of women's rights. Both
the relative scope which Quaker women enjoyed and their
lack of equality with men in the Society's organization tended
to sensitize their minds to the relative position of the sexes.

But it is very unlikely that elderly and eminent Quaker
philanthropists such as Robert Charleton were influenced
by concern for women's rights. They were predisposed in
the agitation's favour by their concern for liberty and their
dislike of any extension in the powers of the state. But their
active support was due to the fact that the Acts recognized
the supposed necessity of prostitution and indirectly sanctioned it by safeguarding the public against its attendant
dangers. Their alternative remedy lay in a general moral
reformation.

The unsavoury subject matter of the agitation alienated
some potential Quaker supporters,[2] but others were probably attracted by the freedom to study and discuss a forbidden subject. The fact that many eminent Victorians—
Gladstone among them—made the reclamation of prostitutes their favourite philanthropy has often aroused speculation, but here the delicacy of the subject is matched by the
tenuousness of the evidence.

Friends identified themselves with the agitation from the
beginning. Josephine Butler claimed, with pardonable
exaggeration, that the 'Ladies' Appeal and Protest' which
inaugurated the movement was signed by 'all the leading

[1] *FQE* (1868), 444ff.; *The Friend* (1873), 15, 35, 203 and 226–8.
[2] *The Shield* (1873), 386.

ladies of the Society of Friends'.[1] The Quaker signatories were 'weighty' Friends—nearly all were, or would become, ministers, elders, or overseers.[2] Robert Charleton, widely respected for his generous almsgiving and his work for peace and temperance, was another early supporter. With another Bristol Friend, Thomas Pease, he organized the movement's first public meeting. He presided at the meeting where a National Association was founded to oppose the Acts, and served as its treasurer until forced by mortal illness to resign. When he died, the movement's organ, *The Shield*, paid him the unique tribute of a front page obituary. A woman Friend, Margaret Tanner, was treasurer of the Ladies' Association. The agitators relied heavily on the representation of Quakers and ex-Quakers in parliament. William Fowler acted as its parliamentary spokesman until he lost his seat in 1874, bringing in bills for the repeal of the Acts in 1870 and 1873.[3] After the election of 1880, the Friends' Association for Abolishing the State Regulation of Vice reflected complacently that there were five Quaker advocates of repeal in parliament.[4] Quakers also supported the working men's League for the repeal of the Acts, and a Friend, William Catchpool, edited its periodical.[5] And from 1870 on, London Yearly Meeting officially committed itself to the cause.

The services which Friends rendered to the agitation against the Contagious Diseases Acts were essentially the same as their services to teetotal temperance. By their early support they helped confer respectability on the movement. They provided the core of its financial support: one Friend, Edward Backhouse, subscribed £1,000 per annum,[6] and when a special Quaker society devoted to the subject was founded in 1873, it immediately raised almost £5,000 in subscriptions.[7] Josephine Butler's own account of the move-

---

[1] Josephine E. Butler, *Personal Reminiscences of a Great Crusade* (London, 1896), p. 20.
[2] Maurice Gregory, *The Crowning Crime of Christendom with a Short History of the Society of Friends for its Abolition* (London, 1896), p. 8.
[3] Butler, *Personal Reminiscences*, pp. 60–1, 63 and 72.
[4] *Annual Report, 1880.*
[5] Gregory, *The Crowning Crime of Christendom*, p. 10.   [6] ibid., p. 8.
[7] *The Shield* (1873), 386.

ment is full of grateful references to Friends. As she travelled on her lecture tours round England, she usually stayed with them, and relied on them to arrange meetings beforehand and consolidate supporters afterwards.[1]

In 1883 the Acts had their teeth drawn by legislation abolishing both compulsory inspection and the special police corps. Three years later, they were formally repealed, and the various organizations which had opposed them sang their Te Deum. The Friends' Association, with much justification, reflected in its last Annual Report: 'In the great and prolonged struggle against State regulated Vice in this country we are thankful to believe that the Society of Friends has taken its full share.'[2]

The struggle, indeed, had an epilogue. In the following year the Friends' Association was reconstituted, to deal with the Contagious Diseases Acts still operating in India, and the indefatigable Quaker, Alfred Dyer, who had gained fame through his investigations of the 'White Slave Traffic' in Belgium, went to India to report on conditions there. But for most Friends the agitation ended in 1886.

In retrospect, the part they played appears one of the more admirable chapters of Victorian Quaker philanthropy. To support the agitation, especially in its early stages, required considerable moral courage. It did not offer the prestige and popular acclaim of so many other Victorian charitable and reforming movements. The Quakers who supported it did so, in the main, out of hatred for the assumption that 'vice is necessary to man'and out of considerations as abstract as liberty and justice.

THE CHANGING FACE OF
LATE VICTORIAN PHILANTHROPY

Beatrice Webb once stated that of all the changes she had known in her lifetime, the most striking was the decline in personal alms-giving.[3] Among Quakers, as in charitable circles generally, the later years of Victoria's reign produced a new awareness of the limitations and shortcomings of

---

[1] Butler, *Personal Reminiscences, passim.*   [2] *Annual Report, 1886.*
[3] Beatrice Webb, *My Apprenticeship* (London, 1926), pp. 194–5, n.1.

philanthropy. This change in attitude was partly due to the influence of the Charity Organisation Society, founded in 1869. The C.O.S. attacked alms-giving with missionary fervour. It claimed that indiscriminating benevolence could not permanently relieve distress, but was more likely to do positive harm, by encouraging pauperism. After a time the C.O.S. became largely discredited, but the negative side of its policy passed into the accepted coin of social thinking.

A second factor which discouraged the philanthropic response to social evils lay in the impact of a whole series of books on the condition of the poor. They ranged in scope and intent from the sensationalism of Mearns, in *The Bitter Cry of Outcast London*, to Charles Booth's enormous systematic survey which showed that thirty per cent of the population lived below a very meagrely defined subsistence level. These studies revealed for the first time the magnitude and permanence of destitution in England, and suggested that it was a problem which could not be solved by the amateur efforts of private benevolence. Young intellectuals such as Edward Grubb, who had a great impact on the Quakerism of his generation, studied socialism and the publications of the Fabians. A Quaker, Isabella Ford, was present at the meeting of sixteen from which the Fabian Society stemmed, and Edward Pease, who left Friends, became its secretary and first historian. In 1898 the Socialist Quaker Society was founded. It had only handful of members but its very existence was symbolic.

Silently and invisibly, a revolution took place in Friends' attitude to traditional philanthropy. When William Allen looked at the destitution caused by the decline of the Spitalfields silk industry, his reaction had been to establish a soup society. He never reflected on the unemployment which created destitution, or on the inadequacy of his remedy to relieve it. Now Friends became more conscious of the social causes of distress. In 1911, Yearly Meeting adopted a new query: 'Do you seek to understand the causes of social evils and to take your right share in the endeavour to remove them?' And there were other grounds for dissatisfaction. Edward Grubb criticized traditional philanthropists for their assumption 'that there must necessarily be a huge class condemned to a kind of life which they would never think of submitting to themselves'.[1] They were condemned, too, for their tendency to draw a moral distinction between the way in which money was made and the use to which it was put. Joseph Rowntree and George Cadbury followed a pattern new among Victorian Quaker philantropists in believing that the first claimants on benevolence should be the workers who helped create the wealth which made benevolence possible. Some, such as Edward Pease and Stephen Hobhouse, an influential convert, believed that all inequalities of wealth were wrong in themselves, and that the riches of the Quaker manufacturers were in themselves an indictment of the class.

This is not to say, of course, that all or most Friends abandoned philanthropy for socialism. But by the 1890s, they could no longer take it for granted that the philanthropist was the ideal Christian, or that alms-giving and support of charitable societies was an adequate response to the social ills of their time. By the nineties, there are fewer Quaker philanthropists of the mid-Victorian mould, wealthy businessmen, serving on a multitude of societies. This is not to say that the genre had disappeared. Men such as John Horniman, who died in 1893, continued to distribute fortunes to charitable societies, and the lives of Quakers such as Joshua Rowntree, with his work for peace, temperance, the anti-opium movement and the Adult School movement recall the many sided benevolence of a Joseph Sturge. Friends raised thousands of pounds, in the nineties, for famine relief, and for the assistance of the Doukhobors, a persecuted Russian sect whose teachings had some similarities with those of Quakerism.[2] But the channels through which the Quaker social conscience acted were changing, though the vigour and sensitivity of that conscience remained.

[1] *The Friend* (1889), 51.   [2] cf. p. 106 above.

IX

A SPECIAL CALLING:
QUAKERS IN ADULT EDUCATION

THE first Sunday Schools, which were established in the last two decades of the eighteenth century, were run by interdenominational committees of well-to-do subscribers for the benefit of the illiterate poor. Paid teachers were employed, and the teaching of reading was combined with religious instruction. In some cases, provision for adults was made, but they concentrated mainly on children.

As the nineteenth century progressed their character changed. Sunday Schools became the responsibility of specific denominations and paid instructors were replaced by the voluntary services of 'the creditable young people belonging to the congregations'.[1] As literacy became more widespread, they came to concentrate exclusively on religious instruction. They also became more respectable, and Sunday School attendance became the norm for middle-class children.[2] By the 1880s, Sunday Schools had adopted their present-day function, that of training the youthful members of a congregation in its principles and practices.

Quaker Sunday Schools, or First Day Schools as they were always called, differed from those of other denominations in three important ways. They were established much later; they were intended not for young Quakers, but for the uneducated poor; and they included many schools which were run for the specific benefit of illiterate adults. The religious education of Quaker children was catered for in subsidized boarding schools. The First Day Schools were thus essentially a branch of philanthropy, but they differed radically from other charitable movements in which Friends were engaged. They became the official responsibility of the

---

[1] Parl. Papers, 1834, ix, Minutes of Evidence, p. 109, question 1429.
[2] The Modern Sunday School [a symposium issued by the Sunday School Union] (London, n.d.), p. 50.

Society. They demanded Friends' participation, not merely as subscribers or committee members, but as teachers; and teachers, unlike committee members, were required by the hundred. And they were to have a profound effect on the Society itself, providing large numbers of potential working-class recruits, who were to present an essentially middle-class church with grave problems.

THE BACKGROUND

Although some Friends had supported the early inter-denominational Sunday Schools,[1] and they had played a decisive role in the early days of the British and Foreign Schools Society, they were very late in developing Sunday Schools of their own. There were only five First Day Schools in the whole of England in 1830.[2] By 1851, the year of the religious census, there were thirty-five—out of a total of 23,137 Sunday Schools.[3] Of course the small size of the Society of Friends necessarily limited the number of schools they could be expected to run. But there were to be over eight times as many First Day Schools by 1900, and it is clear that we must find other explanations for their tardy entry into this field.

From an early date, Friends realized that they were lagging behind other denominations with regard to Sunday School work.[4] Some opposition, within the Quaker fold as outside it, was rooted in hostility to the education of the poor *per se*, since it 'disqualifies them for filling those useful though inferior offices for which, under their circumstances, they appeared to have been designed. . . .'[5] But the essential difficulty lay in Quaker traditions of quietism.[6] To the quietist, the giving of regular instruction, Sunday by Sun-

[1] Thomas Pole, *A History of the Origin and Progress of Adult Schools: with an Account of some of the Beneficial Effects already produced* (privately printed, 1814), *passim*.
[2] *An Account of the First-Day Schools, conducted by Friends, in England, to the end of the year 1847* (Bristol, 1847). This source mentions only three schools. But cf. the *Friends First Day School Association Annual Report*, 1880, p. 5 and 1883, p. 8.
[3] *Parl. Papers, 1852–3*, xc, p. cixix.
[4] *The Friends Monthly Magazine* (1830), 813–14 and (1831), 176–7.
[5] ibid. (1830), 452–3.
[6] Cf. Rowntree, *Quakerism Past and Present*, p. 134 footnote.

day, with no claim to special inspiration, was a denial of the very spirit of Quakerism. An early defence of Quaker Sunday Schools treads delicately round this point: 'it would be difficult to lay down any certain rules for accomplishing [religious instruction]; but the teachers, if persons of serious character, will find in the performance of their several duties abundant opportunities for communicating it.'[1] The evangelical, with his belief in child conversion, and his stress on the Bible, which could, of course, only be studied by the literate, took a very different view. It is no coincidence that the extreme evangelicals who formed the Beaconite schism made provision for a very large Sunday School, or that a First Day School at Leeds collapsed because some of its teachers left Friends with the Beaconites, at that time.The early Quaker advocates of Sunday School teaching were, without exception, evangelicals.

And there were other difficulties. Other denominations, eager to expand their numbers, naturally hoped that their scholars would become church members. Friends had an ambivalent attitude to converts in general, and working-class converts in particular.[2] But if they did not treat their schools as training grounds for potential Quakers, they were left with a problem: should they teach their pupils such specifically Quaker tenets as pacifism or the wrongness of oaths? Most evangelicals sought simply to communicate a core of evangelical teaching, stripped of denominational tenets. This outraged many—'Mantles of Fox, of Penn, of Barclay! where have ye alighted?'[3]—and the dilemma wrecked a strongly supported proposal to establish a First Day School in Manchester in 1842. Once schools were established, Quaker traditions of silent worship proved impracticable for restless children unused to Quakerism, and hymn singing was introduced, to the horror of traditionalists. There were difficulties of this sort at Hull, in 1862: 'It is much to be regretted that some Friends disapprove of the School. . . . First Day B. complained to the Overseers that there had been singing introduced into the school . . . the result is great offence has been given to these

---

[1] *The Friends Monthly Magazine* (1831), 177.
[2] cf. pp. 130–134 above.   [3] *The Irish Friend* (1842), 134.

narrow-minded Friends who threaten to withdraw the use of the Meeting House.'[1]

Friends came late to Sunday School teaching, partly, it seems, through a mixture of snobbery and sheer inertia. Throughout the Victorian period, Sunday School teachers were often criticized for ignorance and incompetence,[2] and Quakers who did undertake the work frequently claimed, not without justification, that their own education and social standing were superior to those of teachers in other denominations.[3] Until perhaps the 1840s, the typical Quaker philanthropist, used to serving on committees and attending Annual General Meetings, simply did not think of Sunday School teaching as a possible and appropriate sphere of Christian service.

THE SPREAD OF FIRST DAY SCHOOLS

It sometimes happened, in Victorian Quakerism, that the ardent advocacy of a single widely respected individual was sufficient to bring a new issue to the favourable attention of Friends in general. The aged George Richardson played such a role in the case of foreign missions, as did Joseph Sturge in that of Sunday School teaching.

The First Day School which Sturge established at Severn Street, Birmingham, in 1845, was not the first Quaker Sunday School, but it was destined to be the most successful and influential. The story of its establishment was retold as often among Friends as the story of Robert Raikes's foundation of the first Sunday Schools, in Gloucester, in the movement generally, acquiring the status of a myth of origin. For Sturge, founding the school was an incident in a busy life. Once it was established, he played little active part in it. At this juncture another Birmingham Quaker, William White, (1820–1890), assumed the mantle of leadership. White was a convert from Wesleyanism, who came to Birmingham in 1848 and established a successful printing business there. He took a class for adults at Severn Street, and henceforth devoted the best energies of a long life to encouraging the

---

[1] Quoted in Chapman-Huston, *Sir James Reckitt A Memoir*, p. 231.
[2] *Parl. Papers*, 1852–3, xc, p. lxxiii.
[3] *One and All* (Oct. 1900), 159 (with reference to the 1850s).

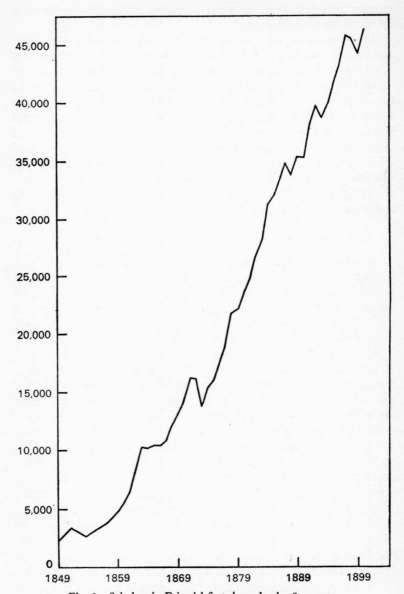

Fig. 8   Scholars in Friends' first day schools 1849–1900

spread of Sunday Schools for adults as the peculiar mission of Victorian Friends.

Two years after Severn Street School was founded, the Friends First Day School Association was established at a conference held in Birmingham. For the next forty-five years, it was to be run by a committee of Bristol Friends, headed by Joseph Storrs Fry. Its work was confined to issuing Annual Reports, and arranging Annual General Meetings and periodic conferences. The expansion of the movement was unplanned, depending on individual initiative. A First Day School teacher would shift to another town, and establish a new school there, or the Friends of a meeting would be stirred to emulation by reports of the successes of other centres in this sphere. But despite this lack of planning, the movement expanded with dramatic rapidity, as the graph illustrating this chapter shows. When the F.F.D.S.A. was founded in 1847, there were seventeen Quaker Sunday Schools. Twenty years later, there were 71 schools, and by 1900, there were 288—91 for children and 197 for adults.[1] After 1870 the scholars outnumbered English Friends themselves. In 1893, for instance, just before the F.F.D.S.A. was reorganized, it embraced 2,153 teachers and 38,591 scholars, a remarkable total when one considers that London Yearly Meeting had at the time only 16,369 members, including children, invalids, housewives, and the aged.

The 1850s were the crucial transition period. The pioneers of the movement liked to reminisce in later years about the opposition they had encountered from Friends at this time.[2] In 1856, several Quaker congregations refused to accept a visit from a deputation expounding the merits of First Day Schools. In 1873, the schools received the official sanction of Yearly Meeting, though their status could still provoke 'rather a hot discussion' in 1876.[3]

How can we explain the rapid growth of the movement, despite its tardy beginning and the considerable opposition it encountered? Why did so many Friends leave their

[1] Statistics of Quaker Sunday Schools used in this chapter, and in the construction of the relevant graph, come from the *F.F.D.S.A. Annual Reports*.

[2] William White in *The Friend* (1897), 837. cf. J. S. Fry, *Liverpool F.F.D.S.A. Conference Proceedings 1859*, p. 5.

[3] Thomas Hodgkin to his wife, 26 May 1876 (MS. in FHL, Portfolio B, 34).

pleasant suburbs, on the only free day of the week, to visit a dingy room in a slum where they undertook a difficult and demanding task for which they had no formal training whatsoever? Indeed, the work tended to overflow into other days of the week as well—Allen Baker's family commented on his Adult School commitments: 'giving up his home life was not only a sacrifice, it was an enduring grief.'[1] The whole question of how philanthropic movements arise, of why some support them while others pay them little attention, is a very obscure one, but if we study the schools' early promoters, certain characteristics become readily apparent. An analysis of those who attended the F.F.D.S.A.'s inaugural conference in 1847[2] shows that they fell into two categories—middle aged philanthropists who took little or no active part in teaching but wished to encourage the movement, and a contingent of teachers, who were mainly men in their twenties. The members of both groups tended to be ardent evangelicals, and teetotalers. Some, such as Arthur Naish, John Whiting, and James, John and Richard Tapper Cadbury were prominent workers in the temperance movement: it was claimed at William White's death that he had been president of every temperance organization in Birmingham.[3] Many were, or subsequently became, prominent in other philanthropic movements. And they included men who were very wealthy, or later became so, such as George Palmer. It was one of the striking features of the movement that famous manufacturers and men well known in public life were often active Sunday School teachers for many years. A satirist who attended a Quaker Sunday School teachers' conference in 1874, commented unfavourably on this aspect:

> Carriages at command,
> Servants a goodly band,
> Foot-stools on every hand,
> This the cross bearing.[4]

[1] Elizabeth Balmer Baker and P. J. Noel Baker, *J. Allen Baker Member of Parliament A Memoir* (London, 1927), p. 67.

[2] They are listed in *The Friend* (1848), 32, footnote. Biographical details were available on 26 out of 43.   [3] *One and All* (Oct. 1900), 147.

[4] S. T. Richardson, '*The Friends' in Council, A Humorous Representation of a Friends' Sunday-School Teachers' Conference, holden in Darlington during the month of August 1874* (2nd ed., Darlington and London, 1875), n.p.

The cocoa manufacturers, George Cadbury, Joseph Rowntree and Joseph Storrs Fry were strong supporters; the Adult School paper, *One and All*, actually urged its readers to drink cocoa, in gratitude for benefits received.[1]

It is not surprising that the schools' promoters tended to be evangelicals and teetotalers; the social philosophy of the temperance movement and of the Adult School movement were much the same. Yet these characteristics alone do not explain their interest in Sunday Schools. The first Quaker apologia for the movement was written by a Bristol doctor, Thomas Pole, in 1814. His book bears the imprint of the tensions and anxieties of the Napoleonic wars. By making the poor religious, he claims, Sunday Schools will lessen crime 'and encourage the principles on which society depends for its security'.[2] The poor will be led to 'industry, frugality, and economy', which will lessen their demands on the philanthropic.[3] Moreover, once literate, the poor will educate their children, thus sparing future generations of philanthropists even the expense of Sunday Schools.[4] Probably, Pole was looking for motives which would attract potential subscribers—but in his emphasis on the material and social blessings the schools would bring he was anticipating the voice of future generations of Sunday School promoters.

The Quakers who pioneered the First Day Schools in the forties and fifties were motivated by distress at the irreligion of the poor—made painfully evident by the 1851 religious census, and by Mayhew's interviews with the London street population—and by a strong, if narrowly focused, desire to help them to improve their material condition. They were influenced by the successes of other denominations, and by a vague and unformulated feeling of duty: 'we had a vague notion that First-day school teaching was a good thing—that a Christian ought to be useful.'[5] Laissez-faire liberals, they believed that the solution to poverty lay in the triumph of individual character over circumstance. The writings of

---

[1] *One and All* (Oct. 1900), 156.

[2] Thomas Pole, *A History of the Origin and Progress of Adult Schools* (Bristol, 1814), p. 18.   [3] ibid., p. 19.   [4] ibid., p. 18.

[5] Quoted in *James Henry Barber: A Family Memorial*, ed. H. M. Doncaster (Sheffield, 1905), vol. i, p. 310.

the movement's leaders, such as William White and Edward
Smith, are full of stories of scholars who have reached the
plateau of respectability through the exercise of the bour-
geois virtues of sobriety, thrift and self-improvement.
Inevitably, they tended to equate piety with prosperity;
one often gets the impression that the outward and visible
signs of inward and spiritual grace are a black cloth coat and
a bank account.[1] It is easy to discern the defects of the Adult
Schools' social evangel now, yet it was shared by many
Victorian labour aristocrats, passionate advocates as they
were of temperance and the Liberal party. And one of the
keynotes of the First Day School movement continued to
be its teachers' firm belief that they had discovered the key
to a new and better society. As late as 1903, a man as
sophisticated as John Wilhelm Rowntree was describing
the Adult Schools as the cure for all social evils, 'healing
with the blessed peace of God, the [unspecified] ailment of
Society'.[2]

The fear of violent revolution, haunted, with good reason,
the more prosperous sectors of mid-Victorian society. It is
unlikely that anyone ever took up Sunday School teaching
in order to exorcize the spectre, but teachers, both Quaker
and non-Quaker, liked, as an additional incentive, to point
out that religion was the best preservative of the *status quo*.
Thus in 1874 a speaker at a Quaker Sunday School teachers'
conference stated that the 1870 Education Act might
'plunge us in anarchy and revolution', and that he and his
colleagues must 'do our part in averting a national ruin'.[3]

The ease with which philanthropic and other enthusiasms
spread among Friends, and the factors which contributed to
this, have been noted repeatedly in this study. A single
'weighty' Friend could easily establish a school and per-
suade or coerce young Quakers into teaching in it. Many
Quaker shop assistants and apprentices were expected by

---

[1] [William] White, *The Development of the Sunday School System in the Direction
of Adult Instruction* (Birmingham and London, [1886]), p. 5, and the various works
of Edward Smith, *Glowing Facts and Personalities, Mending Men* and *Studies in
Men Mended*.

[2] J. Wilhelm Rowntree and Henry Bryan Binns, *A History of the Adult School
Movement* (London, 1903), p. 82.

[3] *Darlington F.F.D.S.A. Conference Proceedings*, 1874, p. 48.

their employers to include First Day School teaching among their duties. The elder Joseph Rowntree was typical of the senior Friends who did much to establish the movement. One of his apprentices, Richard Tatham, took up the work perforce: 'This was to him at first not a willing, but rather an irksome service, united in . . . seeing that most of the young men in his master's employment were so engaged.'[1] Walter Sturge, who became a pillar of the movement, was advised to become a First Day School teacher by Joseph Rowntree, when he was a school boy at York: 'In my secret heart I rebelled against this advice: nevertheless soon after settling down at home I was induced to become a teacher. . . . For some years I do not recollect having any motive other than the wish to please my parents, and to do the same as other young Friends of my station.'[2]

Of the many young Friends who took up the work reluctantly, some continued to dislike it, and gave it up after a time. But many discovered in themselves an unsuspected aptitude for teaching, and sympathy with the problems of the poor. The work was not without its compensations. Scholars were flattered by the attentions of their middle-class and often wealthy teachers, and repaid them with a devotion which often lasted many years. It frequently happened that a popular teacher and his class grew old together. Moreover it offered scope for the energies of young Friends who were practically excluded from taking a responsible role in the affairs of the Society, and strengthened their commitment to Quakerism, and to Christianity. One admitted frankly in 1876 that 'he should not now be a Friend if First-day school work had not given him something to do'.[3]

It seems, then, that the rapidity with which the movement spread was partly due to the ease with which any philanthropic concern spread among Friends. It spread all the more readily because it appealed to their evangelicalism, and their concern for the sufferings of the poor, as well as to their self-help social philosophy. But another problem suggests itself—why, when other denominations taught chil-

---

[1] John Ford, *The Sabbath School Teacher; a Memoir of Richard E. Tatham* (York, 1861), p. 2.
[2] *The Friend* (1888), 255.   [3] *The Monthly Record* (1876), 29.

dren, did Quakers run their schools primarily for the benefit of adults?

This emphasis on the instruction of adults developed slowly. No statistics of the relative numbers of child and adult scholars exist until 1870, but in that year, children were still in the majority. By 1875 adult scholars outnumbered children, but well before then there was a growing tendency to identify First Day Schools with Adult Schools, to such an extent that the terms became practically synonymous. A Friend complained at the 1870 Annual General Meeting of the F.F.D.S.A. that one could hardly tell from its discussions that children's schools existed.[1]

The emphasis on the teaching of adults was largely due to the example of the school at Severn Street, Birmingham, and to the missionary efforts of William White. The school was originally founded for the benefit of adolescents, but soon began to concentrate on the teaching of illiterate adults. It came to enjoy a remarkable and long-lasting success. By the closing years of the century, there were Adult Schools throughout Birmingham, and schools established in other centres closely imitated their Birmingham exemplar. In 1847, only two out of the seventeen First Day Schools in existence made provision for adults. But some of the delegates who met at Birmingham for the F.F.D.S.A.'s inaugural conference in that year were so impressed by the work at Severn Street that they decided to establish Adult Schools, or adults' departments in existing schools.[2] Various factors account for the movement's striking success at Birmingham, the size and vigour of the Quaker community, and the social and economic structure of the city itself. But whatever the cause, its success encouraged Friends to establish similar schools elsewhere.

The concentration on Adult Schools was partly the result of the tireless advocacy of William White, perhaps the only convert to make a real impact on Victorian Quakerism. To White, Adult Schools were the particular mission of Friends,

[1] *The Friend* (1870), 187.

[2] Frederick John Gillman, *The Story of the York Adult Schools from the commencement to the year 1907* (York, 1907), pp. 3–4; cf. *The Friend* (1897), 838 (re Sheffield) and Joseph Storrs Fry, *A Brief Memoir of the Life and Character of Arthur Naish of Bristol* (London and Bristol, 1865), p. 14 (re Bristol).

and he claimed to have spoken on their behalf in every county of England except Rutland. Long before his death, he was universally regarded as the founding father of the movement. Other factors encouraged the emphasis on adult schools. Friends came so late to the work of Sunday School teaching that they had to establish their children's schools in the teeth of opposition from schools which had been there for generations. In the tuition of adults, they were pioneering a relatively new field. Moreover, those who ran children's schools were sometimes embarrassed by the question of why their own children did not attend. Teaching adults was seen as more difficult, demanding, and prestigious than teaching children, hence better suited to Friends' relatively high level of education, and their view of themselves as a religious élite. And they often claimed that working men who would not attend churches run by professional clergy would come to Adult Schools, knowing that the Quakers received no payment for their work.

THE CHANGING CHARACTER OF ADULT SCHOOLS[1]

The first Adult Schools were held either on Meeting House premises, or in a rented room in a slum. Scholars were collected by canvassing in the poorest parts of the town. Essentially, they were offered a bargain: they were taught reading, and usually writing, unless sabbatarian scruples prevented it, and in return accepted Biblical and religious instruction. Quaker theories of inspiration often meant that the latter made little departure from the text of scripture: the Birmingham Annual Report for 1872 stated that 'the Egyptian plagues have been very earnestly and lovingly laid before us.' There was at first no thought of building up a separate institutional life. It was assumed that scholars would leave when they had attained their goal of

[1] This chapter section is based on the proceedings of successive F.F.D.S.A. Conferences, and on the Annual Reports of local schools which often appeared in Quaker periodicals, and in *The Monthly Record* and *One and All*, as well as on the collection of printed and MS. material relating to the Bristol schools in Bristol Record Office. The records of the York schools, in York Public Library, were not consulted—they are analysed by J. F. C. Harrison, in his *Learning and Living 1790–1960. A Study in the History of the English Adult Education Movement* (London, 1961).

literacy, and indeed they were sometimes actually encouraged to do so to make room for new recruits.

By perhaps 1870 a number of changes had occurred, or were taking place. Scholars came to regard the Adult School as a permanent commitment, midway between a church and a club. At first Friends did not understand this tendency, or even resisted it, but soon lifelong attendance became the goal, and a scholar who ceased to attend was pursued by his teacher and his fellow scholars. The schools acquired permanent premises. James Hack Tuke estimated in 1876 that Friends spent £5,000 a year on them.[1] They often erred, however, on the side of austerity. The humane Henry Isaac Rowntree, a pioneer of the coffee-house movement, urged in the same year: 'The school should be the scholar's club, open whenever the public-houses are open, and offering all their legitimate attractions, except the drink . . . don't hang the walls with awful texts and notices, which no teacher would suffer to remain on the walls of his own dining-room for a single instant.'[2] One of the school's earliest subsidiary functions, and one of the most valuable in gaining and keeping support, was their development of savings banks and insurance schemes. Run and automatically guaranteed by wealthy and efficient businessmen, they offered the scholars a measure of financial security without the weaknesses which had always bedevilled friendly societies: inexperienced management and the danger of dishonesty. Many a scholar, having committed himself to one of these schemes, doubtless endured the weekly Bible lesson as the price he paid for his membership. The schools acquired libraries, albeit of a bleak and instructive variety. They had their periodic outings and tea parties, and as time passed they proliferated ever more educational and recreational facilities—sports clubs, rambling clubs, debating clubs and so on. Teetotalism was strongly encouraged, though not compulsory, and most Adult Schools were run in conjunction with a branch of a temperance organization. The process of embourgoisement which had occurred in other educational institutions—the Athenaeums, the Mechanics Institutes, and the Sunday School movement in

[1] *The Friend* (1876), 258.   [2] *The Monthly Record* (1876), 41.

general—also took place in the Adult Schools. Friends had sought their first scholars in the poorest parts of a city. As time passed, they became increasingly respectable, and the very poor felt themselves excluded.[1] Partly as a consequence of this, partly as a result of the growth in literacy in the general community, the instruction in reading and writing which had formed the original attraction of the schools became increasingly unnecessary. Well before the 1870 Education Act had affected literacy levels, some schools reported that they had dropped writing lessons, because they were no longer necessary. This left the problem of how to fill 'the first half hour', which these lessons had occupied. Schools solved the problem in various ways: 'sometimes a book is read aloud, or a lecturette on current events or other matters of general interest is given.'[2] But for many schools, failure to meet the challenge adequately proved a source of weakness.

By the 1880s, the core of the school's programme was the Bible lesson. Teachers viewed themselves as religious leaders and instructors, and scholars attended, partly because of the social and other benefits the Adult Schools offered, and partly because they regarded them as a working men's church. On the one hand, they offered the satisfactions of a club, providing friends and leisure-time activities. 'To such as me', wrote a scholar in 1894, using capitals to stress his point, 'the school is SALVATION FROM DISCONTENTED DONOTHING-ISM.'[3] Friends sometimes feared that this social aspect outweighed the religious, that schools might be turning into 'Sunday clubs, where people just go to meet one another and to pass a pleasant hour'.[4] The Pleasant Sunday Afternoon movement, which had much in common with the Adult Schools in their later phase, met this need much more directly, and robbed the Adult Schools of much support in consequence.

But many attended Adult School meetings in the spirit in which they would have attended a church. In the last decades

[1] *Dublin F.F.D.S.A. Conference Proceedings, 1870*, p. 126; *Birmingham F.F.D.S.A. Conference Proceedings, 1890*, p. 200.
[2] *F.F.D.S.A. Annual Report, 1900*, p. 22.   [3] *One and All* (1894), 38.
[4] *Birmingham F.F.D.S.A. Conference Proceedings, 1890*, p. 22.

of the nineteenth century, the Schools adopted congregational singing and prayer, and the addresses on religious subjects were in effect sermons. Probably most of the scholars who attended over a long period were men who, under other circumstances, would have become staunch supporters of a Dissenting chapel. Charles Booth described the Adult School at Bunhill Fields, in London, as 'a gathering of devoutly inclined men, or more rarely women, for the study of the Bible and for religious and social co-operation on very democratic lines ... there is nothing to attract the ordinary man in the street. The attraction is for those of a religious disposition.'[1] The membership of the Adult School at Newcastle on Tyne has been similarly described: 'Most of these people called themselves Quakers for this was their only religious centre—their Church and Church Hall round which their lives revolved.'[2]

The 'very democratic lines' to which Booth referred grew originally out of necessity. To cope with two perennial problems, the shortage of teachers and differences in educational level amongst the scholars, the Birmingham school had introduced 'elementary teachers', a system not dissimilar to the monitorial system employed in the British and National Schools. Scholars who could read and write taught illiterates, while Quaker teachers supervised them and concentrated on Bible instruction. But these elementary teachers retained the status of scholars, and did not attend Teachers' Meetings. In the 1890s, attempts were made to make the schools more democratic, partly in response to scholars' higher educational levels. Discussion methods became popular, and classes were run by an elected President, who was, of course, the old teacher writ large. But, though the forms adopted became more democratic, and the literature of the movement is full of emphasis on 'good fellowship', its spirit remained, inevitably, profoundly paternalistic. There was a great gulf between the scholars and their middle-class teachers. The former were expected to be grateful and devoted, the latter to be kind. In this relation lay the seeds of ultimate weakness.

[1] Charles Booth, *Life and Labour of the People in London, Third Series*, vol. ii, p. 137.   [2] *Correspondence.*

After 1887 the era of rapid expansion, which Friends had seen as a special mark of divine favour, was replaced by years of stagnation and decline. To some extent, the adoption of a new system of school affiliation in 1893 masks the decline in total membership figures, by giving a false impression of expansion in that year. Those Quakers who were most deeply committed to the movement recognized, more or less clearly, the reasons for the change.[1] They saw that a movement which was closely tied to a small and distinctive church could not hope to expand indefinitely. The respectable working men who formed the core of the movement were shifting to suburbia, leaving behind the school which was centrally situated, often in a slum. They recognized the long-term effects of the Education Act of 1870. The elementary instruction of adults had become unnecessary, and the schools had not succeeded in finding something to take its place. Some members and potential members had been lost to the Pleasant Sunday Afternoon movement. But the most fundamental reasons for the decline were two fold. On the one hand, many of the facilities which the Adult Schools had provided, such as savings banks, libraries, and recreational clubs, were now readily available elsewhere. The F.F.D.S.A.'s Annual Report for 1899 reflected sadly: 'Additional facilities for travel and recreation, the large increase in some districts of Sunday labour, these all tell against our work.'[2] On the other hand, the paternalism of the movement was becoming increasingly unacceptable. Friends themselves realized this, albeit obscurely. A teachers' conference listed thirteen reasons for the movement's decline. They included 'Activity of the Labour movement, and the idea that the Schools are antagonistic to the same'.[3] One does not need to share the Marxism of two critics to sympathize with their comments on the movement: 'We emerge from a perusal of the Adult School literature with the feeling that we have been plunged in a bath of Uplift, of Earnestness, of Undenominational Goodness. But our minds have been given no direction whatever.'[4]

[1] Rowntree and Binns, *A History of the Adult School Movement*, pp. 52–3. *F.F.D.S.A. Annual Report, 1886*, p. 10; and *1898*, p. 17.

[2] ibid., 1899, p. 18.   [3] *F.F.D.S.A. Annual Report, 1898*, p. 17.

[4] Eden and Cedar Paul, *Proletcult (Proletarian Culture)* (London, 1921), p. 43.

By the end of the nineteenth century, the Adult School movement was seriously weakened, but not defunct. An Indian summer of renewed activity awaited it in the years before the First World War, the fruit partly of closer co-operation with similar schools run by non-Quakers, and partly of gifted and devoted leadership, dedicated to the ideal of expansion. It was the First World War, with the conflict of loyalties which Quaker pacifism meant, which heralded its final decline.

The systematic instruction of illiterate adults was a novelty when the Quakers took it up in the 1840s, but the importance of the Adult Schools lies in the context of Quaker history rather than in the history of education. The number of Adult Scholars was always under 29,000, a low total in relation to the population even of a single large English city. But its effect on the Society of Friends was tremendous. It was a source of potential converts, and it forced Friends to adopt certain innovations, such as hymn-singing. For many, regular and intimate contact with the relatively poor opened new horizons, sensitizing their consciences, as nothing else could have done, to the restrictions and hardships of their lives.

THE RELATIONSHIP OF THE SCHOOLS TO QUAKERISM

The main dimensions of the problem which confronted both Friends and Adult Scholars have been outlined in an earlier chapter of this book.[1] The members of a predominantly middle-class church could not contemplate the prospect of large numbers of working-class converts with equanimity, especially since they considered themselves bound to contribute to the support of their poorer members, and subsidize their children's education. Yet the great aim of the Schools was to turn scholars into ardent Christians, and Christianity was regarded as inseparable from some form of church membership. If teachers were sincere in their Quakerism, they could not encourage scholars to join

---

[1] cf. pp. 129ff. above.

another church. Still less could they be satisfied to see them join no church at all.

Some Adult Scholars did become Quakers. Although they formed an important proportion of all converts to Quakerism, they were only a tiny fraction of those who came under the influence of the movement. In 1870, it was estimated that only fifty-four First Day Scholars had ever become Friends.[1] Twenty years later, in 1890, converts from every source totalled 262; but there were over 35,000 child and Adult scholars in Quaker Sunday Schools. In that year, it was suggested that the relatively small number of such converts meant that they suffered from 'religious loneliness and isolation'.[2]

Others—the great majority—had no desire to become Quakers. Some were discouraged by the informal barriers which existed. Many a scholar discovered, when he visited the Meeting House, the difference between benevolence and equality, and that the cheerful bonhomie of the schools was replaced by 'a kind of exclusiveness which was not present in the adult school work'.[3] But even if Victorian Friends had invariably welcomed catechumens, it is unlikely that the silence and constraint of a Quaker Meeting for Worship could ever have appealed to more than a minority. There were therefore two alternatives left for most scholars: to join another denomination, or to regard their Adult School attendance as a form of church membership.

There is no way of knowing how many First Day Scholars joined other denominations. Throughout the second half of the nineteenth century there are recurring complaints that other churches, especially the Wesleyans, the Primitive Methodists, and the Baptists, reaped where Quakers sowed.[4] But many had absorbed enough of Friends' distinctive teachings for this to be impossible. Affection for a Quaker school and Quaker teachers, the power of habit and of sheer inertia inclined them to the latter course. Friends themselves were clearly aware of the situation—the relation-

---

[1] *Dublin F.F.D.S.A. Conference Proceedings, 1870*, p. 142.
[2] *Birmingham F.F.D.S.A. Conference Proceedings, 1890*, p. 189.
[3] ibid., p. 73; cf. *Dublin F.F.D.S.A. Conference Proceedings, 1870*, p. 140.
[4] *The Friend* (1869), 266–7 and (1870), p. 25. *The British Friend* (1905), 169–70.

ship of scholars to the Society formed the main theme of every F.F.D.S.A. Conference—and decided that the best remedy was to expand the religious functions of the schools. The first step was the holding of Sunday evening services, called mission meetings, which, with their prepared addresses and congregational singing, were very much like a nonconformist chapel service, with perhaps half a dozen Friends sharing, at different times, the duties of the minister.

These meetings were especially characteristic of Adult Schools, but were often also held in connection with children's schools. At first it was usual for teachers to take child scholars with them to Meeting for Worship.[1] But the practice proved unsatisfactory—from whose standpoint is not always recorded—and it became usual to hold separate services for children as well as adults.[2]

Most Mission Meetings seem to have been established in the 1860s. By 1875 it was estimated that there were as many Mission Meeting attenders as there were English Quakers.[3] Yet they had their critics, both among scholars and among Friends. Many Friends regarded them with suspicion, because hymn singing and prepared addresses were contrary to Quaker tradition. Moreover, the Mission Meetings diverted the energies of some of the most zealous members of a Meeting, and weakened the attendance at the evening Meeting for Worship. They were still more alarmed by the fact that those active in the movement became convinced of the intrinsic merits of hymn singing and Bible readings, *per se*, and began to advocate their adoption by Friends in general.[4] Arnold Rowntree complained in 1905: 'Half-heartedly and grudgingly we allow the opening of a "Mission Meeting", and then neglect it. It is no wonder that it becomes unquakerly.'[5]

From the standpoint of the scholars who attended them regularly, the Mission Meetings were less than completely satisfactory, for some desired the satisfactions and responsi-

[1] *The Friend* (1847), 37; F.F.D.S.A. *Annual Report, 1849*, p. 12; *Liverpool F.F.D.S.A. Conference Proceedings, 1859*, pp. 43–9.
[2] F.F.D.S.A. *Dublin Conference Proceedings, 1870*, pp. 159–61.
[3] *The Friend* (1875), 146.
[4] *FQE* (1867), 102–13; *Dublin F.F.D.S.A. Conference Proceedings, 1870*, pp. 12–13. [5] *The British Friend* (1905), 170.

bilities of formal membership of a recognized church. In 1870 a conference was held to discuss the problems of the 300 adults attending Mission Meetings in London. One of those present, William Beck, recommended that they should develop into churches, with a formal system of membership, with self government, and with a 'rite' to symbolize union. The 'rite' he recommended consisted simply of monthly fellowship meetings.[1] His suggestions probably had little influence, but he accurately predicted the course of development which was to occur in some areas.

Many, probably most Mission Meetings, never developed into separate churches. But by 1875 it was clear that in some centres: 'the gatherings which take place under the care of our teachers and other Christian workers, are gradually assuming the character of religious organisations or mission churches, and this rather as the natural outcome of their position and felt wants, than as the result of preconceived plans.'[2]

The only systematic account of these churches is to be found in a report presented to the Manchester Conference in 1895.[3] Its author complained of the difficulty of obtaining information about them: the difficulty reflects their spontaneous growth, and their lack of contact with each other. Intending members were expected to be of respectable life and to make an evangelical declaration of faith. When asked whether they expected prospective members to adopt the distinctive views of Friends, the churches' answers varied. The one at Bunhill Fields replied in a single word, 'Fully'. They reported that their services were held on Quaker lines, sometimes with the addition of singing: their practice was obviously coming to resemble that of Friends to an increasing extent. The name they adopted varied, there was a Christian Society, a Friends Mission Church, and a School Society of Friends.

The churches were asked whether they encouraged their members to become Quakers. Here again, their practice varied. So many members of the Norwich Gospel Band joined

---

[1] *The Monthly Record* (1870), 139; *The Friend* (1870), 25.
[2] *F.F.D.S.A. Annual Report, 1875*, p. 8.
[3] *Manchester Conference Proceedings, 1895*, p. 101f.

Friends that the Band ceased to exist, except for the purposes of tract distribution. At Kendal, membership of a Mission Meeting was seen as a stepping stone to Quaker membership. The Bedford Institute reported that its members were encouraged to become Friends 'to a limited extent', and the Christian Society at Birmingham replied, 'Yes, but the bulk are satisfied with their own [membership].' In a ten-year period, 77 of the Christian Society's 1,000 members became Friends.

By the end of the nineteenth century, there were probably at least a score of these mission churches in existence. The largest and the best documented was the Birmingham Christian Society,[1] which had 1,209 members in 1900. The Christian Society grew out of evening services which were instituted for the benefit of the Adult Scholars in 1863. Ten years later, it was given a formal organization of its own, 'to find a spiritual home for those whom we had drawn by our teaching in the Adult Schools, too near Friends to go elsewhere, but whom Friends of that day were not prepared to receive into membership.'[2] Quaker Adult School teachers were also members of the Christian Society, and it is clear that they dominated both its organization and its services.[3] A number of vigorous congregations developed in different parts of Birmingham, which proliferated temperance societies, Mothers' Meetings and so on. The organization adopted a modified and simplified version of Quakerism, with a Monthly Fellowship Meeting, which combined social and administrative functions more overtly than its Quaker prototype.

By the 1890s what was in effect second-class Quakerism was becoming less acceptable to scholars and to Friends themselves. Many of the latter felt conscience stricken by the presence of a large body of men and women on their doorstep, separated only by social barriers. As a wealthy Birmingham Quaker asked himself: 'Are such work as CS

[1] For the early history of the Christian Society, see Samuel Price's account in the *Darlington FFDSA Conference Proceedings, 1874,* p. 103. Its subsequent history is given in Price's, *A Short Sketch of the Severn Street Christian Society, 1873–1907* (Birmingham, n.d.).

[2] Price, *op. cit.,* p. 13.

[3] *Manchester Conference Proceedings, passim.*

work to be kept as outside work of the Soc?, or what can be done to fuse this work with our own. A question for the whole Socy of Friends.'[1]

In the twentieth century, the mission churches declined rapidly. This was partly the result of the decline of the Adult School movement, and partly of the changed attitude of Friends, who encouraged mission church congregations to draw closer to the Society, either by their members' joining it individually, or by the churches' seeking Associate or Congregational Membership.

[1] Barrow Cadbury, Memorandum Book (Oct. 1889–June 1890), notes on a conference on the relationship of mission work to the Society of Friends, 27 Nov. 1889 (MSS. in Bournville Cocoa Works Archives).

CONCLUSION
IMAGE AND REALITY

AMIDST a multitude of changes, permanent or ephemeral, which affected Victorian Friends, one central theme emerges—the transition from the ideal of a Peculiar People, cut off from a corrupting world, to that of one Christian church among many, whose members have a responsibility to society which they may fulfil in many different ways.

When Victoria came to the throne, the Society of Friends in England was a small and exclusive middle-class church. Although its numbers were declining, it showed little interest in attracting converts. Most of its members were interrelated, and could claim generations of Quaker ancestry. They could marry only their fellow Quakers, and were cut off from the rest of society by their distinctive formulae of dress and speech. They had attained eminence in some branches of philanthropy, especially the anti-slavery movement, the British and Foreign Schools Society, and the British and Foreign Bible Society, but many conservative Quakers still frowned upon such activities, and the close cooperation with Christians of other denominations which they entailed. The first Quaker entered Parliament after the passage of the First Reform Act, and, in the years that followed, the Society's traditional condemnation of politics rapidly disappeared. But the chief preoccupation of devout Quakers in the 1830s was theology: the rival claims of quietism and evangelicalism, and the dissensions which these bred. Meetings for Worship were often held in silence, and whoever spoke in them was thought to give direct expression to the intimations of the Holy Spirit.

In the 1890s, many of these characteristics remained the same. The Society was still a small church, though its headlong decline in membership had been replaced by modest but steady expansion. It was still relatively exclusive, and closely linked by friendship and kinship, but these elements had been modified by the abandonment of compulsory group endogamy and the admission of a number of working-class converts from the Adult Schools. It was still predominantly middle-class, with some families of great wealth. Its complex organization had been modified in some details, but remained essentially unchanged. Friends were still pacifists, and still regarded oaths as forbidden and the sacraments as unnecessary. But the prophetic view of the ministry had declined: far more members took part in Meeting for Worship, and when they did so, they adopted a more conversational tone. The ideal of a Peculiar People had vanished. Singularity of dress and speech had practically disappeared, and Friends were active in local and national politics to an extent quite disproportionate to their limited numbers. They supported a network of Home and Foreign Missions, and in their First Day Schools taught a number of child and adult scholars equivalent to two-and-a-third times their own membership. They were still noted for their philanthropy, though the form which this took had undergone a number of metamorphoses. Philanthropy still had its Quaker critics, but they were now inspired by socialism, rather than by quietism. Teetotalism, an innovation in the 1830s, had become an orthodoxy. In theology, the wheel had almost turned full circle. Evangelicalism was declining, and the school of thought which replaced it had much in common with the quietism of an earlier day.

What is the relationship between the analysis of Victorian Quakerism presented in this study and the picture which contemporaries had of the movement? The image which Quakerism presented to the various sectors of Victorian society can be found reflected in many mirrors—in scores of casual references, in the articles on Quakerism which appeared from time to time in periodicals, and in the essays on the decline of Quakerism which were submitted both by Quakers and non-Quakers for a public essay contest in 1859.

One of the most striking factors which emerges is that contemporaries were deeply interested in Quakerism. There are several reasons for this—the distinctiveness of Quakers' outward appearance, and of many of their beliefs and practices, and the public reputation of a few prominent Friends

such as Bright and Elizabeth Fry. Victorian accounts of
Quakerism usually begin by pointing out the enormous
changes which the movement had undergone since the time
of Fox, when Friends were a band of despised and persecuted
visionaries. In Victorian England, Friends were often
described, both by themselves and others, as a spiritual élite:
'We are apt to credit ourselves with a position of superiority
among the churches, and to regard ourselves as the aristocracy of Dissent.'[1] Accounts of Quakerism written before
1860 lay great emphasis on the peculiarities of Quaker
dress and speech. Those written later, stress their abandonment. But practically all accounts by outsiders, whether
casual references or extended analyses, are full of praises
for the Society. F. W. Newman stated that 'Among Christian sects, I have from boyhood, pre-eminently honoured the
Friends.'[2] and an extraordinary diverse range of observers
echoed his words.[3] Articles in periodicals almost invariably
praise them: *The Westminster Review* wrote that 'More
than common philanthropy, generosity, amiability, were
expected from the Quaker in consequence of his clothes.'[4]
The evidence overwhelmingly shows 'a strong (though
often distant) admiration for Quakerism, which is very
general.'[5]

This widespread esteem rested largely on their achievements in philanthropy. Clarkson, writing at the beginning
of the nineteenth century, analysed the ingredients in their
popular image, and began with benevolence: 'I know of no
point, where the judgment of the world has been called
forth, in which it has been more unanimous.'[6] But in addition,
Friends were reputed to possess certain qualities of mind and
spirit—gravity, kindness, tranquillity—as well as an un-

---

[1] *Present Day Papers*, vol. ii, Apr. 1899, p. 22. cf. *The Edinburgh Review*, July,
1891, p. 220 and W. B. Selbie, *Nonconformity: Its Origin and Progress* (London,
n.d.), p. 247.
[2] Quoted in Tallack, *Howard Letters and Memories*, p. 81.
[3] cf., for instance, *The Spectator*, 12 June 1880; Joseph Parker, *A Preacher's
Life: An Autobiography and an Album* (London, 1899), p. 205; *The Hibernian
Essay on the Society of Friends, and the Causes of their Declension. By a Friend of
the Friends* (London, 1859), p. 33; Augustus J. C. Hare, *In My Solitary Life*, ed.
Malcolm Barnes (London, 1953, first published 1900), p. 113.
[4] *The Westminster Review* (1875), 318.   [5] *The Inquirer* (1900), 659.
[6] Clarkson, *A Portraiture of Quakerism*, vol. iii, p. 162.

usual capacity for domestic happiness. There are many parallels to the comment of an early nineteenth century Quaker, that 'There is that to be met with and felt, in the company of and intimacy with Friends, which is better experienced than described—a happy, serene, and calm temper, full of forbearance and love, and affection to all, and well seasoned with sober humility—such as elsewhere I have never been able to find.'[1] Friends were repeatedly described as possessing, to an unusual degree, a spirit of calm and self-control—forged, perhaps, in the patient endurance of innumerable silent meetings. *The Spectator* spoke of their 'elevation of self-restraint . . . into a kind of sacredness',[2] and Josephine Butler described their 'great determination and calmness combined'.[3] And when Carlyle was describing the archetype of the good employer, he called him Friend Prudence.

There was, of course, another side to this shining image. Friends were often accused of complacency and exclusiveness, failings of which they perpetually accused themselves. An anonymous essayist wrote that 'Themselves remain the special object of their own concern; a family of interests . . . a society for combined action, self-protection, and public relations.'[4] In the earlier part of the nineteenth century, they were often criticized for the narrowness of their mental horizons, for lack of culture and intellectual stimulus.[5] They were invariably seen as eminently prosperous and respectable —this was sometimes matter for blame, and sometimes for congratulation, depending on the observer's viewpoint. But the vice which was attributed to them most often was avarice. Almost every general account of Friends claimed that they revered wealth, and devoted their best energies to its accumulation. Clarkson wrote that 'a Money-getting

[1] *Barclay Letters and Papers*, p. 32.
[2] *The Spectator* (12 June 1880); Hancock, *The Peculium*, p. 187.
[3] Butler, *Personal Reminiscences*, pp. 82–3.
[4] *The Quakers, or Friends: Their Rise and Decline* (2nd ed., London, 1859), p. 37, and also pp. 32ff. cf. *An Honest Confession of the Cause of Decadence in the Society of Friends, with a glance at a few of the 'Peculiarities' of the Society. By a Member* (London, n.d. [1859]), p. 9.
[5] Clarkson, vol. iii, pp. 228ff. B.M.Add.MS. 27823 (Place Papers), f.59, Francis Place, 'The Quakers', Dec. 1827. *The Globe*, 22 Nov. 1844, quoted in *The Friend* (1845), 28.

Spirit . . . is considered as belonging so generally to the individuals of this Society, that it is held by the world to be almost inseparable from Quakerism.'[1] A mid-nineteenth century critic claimed that 'WEALTH is pursued with systematic purpose, and all the powers of the mind are bent to serve that end.'[2]

For some observers, the prosperity of Friends was, in itself, a damning indictment of them. Throughout his *Rural Rides*, Cobbett heaped violent and vulgar abuse on Quakers and Jews alike: he called the former 'the pestiferous sect of non-labouring, sleek and fat hypocrites'.[3] Francis Place had little that was good to say about Friends,[4] and *The Poor Man's Guardian* bitterly compared their solicitude for slaves abroad with their position of privilege at home, resting on the labours of the inarticulate poor: 'But the white slavery of Englishmen suits the Quakers; *they* continue to have houses built for them, and to enjoy all the bounties of Providence . . . Let the *Friends* show a sympathy for the white slaves of England.'[5] The same point was made, when a Gurney chaired a charitable meeting, by those whose voices seldom appear in historical records: 'The platform was surrounded by chartists . . . and the cry of 'Think of the slaves at home' was raised more than once.'[6]

Some of the most interesting comments came from those who were not Friends, but worked in close association with them. Some of these, such as Sir George Stephen, in the 1830's, and Josephine Butler, in the 1870s, had nothing but praise for them.[7] Thomas Clarkson, who was intimately associated with Friends during the first phase of the anti-slavery movement, from 1787, wrote a three volume analysis

[1] *Op. cit.*, vol. iii, p. 253, cf. Hancock, *The Peculium*, p. 226. *Observations on some of the Recent Essays on the Supposed Decline of the Society of Friends* (London, 1860), p. 30.
[2] *The Quakers or Friends: Their Rise and Decline*, p. 50.
[3] William Cobbett, *Rural Rides* (London, 1830), p. 430.
[4] cf. p. 285 below.
[5] *The Poor Man's Guardian* (2 March 1833), 71; cf. 27 Apr. 1833, p. 135. I am grateful to Mrs. P. Hollis for drawing my attention to this source.
[6] *The Anti-Slavery Reporter* (1840), 296.
[7] Stephen, *Antislavery Recollections*, p. 65; Butler, *Personal Reminiscences*, *passim*.

in which affection and admiration predominate, but are tempered with criticism. Near the end of his study, he listed the qualities which popular opinion ascribed to Friends, and attempted to determine whether they corresponded to the reality. He decided that the popular image of Friends was 'a strange medley of consistency and contradiction, and of merit and defect'.[1] The favourable attributes, he decided, were accurate: the list begins with 'Benevolence' and 'Quietness of Mind and Manner', and embraces a number of other qualities, such as fortitude, and punctiliousness in fulfilling engagements. Of the adverse attributes ascribed to them, he gave a qualified assent to the lack of intellectual cultivation, 'a Money-getting Spirit' and superstition—the last mentioned, in the sense of looking for the constant interposition of the divine in the ordinary affairs of life. He rejected charges of obstinacy, disregard of truth, 'Want of Animation', and 'Slyness'—though the last attribution is to be found in Pope, and recurs occasionally in Victorian times.[2]

Francis Place came into contact with Friends in 1813–15, through his work on the committee of the British and Foreign Schools Society. The account he wrote of them some years later was essentially hostile: William Allen was the only Friend to whom he felt able to give his unqualified praise.[3] He gave much thought to the discrepancy between his own critical impression of the Society and its glowing public reputation, and decided that the latter was due to their philanthropy, and relative lack of contact with outsiders: 'Their number is small, and they associate with few, very closely, who are not "friends;" They who see them oc-cassionally; see them in the very best light, and can seldom have opportunities of justly estimating them, A considerable share of vulgar charity and some remarkable displays of benevolence, have obtained for them a character as a body far above their merits.'[4]

The Scottish pioneer of teetotalism, John Dunlop, was

---

[1] Clarkson, op. cit., vol. iii, p. 152.
[2] The Greville Memoirs, 1840–60, ed. Lytton Strachey and Roger Fulford (London, 1938), vol. v, p. 85. cf. Clarkson, vol. iii, p. 279.
[3] B.M.Add.MS. 27823, f.58.   [4] ibid., f.59.

another critic of the Society. Apparently he resented the
power and influence which they enjoyed in the temperance
movement: he accused them both of love of power, and of
incompetence in its exercise.[1] Yet after a critical account of a
Quaker meeting, he added, 'It must be admitted that the
Quakers have always been a certain space in advance of the
rest of the population in some things such as anti-slavery,
cure of insanity, peace etc.'[2]

The discrepancies between these various accounts of
Victorian Quakerism are only partly due to the various
biases of different observers. For Victorian Quakerism, of
course, was not a monolithic entity. It embraced men and
women, old and young, rich and poor, devout and nominal
members, over a period of more than sixty years. It included
men with the reputation of saints, such as Joseph Sturge,
and John Tawell, who was executed as a poisoner. It included London bankers, Lancashire manufacturers, and
Lincolnshire agricultural labourers. For all of them, Quakerism was only one element in life, though often an important
one. In making their confident generalizations about their
behaviour and attributes as a group, contemporaries were
essaying a task full of difficulties and ambiguities. Generalization is indispensable for the later historian. But the same
pitfalls, of course, lie in his path.

What is the relationship between these various images of
Victorian Quakerism and the account which has been given
here? There are, of course, points of resemblance:
elements such as their exclusiveness, their activity in
philanthropy, and their prosperity, are amenable to historical
investigation and verification. But the abstract adjectives of
praise and blame, the constant attribution of moral qualities
in which contemporaries dealt so liberally, have no place in
the historian's vocabulary. He cannot decide whether
Quakers were unusually benevolent, calm, obstinate, and so
on, though it is an interesting historical fact that contemporaries thought they were.

And there is another, more important difficulty, which is
intrinsic in every essay in the social history of religion. One
can describe the theological views which were current

---

[1] *The Dunlop Papers*, vol. i, p. 320.   [2] ibid., p. 106.

among Friends, or their economic composition, and yet shed little light on the animating spirit of Victorian Quakerism as a religious movement. One does not explain the spirit of a William Allen or a Joseph Sturge by analysing their opinions, or the external actions of their lives.

This book has studied the anatomy of Victorian Quakerism. But it is the limitation of anatomy that it cannot reveal the secret of the life of any organism. All that this study has attempted to do is to add one piece of detailed research to our knowledge of the outward characteristics of Victorian religion, a phenomenon which has been much described, but is still too little understood.

APPENDIX

The Occupations of Quakers as Listed in Digest of Deaths

TABLE 1: 1840–1841

CLASS I

gentleman	27
manufacturer, mine owner, ship owner	8
banker, stockbroker	6
professional	16
merchant	16
land owner	28
agent (land, insurance or unspecified)	4
brewer, maltster, miller, tanner	6
managerial	1

CLASS II

retailer, small entrepreneur	39
commercial traveller	1
independent craftsman	13
teacher	4
clerk	1
inn keeper	1

CLASS III

shop assistant	1
skilled or semi-skilled worker	34

CLASS IV

unskilled worker	7
agricultural labourer	6
sailor	3

NOT CLASSIFIED BECAUSE OF AMBIGUITY OF
DESCRIPTION
iron founder, machine maker   2

OCCUPATION NOT GIVEN   140

TABLE 2: 1870–1871

CLASS I
gentleman	49
manufacturer, ship owner	7
banker	1
professional	14
merchant	14
land owner	26
agent	2
brewer, miller	5

CLASS II
retailer	12
commercial traveller	2
independent craftsman	8
teacher	3
clerk, bookkeeper	3
foreman	1
other	3

CLASS III
shop assistant	3
skilled or semi-skilled worker	27

CLASS IV
unskilled worker	12
agricultural labourer	1
sailor	1

NOT CLASSIFIED BECAUSE OF AMBIGUITY OF DESCRIPTION	
iron founder, engineer	4

RETIRED	10
OCCUPATION NOT GIVEN	140

TABLE 3: 1900–1901

CLASS I	
gentleman	20
manufacturer, colliery owner, quarry owner	13
banker, stock broker, insurance coy. director	5
professional	10
merchant, publisher	12
land owner	15
miller, printer	6
managerial	2
sea captain	1
other	4

CLASS II	
retailer	21
commercial traveller	5
independent craftsman	12
teacher	4
foreman, overseer, bailiff, small manager	9
clerk	6
missionary	4

CLASS III	
shop assistant	5
skilled or semi-skilled worker	23

CLASS IV

unskilled worker	10
agricultural labourer	2
sailor	2

NOT CLASSIFIED BECAUSE OF AMBIGUITY OF DESCRIPTION	11

RETIRED	24

OCCUPATION NOT GIVEN	11

BIBLIOGRAPHY[1]

MANUSCRIPT SOURCES

LONDON

Friends House Library, Euston Road, London

  1. *Official Quaker Records.*
      Yearly Meeting Minutes (until 1857), after which date they are printed, and referred to as *Yearly Meeting Proceedings.*
      Yearly Meeting Papers. (Bundles of documents laid before successive Yearly Meetings. For the Victorian period, only 1837–55 and 1864–9 survive.)
      Minutes of Meeting for Sufferings.

[1] Unless otherwise stated, Minutes, Annual Reports, periodicals &c., were consulted for the whole Victorian period, or for that part thereof for which they exist.

Minutes of the Parliamentary Committee of Meeting for Sufferings.

Minutes of the Peace Committee of Meeting for Sufferings.

Digest of Deaths, 1837–1901.

Minutes of Yearly Meeting Committee appointed to visit Lancashire Quarterly Meeting, 1835–6 (S113 and S114).

Friends Tract Association Minute Book, 1834–53.

Minutes of the Socialist Quaker Society (two vols, 1898–1909 and 1909–13).

2. *Unofficial accounts of Yearly Meeting proceedings.*

Samuel Alexander (1847 and 1852).

Jacob Henry Cotterell (1846 and 1847).

George Crosfield (1840).

Josiah Forster (1828–70; some years omitted).

Harrison Penney (1870).

John Priestman (?) (1859).

John Stephenson Rowntree (1854, 1856, 1859, 1862, and 1871).

Joseph Rowntree Jnr. (1855, 1857, and 1858).

William Rowntree (1856, 1859, and 1872).

William Smeal (1838).

3. *Journals, Diaries or Memorandum Books.*

Joseph Bevan Braithwaite (four vols: 1865–76, 1882–3, 1883–90, and 1890–1905).

Elizabeth Fry (1780–45; two volumes are missing from this collection, and are in Norfolk and Norwich County Record Office).

Joseph John Gurney (1808–46; transcript, in five volumes, made for and checked by Samuel Gurney, in 1851).

Grover Kemp (two vols.: 1823–9 and 1857–8).

Norman Penney (accounts of his work as a Home Missioner, 1883–8, and 1892–6).

Daniel Pickard (Diary, 1866–1905; there is also a transcript of this, and a MS. *Life* by L. A. Pickard).

Elizabeth Robson (journals of her ministerial journeys. There is also a transcript by Henry Robson, with much additional material).

Thomas Robson ('TR's Acct. of a Western Journey, with his beloved Wife—1833').

4. *Correspondence.*

Elihu Burritt, 1850–6 (vol. S101). Additional material relating to Burritt is collected in Box 8.5, ff. 1–36.

Gurney MSS. A large and valuable collection of the letters of the Gurney family. Many are from the pre-Victorian period.

Joseph Rowntree Snr. Correspondence relating to changes in Quaker marriage regulations (Temp. Box 93/3 and 4).

Joseph and Hannah Sturge (Box 10/3, ff. 1–10).

Correspondence and depositions concerning the Manchester rationalist schism (Box 9).

5. *Miscellaneous single letters.*

There are a number of boxes and bound volumes of individual letters, arranged according to the date of the library's acquisition of them, from different hands and periods. These were searched for relevant material, and the following letters are cited in this study.

John to William Dymond, 8 June 1837 (transcript, Port. 34/3).

Stephen Perry to Hannah Poulter, 8 Aug. 1867 (Port. B.27).

John Bright to John Pease, 26 Dec. 1851 (Temp. Box 24).

Thomas Hodgkin to his wife, 26 May 1876 (Port. B.34).

The Public Record Office.

Original Census returns for Banbury, 1851 (H.O. 107/1753 and 1734) and Bristol, 1861 (R.G. 9/1712ff.).

The British Museum.

Bright Papers. Add.MS.43383–92.

Campbell Bannerman Papers. Add.MS.41215.

Cobden Papers. Add.MS.43649–52 (correspondence with Bright); 43653–4 (correspondence with Henry Ashworth); 43656 (correspondence with Sturge); 43657–9 (correspondence with Henry Richard).

Elizabeth Fry diary, transcript. Add.MS.47456–7. (This was used as well as the original in Friends House, for convenience's sake.)

Fry family correspondence. 1838–72, Egerton MSS. 3675, Parts I–III.

Herbert Gladstone Papers. Add.MS.46058, 45987.

Place Papers. Add.MS.27,810, ff. 99, 128, 132; 27,823, ff. 59–61.

Sturge Papers. Add.MS.43722–3, 43845, and 50131.

University College Library.

Bright's letters to his wife, 1847–78.

BANBURY

Banbury Meeting House. (Records consulted by permission.)
Rough membership list, Banbury Monthly Meeting.

BIRMINGHAM

Birmingham University Library.
   Journal of anonymous Quaker [George Price] 1854–64.
Cadbury MSS. (L.Add. 1144–1188). Of little value.
Bournville Cocoa Works Archives. (Consulted by permission.)
Mainly business records, of little value for this study. The MSS.
used by Gardiner for his life of George Cadbury have apparently
been destroyed. The following are cited in this study:
   Barrow Cadbury. *Memorandum Books.*
   Elizabeth Cadbury to Carl Heath, 13 Sept. 1940.

BRISTOL

Bristol Archives Office
   List of Attenders, 1856 (SF R 3/7).
   List of Members, 1856 (SF R 3/4).
   Membership List, Bristol Monthly Meeting, 1864–1924
      (SF R 3/6)
   National Stock Collection Books, 1853–65 (SF F1/4 and 7).
   New Street Mission Sunday School, Minutes of Teachers'
      Meeting, (two vols. 1872–87 and 1887–1908) (SF/ A9/15).
   Rules, Minutes, &c. of Friends School, the Friars, Bristol,
      1790–1848 (SF A10 1a).

FRITCHLEY, DERBYSHIRE

Fritchley Meeting House. (Records consulted by permission.)
   Fritchley Monthly Meeting Minutes.
   Fritchley General Meeting Minutes.

MANCHESTER

Mount Street Meeting House. (Records consulted by permission.)
   Hardshaw East Monthly Meeting Minutes (1840–1920).
   Guard Books (1912–20).

Manchester City Library.
John Benjamin Smith Papers. (Correspondence with Bright consulted, only.)

NORWICH

Norfolk and Norwich County Record Office.
Norwich Monthly Meeting Minutes, 1840–1920.
Elizabeth Fry diary (two volumes, 1816–18 and 1821–22).
Ten letters from Elizabeth Fry to Louisa Pelly, 1829–46.

OXFORD

Oxford County Record Office.
Banbury Monthly Meeting Minutes (1835–45).
Membership list, Banbury Monthly Meeting (1837–55).

Rhodes House.
British and Foreign Anti-Slavery Society MSS. (Sturge correspondence consulted, only.)

PRINTED SOURCES

1. *Parliamentary Debates and Division Lists.*
   Hansard, Third Series. This was consulted extensively.

2. *Parliamentary Papers and other Official Publications.*
   1816: *Report from Select Committee on the Education of the Lower Orders in the Metropolis, with the Minutes of Evidence.* P.P. 1816, IV.
   1820: *'A General Table, showing the State of Education in England'.* P.P. 1820, xii, p. 341ff.
   1834: *Report from Select Committee on the State of Education, with the Minutes of Evidence.* P.P. 1834, ix.
   1835: *Report from Select Committee on York City Election,* Joseph Rowntree's Evidence, P.P. 1835, x, p. 224ff.
   1835: *Abstract of Answers and Returns relative to the State of Education in England and Wales,* P.P. 1835, xli–xliii.
   1838: *A Collection of the Public General Statutes Passed in the First and Second Year of the Reign of Her Majesty Queen Victoria.*

1851: *Census of Great Britain, 1851. Religious Worship. England and Wales*, P.P. 1852–3, lxxxix.

1851: *Census of Great Britain, 1851. Education, England and Wales*, P.P. 1852–3, xc.

1861: *Report of the Commissioners appointed to inquire into the State of Popular Education in England*, P.P. 1861, xxi.

1911: *74th Annual Report of the Registrar General of Births, Deaths and Marriages in England and Wales*.

3. *Periodicals.*

(a) *Quaker Periodicals.* (Dates are of publication.)

The Annual Monitor, 1813–1920.

The Aurora Borealis, 1833.

The British Friend, 1843–1913.

The Essayist and Friends' Review, 1893.

The Friend, 1843–   .

The Friends Monthly Magazine, conducted by Members of the Society of Friends, 1830–1.

The Friends Quarterly Examiner, 1867–1946.

The Herald of Truth, or Friend of Religion, Literature and Science, 1828–9.

The Inquirer, 1838–40 (Beaconite.)

The Irish Friend: A Monthly Periodical devoted Chiefly to the Interests of Friends, 1837–42.

The Journal of the Friends Historical Society, 1903–   .

The Lindfield Reporter or Philanthropic Magazine; being a Repository for Hints and Suggestions, calculated to promote the Comfort and Happiness of Man, 1835–42.

The Manchester Friend, Dec. 1871–Dec. 1873.

The Monthly Record. A Journal of Home and Foreign Missions. First-Day Schools, Temperance, and other Christian work in the Society of Friends, 1869–91.

One and All. The Organ of the Midland Adult School Association, 1891–?

The Philanthropist: or Repository for Hints and Suggestions Calculated to promote the Comfort and Happiness of Man, 1811–19.

The Ploughshare, 1912–20.

Present Day Papers, 1898–1902.

The Quarterly Magazine and Review. Chiefly designed for the use of the Society of Friends, 1832.

The Yorkshireman. A Religious and Literary Journal by a Friend, 1833–7.

(b) *Other.* (Those marked* were studied systematically.)

*The Anti-Corn Law League Circular.**

*The Anti-Bread-Tax Circular.**

*The Anti-Slavery Reporter.**

Bond of Brotherhood (Elihu Burritt's periodical).

The Bournville Works Magazine, 1902–4.

*The British and Foreign Anti-Slavery Reporter.**

*The British Emancipator.**

*Cake and Cockhorse. The Magazine of the Banbury Historical Society.**

The Christian World, 1904.

The Daily Telegraph, 1891–9. (Studied for its lists of philanthropic wills.)

The Eclectic Review, 1848, 1851, 1857.

The Edinburgh Review, 1891.

*The Herald of Peace.**

The Labour Leader, 1899.

*The League.**

The Poor Man's Guardian, 1833.

*The Nonconformist and Independent.**

The Quarterly Review, 1849.

Reynold's Newspaper, 1900.

The Saturday Review, 1856–60, 1911.

The Spectator, 1880.

The Shield. The Organ of the National Association for the Repeal of the Contagious Diseases Acts, 1872–3.

*The Staunch Teetotaler.**

The Times. (Extensively consulted for comment on specific issues and events, partly with the help of *The Times Index.*)

The Warrington Examiner, 1928.

The Weekly Record of the Temperance Movement, 1861.

The Western Temperance Herald. The Organ of the West of England and South Wales Temperance League, 1868, 1871.

The Westminster Review, 1875.

(c) *Press Cuttings.* There is a very useful collection in Friends House Library.

4. *Annual Reports and Conference Proceedings.*

British and Foreign Anti-Slavery Society Annual Reports.

Minutes of the Proceedings of the General Anti-Slavery Convention, called by the Committee of the British and Foreign Anti-Slavery Society, held in London on the 12th June, 1840.

British and Foreign Bible Society Annual Reports.

British and Foreign Temperance Society Annual Reports (1832–5).

Friends Association for Abolishing the State Regulation of Vice Annual Reports, 1873–1909.

Friends First-Day School Association Annual Reports, 1847–1900.

Report of the Proceedings of a Conference of Teachers in Friends' First-Day Schools, Liverpool, 1859.

Report of a Conference of Teachers held at Birmingham. First Month, 1867.

Report of the Proceedings of a Conference of Teachers in Friends' First-Day Schools, held in Dublin, on the 1st, 2nd, and 3rd of Eighth Month, 1870.

Report of a Conference of Teachers held in Darlington, Eighth Month, 1874.

Report of the Proceedings of a Conference of Teachers in Friends' First-Day Schools, held at Manchester, on the 16th and 18th of Second Month, 1885.

Report of the Proceedings of a Conference of Teachers in Friends' First-Day Schools, held at Birmingham, on the 13th, 14th, and 15th of Tenth Month, 1890.

Friends Temperance Union Annual Reports, 1892–1920.

Howard Association Annual Reports.

Peace Congress Reports, 1849–1903.

Peace Society Annual Reports, 1870–1902.

Peace Society, Speeches and Statements at the Annual Meeting, May 1870.

The Sixth Report of the Committee of the Society for the Improvement of Prison Discipline, and for the Reformation of Juvenile Offenders, 1824.

Society of Friends:
    Extracts from the Minutes and Proceedings of the Yearly Meeting of Friends, held in London, 1857 onwards.
    A Report of the Proceedings of the Yearly Meeting of the Society of Friends, reprinted, with corrections and Additions, from the 'Christian Advocate' Newspaper, 1836.
    The Proceedings of the Yearly Meeting of the Society of Friends . . . 1837 (reprinted from *The Patriot*).
    Report of the Proceedings of the Conference of Members of the Society of Friends . . . in Manchester . . . 1895.
    The Society of Friends, Report on the Proceedings of the Conference at Darlington on Foreign Missions held, by direction of London Yearly Meeting, 1896.
    United Kingdom Alliance Annual Reports.

5. *Quaker biography, autobiography, family memoirs and printed journals.*[1]

ALEXANDER, Horace G., *Joseph Gundry Alexander*, n.d. [1920].

ASH, Edward, *A Retrospect of my Life*, Bristol, 1874.

BAKER, Elizabeth Balmer and P. J. NOEL BAKER, *J. Allen Baker, Member of Parliament A Memoir*, 1927.

BASSETT, Arthur Tilney, *The Life of the Rt. Hon. John Edward Ellis M.P.*, 1914.

BAYLY, Mrs., *The Life and Letters of Mrs. Sewell*; 3rd ed., 1889.

Biographical Catalogue being an Account of the Lives of Friends and others whose Portraits are in the London Friends' Institute, 1888.

BOYCE, Anne Ogden, *Records of a Quaker Family: the Richard-sons of Cleveland*, 1889.

BRAITHWAITE, Joseph Bevan, *Memoirs of Joseph John Gurney*, 1854.

Braithwaite, J. Bevan, A Friend of the Nineteenth Century. By His Children, 1909.

BRIGGS, Asa, *Social Thought and Social Action A Study of the Work of Seebohm Rowntree 1871–1954*, 1961.

BRYANT, S. E. and G. P. BAKER (eds.); *A Quaker Journal being the Diary and Reminiscences of William Lucas of Hitchin (1804–1861) A Member of the Society of Friends*, 1934.

BUDGE, Frances Anne, *Isaac Sharp, An Apostle of the Nineteenth Century*, 1898.

BUXTON, Charles, (ed.); *Memoirs of Sir Thomas Fewell Buxton, Bart.*, 2nd ed., 1849.

CHAPMAN-HUSTON, Desmond, *Sir James Reckitt A Memoir*, 1927.

CORDER, Percy, *The Life of Robert Spence Watson*, 1914.

CREIGHTON, Louise, *Life and Letters of Thomas Hodgkin*, 1917.

DE BUNSEN, Victoria, *Charles Roden Buxton A Memoir*, 1948.

DONCASTER, H. M. (ed.); *James Henry Barber: A Family Memorial*, Sheffield, 1905.

DONCASTER, Phebe, *John Stephenson Rowntree: His Life and Work*, 1908.

---

[1] This section includes several who were not Quakers, but were closely linked with them. In this and subsequent sections, the place of publication is London, unless otherwise stated.

DUDLEY, James, *The Life of Edward Grubb 1854–1939 A Spiritual Pilgrimage*, 1946.

DYMOND, Charles William, *Memoirs Letters and Poems of Jonathan Dymond with Bibliographical Supplements*; privately printed, 1911.

ELLIS, Margaret, *Letters and Memorials of Eliza Ellis*, Leicester, 1883.

EVANS, Jonathan, (ed.), *A Journal of the Life, Travels and Religious Labours of William Savery*, 1844.

FLYNN, John Stephen, *Sir Robert N. Fowler Bart., M.P. A Memoir*, 1893.

FORBUSH, Bliss, *Elias Hicks Quaker Liberal*, New York, 1956.

FORD, John, *Memoir of Thomas Pumphrey*, 1864.

— *The Sabbath School Teacher: A Memoir of Richard E. Tatham*, York, 1861.

ROBSON, S. E., *Joshua Rowntree* (Adult School ed.), 1916.

ROWNTREE, John S., *A Family Memoir of Joseph Rowntree*, privately printed, 1868.

SCOTT, Richenda, *Elizabeth Cadbury 1858–1951*, 1955.

A Selection of the Letters and Papers of the late John Barclay; 1st American ed., from 2nd. London ed., Philadelphia, 1847.

A Selection from the Letters of the late Sarah Grubb (formerly Sarah Lynes), Sudbury, 1848.

Selections from the Diary and Correspondence of John G. Sargeant, Newport, 1885.

SMITH, Charlotte Fell, *James Nicholson Richardson of Bessbrook*, 1925.

SMITH, Logan Pearsall (ed.), *A Religious Rebel, The Letters of 'H.W.S.' (Mrs. Pearsall Smith)*, 1949.

— *Unforgotten Years*, 1938.

SOUTHALL, Celia, *Records of the Southall Family*, privately printed, 1932.

SOUTHALL, Isabel, *Memorials of the Prichards of Almeley and their Descendants*, 2nd. ed., privately printed, 1901.

STURGE, M. Carta, *Some Little Quakers in their Nursery*, 1929; first pub., 1906.

STURGE, William, *Some Recollections of a long life*; privately printed, 1893.

SWIFT, David E. *Joseph John Gurney; Banker, Reformer, and Quaker*, Middletown, Connecticut, 1962.

TALLACK, William, *Howard Letters and Memories*, 1905.

— *Peter Bedford. The Spitalfields Philanthropist*, 1865.

TANGYE, Richard, *The Growth of a Great Industry. 'One and

All' An Autobiography of Richard Tangye of the Cornwall Works, Birmingham, 1889.

TAYLOR, Maria, *Memorials of Samuel Bowly*, privately printed, 1884.

TREVELYAN, George Macaulay, *The Life of John Bright*, 1913.

A Tribute to the Memory of Mr. William Rathbone, of Liverpool, Liverpool, 1809.

VERNON, Anne, *A Quaker Business Man. The Life of Joseph Rowntree 1836–1925*, 1958.

VINING, Elizabeth Gray, *Friend of Life, The Biography of Rufus M. Jones*, 1959.

VIPONT, Elfrida, *Arnold Rowntree. A Life*, 1955.

WALLING, R. A. J. (ed.), *The Diaries of John Bright, with a Foreword by Philip Bright*, 1930.

WEDMORE, Edmund Tolson, *Thomas Pole M.D. (Journal of the Friends Historical Society Supplement, 7)*, 1908.

— *Richard Reynold Philanthropist*, Bristol, 1907.

WHITE, William, *A Brief Memoir of Joseph Clark, for nearly twenty years Superintendent of Severn Street First-Day School, Birmingham*, Birmingham, 1867.

WHITNEY, Janet, *Geraldine S. Cadbury, 1865–1941. A Biography*, 1948.

WOOLF, Virginia, *Roger Fry, A. Biography*, 1940.

WOOLMAN, John, *A Journal of the Life and Travels of*; 3rd ed., 1838.

6. *Books by and/or about Friends, published before or during 1910.*[1]

An Account of the Times and Places of holding the meetings for Worship and Discipline of the Society of Friends in Great Britain and Ireland for . . .1854.

An Account of the First-Day Schools, conducted by Friends, in England. To the end of the Year 1847, Bristol, 1847.

An Address to the Members of the Society of Friends on their aversion to War, and Support of the Peace Society, n.d. [1833].

ALLEN, William, *Brief Remarks upon the Carnal and Spiritual State of Man*, 1817.

ASH, Edward, *The Christian Profession of the Society of Friends, Commended to its Members*, 1837.

—, *Four Essays on Theological Subjects*, 1864.

[1] This list excludes books by Friends on secular subjects—it deals only with books on Quakerism, or closely related topics, such as philanthropy. The date 1910 was chosen arbitrarily, as roughly corresponding to the line of demarcation between primary and secondary sources.

ASH, Edward, *Quakerism: Its Place and Service in Christ's Church: with Thoughts on Christian Ministry, as exercised in the Society of Friends*, 1865.

——, *Seven Letters to a Member of the Society of Friends*, 1855.

BARCLAY, Robert, *An Apology for the true Christian Divinity, as the same is held forth, and preached by the people in scorn called Quakers*; 14th ed., Glasgow, 1886.

BEWLEY, Thomas, *An Inquiry into the Right Place and Authority of Holy Scripture*; privately printed, 1867.

The Book of Christian Discipline of the Religious Society of Friends in Great Britain; 5th ed., 1883.

The Book of Meetings of the Society of Friends in Great Britain and Ireland, 1904ff.

BRAITHWAITE, William Charles, *Spiritual Guidance in the Experience of the Society of Friends*, 1909.

CHARLETON, Robert, *Brief Thoughts on the Atonement*, 1878.

Christian Discipline of the Religious Scoiety of Friends in Great Britain and Australia, 1906.

CLARKSON, Thomas, *A Portraiture of Quakerism*; 2nd ed., 1807.

COOPER, Frederick, *The Crisis in Manchester Meeting, With a Review of the Pamphlets of David Duncan and Joseph B. Forster*; privately printed, 1869.

CREWDSON, Isaac, *A Beacon to the Society of Friends*, 1835.

——, *Glad Tracts for Sinners*; privately printed, 1845.

CROSFIELD, John Dymond, *The Straws on the Camel's Back, or the Financial Pressure exercised from Devonshire on the Members of the Society of Friends*, n.d. [1898].

DUNCAN, David, *Can an Outward Revelation be Perfect? Reflections upon the claim of Biblical Infallibility*, 1863.

——, '*Essays and Reviews*'. *A Lecture*, Manchester, 1861.

[DYMOND, Jonathan] *An Enquiry into the Accordancy of War with the Principles of Christianity, and an Examination of the Philosophical Reasoning by which it is Defended*; anonymous 1st ed., 1823.

Extracts from the Minutes and Advices of the Yearly Meeting of Friends held in London, 1822.

An Essay on the Causes of the Decline of the Society of Friends. '*Quantum Mutatus*', n.d. [1859].

Epistles from the Yearly Meeting of Friends held in London to the Quarterly and Monthly Meetings in Great Britain, Ireland and elsewhere: from 1681 to 1857, inclusive, 1858.

A Faithful Letter to the Quakers, 1879.

FORSTER, Joseph B., *On Liberty. An Address to the Members of the Society of Friends*, 1867.
— *The Society of Friends and Freedom of Thought in 1871*, 1871.
FOTHERGILL, Samuel, *Essay on the Society of Friends: Being an Inquiry into the Causes of their Diminished Influence and Numbers, with Suggestions for a Remedy*, 1859.
Fox, Joseph John, *The Society of Friends: an Enquiry into the Causes of its Weakness as a Church*, 1859.
FRY, Elizabeth, *Observations on the Visiting, Superintending, and Government, of Female Prisoners*; 2nd ed., 1827.
GILLMAN, Frederick John, *The Story of the York Adult Schools from the Commencement to the Year 1907*, York, 1907.
GREGORY, Maurice, *The Crowning Crime of Christendom. With a Short History of the Efforts of the Society of Friends for its Abolition*, 1896.
GREEN, Joseph J. (ed.), *Quaker Records: being an Index to 'The Annual Monitor', 1813–1892*, 1894.
GRUBB, Edward, *Authority and the Light Within*, 1909.
GURNEY, Joseph John, *Chalmeriana: or, Colloquies with Dr. Chalmers*, 1853.
— *Essays on the Evidences, Doctrines, and Practical Operation, of Christianity*, 1825.
— *Hints on the Portable Evidence of Christianity*, 1825.
— *A Letter to a Friend on the Authority, Purpose, and Effects of Christianity, and especially on the Doctrine of Redemption*; 3rd ed., 1824.
— *Observations on the Distinguishing Views & Practices of the Society of Friends*; 7th ed., 1834.
HANCOCK, Thomas, *The Peculium: an Endeavour to throw light on some of the Causes of the Decline of the Society of Friends, especially in regard to its Original Claim of being the Peculiar People of God*, 1859.
The Hibernian Essay on the Society of Friends, and the causes of their Declension. By a Friend of the Friends, 1859.
HODGKIN, J. B., *The Public Worship of the Society of Friends*, 1908.
HODGSON, William, *The Society of Friends in the Nineteenth Century: A Historical View of the Successive Convulsions and Schisms therein during that period*, Philadelphia, 1875.
An Honest Confession of the cause of Decadence in the Society of Friends. . . . By a Member, n.d.
HOWARD, Robert, *A Few Words on Corn and Quakers*; 2nd ed., 1800.

MacNair, Robert, *The Decline of Quakerism: An Enquiry into the Causes which have led to the Present Moral and Numerical Weakness of the Society of Friends*, 1860.

Maurice, Frederick Denison, *The Kingdom of Christ: or, Hints to a Quaker, respecting the Principles, Constitution, and Ordinances of the Catholic Church*; 2nd ed., 1842.

Pickard, Daniel, *A Brief Reply to Thomas Bewley's Pamphlet entitled 'An Inquiry into the right place and authority of Holy Scripture*, Gloucester, 1867.

— *An Expostulation on behalf of the Truth, against Departures in Doctrine, Practice, and Discipline*, 1864.

Pike, Richard, (ed.), *Quaker Anecdotes*, 1880.

Pole, Thomas, *A History of the Origin and Progress of Adult Schools with an Account of some of the Beneficial Effects already produced*, privately printed, 1814.

Price, Samuel, *A Short Sketch of the Severn Street Christian Society, 1873–1907*, Birmingham, n.d.

The Quakers, or Friends: Their Rise and Decline; 2nd ed., 1859.

Quakerieties for 1838, by An Embryo 'Harvest Man', 1838.

Rathbone, William, *A Memoir of the Proceedings of the Society called Quakers, belonging to the Monthly Meeting of Hardshaw, in Lancashire, in the case of the Author of a Publication entitled a Narrative of Events, &c.*, Liverpool, 1805.

— *A Narrative of Events that have lately taken place in Ireland, among the Society called Quakers*, 1804.

Some remarks on a Recent Publication entitled Seven Letters to a Member of the Society of Friends, 1855.

A Reasonable Faith. Short Essays for the Times by Three 'Friends', 1884.

Richardson, S. T., *'The Friends' in Council, a Humorous Representation of a Friends' Sunday-School Teachers' Conference, holden in Darlington during the month of August, 1874*, 1875.

R. [owntree], J., *Statements connected with the Marriage Regulations of the Society of Friends*; privately printed, 1858.

Rowntree, John Stephenson, *Quakerism Past and Present: being an Inquiry into the Causes of its Decline in Great Britain and Ireland*, 1859.

Rowntree, Joshua (ed.), *John Wilhelm Rowntree, Essays and Addresses*, 1905.

Rowntree, J. Wilhelm and Henry Bryan Binns, *A History of the Adult School Movement*, 1903.

Rules of Discipline of the Religious Society of Friends, with Advices, 1834.

SESSIONS, Frederick, and F. DYMOND. *Friends Temperance Union, Handbook of Practical Methods*, 1895.

Sketch of the Origin and Results of Ladies' Prison Associations, with Hints for the Formation of Local Branches, 1827.

SMITH, Edward, *Mending Men. Adult School Process*, n.d.

— *Glowing Facts and Personalities chiefly associated with the Birmingham Adult School Movement and the late Alderman William White, First President of the Midland Adult School Union*, 1916.

— *Studies of Men Mended*, n.d.

Socialist Quaker Society Publications, 1898–1913. (Bound volume of eight pamphlets, in FHL.)

STEEL, John W., '*Friendly' Sketches Essays Illustrative of Quakerism*, 1876.

STEPHEN, Caroline Emelia, *Quaker Strongholds*; first pub., 1890; 4th ed., 1939.

[TALLACK, William], *The Friends and Capital Punishment*, 1883.

THORP, Fielden, *A Review of a Lecture on 'Liberty'*, 1867.

THURNAM, John, *Observations and Essays on the Statistics of Insanity*, 1845. (Appendix II, 'Contributions to the Statistics of the Society of Friends'.)

To the Glory of God. An Address to Members of the Society of Friends. (Friends Temperance Union pamphlet.) 1891.

TURNER, Frederick Storrs, *The Quakers. A Study Historical and Critical*, 1889.

WHITE [William] *The Development of the Sunday School System in the Direction of Adult Instruction. A Paper read at the Autumnal Convention of the Sunday School Union, 29th Sept. 1886.*

— *Our Jubilee Year, 1895. The Story of the Severn Street and Priory First-Day Schools, Birmingham*, 1895.

WHITING, Mary Lucy, *Types of Sunday Evening Meetings and their Respective Values* (Friends Home Mission and Extension Committee pamphlet), 1908.

The Whole Correspondence between the Committee of the Yearly Meeting of Friends, and Isaac Crewdson, 1836.

WILKINSON, John, *Quakerism Examined: In a Reply to the Letter of Samuel Tuke*, 1836.

William Beck and the Bedford Institute, n.d.

WORSDELL, Edward, *The Gospel of Divine Help. Thoughts on Some First Principles of Christianity Address Chiefly to the Members of the Society of Friends*; 2nd ed., 1888.

7. *Books about Quakerism, published after 1910.*

A Brief Account of the Rise of the Religious Society of Friends, their Original Principles and Church Government, with some Observations on the present state of the Society, 1925; issued by Fritchley Friends.

BRAITHWAITE, William C. *The Beginnings of Quakerism*; 2nd revised ed., 1961.

— *The Second Period of Quakerism*; 2nd revised ed., Cambridge, 1961.

BRINTON, Anna (ed.), *Then and Now. Quaker Essays Historical and Contemporary by friends of Henry Joel Cadbury on his Completion of Twenty-two Years as Chairman of the American Friends Service Committee*, Philadelphia, 1960.

DAVIS, R. (ed.), *Woodbrooke, 1903–1953*, 1953.

DONCASTER, L. Hugh, *Quaker Organisation and Business Meetings*, 1958.

EMDEN, Paul, H., *Quakers in Commerce. A Record of Business Achievement*, 1939.

Facing the Facts being the Report of the Conference on 'The Society of Friends and the Social Order' held in London 19–22 October, 1916.

FLEMING, Horace, *The Lighted Mind: The Challenge of Adult Education to Quakerism*, 1929.

FRY, A. Ruth, *A Quaker Adventure. The Story of Nine Years' Relief and Reconstruction*, 1926.

— *Quaker Ways*, 1933.

GRAHAM, John W., *War from a Quaker Point of View*, 1916.

GRUBB, Edward, *Christianity and Business*, 1912.

— *Eldership A Definite Service*, 1924.

— *Separations. Their Causes and Effects: Studies in Nineteenth Century Quakerism*, 1914.

GRUBB, Isabel, *Quakerism and Industry before 1800*, 1930.

HARVEY, William Fryer, *Quaker Byways and Other Papers*, Weybridge, 1929.

HIRST, Margaret E., *The Quakers in Peace and War. An Account of their Peace Principles and Practice*, 1923.

HUNT, N. C. *Two Early Political Associations: the Quakers and the Dissenting Deputies in the Age of Sir Robert Walpole*, Oxford, 1961.

JAMES, Sydney V., *A People Among Peoples. Quaker Benevolence in Eighteenth Century America*, Cambridge, Mass., 1963.

JONES, Lester M., *Quakers in Action. Recent Humanitarian and Reform Activities of the American Quakers*, New York, 1929.

JONES, Rufus M., *The Later Periods of Quakerism*, 1921.
JORNS, Auguste, *The Quakers as Pioneers in Social Work* (trans. Thomas Kite Brown, Jr.), New York, 1931.
Jubilee Souvenir Luton Adult School 1862–1912, Luton, 1912.
London Yearly Meeting during 250 Years (*by various authors*), *1919*.
LLOYD, Arnold, *Quaker Social History 1669–1738*, 1950.
LOUKES, Harold, *The Discovery of Quakerism*, 1960.
MARSH, Edward, *Facts about Friends. A Study of the Statistics of London and Dublin Yearly Meetings 1861–1911*, n.d. [1911].
McKENZIE, Isabel, *Social Activities of the English Friends in the first Half of the Nineteenth Century*, privately printed, New York, 1935.
Mount Street 1830–1930, (various authors), 1930.
PENNEY, Norman (ed.), *Pen Pictures of London Yearly Meeting 1789–1833, being Extracts from the Notes of Richard Cockin, and others*, 1930.
PLATT, Joan (from materials supplied by A. J. Eddington), *The Quakers in Norwich*, Norwich, 1926.
Quakerism and Industry being the full record of a Conference of Employers chiefly Members of the Society of Friends, held at Woodbrooke near Birmingham, 11th–14th April, 1918 Together with the Report issued by the Conference, Darlington, 1918.
RAISTRICK, *Quakers in Science and Industry, being an Account of the Quaker Contributions to Science and Industry during the 17th and 18th Centuries*, 1950.
ROWNTREE, Arnold S., *Woodbrooke: Its History and Aims*, 1923.
Social Thought in the Society of Friends (issued by War and Social Order Committee), 1922.
Some Facts about the F.F.M.A., n.d. [1917].
STEWART, W. A. Campbell, *Quakers and Education as seen in their Schools in England*, 1953.
TOLLES, Frederick B., *Quakers and the Atlantic Culture*, New York, 1960.
WRIGHT, Luella M., *Literature and Education in Early Quakerism*, Iowa City, 1933.

8. *Other Books, published before 1910.*
ALEXANDER, Joseph G., *Sixty Years against Slavery. A Brief Record of the Work and Aims of the British and Foreign Anti-Slavery Society, 1839–1899*, n.d.

ARNOLD, Matthew, *Culture and Anarchy* (ed. J. Dover Wilson), Cambridge, 1950; first pub., 1869.

ARNOLDSON, K. P. *Pax Mundi A Concise Account of the Progress of the Movement for Peace by means of Arbitration, Neutralisation, International Law and Disarmament*, 1892.

ASHWORTH, Henry, *Recollections of Richard Cobden, M.P., and the Anti-Corn Law League;* 2nd ed., n.d.

AXON, William E. A., *The Annals of Manchester: A Chronological Record from the Times to the end of 1885*, Manchester, 1886.

The Baptist Handbook, 1890–1900.

BAYNE, A. D., *A Comprehensive History of Norwich*, 1869.

BEESLEY, Alfred, *The History of Banbury; Including copious historical and antiquarian notices of the neighbourhood*, 1841.

BLUNT, John Henry, *The Book of Church Law;* revised ed., 1872.

BOOTH, Charles, *Life and Labour of the People in London,* Third Series, *Religious Influences*, 1902.

BOSS, Thomas Ward, *Reminiscences of Old Banbury*, Banbury, 1903.

BROWNE, George, *The History of the British and Foreign Bible Society, from Its Institution in 1804, to the close of its Jubilee in 1854*, 1859.

BURNS, Dawson, *Temperance History. A Consecutive Narrative of the Rise, Development, and Extension, of the Temperance Reform with an Introductory Chapter*, n.d.

BURRITT, Elihu, *Ten Minute Talks on all sorts of Topics, with Autobiography of the Author*, 1874.

BUTLER, Josephine, *Personal Reminiscences of a Great Crusade*, 1896.

— (ed.), *Woman's Work and Woman's Culture. A Series of Essays*, 1869.

BUTTERWORTH, James, *The Antiquities of the Town, and a complete History of the Trade of Manchester*, Manchester, 1822.

BUXTON, Thomas Fowell, *An Inquiry whether Crime and Misery are produced or prevented by our Present System of Prison Discipline;* 6th ed., 1818.

CANTON, William, *A History of the British and Foreign Bible Society*, 1904–10.

COBBETT, William, *Rural Rides*, 1830.

The Congregational Year Book.

COULING, Samuel, *History of the Temperance Movement in Great Britain and Ireland; from the earliest date to the present time, with biographical notices of departed Temperance Worthies*, 1862.

CRIPPS, Henry William, *A Practical Treatise on the Law relating to the Church and Clergy*; 5th ed., 1869.

DALE, A. W. W., *The Life of R. W. Dale of Birmingham*, 1898.

DALE, R. W., *The Old Evangelicalism and the New*, 1889.

DAVIES, C. Maurice, *Unorthodox London: or Phases of Religious Life in the Metropolis*, 1873.

— ibid., Series II, 1875.

EDWARDS, E., *Personal Recollections of Birmingham and Birmingham Men*, Birmingham, 1877.

ESPIN, Rev. Canon, *The Pastoral Aspect of Sunday School Work*, 1876.

EVANS, Howard, *Sir Randal Cremer. His Life and Work*, 1909.

GOBLET, d'Alviella, *The Contemporary Evolution of Religious Thought in England, America and India* (trans. J. Modern), 1885.

GOSSE, Edmund, *Father and Son*, 1958; first pub., 1907.

GOUGH, John B., *Autobiography and Personal Recollections*, 1870.

GREGORY, Alfred, *Robert Raikes: Journalist and Philanthropist. A History of the Origin of Sunday Schools*, 1877.

GRISCOM, John, *A Year in Europe*, New York, 1823.

HARE, Augustus J. C., *The Story of My Life*; first pub., 1896–1900; two vol. abridgement by Malcolm Barnes, *The Years With Mother*, 1952, and *In My Solitary Life*, 1953.

HAWKINS, C. B., *Norwich. A Social Study*, 1910.

HUDSON, J. W., *The History of Adult Education*, 1851.

The Hundredth Year. The Story of the Centenary Celebrations of the Sunday School Union, 1903, 1903 (ed. M. Jennie Street).

JOHNSON, George W. and LUCY A. (eds.), *Josephine E. Butler An Autobiographical Memoir*, Bristol, 1909.

JOHNSON, William Ponsonby, *The History of Banbury and its Neighbourhood*, Banbury, n.d.

MACKIE, Charles, *Norfolk Annals. A Chronological Record of Remarkable Events in the Nineteenth Century*, vol. I, 1801–1850, Norwich, 1901.

MARTINEAU, Harriet, *Biographical Sketches*. 1852–68; 2nd ed., 1869.

— *Harriet Martineau's Autobiography with Memorials by Maria Weston Chapman*, 1877.

MASTERMAN, C. F. G., *The Condition of England*, 1911; first pub., 1909.

Mathew's Annual Directory for the City and County of Bristol, including Clifton, Bedminster, and surrounding villages, 1863, 1864.

MAYHEW, Henry, *London Labour and the London Poor; a cyclopedia of the condition and earnings of those that will work, those that cannot work and those that will not work,* 1851.

MIALL, Arthur, *Life of Edward Miall Formerly Member of Parliament for Rochdale and Bradford,* 1884.

MIALL, Charles S., *Henry Richard, M.P. A Biography,* 1889.

Minutes of the Conference of the Methodist New Connection, Minutes of the Conference of the Wesleyan Methodists.

The Modern Sunday School, various authors, n.d.

MORLEY, John, *The Life of Richard Cobden;* 11th ed., 1903.

MUDIE-SMITH, Richard (ed.), *The Religious Life of London,* 1904.

The Nonconformist's Sketch-Book; a Series of Views, Classified in Four Groups, of a State–Church and its Attendant Evils, 1842.

'*Nonconformity and Politics' by a Nonconformist Minister,* 1909.

OWEN, John, *The History of the Origin and first ten years of the British and Foreign Bible Society,* 1816.

RITCHIE, J. Ewing, *The Religious Life of London,* 1870.

ROWNTREE, B. Seebohm, *Poverty. A Study of Town Life;* 2nd ed., 1902.

ROWNTREE, Joshua, *The Imperial Drug Trade. A Re-Statement of the Opium Question, in the Light of Recent Evidence and New Developments in the East;* 3rd ed., 1908.

RUSSELL, George, W. E. (ed.), *Sir Wilfrid Lawson. A Memoir,* 1909.

Sketches of the Religious Denominations of the Present Day with the Number of Sects in England and Wales, and an Introductory Sketch of the Progress of Religious Opinions in England till the Period of the Revolution of 1688, and the Census . . . abridged from the official Report made by Horace Mann, Esq., 1854.

SLUGG, J. T., *Reminiscences of Manchester Fifty Years Ago,* Manchester, 1881.

STEPHEN, George, *Anti-slavery Recollections: in a Series of Letters Addressed to Mrs. Beecher Stowe,* 1854.

The Sunday School and its Relations, various authors, 1896.

WALLAS, G., *The Life of Francis Place,* 1771–1854; 4th ed., 1925; first pub., 1898.

WATSON, Robert Spence, *The National Liberal Federation from its commencement to the General Election of 1906*, 1907.

WATSON, W. H., *The First Fifty Years of the Sunday School*, n.d.

—— *The History of the Sunday School Union*, 1853.

WHITTAKER, Thomas, *Life's Battles in Temperance Armour*, 1884.

WILBERFORCE, Robert Isaac and Samuel, *The Life of William Wilberforce*; 2nd ed., 1839.

WINSKILL, Peter T., *Temperance Standard Bearers of the Nineteenth Century*, Manchester, 1897.

WRIGHT, Thomas, *Our New Masters*, 1873.

9. *Other Books, published after 1910.*

Adult Education Committee Final Report Ministry of Reconstruction, 1919.

ANNAN, Noel Gilroy, *Leslie Stephen. His Thought and Character in Relation to his Time*, Cambridge, Mass., 1952.

ARMYTAGE, W. H. G., *Heavens Below, Utopian Experiments in England, 1560–1960*, 1961.

ARNSTEIN, Walter L., *The Bradlaugh Case*, Oxford, 1965.

BANKS, J. A., *Prosperity and Parenthood*, 1954.

BEALES, A. C. F., *The History of Peace. A Short Account of the Organised Movements for International Peace*, 1931.

BELL, E. Moberley, *Josephine Butler, Flame of Fire*, 1963; first pub., 1962.

BRIGGS, Asa, *Victorian Cities*, 1963.

BROWN, Alan Willard, *The Metaphysical Society, Victorian Minds in Crisis, 1869–1880*, New York, 1947.

BROWN, Ford K., *Fathers of the Victorians, The Age of Wilberforce*, Cambridge, 1961.

BURGESS, Henry James, *Enterprise in Education. The story of the Work of the Established Church in the education of the people prior to 1870*, 1958.

BURN, W. L., *The Age of Equipoise. A Study of the Mid-Victorian Generation*, 1964.

—— *Emancipation and Apprenticeship in the British West Indies*, 1937.

BUTLER, A. S. G., *Portrait of Josephine Butler*, 1954.

CARPENTER, S. C., *Church and People, 1789–1889. A History of the Church of England from William Wilberforce to 'Lux Mundi'*, 1933.

CARTER, Henry, *The English Temperance Movement. A Study*

in Objectives, Vol. I, *The Formative Period 1830–1899*, 1933; Vol. II never published.

CHADWICK, Owen, *The Victorian Church*, 1966.

CHAMPNESS, Ernest, *Adult Schools. A Study in Pioneering*, Wallington, Surrey, 1941.

CHAPMAN-HUSTON, Desmond and Ernest E. CRIPPS, *Through a City Archway. The Story of Allen & Hanburys 1715–1954*, 1954.

A Chapter in the History of Drug Grinding, Oil Distilling and Oil Pressing, Apropos of the Foundation and Progress of Stafford Allen & Sons' Business, n.d.

CHECKLAND, S. G., *The Rise of Industrial Society in England 1815–1885*, 1964.

CHORLEY, Katherine, *Manchester Made Them*, 1950.

CLARKSON, G. Kitson, *The Making of Victorian England*, 1962.

COLE, G. D. H., *Chartist Portraits*, 1941.

COUPLAND, R., *The British Anti-Slavery Movement*, 1933.

COWHERD, Raymond, G., *The Politics of English Dissent*, 1959.

CURRIE, Martin G., *The Adult School Movement. Its Origin and Development*, 1924.

DAY, Clive, *The Distribution of Industrial Occupations in England, 1841–1861*, Trans. Connecticut Academy of Arts and Sciences, March 1925, pp. 79–235.

DENT, J. J., *Hodgson Pratt, Reformer: An Outline of His Work*, Manchester, 1932

The Dunlop Papers, Vol. I, *Autobiography of John Dunlop*, privately printed, 1932.

ELLIOTT-BINNS, L. E., *English Thought 1860–1900, The Theological Aspect*, 1956.

ENSOR, R. C. K., *England 1870–1914*, Oxford, 1936.

ERICKSON, Charlotte, *British Industrialists Steel and Hosiery 1850–1950*, Cambridge, 1959.

EVERSLEY, D. E. C., Peter LASLETT, and E. A. WRIGLEY, *An Introduction to English Historical Demography from the Sixteenth to the Nineteenth Century*, 1966.

FAIRHOLME, Edward G., and Wellesley PAIN, *A Century of Work for Animals. The History of the R.S.P.C.A., 1824–1934*, 1934.

FAWCETT, Millicent, and E. M. TURNER, *Josephine Butler Her Work and Principles and their Meaning for the Twentieth Century*, 1927.

GASH, Norman, *Politics in the Age of Peel. A Study in the Technique of Parliamentary Representation 1830–1850*, 1953.

GILLISPIE, Charles Coulston, *Genesis and Geology. A Study in the Relation of Scientific Thought, Natural Theology, and Social Opinion in Great Britain, 1790–1850*, Cambridge, Mass., 1951.

GLASS, D. V. (ed.), *Social Mobility in Britain*, 1954.

GLOVER, Willis B., *Evangelical Noncomformists and Higher Criticism in the Nineteenth Century*, 1954.

The Greville Memoirs 1814–60, ed. Lytton Strachey and Roger Fulford, 1935.

GRIGGS, Earl Leslie, *Thomas Clarkson The Friend of Slaves*, 1936.

GUTTSMAN, W. L., *The British Political Elite*, 1963.

HAMMOND, J. L., and Barbara, *Lord Shaftesbury*, 1923.

HANHAM, H. J., *Elections and Party Management. Politics in the time of Disraeli and Gladstone*, 1959.

HARRISON, J. F. C., *Learning and Living 1790–1960. A Study in the History of the English Adult Education Movement*, 1961.

HAYTER, Mark H. C., *The Vision of a Century 1853–1953*, 1953.

HEASMAN, Kathleen, *Evangelicals in Action. An Appraisal of their Social Work*, 1962.

HERBERT, George, *Shoemaker's Window: recollections of a Midland town before the railway age*, ed. Christiana S. Cheney, Oxford, 1948.

HERTZ, Gerald Berkeley, *The Manchester Politician 1750–1912*, 1912.

HOBSBAWN, E. J., *Labouring Men Studies in the History of Labour*, 1964.

HOBSON, J. A., *Richard Cobden The International Man*, 1918.

HOUGHTON, Walter, E., *The Victorian Frame of Mind 1830–1870*, 1957.

HOUSE, Humphry, *The Dickens World*; 2nd ed., 1950.

HUTIN, Serge, *Les Disciples Anglais de Jacob Boehme aux XVIIe et XVIIIe siècles*, Paris, 1960.

INGLIS, Kenneth S., *The Churches and the Working Classes in Victorian England*, 1963.

IRVINE, William, *Apes, Angels and Victorians. A Joint Biography of Darwin and Huxley*, 1955.

JAEGER, M., *Before Victoria. Changing Standards and Behaviour 1787–1837*, 1956.

JONES, M. G., *The Charity School Movement. A Study of Eighteenth Century Puritanism in Action*, Cambridge, 1938.

JONES, R. Tudur, *Congregationalism in England 1662–1962*, 1962.

KELLY, Thomas, *A History of Adult Education in Great Britain*, Liverpool, 1962.

KENDALL, Guy, *Robert Raikes. A Critical Study*, 1939.

KENT, John, *Elizabeth Fry*, 1962.

KLINGBERG, Frank J., *The Anti-Slavery Movement in England. A Study in English Humanitarianism*, New Haven, 1926.

MANNING, Bernard Lord, *The Protestant Dissenting Deputies*, Cambridge, 1952.

MARTIN, David A., *Pacifism. An Historical and Sociological Study*, 1965.

MARTIN, Hugh (ed.), *Christian Social Reformers of the Nineteenth Century*, 1927.

MATHIAS, Peter, *The Brewing Industry in England 1700–1830*, Cambridge, 1959.

MATTHEWS, P. W., and Anthony W. TUKE, *History of Barclay's Bank Limited. Including the many private and Joint Stock Banks amalgamated and affiliated with it*, 1926.

McCORD, Norman, *The Anti-Corn Law League 1838–1846*, 1958.

Moss, Arthur W., *Valiant Crusade. The History of the R.S.P.C.A.*, 1961.

MUIRHEAD, J. H. (ed.), *Birmingham Institutions*, Birmingham, 1911.

MUSSON, A. E., *Enterprise in Soap and Chemicals, Joseph Crosfield & Sons, Limited, 1815–1965*, Manchester, 1965.

NEWSOME, David, *The Parting of friends: a study of the Wilberforces and Henry Manning* (1966).

NIEBUHR, H. Richard, *The Social Sources of Denominationalism*, New York, 1957; first pub., 1929.

1825–1925. One Hundred Years' History of Shoes and Sheepskin Rugs at Street, Somerset, n.d.

OWEN, David, *English Philanthrophy 1660–1960*, Cambridge, Mass., 1965.

PAUL, Eden and Cedar, *Proletcult (Proletarian Culture)*, 1921.

PELLING, Henry, *Origins of the Labour Party, 1880–1900*, 1954.

PHELPS, Christina, *The Anglo-American Peace Movement in the mid-Nineteenth Century*, New York, 1930.

PHELPS BROWN, E. H., *The Growth of British Industrial Relations. A Study from the standpoint of 1906–14*, 1959.

POIRIER, Philip P., *The Advent of the Labour Party*, 1958.

POTTS, William, *Banbury through a Hundred Years. The*

Development of the town in the Nineteenth Century and After.
Banbury, 1942.

QUINLAN, Maurice J., *Victorian Prelude. A History of English Manners, 1700–1830*, New York, 1941.

RECKITT, Basil N., *The History of Reckitt and Sons, Limited,* 1951.

RECKITT, Maurice B., *Maurice to Temple. A Century of the Social Movement in the Church of England*, 1947.

ROE, James Moulton, *A History of the British and Foreign Bible Society 1905–1954*, 1965.

ROSE, Gordon, *The Struggle for Penal Reform, The Howard League and its Predecessors*, 1961.

RUSSELL, George W. E., *A Short History of the Evangelical Movement*, 1915.

RUSSELL, Rex C., *A History of Schools and Education in Lindsey, Lincolnshire 1800–1902, II Sunday Schools in Lindsey*, Lindsey, 1965.

SALT, Henry S., *Seventy Years Among Savages*, 1921.

SAMUELSSON, Kurt, *Religion and Economic Action*, ed. D. C. Coleman, trans., Geoffrey French, Stockholm, 1961.

SIMEY, Margaret, *Charitable Effort in Liverpool in the Nineteenth Century*, Liverpool, 1951.

SOUTHGATE, Donald, *The Passing of the Whigs, 1832–1886*, 1962.

STORR, Vernon F., *The Development of English Theology in the Nineteenth Century 1800–1860*, 1913.

STRACHEY, Lytton, *Eminent Victorians*, Glasgow, 1959; first pub., 1918.

TAYLOR, Audrey M., *Gilletts Bankers at Banbury and Oxford*, Oxford, 1964.

TAYLOR, Gordon Rattray, *The Angel-Makers. A Study in the Psychological Origins of Historical Change 1750–1850*, 1958.

THOMAS, J. A., *The House of Commons 1832–1901. Study of Its Economic and Functional Character*, Cardiff, 1939.

TOWNSEND, W. J., H. B. WORKMAN, and George EAYRS (eds.), *A New History of Methodism*, 1909.

TROELTSCH, Ernst, *The Social Teaching of the Christian Church*, trans. Olive Wyen, 4th impression, 1956, vol. II, only.

TUTTLE, Elizabeth Orman, *The Crusade against Capital Punishment in Great Britain*, 1961.

VINCENT, John, *The Formation of the Liberal Party 1857–1868*, 1966.

WARD, J. T., *The Factory Movement 1830–1855*, 1962.

WARNER, Wellman J., *The Wesleyan Movement in the Industrial Revolution*, 1930.

WEARMOUTH, Robert F., *Methodism and the Working-Class Movements of England 1800–1850*, 1937.

WEBB, Beatrice, *My Apprenticeship*, 1926.

WEBB, Clement, C. J., *A Study of Religious Thought in England from 1850*, Oxford, 1933.

WEBB, R. K., *Harriet Martineau, A Radical Victorian*, 1960.

WICKHAM, E. R., *Church and People in an Industrial City*, 1957.

WILLIAMS, Eric, *Capitalism and Slavery*, 1964; first pub., 1944.

WILLIAMS, Iolo A., *The Firm of Cadbury 1831–1931*, 1931.

WOOD, H. G., *Belief and Unbelief since 1850*, Cambridge, 1955.

WOODROOFE, Kathleen, *From Charity to Social Work in England and the United States*, 1962.

YOUNG, A. F., and E. T. ASHTON, *British Social Work in the Nineteenth Century*, 1956.

10. *Works of Reference.*
    Debrett's Illustrated House of Commons and the Judicial Bench, 1867 ff.

    Dod's Parliamentary Companion, 1833 ff. (volumes before 1865 have slightly different titles).

    The Financial Reform Almanack, 1872–94.

    Who's Who.

    Who Was Who, 1897–1916.

    LOCH, C. S., *The Charities Register and Digest*, 1882.

    LOW, Sampson, *The Charities of London. Comprehending the Benevolent, Educational, and Religious Institutions. Their Origin and Design, Progress, and Present Position*, 1850.

11. *Unpublished Theses and Monographs* (consulted by permission, where necessary).
    BAILEY, Maurice, H., *The Contribution of Quakers to some Aspects of Local Government in Birmingham 1828–1902* (Univ. of Birmingham M.A. thesis, 1952).

    BEAMISH, Lucia Katharine, *The Quaker Understanding of the Ministerial Vocation with special reference to the Eighteenth Century* (Univ. of Oxford B.Litt. thesis, 1965).

    EDDINGTON, J. Arthur, *The Gurney Manuscripts Synopsis of the Contents*, 1933 (typescript in FHL).

    ELLIS, George Mark, *The Evangelicals and the Sunday Question 1830–1860: Organised Sabbatarianism as an Aspect of the Evangelical Movement* (Univ. of Harvard Ph.D. thesis, 1951).

HARRISON, Brian, *The Temperance Question in England 1829–1869* (Univ. of Oxford D.Phil. thesis, 1965).

HOWARD, Bernard, *A Luke Howard Miscellany compiled by his Great Grandson,* 1959 (typescript in FHL).

INGLIS, K. S., *English Churches and the Working Classes, 1880–1900, with an Introductory Survey of Tendencies earlier in the century* (Univ. of Oxford D.Phil. thesis, 1956). This thesis has been published.

MACINTOSH, William H., *The Agitation for the Disestablishment of the Church of England in the Nineteenth Century (Excluding Wales) with special reference to the Minutes and Papers of the Liberation Society* (Univ. of Oxford D.Phil. thesis, 1955).

MARTINEAU, Erica, *Quakerism and Public Service chiefly between 1832 and 1867 being a study of the emergence of the Society of Friends and its Members into social and political activities* (Univ. of Oxford B.Litt. thesis, 1938).

MEIR, J. Kenneth, *The Origin and Development of the Sunday School movement in England from 1780 to 1880, in relation to the State Provision of Education* (Univ. of Edinburgh Ph.D. thesis, 1954).

MURPHY, Howard R., *The Origins of the Humanitarian Ethos in England with special Reference to the History of Ethical and Theological Ideas, 1700–1870* (Univ. of Harvard Ph.D. thesis, 1951).

PEETZ, E. A. Otto, *Friends Mission Work in Madagascar up to 1927 and its Doctrinal Implications* (Univ. of Oxford B.Litt. thesis, 1960).

ROSE, A. Gordon, *The History of the Howard League for Penal Reform* (Univ. of Manchester Ph.D. thesis, 1960).

STUART, F. C., *A Critical Edition of the Correspondence of Sir Thomas Fowell Buxton, Bart., with an Account of His Career to 1823* (Univ. of London M.A. thesis, 1957).

SUTTON, George Barry, *Shoemakers of Somerset. A History of C. and J. Clark 1833–1903* (Nottingham M.A. thesis, 1959).

TEMPERLEY, Howard R., *The British and Foreign Anti-Slavery Society,* 1839–68 (Univ. of Yale Ph.D. thesis, 1960).

WALSH, J. D., *The Yorkshire Evangelicals in the Eighteenth Century: with especial reference to Methodism* (Univ. of Cambridge Ph.D. thesis, 1956).

WHITBY, A. C., *Matthew Arnold and the Nonconformists. A Study in Social and Political Attitudes* (Univ. of Oxford B.Litt. thesis, 1954).

12. *Articles in Learned Journals.*

HINE, Reginald L., 'Samuel Lucas (1805–1870) His Life and Art-Work', *Walkers Quarterly*, 27.

INGLIS, K. S., 'Patterns of Religious Worship in 1851', *The Journal of Ecclesiastical History*, II, 1960.

ISICHEI, Elizabeth Allo, 'From Sect to Denomination in English Quakerism', *The British Journal of Sociology*, 15, 1964.

— 'Organisation and Power in the Society of Friends (1852–1859)', *Archives de Sociologie des Religions*, 19, 1965.

PASSY, Frédéric, 'Peace Movement in Europe', *The American Journal of Sociology*, 1896.

INDEX